To Rob: Never be a slave to fashion,
always have the courage of your convictions,
and always throw the 4-seam fastball up and in.

—Your favorite dad (Doug Rosenberg)

Contents at a Glance

Contents

Emperor's New Code (a Story)

SATIRE WARNING (octagonal badge)

ONCE UPON A TIME there lived a project manager (named, curiously enough, Fred Emperor) whose only worry in life was to keep up with the latest trends in development techniques. He changed methodology almost every project and loved to show off his knowledge to management.

Word of Emperor's habits spread over his department and beyond into Internet newsgroups. Two gurus who had heard of the project manager's fashion-consciousness decided to take advantage of it. They introduced themselves via e-mail with a scheme in mind.

"We are a pair of very good programmers, and after many years of research we have invented an extraordinary development process of such agility that the cost of changing requirements has been reduced nearly to zero. As a matter of fact, we have flattened out the famous cost-to-fix-defect exponential curve that Barry Boehm presented in *Software Engineering Economics*!" they wrote.

One of Emperor's programmers heard the gurus' strange story and notified Emperor, whose curiosity got the better of him. He decided to see the two scoundrels.

"Besides reducing the cost of changing requirements, sir, we've eliminated the need for up-front design (this is such a silly concept with our new method that we call it BDUF, short for 'Big Design Up Front') and, of course, your programmers will never have to waste any time documenting their work, for all the code is self-documenting. One important thing, though: You must be aware that closed-minded people on your staff might tell you that this approach can't possibly work. Always remember that this is a sure sign that these people are afraid, and do not take these fearful opinions seriously. In fact, you'd be better off getting rid of these cowards," the two gurus informed Emperor.

Emperor gave the two men a contract to build a payroll system in exchange for their promise to begin working on the project immediately. "Tell us what you need to get started and we'll give it to you. Just remember, the payroll system must be done in 4 years before our mainframes drop dead," said Emperor.

The two gurus asked for a big room with lots of computers running Smalltalk and a large stack of index cards, and then began working. They also asked for a full-time "customer," who they called a "goal donor," to live in the room with the Smalltalk programmers. The project manager looked around and, finding all of his key employees busy, he grabbed the first person he could find hanging around near the coffee machine and tossed him in the room with the programmers.

Emperor thought he had spent his money quite well—in addition to getting a new project completed that he could feel forever free to change the requirements of at any time, he would discover which of his programmers could churn out the most code in the shortest time, and which of his programmers were cowardly dogs, so he could get rid of them. A few days later, he called the old and wise chief technical officer (CTO), who was considered by everyone to be a man with common sense. "Go and see how the work is proceeding," Emperor told the CTO, "and come back to let me know."

The CTO was welcomed by the two gurus.

"We've built and tested the system 17 times since Tuesday," they said. "We're almost finished, but we need a few more cases of Pepsi, more computers to run our regression test suites on, some chocolate-chip cookies (coding is hungry work, indeed), and special desks with two chairs, for we always program in pairs to compensate for not doing any up-front design. We've made extra certain to turn a blind eye toward future requirements and only to build what we need today. Here, Excellency! Admire the test scores—feel the agility of the process!"

The CTO bent over the stack of index cards and tried to see the architecture that was not there. He felt cold sweat on his forehead.

"I can't see any architecture," he thought. "If I see nothing, that means I'm stupid! Or worse, incompetent!" If the CTO admitted that he didn't see anything, Emperor might claim he was incompetent and try to take his job.

"What a marvelous architecture," he said. "I'll certainly tell Mr. Emperor."

The two gurus rubbed their hands gleefully. They had almost made it. More Pepsi, 18 bags of potato chips, and a couple of ping-pong tables were requested to finish the work.

Finally, Emperor received the announcement that the two gurus had the payroll system up and running. They came to Emperor's office to demonstrate it for him.

"Come in," said Emperor. Even as they bowed, the two gurus pretended that their system, which had been designed to DoTheSimplestThingThatCouldPossiblyWork and could thus only pay a small percentage of the employees, would scale to handle all of the requirements.

"Here it is, Mr. Emperor, the result of our labor," the gurus said. "We have worked night and day (well, actually we knock off at 5:00 PM every day because we want to stay fresh) but, at last, the most agile process in the world is ready for you. Smell the code and experience how fine it is."

Of course, Emperor did not smell anything except a faint odor of bubble gum and Scotch tape, and he could not see any architecture between his fingers. He panicked and felt like fainting. Luckily, his chair was right behind him, so he sat down. But when he realized that no one could know that he did not see the architecture, he felt better. Nobody could find out he was stupid and incompetent. And Emperor didn't know that everybody else around him thought and did the very same thing.

The farce continued as the two gurus had foreseen it. "Mr. Emperor, you'll have to give us an open-ended variable-scope contract in order for us to complete the payroll system," the two gurus said. "Our new process doesn't operate well with fixed schedules or budgets—fixed schedules give the code a funny smell." Emperor was annoyed, as he usually only used fixed-price contracts, but because none of his bystanders seemed upset, he felt relieved.

"Yes, this is a beautiful process and it feels very agile to me," Emperor said, trying to look comfortable. "You've done a fine job."

The two gurus immediately started approaching publishing companies about getting book contracts to popularize their new process.

"Mr. Emperor," they said, "we have a request for you. The people have found out about this extraordinary process and they are anxious to learn more about it. Might we have permission to publish a dozen or so books about our process that reference the work we've done for you?" Emperor was doubtful about showing the details of his project to the people, but then he abandoned his fears. After all, no one would know about it except the ignorant and the incompetent.

"All right," he said. "I will grant the people this privilege." Book contracts were signed, magazine articles were written, and user conferences were scheduled in Italy. The gurus' process was given great credibility based on the claims of success on Emperor's project. Magazine editors and conference coordinators anxiously scrutinized the ideas of the programmers across the industry. Everyone wanted to know how stupid or incompetent his or her neighbor was but, as the details of Emperor's project were revealed, a strange murmur rose from the crowd.

Alas, the goal donor whom Emperor had found by the coffee machine turned out to be a new hire, right out of school, who really didn't understand the requirements of the payroll system and completely missed the point that the mainframes were going to die in 4 years' time. Encouraged by the gurus that changing requirements was no problem due to the variable-scope contract they had received, the project continued to consume soda, chips, and cookies for several years while they were refactoring code, without actually progressing toward completion. The two gurus assured the goal donor that this was no problem, because SoftwareIsNeverDone. And ultimately Emperor had to cancel the project, unfinished, which he did as soon as he realized that his mainframe didn't die.

Everyone said, loud enough for the others to hear, "Look at Emperor's new process. It's the essence of agility!"

"What marvelous productivity!"

"And the architecture! The architecture that has emerged from the code! I have never seen anything like it in my life."

They all tried to conceal their disappointment at not being able to see the architecture or smell the code, and because none of them was willing to admit their own stupidity and incompetence, they all behaved as the two gurus had predicted.

A young Java programmer from London, who was not afraid and could only see things his eyes showed to him, put up a small Web site with a contrary opinion. "Emperor's process of DesignAfterFirstTesting is DAFT," he said. "ConstantRefactoringAfterProgramming is CRAP. The whole thing is a bunch of daft crap, actually."

"Fool!" he was reprimanded on the newsgroups. "You're afraid of agility!"

But the young programmer's remarks, which had been heard by the bystanders, were repeated over and over again until everyone cried, "This is just a bunch of daft crap!"

The book publishers realized that the people were right but couldn't admit to that. They thought it better to continue the book series under the illusion that anyone who couldn't smell the code was either stupid or incompetent. And so books continued to roll off the printing press.

Preface

I FIRST HEARD OF EXTREME PROGRAMMING (XP) a few years ago when I used to spend lots of time on an e-mail list forum called the Object Technology User Group (OTUG) and began to see claims that the "cost-to-fix-defect curve" had been flattened.

For those of you who may not be familiar with this curve, it was published in a landmark book called *Software Engineering Economics* by Barry Boehm some 20 years ago, and it basically states that the cost of removing a defect (fixing a bug) increases exponentially as we progress through the life cycle from requirements analysis through design, coding, testing, and release of a system. So suddenly we were all made aware of this new phenomenon that promised to "embrace change" and flatten this curve.

My sensitive nose immediately detected a "hype smell," and I decided to do a little investigating. Sure enough, I rapidly discovered that the claims of a flat cost of change across the life cycle were the result of eliminating those life cycle phases where the cost of fixing a defect was lower—that is, no requirements analysis, no design before coding. Just code, test, and refactor, and the cost of making a change is flat across the life cycle! Miraculous, and completely based on circular logic. But man, did the combination of hype and circular logic ever sell books!

Before long, nearly every question anyone posted to OTUG was answered with an advertisement for XP, and for a while I'd get into the discussions when I wasn't too busy. But it seemed like some of the more prominent XP gurus did nothing but post messages to newsgroups, as there would routinely be 15 or more posts a day by these folks. And, of course, I always enjoyed the hate e-mail I received from zealots when I dared challenge any of the circular reasoning that was presented. When I did engage in the discussions, I spent a bunch of time surfing through some of the prominent XP Web sites, including, of course, the C2 Wiki Web. During this period, I was also involved in putting together a keynote speech for the UML World conference titled "Alice in Use Case Land." I decided to capture some of the "through the looking glass" guidance I discovered on my journey through the C2 Wiki Web and other XP sites in that talk. (You can read the complete script for "Alice" at http://www.iconixsw.com/aliceinusecaseland.html.)

Eventually, I grew bored with discussing XP on the newsgroups, got too busy with other projects (including my second book, *Applying Use Case Driven Object Modeling with UML*), and gave it up as a pastime. I returned to the sport briefly upon learning of the termination of the C3 project at Chrysler and reading on the C2 Wiki Web the reasons for the termination (the goal donor, happily embracing change, wanted to add new features, and the gold owner wanted to turn off the mainframes), and it irritated me that C3 was still being touted as a fabulous success on the newsgroups.

Why did this irritate me? Because, if you look on the C2 Wiki Web (read it yourself at `http://c2.com/cgi/wiki?CthreeProjectTerminated`), you'll find this quote (referring to Frank Gerhardt from Chrysler speaking at the XP 2000 conference):

> *"If I remember correctly Frank said words to the effect that, at DaimlerChrysler these days the terms: 'C3', 'ExtremeProgramming' and especially 'PlanningGame', and to some extent 'SmallTalk', 'GemStone' and 'object-oriented' are now unutterable by anyone wishing management there to take them seriously. He got a rather nervous sounding chuckle from the audience with the line 'Chrysler has done XP OnceAndOnlyOnce'."*

To paraphrase Churchill, "Never has so much hype been achieved by so few, over such a dismal failure."

At last count, there were well over 20 XP books on the market, which, if you think about it, were all spawned by the "success" of C3. Incredible.

Some months later, somebody forwarded me Matt Stephens' article titled "The Case Against Extreme Programming" (`http://www.softwarereality.com/ExtremeProgramming.jsp`), and I immediately recognized a kindred spirit. As I was reading Matt's article, I came upon a section where he was picking apart one of the XPers' favorite fallacious arguments, that unless you had actually tried a particular technique (I think in this case it was pair programming), you weren't qualified to say you wouldn't like it. This argument had always reminded me of a roommate I had in college when I was 17 years old, who had been trying to convince me to try LSD. (His words still stick in my mind: "But how do you know you won't like hallucinogenic drugs if you've never tried them?")

I can remember my reaction as I read Matt's words:

> *"Luckily us* [sic] *humans have pre-cognitive dissonance . . .* ["What?" I said to myself.] *I have never tried sticking my head in a bucket of sh—, I have never tried constant pair programming. But I know in advance that 'NO sir I wouldn't like it.' I know in advance, having seriously considered it, that constant pair programming is a totally warped idea."*[1]

Well, I almost fell off my chair laughing, and I remember saying out loud (to nobody in particular), "I *have* to write a book with this guy." A few months later (as we were bouncing this book proposal off the second possible publisher, who

---

1. Matt Stephens, "The Case Against Extreme Programming," `http://www.softwarereality.com/lifecycle/xp/key_rules.jsp`, August 26, 2001.

wanted us to write a pro-XP book instead), I found myself over in England teaching a couple of classes, and I got to spend some time with Matt, whereupon we decided that we should write the book we wanted to write and hopefully somebody would show up and publish it.

Ultimately, it was inevitable that I wound up writing this book with someone from England, because the subject matter is so well suited to the British sense of humor. The idea of a roomful of programmers, coding in pairs, working with stories scribbled on index cards, writing unit tests instead of doing architecture and design, and continually refactoring their code until it smells good just always made me envision "Monty Python's Extreme Programming Circus." To that end, I offer a sketch called "The Ministry of Code Smells":

> *John Cleese sits at a desk, in a suit. The desk has a sign on it that reads "Ministry of Code Smells". In walk a pair of programmers, Eric Idle and (dressed as a woman) Terry Jones. They are carrying a computer printout.*
>
> **Cleese:** Good morning. We'd like to smell your code, please.
>
> **Idle:** Good morning, sir. Yes, we've got it right here.
>
> **Jones:** *[Whispers in a falsetto voice]* Did you use deodorant on the code this morning, dear?
>
> **Idle:** *[Whispers]* Yes, yes, of course I did.
>
> **Cleese:** Well I'll be the judge of that. Let's have it.
>
> **Idle:** *[Hands over the code]* Yes, sir.
>
> **Cleese:** *[Takes a whiff]* No, that won't do at all. *[Sniffs again]* No, that will never do. That is definitely a "code smell."
>
> **Idle:** But I washed it twice, and then used deodorant.
>
> **Cleese:** No, sorry, you'll just have to refactor that.
>
> **Jones:** *[Shrieks]* But I worked all day on that code!
>
> **Cleese:** Now look here, madam–
>
> **Jones:** *[Gets up and pounds purse on Cleese's desk]* No, no, no, noooooooo!

As things developed, we finally found a publisher (thanks, Gary!) who told us we could write the book we wanted to write. Along the way (starting from the version of "Imagine" that I wrote for the Alice talk), my son, Rob, and I started rewriting lyrics to Beatles songs to parody some of the more amusing aspects of XP as I was driving him to school in the morning, and we hope you'll enjoy the "Songs of the Extremos" that you'll find sprinkled throughout the book.

At any rate, Matt and I share a common bent for satire that lends its tone to this book. We think there's a whole lot of material that needs parodying, and we hope you'll enjoy our efforts. But there's also a lot of serious stuff in this book, too, and we hope that doesn't get lost among the chuckles.

On a very serious note, I've persisted with this idea (despite many people encouraging me to give it up) based on a very strong personal conviction: I don't want to be nearby when somebody decides to deploy an air traffic control system or some missile-targeting software that has been developed with no written requirements, and where the programmers made the design up as they went along.[2]

Doug Rosenberg
Santa Monica, California
June 25, 2002

---

2. By coincidence, not long after writing the closing comment for this preface, I discovered this July 2002 article: http://www.technologyreview.com/articles/wo_sherman071902.asp. It describes a team that is faithfully applying XP to a collision-detection system for the airline industry! In that particular project, XP is being used to address the issue of code quality. The article describes XP as a "coding discipline." The worrying aspect of this particular article (aside from the fact that XP is being used on this type of project) is that the team is viewing its problems at the buggy code level. Acknowledging that the team needs to "lose the cowboy attitude and learn to cooperate" is an important first step. However, the team should be taking a much bigger step back and viewing its organization, its culture, and itself. Coding discipline is important; however, as we discuss later, it is only a relatively minor part of the overall picture (as the C3 team discovered to its peril).

About the Authors

Matt Stephens first discovered programming at the age of 11 and has continued ever since (he's now in his 30s). He has architected and led projects to create cinema ticket issuing systems, financial payment systems, enterprise alerting software, a graphical CASE tool for configuring an Enterprise Application Integration (EAI) server, and numerous other products. In his current role he is a technical team leader, architect, and agile process mentor for a technology start-up in Central London.

Matt pair-programs with his 7-month-old daughter, Alanah.

On the Web, Matt's "home page" is http://www.SoftwareReality.com, a satirical Web site for software developers.

Doug Rosenberg of ICONIX Software Engineering, Inc. (http://www.iconixsw.com) spent the first 15 years of his career writing code for a living before moving on to managing programmers, developing software design tools, and teaching object-oriented analysis and design.

Doug has been providing system development tools and training for nearly two decades, with particular emphasis on object-oriented methods. He developed a unified Booch/Rumbaugh/Jacobson design

Doug is listening for the sound of one man coding.

method in 1993 that preceded Rational's UML by several years. He has produced more than a dozen multimedia tutorials on object technology, including COMPREHENSIVE COM and COMPLETE CORBA, and is the author of *Use Case Driven Object Modeling with UML* (Addison-Wesley, 1999) and *Applying Use Case Driven Object Modeling with UML* (Addison-Wesley, 2001).

Recently, Doug has been spending increasing amounts of time shooting QuickTime VR (virtual reality) photography for fun and profit. You can see his VR photography online at http://www.VResorts.com.

Matt and Doug are collaborating on another book, *Agile Modeling with the ICONIX Process* (with Scott Ambler and Mark Collins-Cope), due out shortly from Apress.

Acknowledgments

FIRST OFF, THANK YOU to Gary Cornell at Apress, without whose permission to "go for it" there would have been no book—at least not the book we wanted to write. After two other publishers got cold feet, it was refreshing to see that Apress is prepared to let us say the things we feel need to be said!

Also thanks to our secret third author—Doug's son, Rob—for his help with the "Songs of the Extremos" and many of the satire pieces (especially the Camp Regretestskiy sketch).

Thank you to all the "Voice of eXPerience" (VoXP) contributors for joining us in speaking what's on our minds. The nonanonymous ones are David Van Der Klauw, Timothy Fisher, and Robin Sharp.

Over at Apress, thanks to Tracy Brown, Nicole LeClerc, Beth Christmas, Kari Brooks, and Kurt Krames.

Thanks to all the people who read and reviewed the book leading up to its publication, and in doing so helped us immeasurably to beat the manuscript into shape, in particular, Dino Fancellu, Robin Sharp (again), Alex Chaffee, John Zukowski, Philip Nortey, Mark Collins-Cope, Jim McKinney, Gary A. Ham, Andy Carmichael, Tim Axelrod, and Steve McConnell.

Matt would especially like to thank his wife, Michelle, for her patience and encouragement to finish the book. And, of course, he'd like to thank Doug for getting him involved in this book-writing thing in the first place. And in which case, Doug would like to thank Matt for having the courage of his convictions to write his "The Case Against Extreme Programming" article in the first place and for keeping the courage of his convictions all the way through.

Thanks to Allen Matheson for letting us use his photo of the Atlas statue at Rockefeller Center; thanks to Chris Starczak at ICONIX; and a big thanks to Arthur Marx, DeDe Merrill, and Bob Finklestein of Groucho Productions for kindly allowing us to use the Groucho icon that appears frequently throughout the book.

And for inspiration, how could we possibly forget

- John, Paul, George, and Ringo

- Mick and Keith

- Randy Newman

- Groucho, Harpo, Chico, and Zeppo Marx

- John Cleese, Eric Idle, Terry Jones, Michael Palin, and Terry Gilliam (aka Monty Python's Flying Circus)

Introduction

BEFORE WE GET STARTED, we want to draw attention to some of this book's very unique elements. This isn't your normal, run-of-the-mill computer science book! The subject matter is, we feel, worthy of a satirical treatment, so that's what we've set out to give it. In addition to the satire, there's also lots of dry humor. We do occasionally get serious and give a systematic breakdown of the flaws and dangers inherent in Extreme Programming (XP).

Having said that, this book isn't an outright "slam" piece. As we point out later, not all of XP is bad. So we do aim to provide a balanced critique and to signpost the parts of XP that we feel can be salvaged or refactored into something that achieves the same agile goals in a more robust kind of way.

XP has received more than its fair share of hype, and new XP books continue to appear at an incredible rate. The industry is being affected by the inflated claims surrounding XP in all sorts of ways (some of them positive, as we explore, but many of them negative). With this in mind, we feel a book that swims against the tide and rejects XP is important.

Here's one small example of how XP is affecting the industry. Matt (intrepid coauthor of this book) received an e-mail from a consultant who had just recently lost an important contract because he refused to launch into a project without doing some detailed requirements analysis and up-front design first. The customer had read about XP and told the consultant that "if XP says it's okay to run a project like that, then we'll find someone who *will* skip requirements and up-front design!"

Although some businesspeople hear about XP and instantly go insane (as the consultant story seems to suggest), others dig their heels in and reject change. In fact, a major problem faced by teams wanting to introduce XP into their organization is that XP requires a significant mind shift in the entire organization, from the way teams are organized to the way the company does business with its customers. This book analyzes XP's flaws and proposes an alternative approach to agility that requires much less change in existing organizations, while still retaining XP's agile goals. You can use this "alternative approach" as a crib sheet for when you tailor your own agile methodology. (Near the end of the book, we also provide some pointers to other agile processes that we feel to be more rigorous than XP.)

Most of all, though, this book aims to shatter some of the myths that are beginning to spring up in the wake of the XP tidal wave, such as it's okay not to document your work, an on-site customer and a bunch of automated tests are a sufficient replacement for a written requirements spec, the needs and comfort of the individual are secondary to the project (i.e., "pair-program with us or get another job"), and so on. And we aim to do this in an entertaining and humorous way because . . . well, because the subject matter calls for it.

Who Should Read This Book?

XP is often introduced into organizations by the programmers. This isn't surprising, because XP is a remarkably "programmer-friendly" methodology. It raises the profile of programmers (not a bad thing in itself) and puts them on a level footing with the customer. So if you're a manager or a customer who is being sold the idea of using XP in the next project, this book provides a valuable contrary viewpoint.

If you're a programmer who is introducing XP into an organization, this book should help because it outlines a lot of the dangers that tend to get brushed over in other XP books but that can be potential project-killers.

If you're thinking about tailoring XP to extract all its good bits, but you want to avoid the "house of cards" effect, where one small change to the process brings the whole lot crashing down, this book provides some valuable guidance.

Also, if you're a software developer and just want to read some good old sidesplitting satire, this book should fit the bill!

How to Read This Book

There are several different ways that this book can be read (aside from the usual sitting in a chair and turning the pages). Cover to cover is, of course, the method we recommend, because we introduce themes that get revisited later—each chapter builds on the previous chapter, to an extent.

Alternatively, if you're looking for a particular theme, it's possible to skip through the book looking for the appropriate icons (see the icon key in the next section).

For example, if you'd like to piece together our "refactored process" (which we describe in Chapter 15), flip through the book looking for the Happy Fangs icons (these tend to be at the end of chapters, but not always).

We've also indexed all the satire pieces, "Voice of eXPerience" (VoXP) stories, and "Songs of the Extremos," so these will hopefully provide some handy trails through the book.

Key to Icons

There are several different themes running throughout this book. The important ones are delineated by their own icons, as follows:

WARNING *The meaning of Fangs (the slippery slope serpent) should become clear after reading Chapter 3. Most chapters end with a summary of certain high-risk XP practices. Look for the Angry Fangs icon.*

 SOLUTION *But it's not all doom and gloom. We also show how to reduce risk in XP. Fangs gets, well, defanged.*

 As we discuss in Chapter 4, certain Extremo quotes define XP in almost Marxist terms. These get a Karl Marx icon.

 Then there's the other Marx. Extremo quotes that we feel to be particularly special or outrageous get "awarded a Groucho."

 SATIRE WARNING *The book is filled with dry humor and sarcasm, but some parts are outright satirical. This icon delineates what is satire and what is genuinely XP.*

 VOXP *We also provide some real-life anecdotes from people who have worked on XP projects. You'd be forgiven for thinking that some of this stuff is satire, so the Voice of eXPerience (VoXP) icon helps to set these stories apart from the "real" satire.*

 Every now and again we encounter some circular logic in the Extremo world. If it's dark, just look for the light bulb. But then if there's a light bulb, it wouldn't be dark, right?

 Quotes that we feel to be particularly hype inflated, if they weren't already awarded a Groucho, get our ultrashiny, new-and-improved Hype! icon.

Satire Stories

Just looking for the satire? This list should help:

Voice of eXPerience (VoXP) Stories

You'd be forgiven for thinking that some of these stories are satire (like the "no coffee before 10:30 AM" incident). But each VoXP story listed here is a real-life account of experiences on an XP project.

Songs of the Extremos

Surely, no critical expose of Extreme Programming would be complete without some Songs of the Extremos! Here's a complete list of all the songs in this book:

Part I

Another Fine Mess You've Gotten Me Into (Laurel and Hardy Take Up Programming)

CHAPTER 1

XP in a Nuthouse (Oops, We Mean Nutshell)

You Say Design, I Say Just Code
(Sing to the tune of "Hello Goodbye" by The Beatles)

We write tests
We write code
Up-front design
No no no no no

We just . . . write code
You say design
I say write code

Just code, just code
I don't know why you say design
I say just code

Requirements
Are just code
So's design
Code is all we know

QA . . . smell the code
You do design
I just write code

Just code, just code
I don't know why you do design
I just write code

Extreme Programming (XP) has become something of a phenomenon. Currently, almost 20 books are available on XP, with more on the way. A quick search on the Web reveals a world of activity and discussion surrounding XP. In many ways, XP is the new pop-culture software process, increasingly trendy with programmers all around the world and vociferously defended by its followers.

In this book, we examine the sorts of problems that XP is trying to solve, and we discuss why we feel XP is more fragile than other agile methodologies. Think of this book as a lighthouse for wary travelers.

It would be wrong of us to suggest that XP can't possibly work, because reports of successful XP projects do surface every now and again. Even a stopped clock is right twice a day. So we're not saying that XP can't possibly work, because sometimes it does (although we refer you to the "night gunner" scene in Chapter 8 for our thoughts on this. In addition, bear in mind that the most loudly proclaimed XP "success story" was rather dubious to say the least. We analyze that particular project in Chapter 2).

So our primary message in this book is that XP is inherently high-risk, brittle, and prone to certain failure modes. It's also suited only to a very small number of project types (mostly small-scale projects with a very small team of programmers). We explore these points in more detail in the upcoming chapters.

To round off the book, in Chapter 15 we explore various ways to achieve the goals that XPers aspire toward (software agility, rapid development, simple design, feedback, customer satisfaction, and so on) using safer processes that XPers claim to be unworkable but that we've used successfully and seen used successfully over and over again.[1] We also present a case study of a real-life project that is in many ways "XP-like" and fits the agile bill, but that has been tailored to address XP's many failure modes.

Extreme Programming in Theory

Before we go into detail about the dangers of XP, it's worth spending a little time covering the actual XP values, practices, and so forth. As you're reading this book, it's likely that you've read some of the "official" XP books. Just in case, though, here's a quick summary of XP.

---

1. We include a summary of our refactored process at the end of this chapter.

The Central Premise of XP

The following quote is from XP author Kent Beck:

> *"One of the universal assumptions of software engineering is that the cost of changing a program rises exponentially over time."*[2]

This "cost of change curve" is the primary reason software developers try to get the requirements and the design right as early as possible. XP attempts to turn this on its head, and in fact this turns out to be possibly the single most controversial aspect of XP.

XP's central technical premise is that all its practices work and are effective because the cost of change curve is flattened. The theory goes something like this: Traditionally, the later in a project a change is made, the more costly the change will be. If a process could be put in place that prevents the cost of change from rising over time, then (the theory goes) you could afford to delay big decisions until later.

In effect, if this is true, then (the Extremos believe) you can afford to skip the up-front requirements analysis and design phases, and instead "drip-feed" the project with new requirements incrementally throughout its lifetime. In theory, XP "works" because it doesn't cost significantly more to add new features in later than it would to add them in now.

XP is defined by four sets of things: values, practices, activities, and roles. Pretty much all of these are geared toward flattening the cost of change curve.

The Values

The four values in XP are as follows:

- Communication

- Simplicity

- Feedback

- Courage

---

2. Kent Beck, *Extreme Programming Explained: Embrace Change* (New York, NY: Addison-Wesley, 2000), p. 21.

Communication

If everyone is in the same room and communicating well, then there's less chance of misunderstandings or "but I thought you meant . . ." arguments cropping up.

XP takes the stance that the most expressive form of communication is verbal and that *verbal communication is less prone to error and misunderstandings than written communication.* Later in the book (trying to keep a straight face), we analyze this approach in more detail.

Simplicity

Simplicity in everything is key: Always try to do the simplest thing that could possibly work. It usually takes less time than, say, doing a complicated thing to achieve the same goal.

It's worth mentioning that even when you follow the simplicity value, absolute simplicity isn't always the best solution. Sometimes a complex problem does require a slightly complex solution. For example, an autopilot on a commercial airliner would work fine with the simplest design, but an airline customer would probably want some extra stuff, such as a backup system, failsafe devices, monitoring software, software that monitors the monitoring software, and so on.

Nonfunctional requirements (such as high availability) all affect the design. So the simplest thing that could possibly work might actually turn out to be quite a complex solution. It's still a good rule of thumb, though.

Feedback

Does this screen really work the way the customer expects it to? Hey, why not ask him—he's just over there. Feedback in all things is useful and catches misunderstandings early. Often, feedback from others helps to improve your code, your design, your hairstyle, and so on.

Feedback also refers to the way that software design is approached in XP: Build a "first-effort" prototype of the system (one small part at a time), test it, and adjust the design until it's right. The first version is bound to be slightly off, but it allows you to make a quick start so that you can later fine-tune the design.

In *Agile Software Development*, Alistair Cockburn recounts a story about Seymour Cray (the famous inventor of various supercomputers) and an early experience he had with using feedback as part of the design process:

> *"Seymour Cray illustrated that a little bit of feedback can replace a lot of analytical work. Of all the published methodologies, Extreme Programming (XP) perhaps puts the most emphasis on feedback, both during design and in the overall project."*[3]

---

3. Alistair Cockburn, *Agile Software Development* (New York, NY: Addison-Wesley, 2001), p. 66.

In addition, the planning game (which we cover shortly) gives feedback to and from the customer, allowing him to "steer" the project.

Courage

Have the courage to ski off-piste, to base-jump off a ridiculously tall cliff somewhere in Norway, and to make a small design change in your payroll project.

We discuss courage in a bit more detail in the "Fear" section in Chapter 4.

The Practices

The 12 practices in XP are as follows:

- Test-driven development (via unit tests and customer tests, aka acceptance tests)

- The planning game

- Whole team (was on-site customer)

- Small releases

- Metaphor

- Simple design

- Refactor mercilessly

- Collective ownership

- Pair programming

- Continuous integration

- Sustainable pace

- Coding standards

The list changes occasionally; for example, "40-hour week" was renamed to "sustainable pace" so that it would make sense in work cultures outside the United States. These pages are probably the best places to check for the most up-to-date version of the list: `http://c2.com/cgi/wiki?ExtremeProgrammingCorePractices` and `http://www.xprogramming.com/xpmag/whatisxp.htm`.

An important XP practice that didn't make it into the official list of 12 is emergent design.

We discuss emergent architecture and design in Chapter 12.

Another XP practice that wasn't on Kent Beck's original list but has since become central to XP (in the form of the whole team practice), is that of *colocating* teams—that is, the entire team (programmers, coach, customer, and so on) must be able to squeeze into one room.

We discuss how colocated teams affect scalability in the section "When XP Starts to Fail," in Chapter 14.

Test-Driven Development

This practice is a combination of the practice of testing the code and the design (unit testing) and the practice of testing that all the requirements have been implemented (acceptance testing). *Unit tests* (aka *programmer tests*) are always written by the programmers, and *acceptance tests* (also known as *functional tests* and *customer tests*) are, if possible, written by the customer.

XP takes a "test-first" approach to programming. That is, for each class (or task), you first write the unit tests, run them, see that they fail, and then write the code that's necessary to prevent the unit tests from failing.

An increased emphasis on unit testing and on the use of automated testing tools is probably the most useful benefit to have emerged from the XP phenomenon. In fact, test-driven development (aka test-first design) is beginning to take on a life of its own that's increasingly distinct from XP.[4] Unit testing has been around far longer than XP, of course, but there's no doubt that the Extremos have raised consciousness across the industry about the importance of this practice, and they deserve credit for this.

---

4. See `http://www.objectmentor.com/writeUps/TestDrivenDevelopment` and Kent Beck, *Test-Driven Development: By Example* (New York, NY: Addison-Wesley, 2002).

The Planning Game

Planning in XP involves eliciting the right decisions from the right people. Business-people need to decide about scope, priority, what each release will consist of, and the release dates. Technical people need to decide about estimates, consequences, process, and detailed scheduling.

The *planning game* involves breaking the project into very short 1- to 3-week iterations and taking the project one iteration at a time. For each iteration, the customer needs to decide which user stories to include and which to leave until a future iteration.

Any piece of work that takes time is written up as a *user story* and assigned its own little piece of cardboard (the *story card*). User stories must be testable and estimable. In addition, every user story must provide business value to the customer (i.e., design details wouldn't be written as user stories).

Each story represents a week or two of work. To make work allocation and estimating easier, each story is broken down into smaller tasks that the programmers sign up for, where each task represents a day or two of work.

The story cards themselves shouldn't contain much detail: They're really placeholders for conversations or "promises for future conversations with the customer."

If the customer (or higher management) requests some documentation, it's assigned as a user story, and a cost estimate is attached. Changes in requirements are handled in a similar way. Every change is given an assigned cost. For any iteration, to schedule a change the customer must remove some other change of equal cost.

As the project progresses, estimating of user stories, in theory, becomes more accurate. The rate of user stories completed per fixed iteration is known as the *project velocity*. A key goal in an XP project is to maintain a consistent (therefore predictable) velocity.

As we'll see in Chapter 11, some Extremos regard "constant velocity" as more important than deadlines.

Whole Team (Was On-site Customer)

From *Extreme Programming Explained*:

> *"A real customer must sit with the team, available to answer questions, resolve disputes, and set small-scale priorities. By 'real customer' I mean someone who will really use the system when it is in production."*[5]

The definition of an XP "customer" has actually changed since the preceding quote was published in 2000. The new-testament definition is that the XP customer is simply a representative of the real customer. If you can get the real thing, then so much the better; otherwise, a proxy will do.

The following quote is from XP author Michael Feathers:

> *"Some larger teams doing XP have teams of customers. The important thing isn't so much that there is a single customer, but that the 'customer speaks with one voice.'"*[6]

This is an important aspect of the XP customer (in fact, of any customer in any project). The customer must speak with one voice—that is, the programmers must receive clear, unambiguous, nonconflicting instructions on what to create.

The Feathers quote also indicates that the concept of the customer role has evolved still further, that the "customer" may be an entire team. In his foreword to Pete McBreen's *Questioning Extreme Programming*, Kent Beck writes:

> *"I will suggest that as you read this, you keep in mind one mistake of early XP thinking for which I am entirely responsible—'the customer' doesn't mean one person. It means a team, as big or bigger than the development team."*[7]

Beck doesn't specify whether the customer team should be in the same room as the development team. This raises some questions about how the XP "customer" can still speak with a single voice. If they're colocated in the same room, it would be rather difficult to mandate that only one of them ever speaks to the developers. The rest must surely be gagged!

---

5. Beck, *Extreme Programming Explained*, op. cit., p. 60.
6. Michael Feathers posting to the newsgroup `comp.software.extreme-programming`, subject: "Re: On-site Customer Liaison; was The Case against XP," December 29, 2001.
7. Pete McBreen, *Questioning Extreme Programming* (New York, NY: Addison-Wesley, 2002), p. xvi.

Small Releases

Back to *Extreme Programming Explained*:

> *"Put a simple system into production quickly, then release new versions on a very short cycle."*[8]

Although this approach does have advantages, there are also certain risks that must be contained (these are discussed later). In fact, we've noticed a small caveat being added onto this practice more recently: The (typical) 2-week iteration doesn't necessarily result in a production release (i.e., a program that will be used in a live system by "real" users). It may instead simply be a small release aimed at the internal customer, primarily to gain early feedback and hopefully find any defects that need to be corrected.

Also from *Extreme Programming Explained*:

> *"It is far better to plan a month or two at a time than six months or a year at a time. A company shipping bulky software to customers might not be able to release this often. They should still reduce their cycle as much as possible."*[9]

The theory behind small releases is that valuable functionality is placed into the user's hands as soon as possible and that the system never gets too far removed from what the customer really wants. That is, if users are going to say, "Yes, but that's not really what I wanted. . . ." when they see the finished software, they get to say this after a couple of weeks of development work has gone by, not after a couple of years. This ties in with XP's feedback value.

System Metaphor

In XP, the software architecture is complemented with a single unifying metaphor. The *system metaphor* is a simple shared story of how the system works. All naming and design theories stem from that one story. For example, "the system is a bakery," therefore we have ovens, bakers, trays, shop counters, tins, and so forth.

Similarly, a contract management system would be spoken of in terms of contracts, customers, and endorsements, and an online e-commerce system would be described in terms of products, a shopping cart, and a checkout procedure.

---

8. Beck, *Extreme Programming Explained*, op. cit., p. 54.
9. Beck, *Extreme Programming Explained*, op. cit., p. 56.

The system metaphor is often a bone of contention because it's seen as a direct replacement for a system architecture. Usually this confusion arises because "vanilla" XP projects don't produce a documented architecture model; thus, source code written to a particular common metaphor is about the closest they get. In reality, however, it's the system metaphor *and all the other design activities* that replace the documented architecture.

Simple Design

A simple design is quicker to code and easier to maintain than a complex design.

In XP, a driving design maxim is "Always do the simplest thing that could possibly work." This means not designing or coding for something that won't be included in the current iteration. This philosophy of "coding for today" gets taken to, well . . . extremes in XP.

Emergent Design

As we mentioned earlier, a fundamental XP practice, which didn't make it into the original list of 12 practices but was added later, is *emergent design*, the concept of "growing" a design as your understanding of the problem (and best solution) evolves. Emergent design is discussed in an article by Ron Jeffries on his Web site (http://www.xprogramming.com). It could be thought of as a combination of refactoring, test-driven development, simple design, and metaphor, and of the XP "designing" activity.

We discuss emergent design in Chapter 12.

Refactoring

Refactoring is the practice of improving the design of existing code. XP advises that you strive for simple designs. Therefore, refactoring in XP means looking for ways to simplify the design of existing code while still running all of the tests. And, because XP eliminates up-front design before coding (aka "big design up front" [BDUF]) you've always got plenty of code that needs improving. We like to call this "Constant Refactoring After Programming."

XP does recommend that you only refactor code that really needs it (e.g., where there is duplicated code). The way that XP recommends you identify such code is to look out for *code smells*—parts of the code that have become "crufty" and need to be improved.

Although the code is "existing," it might have been written only a few seconds ago. The theory is that refactoring is a constant and integral part of programming. By continuously thinking about how to simplify your code (and of course doing it), you theoretically end up with a better code-level design (or, in Extremo jargon, "better smelling code").

More on refactoring in Chapter 9.

Collective Ownership

Everyone is responsible for the entire code base. If a programmer sees something she doesn't like about any piece of code in the project, she (and her pair-programming buddy) can go in and change it.

Although XP has collective code ownership, it has individual task ownership.[10] This means that each programmer signs up for tasks at the start of each iteration and is responsible for completing that task by the end of the iteration. Usually, a programmer will sign up for tasks that interest him or that fall under his own core skill set (e.g., an SQL expert will most likely sign up for those tasks that involve writing SQL). However, as we'll see shortly, programmers in XP are required to rotate around frequently.

We discuss collective ownership in the "What If Programmers Take Ownership of Code?" section in Chapter 3.

Pair Programming

You can code on your own for "nonproduction" code[11] such as prototypes. For all production code, though, XP recommends that everyone on the team program in pairs. Pairing up is an effective way of catching errors and helping each other to identify ways of further simplifying the code.

To keep pairs from becoming stale, and to facilitate collective ownership, XP encourages people to move around and switch partners frequently. This "pair promiscuity" (more commonly known as *pair rotation*) is intended to prevent knowledge bottlenecks from appearing. A common situation is where only one

---

10. See `http://www.jera.com/techinfo/xpfaq.html`.

11. In this book we use "production code" to mean source code that's being targeted for delivery to be used in a live system (as opposed to, say, prototype or "spike" code, which would be used for exploration and experimentation and then thrown away).

person knows about one part of the system, hence that person becomes virtually indispensable. If that person isn't around, then a bug in her niche area simply can't be fixed (at least not satisfactorily).

When people are allowed to choose their own pairs, they'll usually choose to work on parts of the project that interest them most or that they're most suited to. If you like to write stored procedures, then whenever a user story comes up involving a stored procedure task, chances are pretty good that you'll choose to work on it. Hence, "pair promiscuity" shouldn't necessarily lead to problems where someone is doing something he doesn't want to (except maybe pair programming).

The XP literature is quite clear that pair programming is mandatory for all production code. That is confirmed online by XP author Robert C. Martin:

> *"The only constraint that XP puts on you is that any production code has be [sic] written by a pair. Your preferences and comfort do not supercede the delivery of quality to the project, or your parcitipation [sic] in the team."[12]*

Alternatively, you could take XP author Ron Jeffries' advice:

> *"XP says that 'all production code is written by two people sitting together at one machine'. That's the rule. As far as I know, no project has ever done that, including many that I consider to deserve the name XP. So what's the rule about? It's an ideal. It's what we strive for. It is a stretch goal."[13]*

Elsewhere, to confuse us even more, Ron also says:

> *"The definition of doing Level 0 XP is quite unambiguous and clear: the 12 practices, all the time."[14]*

Whichever XP author's advice (Ron's or his evil twin's) you choose to follow, if you strive for pair programming, then you might find that the "pairing up" mindset becomes habitual: *Extreme Programming Explained* even recommends pair integrating.

We discuss pair programming further in Chapter 6.

---

12. Robert C. Martin posting to the newsgroup comp.object, subject: "Re: Pair Programming—Yuck!" October 28, 2001.

13. Ron Jeffries, "Misconceptions About XP," http://www.xprogramming.com/xpmag/Misconceptions.htm, January 21, 2002.

14. See http://www.c2.com/cgi/wiki?IfXpIsntWorkingYoureNotDoingXp.

In Chapter 13, a practicing (though skeptical) XPer describes a project in which "pair progress-bar watching" was mandatory for all.

Continuous Integration

Code is integrated and tested after a few hours—a day of development at most. If by the end of the day your code isn't yet working, you're encouraged to toss it away, "go home clean," and start afresh the following morning.

As mentioned previously, pair programming can lead to habitual pairing in other aspects of XP, including pair integrating:

> *"When the machine is free, a pair with code to integrate sits down, loads the current release, loads their changes (checking for and resolving any collisions), and runs the tests until they pass (100% correct)."*[15]

Sustainable Pace

The more tired a programmer is, the more mistakes she'll make. Programmers who code through the night, fired up on "free" pizza and too much Dr Pepper, might think they're doing the company a favor, but in reality they're creating "negative work"—doing more harm than good. The bugs that they're inevitably introducing, in their barely awake daze as they stare bleary-eyed at the flickering screen, will probably take a lot longer to track down and fix than any time they gained, assuming they actually managed to produce any useable code at all between midnight and 5:00 AM.

The upshot is that a "40-hour week" (as this practice used to be known) is quite a good thing, really. *Sustainable pace* will result in higher productivity levels in the long run than making frequent "mad dashes" that quickly burn out your programmers.

Coding Standards

Coding standards are important in any programming project, and more so in an XP project, because any pair of programmers can change any part of the code at any time.

Coding standards also help a lot in making your code clearer, as in easier to read and decipher. Encouraging programmers to give their variables and methods meaningful names helps to make your code self-documenting. For example,

---

15. Beck, *Extreme Programming Explained*, op. cit., p. 59.

call a method calculateTaxGains() rather than multiplyAWithB(), or even worse mltVals(). This in turn means that your code needs fewer (if any) comments. In fact, the presence of code comments (according to Extremo theory) should be taken as a signal that the code could be made clearer.

The Activities

The four basic activities within XP are as follows:

- Coding

- Testing

- Listening

- Designing

Kent Beck, author of *Extreme Programming Explained*, posits that these four activities are all there is to software development:

> "**L**istening, **T**esting, **C**oding, **D**esigning. *That's all there is to software. Anyone who tells you different is selling something.*"[16]

This is a rather minimalist way of looking at software development, and it also sets the tone for the "my way or the highway" rhetoric that surrounds XP. Is it really all there is to it, though? We revisit this quote in the final chapter.

Coding

Without code, we don't have a program, so it's a fair assumption that a software project will involve coding at some stage. In XP, the "stage" is pretty much the entire project.

Testing

Write the test, then write the code. Keep changing the code until the test passes. Rinse and repeat until all the tests are written and pass with flying colors.

By placing such a high emphasis on testing (particularly when refactoring the design), XP ensures that the project always inches forward—it never slips back (although it might be moving "forward" in a circle).

---

16. See http://www.c2.com/cgi/wiki?ExtremeProgramming.

See Chapters 9 and 13 for some good reasons why we feel XP projects are in danger of inching forward in circles. And see Chapter 2 for a discussion of a project in which the signs suggest that it was doing just that.

Of course, the trade-off is also that the project is always inching, never leaping. If you look first, then sometimes it's okay to leap.

We discuss the benefits of looking before you leap further in Chapter 12.

Samurai Debugging

Doug once worked with a guy who had a technique that he called "Samurai debugging" (this was back around 1981/1982). When you follow the Samurai debugging technique, you start with a blank screen. That's not what you want, so you start debugging it, and you continue debugging until your program does exactly what you want it to do.

It's similar to Michelangelo's "All you do is start with a block of marble and chip away everything that doesn't look like David," but it's also not so unlike XP today.

Listening

The customer tells the programmer what he wants the system to do; the programmer writes the system. Because it's human nature to base our interpretations on our own prior experience, everyone will "hear" the customer's requirements slightly differently (we expect this to get especially interesting now that XP has changed the definition of "customer" from a single customer to a customer team). To get past this, programmers must try to put their preconceptions to one side and listen to what the businesspeople are really telling them. It's more difficult than it sounds, but it's worth persevering with.

Also see the "Listening Without Preconceptions" sidebar in Chapter 10.

It's worth noting that there has never been an instance in recorded history of a programmer "hearing" what was most convenient to code. Therefore the silly, archaic practice of writing requirements down in detail can be safely discarded.

Designing

XP involves design. Well, sort of. It doesn't involve design in the traditional sense (plan out your overall architecture, draw lots of lines and boxes, create models, and derive code from models). Instead XP involves a *little* up-front design (at least 5 to 10 minutes before coding; see Chapter 12), and the rest is sort of an integral part of the day-to-day programming process.

Design in XP mainly involves thinking, how can we simplify this? In other words, it's tightly coupled with the practice of constant refactoring. Design in XP is summed up by these two Extremo quotes:

"Get a few people together and spend a few minutes sketching out the design. Ten minutes is ideal—half an hour should be the most time you spend to do this. After that, the best thing to do is to let the code participate in the design session—move to the machine and start typing in code."[17]

"You must remember that XP does not recommend that its practitioners leap into code without a specification. Rather XP recommends the use of user stories and CRC cards as the means of specifying the work up front."[18]

We discuss "letting the code participate in the design" and other catchy Zen-like concepts in Chapter 16.

---

17. Ron Jeffries, Ann Anderson, and Chet Hendrickson, *Extreme Programming Installed* (New York, NY: Addison-Wesley, 2000), p. 70.

18. Robert C. Martin posting to the newsgroup `comp.software.extreme-programming`, subject: "Re: How XP and Microsoft are similar," September 11, 1999.

The Roles

As defined in *Extreme Programming Explained*, the basic roles within XP are as follows:

- Programmer
- Coach
- Tester
- Consultant
- Tracker
- Big boss

Notice that the on-site customer isn't included as a role. In *Extreme Programming Explained*, the on-site customer is actually described as a practice. This more recent description of the on-site customer is also given by Kent Beck:

> *"In XP, the customer side of the team (which is generally around half of the team) accepts responsibility for the scope of the project, including system-level testing. Effective customer sides combine domain experts, testers, analysts, and marketers. Depending on the organization, you might also include customer service representatives, sales engineers, and interaction designers."*[19]

Remember that all these people must be able to squeeze into a single room (all day, every day) for the whole project! Note that this is considerably more "togetherness" than in most families. So, breath mints and deodorant are vitally important on an XP project.

 See the song "Coder's Little Helper" in Chapter 6 for more about the personal hygiene aspects of XP.

The XP Life Cycle

An aspect of XP that many people find compelling is that it has eschewed the "traditional" waterfall approach to software life cycles. A *waterfall* project is characterized by the way in which it's divided into discrete phases. Each phase provides input into the next phase. The requirements-gathering phase usually involves some rapid prototyping, which helps to avoid the problem of unexpected issues cropping up during design and build, which people normally associate with waterfall projects.

With XP, there are no "phases" as such. The design evolves in concert with the requirements. The code is developed in concert with the design. Put another

---

19. Kent Beck posting to the newsgroup `comp.software.extreme-programming`, subject: "The Customer," May 7, 2002.

way, the requirements drive the code; the code is the design. And it all sort of happens at the same time.

This is normally referred to as *evolutionary* development, because the code base is being grown, or evolved, rather than being planned, designed in full, and then built. This contrasts with the approach taken by other modern processes, such as Rational Unified Process (RUP), which tend to be "iterative and incremental" (i.e., the project is broken down into mini-waterfalls, so that there's still at least a significant element of looking before you leap).

With XP, the project is divided into iterations of 1 to 3 weeks, with a deliverable handed to the customer at the end of each iteration (the customer also decides whether each deliverable will be released to the end users).

Each iteration begins with a planning meeting that involves the programmers and the customer. In this meeting, the participants decide what functionality to include and what to leave out for now. The customer describes what she wants (in the form of user stories), and the programmers estimate how long each story will take to implement.

In reality, XP does have waterfall-style "micro-phases," but they are very short: The "Requirements ➤ Design ➤ Code ➤ Integrate ➤ Test ➤ Deploy" life cycle takes place in a single iteration (1 to 3 weeks). The "inner phases" (Design ➤ Code ➤ Integrate ➤ Test) are repeated several times a day, and the boundaries between designing, coding, and testing are blurred to the extent that they're almost indistinguishable. In fact, Kent Beck describes the XP life cycle as "a waterfall run through a blender."

The requirements phase in XP is referred to as *exploration*. The purpose of exploration is to identify, prioritize, and estimate requirements. This would typically take place in the first day or two of each iteration:

> *"Exploration takes the place of a written requirements document. The programmers and the customer assemble and discuss the customer's needs. The customer writes stories describing these needs. In discussion with the customer, the programmers remove ambiguity from the stories by making sure that they are testable and estimable. Customers make sure that stories are meaningful by ordering them in terms of their business value."[20]*

The initial set of stories (handwritten on story cards) won't contain much detail. They're roughly equivalent to a set of use case outlines (although user stories differ in that they aren't limited to describing a user's interaction with the system).

---

20. James Newkirk and Robert C. Martin, *Extreme Programming in Practice* (New York, NY: Addison-Wesley, 2001), p. 9.

See Chapter 10 for a definition of use cases (and comparison with user stories).

Later, in each iteration, the customer writes automated acceptance tests that form the actual detail. This is roughly equivalent to—well, hell, I don't think there's an equivalent to asking the customer to define their requirements in scripted code.

What Problems Are Being Targeted by XP?

The answer to this question depends on the meaning of the question (at the risk of sounding lawyerly). There are two possible interpretations to the question (that we can see), namely

- What problems that manifest in your typical software project are being targeted by XP?

- What problems with existing methodologies are being targeted by XP?

What Problems That Manifest in Your Typical Software Project Are Being Targeted by XP?

Typical problems that threaten to afflict just about every software project include the following:

- Lack of communication between programmers.

- Lack of communication between programmers and the customer.

- Sometimes the customer doesn't know what he wants until he sees it.

- Customer requirements aren't static. They're likely to change during the project, either because they have genuinely changed (e.g., the market has shifted) or because they weren't right in the first place.

- Much time is often wasted on writing functionality that turns out not to be needed after all, either because the design evolved in a different direction or because the requirements changed.

- Documentation quickly becomes out-of-date.

- Sometimes, when a project takes a very long time to complete, it's obsolete before it has even been finished.

This isn't an exhaustive list, but it gives a good idea of the type of "problem project" that XP is aimed at. Whether it succeeds in solving these problems is wide open to debate, of course. We return to this list later in the book.

XP isn't alone in identifying these as common problems. Even traditional waterfall-based projects have ways of solving many of these problems (e.g., they have a prototyping phase that helps to identify the best design and gives the customer a chance to see roughly what she's going to get).

There's an increasing trend in modern processes to "travel light." For example, the ICONIX Process[21] is concerned with getting from use cases to code in as few steps as possible. ICONIX also identifies which documents are transitory (i.e., which documents can be abandoned once used), and which documents should be kept up-to-date. XP places an even higher emphasis on temporary documents, to the extent that the only deliverable that really "matters" is the source code.

What Problems with Existing Methodologies Are Being Targeted by XP?

XP is typically seen as the antithesis to "high-ceremony" methodologies (i.e., prescriptive software processes that demand large amounts of paperwork and many hoops to jump through before any code gets written). The problems with such methodologies include the following:

- There are often too many hoops to jump through before any code gets written. Having a few hoops (e.g., defining the requirements) is good and is commonly known as looking before you leap. Some types of project do benefit from these additional stages, though (e.g., life-critical systems, space shuttle navigation systems, payroll systems).

- Much time is often wasted on creating documents that nobody ever reads.

- Excessive documentation is more likely to result in out-of-date documents.

- All projects are not the same. One methodology just can't fit all possible project types.

---

21. Doug Rosenberg with Kendall Scott, *Use Case Driven Object Modeling with UML: A Practical Approach* (New York, NY: Addison-Wesley, 1999).

That last problem is also true of XP, of course. For example, XP is best suited to small-scale projects of up to 12 programmers. As soon as you have too many programmers to fit into one room, you'll need to add some additional layers of process to assist in communication between teams. At this point, the methodology essentially ceases to be XP.

We explore the problem of squeezing too many programmers into one room in Chapter 14.

Extreme Programming in Practice: The Voice of eXPerience

Well, we've given you a quick overview of the theory underlying XP and we've tried not to interject too much commentary thus far. But, as you might have guessed from the title of the book, we've got some pretty good reasons to believe that XP in practice is often radically different from XP in theory. Scattered throughout the book you'll see sidebars containing descriptions of real XP project experiences. Some of the people who submitted these descriptions have asked to be kept anonymous, for fear of incurring the wrath of their employers or XP teammates.

The concerns of the people who wished to remain anonymous aren't entirely unreasonable, as we'll discover in Chapter 4.

As we discuss later, XP's idealistic practices tend not to gel particularly well with real-world project conditions. The result is often a bastardized adaptation of XP, in which the process becomes warped into something altogether scarier. This experience shows through in pretty much all of these descriptions.

One thing to note about the Voice of eXPerience (VoXP) contributions you'll read in this book: When we started the book, we had no plans for any of them. As word began to spread that we were writing the book, people started sending us their contributions. To the occasional consternation of our publisher, we adjusted our schedule and increased the length of the book by about 25 pages to make room for these firsthand accounts because we feel they're tremendously important.

To kick off, the description in the "XP from the Trenches" sidebar comes from an XPer who has asked to use a pseudonym. Note that not everything described here is "pure" XP—but that in itself gives a good indication of what really happens when XP hits the mainstream.

XP from the Trenches

by "Rich Camden"

The opinions I share with you aren't those of someone who has simply read some of the XP books and disliked their content; rather, they're the opinions of someone who has read the books, practiced XP for over 7 months, and participated in XP user groups.

It's also worth noting that I'm not someone who came into this work with a negative opinion of XP and an attitude set to prove my opinion correct—quite the opposite is true. Although I had never practiced XP prior to joining my current company, I came on board enthusiastically and excited that I would get an opportunity to use XP on a real project. I had read one XP book prior to joining the company. It's directly through experience with the XP methodology that my negative opinions of it were formed.

XP is a methodology created by programmers who are sick of management telling them that they can no longer just code, but they must follow a formal methodology. XP's main tenets are all very programmer-centric and often fail to consider the larger scope of a software development project. XP programmers typically spend little time considering design and analysis issues at a project scope level.

Here are some of my opinions on a number of the main tenets of the XP methodology:

- **On-site customer:** This is a utopian dream. Sure, every development project would love to have a customer full-time at their location participating with the development team, but in the vast majority of projects, this is simply unrealistic. Thus, this ends up being a tenet that is quoted to make XP look good but it's seldom practiced.

- **Pair programming:** This is the worst of the XP tenets. To recommend pair programming across the board for all developers involved in XP is to not understand the people/personality side of programming. Yes, there are those who will benefit from having another programmer constantly sitting next to them, assisting and reviewing their work. But, there are many more who will feel uncomfortable and restrained with another programmer watching everything they do. Unfortunately, this tenet above all others tends to dampen creativity and heroics in XP. Many of the best programming gems come after absorbing oneself in a problem and much deep thinking. This doesn't occur when you have another programmer sitting next to you, trying to take control of the keyboard.

- **Unit testing:** This is a tenet that I do support completely. I believe that thorough unit testing increases the quality of any software project. XP programmers truly are good at religiously writing unit tests. This should be transitioned to non-XP projects as well.

- **Continuous integration:** I have few problems with this tenet. I do believe that integration should be done in small steps as opposed to only at the end of a software project, which is the heart of this tenet.

- **Do The Simplest Thing That Could Possibly Work (DTSTTCPW):** The biggest problem with this statement is that it doesn't stand up well on its own. Sure, if defined properly this could be a good thing, but I have seen XP shops paste this "motto" on their walls and disassociate it from a deeper explanation. Taken alone, this statement leads to poorly designed, difficult to maintain, low-quality software. Following a good design is often not the simplest thing to do at the time, but strategically it's quite often the superior thing to do. This tenet seems to be borne out of programmers who are averse to strategic design, analysis, and modeling and simply want to code.

- **40-hour week:** This is an admirable goal that I support. Unfortunately, I believe this becomes too engrained in XP programmers' heads, and even on projects in danger they don't feel the motivation to put in extra work hours.

A big problem that I see with XP projects is that they tend to be very code-centric. Because of the lack of focus on design and analysis in XP projects, all decisions made related to the development are very code-centric and often neglect to take into account a larger project scope. What you end up with is code that may look very good under a microscope, but the further you step away from the code modules, the bigger the mess you have. You end up with poorly documented and poorly designed applications.

Documentation on XP projects is poor. XP advocates that the software documentation be the code itself. They say that the code along with its tests should be sufficient documentation for any code module. Well, the reality of this is that yes, the code plus its tests provide the equivalent of very detailed documentation for how the module works. What's missing is the bridge to that level of understanding, though. Someone coming onto an XP project that relies upon code to document its modules is in for a very difficult time in trying to grasp the structure of the code and its higher-level functionality.

XP's philosophy is that all programmers should be well balanced on all technologies employed by the application. Again, although this sounds admirable as a goal, the reality of this is that you kill the enthusiasm of an expert and encourage a mediocre understanding of all technologies in all your programmers. It's simply not realistic for all programmers to become experts in all of a project's technologies. Individuals who want to gain expertise in a specific technology, such as security, GUI design, databases, and so on, are discouraged.

XP's popularity is growing not because it's converting followers of other software methodologies, but because it's attracting all the programmers who previously adhered to no formal methodology and now proudly tout that they adhere to XP methodology. I believe this is essentially a "way out" for them. They get to claim a methodology while adjusting their programming style very little.

Finally, XP hasn't been around long enough for many of those projects to have reached maintenance phases. This is where I believe many of the flaws in XP will become apparent.

I've become convinced that XP isn't a methodology that benefits customers in the long run.

Knocking It Down . . . and Then Rebuilding It

At this point we should remind ourselves that the title of this book is *Extreme Programming Refactored*, meaning that we intend to tweak and hone the XP practices into something that's semantically the same because it still achieves XP's agile goals, but does so in a much more rigorous and less risky manner. The process that we'd like to end up with should also be applicable to a much wider variety of projects and shouldn't require significant organizational change.

To get there, we analyze the not-so-good aspects of XP (in fact, most of this book analyzes the not-so-good aspects of XP, although we make no apologies for this because there are already plenty of positive books about XP out there). As a sneak preview, we present here a quick summary of the refactored process that we're aiming for.

If you'd like to read the more detailed description of the refactored process, skip ahead to Chapter 15. That chapter also contains a case study of an "XP-like" project that is very close to our refactored process.

Some of what we describe here is XP, and some of it isn't. We emphasize that this is intended as a discussion point, possibly a crib sheet for when you're tailoring a methodology for your own project—but this is far from being a methodology in itself.

The Values

XP's practices are predicated upon its values. As a set of high-level guidelines for running a software project, there's nothing particularly wrong with these. So no major changes here, then (except we've replaced "courage" with "confidence"— see the "The Values" section in Chapter 15):

- Communication

- Simplicity

- Feedback

- Confidence

The Activities

Not much to say here, except that these are all vital aspects of software development, but they aren't all there is to it:

- Coding

- Testing

- Listening

- Designing

The Other Stuff

This is where the bulk of the refactoring takes place. Here we make some changes to XP's practices, tenets, and general recommendations. Plus we mix in a few practices of our own:

- **Interaction design:** Hire an interaction designer to get the usability aspects of the software right *before* it's written, and revisit usability incrementally throughout the project.

- **Planning game:** Plan in detail for the next iteration and in less detail (milestones) further into the future.

- **Short iterations:** Use fixed 1-month iterations, but track progress on a weekly basis.

- **Small releases:** Release early and often to the customer, but beware of putting the project into maintenance mode too early.

- **Metaphor:** Complement domain models, architecture, and design with a unifying metaphor.

- **Simple design:** Always keep it simple, but don't turn a blind eye toward what you *know* you'll need to add soon.

- **Refactoring:** Refactor when necessary, but not as a replacement for up-front design.

- **Testing:** Automated tests are good, but try not to rely too heavily on them repeatedly "saving the day."

- **Programmers write their own tests:** This gets programmers thinking about code quality.

- **Quality assurance:** A separate QA team is a vital component of software development.

- **Collective ownership** *or* **individual ownership?:** Leave this to your team to decide.

- **Requirements documentation:** Define the requirements in detail, but break into subprojects.

- **Design documentation:** The documentation should be virtually a by-product of the design process.

- **Colocated team:** This is a "nice-to-have," but don't count on it always being possible.

- **On-site customer:** The colocated customer isn't a replacement for a detailed requirements spec. Specifications save projects!

- **Pair programming:** Program in pairs for difficult tasks, but don't force people to pair up!

- **Programmers do design:** Whoever designs the software should also be involved in its implementation.

- **Spikes:** Use occasional *spikes* (small ad-hoc prototypes) if necessary.

- **Continuous integration:** Integrate and fully unit-test the entire system at least once a day.

- **Sustainable pace:** Work at a sustainable pace, but do be prepared to work some extra hours every now and again.

- **Collaborative coding standards:** Get the programmers involved in defining their own coding standards, and then make sure they stick to them.

Summary

In this chapter, we provided a lightning-fast tour of the XP methodology. We also briefly discussed the problems that XP is attempting to solve and gave some indication of the way that these problems would be solved in a non-XP project.

As you probably noticed, there is some crossover between the two. This is because most of the XP practices aren't new. What sets XP apart is that it is the first methodology to have put all these practices in one place and wrap them up into one lightweight (anorexic, even!) process. (As we discuss later, XP presents a curious paradox: It's *lightweight* in the sense that it contains a small number of easy-to-remember practices, but it's *heavyweight* because adhering to its practices involves lots of unrelenting effort and discipline from the entire team for the whole project.)

We spend much of this book analyzing these practices and examining them in the context of real-world projects. Toward the end of the book (as you saw from the "sneak preview" in the preceding section), we discuss ways in which you can refactor XP as a process without causing your whole project to topple over.

CHAPTER 2

Where Did XP Come From? (Chrysler Knows It Ain't Easy . . .)

Chrysler Knows It Ain't Easy
(Sing to the tune of "The Ballad of John and Yoko" by The Beatles)

We're not on the imagined schedule
The goal donor's been gone for a week
Won't our faces be red
When the mainframes drop dead
Chrysler's really gonna be up the creek

Chrysler knows it ain't easy
They know how hard it can be
The way things are goin'
They're gonna cancel C3

Think I'd better dust off the resume
The gold owner is getting real tweaked
Some people say
The project's goin' away
Ya know the mainframe's gonna die in a week

Chrysler knows it ain't easy
They know how hard it can be
The way things are goin'
They're gonna cancel C3

Everybody here is coding for today
'Cause we all know that change is free
Last night someone said
Don't write a thing down
We won't leave nothing for them but the code

Project's goin' south in a hurry
But I figure "hey, why be meek"
Let's go to the press
And just claim success
We'll have four book contracts in a week

Chrysler knows it ain't easy
They know how hard it can be
The way things are going
They're gonna cancel C3

C3 was the seminal XP project in which complementary practices and ideals were brought together and honed to form a single process. The practices had been around for a while, but C3 was the primordial soup that sparked the birth of XP as a single documented process. It's safe to say that were it not for the widespread perception of C3 as an XP success story, there would be no XP phenomenon today, and we wouldn't have felt the need to write this book. So, we feel that the C3 story is really quite important.

The story of C3 is one of high hopes, hype, and ultimately failure. It can be summed up by the following quotes (all cited later in this chapter, emphasis ours):

"The best software development team on the face of the earth."

—Chet Hendrickson

"As of the first of February, 2000, the C3 project has been terminated without a successful launch of the next phase.*"*

—From the C2 Wiki[1]

"The C3 system now provides correct monthly payroll information for more than 86,000 employees. It's [sic] *success is ascribed to Mr Beck's golden rules."*
—*The Economist*, December 2000

"It paid somewhere just under 10,000 [employees]. *It was hoped that it would pay all Chrysler employees, somewhere around 100,000."*

—Ron Jeffries

---

1. For a description of the C2 Wiki, see the "Big Words Like Constantinople and TerminationCanBeSuccess" section in Chapter 4.

> *"The impression amongst the folk I spoke to was that in the view of DC's management C3 was a disastrous project, and never the like shall be seen again there."*
>
> —From the C2 Wiki

> *"None of this actually matters, because building a payroll systems [sic] was C3's secondary goal."*
>
> —Chet Hendrickson

> *"Never has so much hype been achieved by so few over such a dismal failure."*
>
> —Doug Rosenberg

In this chapter we piece together, from information that's freely available on the Web, the events that unfolded during and after the C3 project. We also analyze just why C3 failed and why many XPers still cling to the idea that it didn't really fail (despite having been cancelled when it was only one-third complete and late by several years).

Although XP has progressed since C3, its core elements are still essentially the same (a description of XP as used on C3, in much rawer form than the practices described in the XP books, can be found here: http://www.xprogramming.com/Practices/xpractices.htm). It's worth taking a look at that first project in some detail, because it highlights some of the major risks that are inherent in XP—even today. In fact, reports suggest that the experience left a bad taste in the customer's mouth, to the extent that "XP" is still considered a dirty word in that particular organization.

There have been reports of successful XP projects since, most of them very small-scale. For the most part, however, the XP values and practices haven't changed, therefore the same risks still apply.

Overview of C3

C3, or Chrysler Comprehensive Compensation, was the XP "poster-child" project. Many of the claims about XP working on larger projects were based on the reputed success of the C3 project. In fact, many of the people (Kent Beck, Ron Jeffries, Martin Fowler, Chet Hendrickson, Don Wells) who wrote the XP books available on the market today worked on C3. Most of the initial 2 years' worth of hype about XP came from the purported "success" of C3. Quite naturally, programmers who had no interest in doing design or documenting their work began jumping on the bandwagon. After that, XP books started coming out by the dozen, and the whole thing gained an aura of respectability.

To claim C3 as a success when it was a failed payroll replacement project that got cancelled after 4 years is, we feel, a total distortion of the truth. However, if you repeat often enough that a failed project was really a success, and you say it with enough conviction and *gusto*, over and over again (the marketing term for this is *proof by repeated assertion*, as in "Cigarettes don't cause cancer"), then people will of course start to believe you.

If you look on the C2 Wiki's Cthree Project Terminated page (http://c2.com/cgi/wiki?CthreeProjectTerminated), you can find a very interesting discussion about this project and the impression it left on the folks at Chrysler. The Chrysler Comprehensive Compensation page (http://c2.com/cgi/wiki?ChryslerComprehensiveCompensation) is also interesting. Everybody should read these pages!

The XP Project Life Cycle (As Illustrated by the Activities at C3)

The "project life cycle" in Figure 2-1 is our interpretation of the events that took place during and immediately after the C3 project. We've based this diagram on information that is publicly available on the Portland Patterns Repository "Wiki" site (the C2 Wiki site at http://www.c2.com/cgi/wiki), magazine and Web site articles including interviews with the XP authors, and various Internet discussion groups (including comp.software.extreme-programming) where the people involved in the project have posted copious messages.

In this section, we trace the C3 project life cycle from its beginnings to its "controversial cataclysmic cancellation"[2] in February 2000, using the activity diagram in Figure 2-1 as a guide. We tell the story here using mostly screen shots, quotes, and song lyrics, and then we provide the commentary and analysis afterward. Think of this as a sort of simulated multimedia story trail. Everybody sing along now. . . .

---

2. Of course, this is just our opinion! As we attempt to demonstrate in this chapter, the level at which a project really "fails" is entirely dependent on your point of view. One person's failure is another person's roaring success.

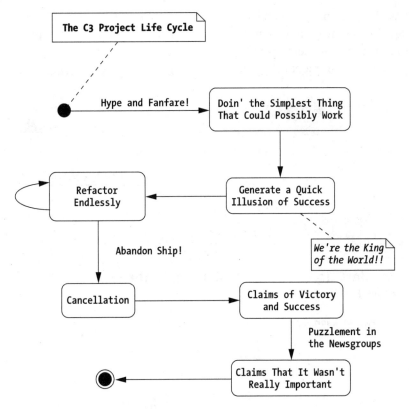

Figure 2-1. Activities during and after C3

We All Met on a Project Called C3
(Sing to the tune of "Yellow Submarine" by The Beatles)

On the Project called C threeeeeee
We told Chrysler
That change was free
'Cause we could code so rapidly
And refactor endlessly

We all met on a project called C3 . . .

Hype and Fanfare

XP is announced to the world with a flourish, with grandiose claims such as "The Best Team in the World," as we see in Figure 2-2.

C3 began in January 1995 as a fixed-price contract. The majority of the project was finished by early 1996, but it consisted mostly of a lot of GUI screens and some functions that were calculating peoples' taxes wrongly. In March 1996, the

C3 project was floundering. So Chrysler brought in Kent Beck, who in turn brought in Ron Jeffries, who in turn brought in his crack team of XPers (except then, of course, they weren't known as "XPers").

Beck's plan was to courageously throw everything away and start again.

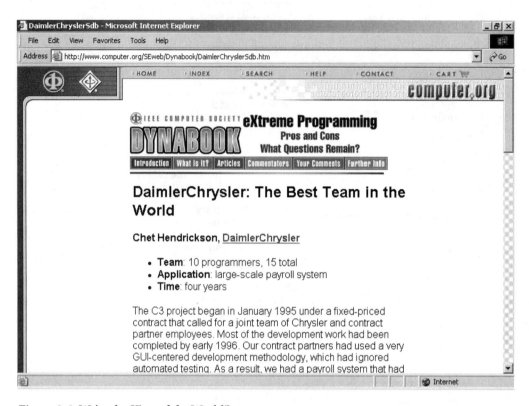

Figure 2-2. We're the King of the World![3]

When You Talk the Talk You Know the Talk That You Talk Is Really Big Talk
(Sing to the tune of "Downtown" by Petula Clark)

When you talk the talk
You know the talk that you talk is really
Big talk
Big talk

As with many doomed software projects, C3 (having been relaunched with its new Extremo power team) started out with high hopes and enthusiasm. And they were courageously "Doin' the Simplest Thing That Could Possibly Work"!

---

3. Chet Hendrickson, "DaimlerChrysler: The Best Team in the World," http://www.computer.org/SEweb/Dynabook/DaimlerChryslerSdb.htm (reprinted from *Computer*, Vol. 32, No. 10, October 1999).

Doin' the Simplest Thing That Could Possibly Work

The team was busy shaping the XP practices and doing the simplest thing possible to get today's piece of work done (see Figure 2-3).

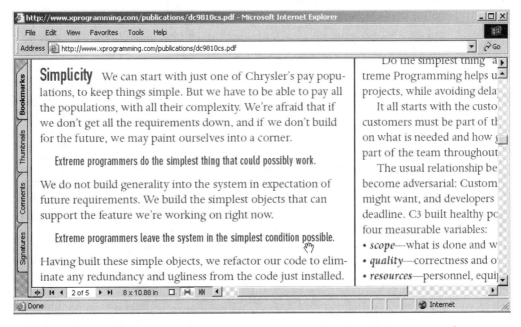

Figure 2-3. Do not build generality into the system in expectation of future requirements.

This description is from an article by Chet Hendrickson:

"Fear is the Mind Killer

"The lack of courage—what I like to call 'fear'—is self perpetuating and can most often be traced to an initial lack of one or more of the other three values [communication, feedback, and simplicity]. A group of progammers [sic] who fear doing the simplest thing that could possibly work because they do not have adequate acceptance testing (a lack of feedback) may later lack the courage to optimize performance due to the systems complexity. Fear will prevent you from doing the right thing, it reduces your degrees of freedom and will eventually drag your project to a halt. This is the antithesis of Extreme Programming."[4]

---

4. Chet Hendrickson, "When is it not XP?" http://www.xprogramming.com/xpmag/NotXP.htm, December 5, 2002.

Generate a Quick Illusion of Success

About halfway through the ill-fated project (with another 2 years to go), the article shown in Figure 2-4 appeared in *Distributed Computing* magazine. The following is excerpted from the article:

> *"We have been paying a pilot group since August 1998 and will roll out the rest before the Y2K code freeze in November 1999."*[5]

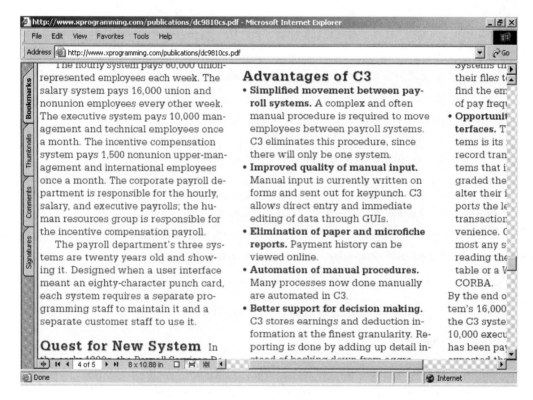

Figure 2-4. Legitimacy is achieved for the Extremos by citing success on the C3 project.[6]

In 1997, Ron Jeffries (C3's XP coach and later coauthor of *Extreme Programming Installed*) posted this message regarding the suitability of

---

5. Chet Hendrickson, "DaimlerChrysler: The Best Team in the World," op. cit.

6. The "C3 Team," "Chrysler Goes to 'Extremes,'" *Distributed Computing*, October 1998, p. 4 (reprinted on http://www.xprogramming.com/publications/dc9810cs.pdf).

Smalltalk (which some would argue was the first useful object-oriented language) for a payroll system:

"I'd never have said it, but it turns out payroll is so complicated that it is very interesting finding the inner simplicities that make it possible to write a program that works. Objects are perfect for it. Smalltalk is perfect for it. That's just part of why we call C3 Payroll the best project in the world."[7]

During and shortly after C3, a blaze of publicity surrounded the project's purported success, bouncing XP onto the software engineering stage. Here are some examples:

"The methodology was invented in 1996, when automaker Chrysler called upon Kent Beck, a software developer, to save a project known as Chrysler Comprehensive Compensation, or C3. Kurt Beck [sic] developed the method and succeeded with the project at Chrysler. The C3 system now provides monthly payroll information for Chrysler employees."[8]

"We have focused on communication here, but many Extreme Programming practices have contributed to C3's success: . . ."[9]

In retrospect it would appear that the claims of success were somewhat premature. Note that, although Ron Jeffries later claimed that the project wasn't on an "imagined schedule,"[10] the early hype surrounding the project would seem to indicate otherwise:

"By the end of October, the salary system's 16,000 employees will be paid by the C3 system. They will be joining the 10,000 executive system employees C3 has been paying since May of 1997. It is expected that the remaining 60,000 employees will move to C3 in mid-1999."[11]

They never made it. Why not? We think it might have been because they were refactoring endlessly.

---

7. Ron Jeffries posting to the newsgroup `comp.lang.smalltalk`, subject: "No One Does Payroll in Smalltalk," August 3, 1997.

8. Juergen Daum, "How to make software developers more productive through 'Extreme Programming,'" `http://www.juergendaum.com/news/04_11_2001.htm`, April 2001.

9. The "C3 Team," op. cit.

10. Ron Jeffries posting to OTUG (`http://www.rational.com`), subject: "C3 Project Terminated," October 10, 2000.

11. The "C3 Team," op. cit.

Refactor Endlessly

Without deadlines, a clear set of implementation milestones, and a documented architecture, the result is bound to be something like this (also see Figure 2-5):

"About every 3 or 4 iterations we do a refactoring that causes us to toss or otherwise radically modify a group of classes."[12]

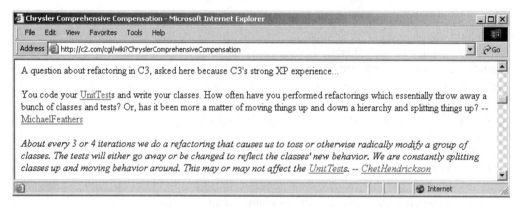

Chrysler Comprehensive Compensation - Microsoft Internet Explorer

File   Edit   View   Favorites   Tools   Help

Address http://c2.com/cgi/wiki?ChryslerComprehensiveCompensation

A question about refactoring in C3, asked here because C3's strong XP experience...

You code your UnitTests and write your classes. How often have you performed refactorings which essentially throw away a bunch of classes and tests? Or, has it been more a matter of moving things up and down a hierarchy and splitting things up? -- MichaelFeathers

About every 3 or 4 iterations we do a refactoring that causes us to toss or otherwise radically modify a group of classes. The tests will either go away or be changed to reflect the classes' new behavior. We are constantly splitting classes up and moving behavior around. This may or may not affect the UnitTests. -- ChetHendrickson

Internet

Figure 2-5. The C3 team reveled in Constant Refactoring After Programming.

Is this a recipe for an overdue project? We think that events prove it to be so. From *Extreme Programming Installed*:

"What if you don't have all the stories? Don't worry—you don't have all the stories. Things will change and all the stories will come to you. You can substitute stories at the beginning of any iteration. Just get the programmers to estimate them, and stick them into the planning process when their cost and value dictate. Grab a few cards, write down the new stories, and act like you had them all the time. No one will ever notice."[13]

12. Chet Hendrickson posting to the C2 Wiki page Chrysler Comprehensive Compensation, http://c2.com/cgi/wiki?ChryslerComprehensiveCompensation.

13. Ron Jeffries, Ann Anderson, and Chet Hendrickson, *Extreme Programming Installed* (New York, NY: Addison-Wesley, 2000), p. 30.

Although the XP practices were supposedly tailored around the needs of the C3 project, it's debatable whether a process that's optimized toward code maintenance and volatile requirements was really the best choice for replacing a legacy payroll system.

We discuss why we feel that XP is optimized toward code maintenance in Chapter 9 and in the section "Release Early, Release Often" in Chapter 13.

Was the C3 payroll really more complex than other payroll systems? C3 was being powered along by XP and a team that called itself "the best software development team on the face of the earth," shouting "BDUF!" and "YAGNI!" at each other, yet after 4 years C3 was only one-third complete.

See Chapter 8 for a definition of BDUF and Chapter 12 for a definition of YAGNI.

One area of complexity that C3 did need to encompass was the myriad of rules and procedures from many different payroll systems within Daimler-Chrysler. Rome would not be redesigned in a day. However, this does rather imply that all the requirements, all the rules, all the procedures, were already well known in existing systems—in other words, they were defined using the XPers' favorite form of documentation: source code! (Smell the COBOL!) For them, integrating these disparate payrolls should have been a breeze. More to the point, they didn't need to use a process that places such a high emphasis on change.

A more suitable process would have been one that uses the best parts from XP—unit tests, refactoring, pair programming (in moderation)—and combined these with an effective design process (the ICONIX Process springs to mind) that catches out all the misunderstandings and design oddities at an early stage (before the code has been written), and then allows the team to go full steam ahead with the testing and coding. Oh, well. They'll know better next time.

Abandon Ship!

As the months and years flew by from the salad days of 1996, the millennium and the much-dreaded Y2K deadline approached rapidly while the team continued refactoring. It became increasingly clear that the team wasn't going to make the "imagined schedule."

In the latter stages of C3, Alistair Cockburn posted this message to the C2 Wiki:

"I consider XP a HighDisciplineMethodology, one in which the people will actually fall away from the practices if they don't have some particular mechanism in place to keep them practicing. Ron is that mechanism at the moment. Should (when) Ron leave, then unless he is replaced in his role, I quite expect to see the team not following the practices properly in less than 6 months."[14]

(Much) Further down the same page, after much discussion and offense-taking to Alistair's suggestion that not everyone on the C3 project was perfect, Ron Jeffries posted this message:

"I'm no longer on C3 full time. Alistair's six-month clock has started."

About 6 months later, perhaps by unfortunate coincidence, C3 was cancelled.

Cancellation

The Project Called C3 (Second Verse)
(Sing to the tune of "Yellow Submarine" by The Beatles)

Oh the project called C3
Was cancelled inexplicabl-eee
So we all
Claimed victory
But at Chrysler
They didn't quite see
It was cancelled inexplicably
Inexplicably, inexplicably
It was cancelled inexplicably
Inexplicably, inexplicably

The Cutter Consortium's February 2000 newsletter included an interview with Ron Jeffries in which he was asked about the "success" of the C3 project:

"As we talked, I asked Jeffries how success on the C3 project translated into XP use on other Chrysler IT projects. His grin told me all I needed to know."[15]

---

14. Alistair Cockburn posting to the C2 Wiki page "High Discipline Methodology," http://www.c2.com/cgi/wiki?HighDisciplineMethodology.

15. Jim Highsmith, "Extreme Programming," http://www.cutter.com/freestuff/ead0002.pdf, p. 4. (This article originally appeared in the February 2000 edition of Cutter Consortium's "e-Business Application Delivery" newsletter.)

The author of the Cutter Consortium article evidently thought that the C3 project was a success. However, we occasionally wonder what Ron was grinning about because, that very same month, disaster struck:

"As of the first of February, 2000, the C3 project has been terminated without a successful launch of the next phase."[16]

(The page that contains this quote then adds, "But bear in mind that termination can be success." Groovy baby, yeah!)

A postmortem is given on the Cthree Project Terminated page[17] (see Figure 2-6).

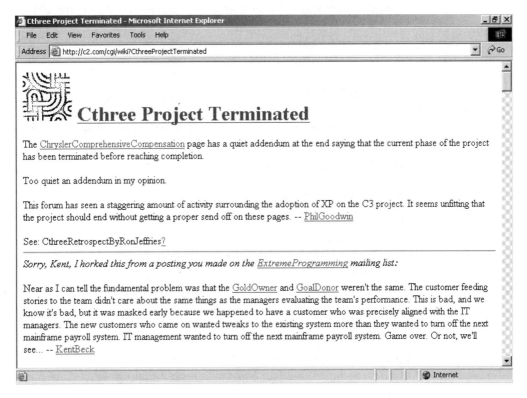

Figure 2-6. C3 project terminated

Originally intended as a Y2K payroll replacement project, the year 2000 arrived with nary a whimper. The portents of millennium bug doom that the world had been dreading simply didn't manifest into anything more than a couple of ATM cards being chewed up and a battered 20-year-old digital watch unexpectedly seizing up somewhere in Wootton Bassett, England. Meanwhile at

---

16. See http://c2.com/cgi/wiki?ChryslerComprehensiveCompensation.

17. See http://c2.com/cgi/wiki?CthreeProjectTerminated.

Chrysler, the mainframes that ran their payroll failed to keel over as anticipated. Because C3 was still not paying 76,000 out of 86,000 employees, we suspect it became expendable. The cancellation has, however, been cited as "inexplicable" by the Extremos. Seems pretty explicable to us. How much did C3 manage to achieve in its 4 long years? On the `comp.software.extreme-programming` newsgroup, Ron Jeffries wrote (on January 4, 2002):

> *"It paid somewhere just under 10,000 [employees]. It was hoped that it would pay all Chrysler employees, somewhere around 100,000. It had demonstrated the ability to pay the next batch correctly (I forget, another 20,000 or something) and those people had essentialy [sic] the same pay rules as the biggest group."*[18]

Claims of Victory and Success

By the time C3 was cancelled, XP was well on its way to becoming the phenomenon that it is today (for example, see Figure 2-7). Beck, Jeffries, Hendrickson, and others had book contracts in hand. Cries of YAGNI, BDUF, and oral documentation were sweeping the land. And something as trivial as the project's cancellation couldn't stand in the way.

It's Been Four Long Years
(Sing to the tune of "Norwegian Wood [This Bird Has Flown]" by The Beatles)

It's been four long years
And we can't get
The payroll to run

But we're not in tears
'Cause we're having
Way too much fun

We like refactoring code till it smells like it should
And we're writing all kinds of books that make us look good

But it's been four long years
And the payroll
Still doesn't run
But we have no fears
'Cause we've convinced most every one

We're really agile and others are merely afraid
Our checks don't come from C3, so we still get paid!

---

18. Ron Jeffries posting to the newsgroup `comp.software.extreme-programming`, subject: "C3 as XP Poster child," January 4, 2002.

But it's been four long years
And we can't get the payroll to run
Now we're all famous
Isn't it great?
Isn't it fun?

The following quote from Alistair Cockburn could just about be attributed to his enthusiasm for XP leading him to exaggerate the "success" of C3 and the part that XP played in C3's "success":

"The recently completed Chrysler Comprehensive Compensation (C3) experi-
ence exemplifies the above discussion. After 26 people failed to deliver what
was considered a large system, an eight-person subset of the team restarted,
using eXtreme Programming (XP), an extremely light and rigorous methodol-
ogy. The eight people successfully delivered in a year what the larger team
with heavier methodology had failed to deliver. Part of the success was its
adherence to Principle 4."[19]

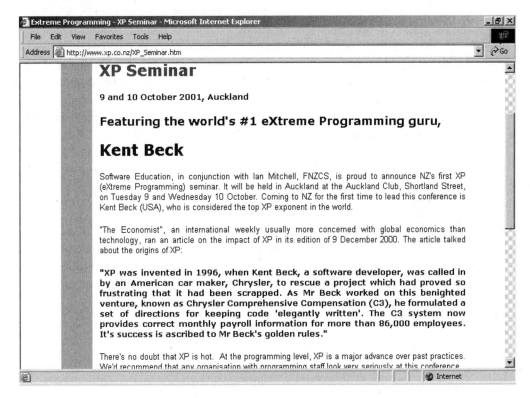

Figure 2-7. XP's success is ascribed to Mr. Beck's golden rules

---

19. Alistair Cockburn, "Selecting a Project's Methodology," *IEEE Software* (http://www.eee.metu.edu.tr/~bilgen/Cockburn647.pdf), July/August 2000.

However, the following quote from *The Economist*, which appeared *almost a year after C3 had been cancelled*, strikes us as being, well (insert tongue firmly in cheek) . . . um, slightly inaccurate:

> *"XP was invented in 1996, when Kent Beck, a software developer, was called in by an American car maker, Chrysler, to rescue a project which had proved so frustrating that it had been scrapped. As Mr Beck worked on this benighted venture, known as Chrysler Comprehensive Compensation (C3), he formulated a set of directions for keeping code 'elegantly written'. The C3 system now provides correct monthly payroll information for more than 86,000 employees. It's [sic] success is ascribed to Mr Beck's golden rules."*[20]

Puzzlement in the Newsgroups

After C3's cancellation, the C3 pages on the Wiki, which had been very active, went rather quiet for a while. Then some sheepish explanations began to appear, some of which contradicted each other (our favorite came from Chet Hendrickson, claiming that C3 was just a research project—more on this later). After that, there was noticeable confusion in various discussion groups (such as the Object Technology User Group [OTUG] and `comp.software.extreme-programming`) and the C2 Wiki (see Figure 2-8), because in some places XP was still being promoted on the back of C3's alleged "success."

In a discussion that took place on the OTUG forum, XP author Robert C. Martin gave this explanation for the cancellation of C3:

> *"Who knows what they are going to do? Certainly not you nor I. Who knows why they did what they did; again, certainly not you nor I. The only facts we really have in evidence are that the project was moving at a predictable rate that everyone was aware of, that it was paying 1/3 of the employees and ready to pay the next third. That it was inexplicably cancelled."*[21]

20. "Extreme measures," *The Economist Technology Quarterly*, December 7, 2000. (Also referenced at `http://www.xp.co.nz/XP_Seminar.htm`.)
21. Robert C. Martin posting to OTUG (`http://www.rational.com`), subject: "The Doug and Ron Show: An analysis of the termination of C3," October 11, 2000.

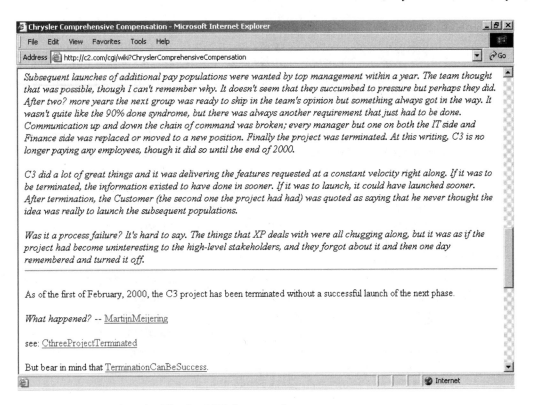

Subsequent launches of additional pay populations were wanted by top management within a year. The team thought that was possible, though I can't remember why. It doesn't seem that they succumbed to pressure but perhaps they did. After two? more years the next group was ready to ship in the team's opinion but something always got in the way. It wasn't quite like the 90% done syndrome, but there was always another requirement that just had to be done. Communication up and down the chain of command was broken; every manager but one on both the IT side and Finance side was replaced or moved to a new position. Finally the project was terminated. At this writing, C3 is no longer paying any employees, though it did so until the end of 2000.

C3 did a lot of great things and it was delivering the features requested at a constant velocity right along. If it was to be terminated, the information existed to have done in sooner. If it was to launch, it could have launched sooner. After termination, the Customer (the second one the project had had) was quoted as saying that he never thought the idea was really to launch the subsequent populations.

Was it a process failure? It's hard to say. The things that XP deals with were all chugging along, but it was as if the project had become uninteresting to the high-level stakeholders, and they forgot about it and then one day remembered and turned it off.

As of the first of February, 2000, the C3 project has been terminated without a successful launch of the next phase.

What happened? -- MartijnMeijering

see: CthreeProjectTerminated

But bear in mind that TerminationCanBeSuccess.

Figure 2-8. It wasn't quite like the 90% done syndrome.

Inexplicably? They start a Y2K project in 1996, and by February 2000 it's only one-third deployed. So it gets cancelled.

In the same message, Martin adds:

> *"OK Doug, you can once again repeat the litany of: 'In four long horrible drought-filled years XP delivered only one meager third of the required functionality, and has placed DC in the position of having to throw everything away and pay gazillions of dollars for a replacement.' But it's a pretty lame argument."*

Actually, that seems like a pretty concise statement of the facts. What exactly makes it lame other than the reality that it doesn't support the XPers' marketing efforts?

An interesting summing up of the C3 project life cycle is given on the Wiki site (our emphasis):

"Written in 2002: The original estimate done by the C3 team in March 1996 was that the project would be ready to ship in about a year. It launched in about a year . . . Subsequent launches of additional pay populations were wanted by top management within a year. The team thought that was possible, though I can't remember why. It doesn't seem that they succumbed to pressure but perhaps they did. After two? more years the next group was ready to ship in the team's opinion but something always got in the way. It wasn't quite like the 90% done syndrome, but there was always another requirement that just had to be done. Communication up and down the chain of command was broken; every manager but one on both the IT side and Finance side was replaced or moved to a new position. Finally the project was terminated. At this writing, C3 is no longer paying any employees, though it did so until the end of 2000."[22]

Is this a predictable outcome of scope creep due to not writing requirements down? We think so. This is *exactly* why we write specifications. Forty years of software engineering experience has taught us that major problems happen when you don't write the requirements down and just let a team[23] build what it likes. It is *sheer lunacy* to ignore this experience. But anyone who suggests otherwise is branded a coward in the Extremo culture. The inmates are running the asylum.

The explanation from Kent Beck is as follows:

"Near as I can tell the fundamental problem was that the GoldOwner and GoalDonor weren't the same. The customer feeding stories to the team didn't care about the same things as the managers evaluating the team's performance. This is bad, and we know it's bad, but it was masked early because we happened to have a customer who was precisely aligned with the IT managers. The new customers who came on wanted tweaks to the existing system more than they wanted to turn off the next mainframe payroll system. IT management wanted to turn off the next mainframe payroll system. Game over. Or not, we'll see . . ."[24]

---

22. See http://c2.com/cgi/wiki?ChryslerComprehensiveCompensation.

23. That includes the on-site customer representative—just one of the project's many masters.

24. Kent Beck posting to the C2 Wiki page Cthree Project Terminated, http://c2.com/cgi/wiki?CthreeProjectTerminated.

It seems pretty clear from reading this. The "GoalDonor" was told by the XP team that they should "embrace change" and that "change is free." So what did they do? They told the programmers to fiddle with features. The "GoldOwner" wanted to still be able to pay their employees on January 2, 2000, and had started the project (in 1996!) because they were afraid the mainframes would die on January 1, 2000.

It got cancelled "inexplicably" in February 2000 when the mainframes didn't die as expected. Their "agile" techniques failed to replace a mainframe payroll system in 4 years (4 years!). How is this an increase in productivity?

When Ron Jeffries was asked this question on OTUG, he replied

"XP doesn't claim 'fabulous productivity gains.' We claim to tell you where you are. Have I published something to the contrary? Let me know, I'll correct it."[25]

Riiiiiiiiiight.

This is from Jeffries' book *Extreme Programming Installed*:

"We give you the ability to move very rapidly, and to change your requirements any time you need to."[26]

Meanwhile, one is inclined to wonder what the management at Chrysler made of all this. At the time of this writing, we heard that Chet Hendrickson is involved in a new XP project in a different part of Chrysler. However, the initial reaction of the Chrysler management appears to have been far from favorable (see Figure 2-9 for an example of the discussion of C3's termination on the Wiki site).

---

25. Ron Jeffries posting to OTUG (http://www.rational.com), subject: "C3 Project Terminated," October 10, 2000.

26. Ron Jeffries et al., *Extreme Programming Installed*, op cit., p. 33.

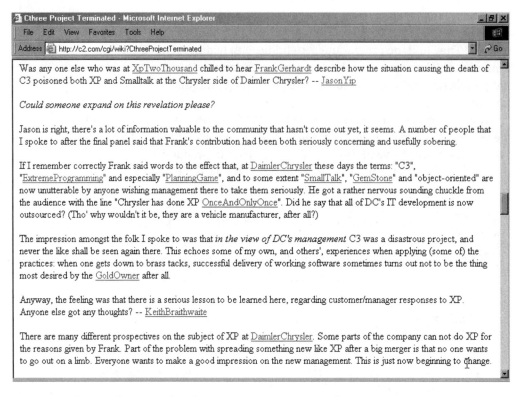

Figure 2-9. "... in the view of DC's management C3 was a disastrous project ..."

Claims That It Wasn't Really Important

The original description of C3 by Kent Beck

> *"I am involved in a GemstoneProject at ChryslerCorporation to replace their
> many payroll applications with a single application. The project has been going
> on for a couple of years. I was brought in to help with PerformanceTuning, but
> ended up as a sort of HeadCoach of an effort to StartFresh."*[27]

differs somewhat from the following postmortem descriptions by various other
XP authors who were involved in the project.

---

27. Kent Beck posting to the C2 Wiki page Chrysler Comprehensive Compensation,
    http://c2.com/cgi/wiki?ChryslerComprehensiveCompensation.

In defense of C3, Chet Hendrickson posted this to the C2 Wiki (our emphasis):

"None of this actually matters, *because building a payroll systems* [sic] *was C3's secondary goal. I don't think anyone has written about this before, mostly because it happened before RonJeffries joined the team. The team's original charter, and it was reiterated when the decision to bring in KentBeck was made, was to learn how to use object technology, to learn how to manage projects that use it and if we built a new payroll system, that would be gravy.*"[28]

Hendrickson also posted this to `comp.software.extreme-programming` in January 2002 (also see Figure 2-10):

"*The truth is that all software projects run until they are cancelled. The successful ones deliver value before the plug is pulled. If you think 4 years is a long time for a payroll system, think about how long the Microsoft Word project has been going on. Its [sic] been about 10 years and they are not done yet! That is an awfully long time to build an [sic] text editor.*"[29]

And this is from Robert Martin (who wasn't on the C3 project) in the same thread:

"*C3 was a project that was started by the IT group as a 'research' project. They wanted to understand the benefits of using OO. So they commissioned C3 to be done in Smalltalk. Eventually IT learned what they wanted to learn. OO doesn't naturally deliver. It requires a gelled team to deliver. IT did not want to continue paying for the team since it was not their responsibility to replace the payroll system. The finance department was not interested in paying for the team either. They had a payroll system already. So, in the end, IT decided to shut down the team.*"

---

28. Chet Hendrickson posting to the C2 Wiki page Cthree Project Terminated, `http://c2.com/cgi/wiki?CthreeProjectTerminated`.

29. Chet Hendrickson posting to the newsgroup `comp.software.extreme-programming`, subject: "About C3," January 16, 2002.

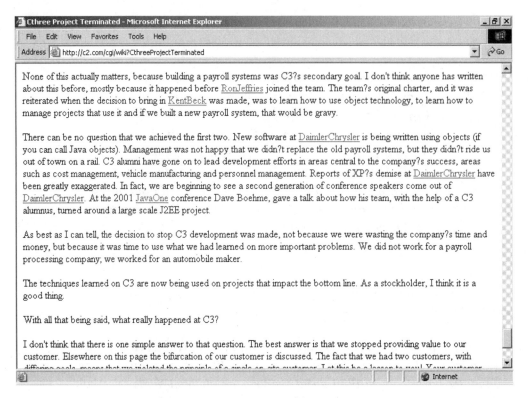

Figure 2-10. Building a payroll system was C3's secondary goal.

An earlier description of C3 (around 2000, after the project had been cancelled) as a research project prompted this slightly puzzled response from someone who was on the original C3 team (before the crack XP squad took over):

"When did C3 become a 'research' project? When I was part of the group that got involved in delivering it in 1994 it wasn't a research project—it was a fixed price (and fixed delivery date (in 1995 I believe)) project. Could someone more knowledgeable of the project evolutions since 1995 react to the late C3 project's characterization as 'research'?"[30]

Ron Jeffries responded as follows:

---

30. Charles Marcus Durrett posting to the newsgroup comp.software.extreme-programming, subject: "C3 dead," July 15, 2000.

"It was always a research project in that it was funded by IT rather than by the customer as are most projects there. It was a research project with the intention of delivering a product, however, and the negotiation of the transition never took place between Finance and IT. This was but one of the weird things that happened."[31]

This insightful message was posted by somebody in response to Jeffries' message:

"If you all had talked extensively with domain experts from Finance about payroll, it seems likely that you all would have found out that what IT had you doing was not fulfilling the real needs of Finance wrt payroll. This seems to validate RUP's approach of doing deeper and more thorough investigation of the domain and requirements before high level production coding."[32]

A good point was made by someone in the later (2002) thread:

"Isn't it almost asinine to use an 'agile' methodology on a task (Payroll) which CAN be completely specced out in advance, so far in advance that 10 yr old mainframe software still fits the bill?"[33]

And here's Robert Martin's carefully considered response:

"No."

Problems with C3

The main problem that beset C3, of course, was that the team didn't come close to getting it done in 4 years (although some XPers have since argued—spuriously, we feel—that this was really a sign of its success[34]).

---

31. Ron Jeffries posting to the newsgroup `comp.software.extreme-programming`, subject: "C3 dead," July 18, 2000.
32. Elliott posting to the newsgroup `comp.software.extreme-programming`, subject: "C3 dead," July 19, 2000.
33. Jordan Bortz posting to the newsgroup `comp.software.extreme-programming`, subject: "C3 as XP Poster child..was Re: The case against Hype — woops other reply was blank," January 3, 2002.
34. See `http://www.c2.com/cgi/wiki?AnAcceptableWayOfFailing`.

We discuss the problem of schedule overrun (which is a high risk in any XP project) in Chapter 11.

C3 could be thought of as a testing ground for the XP practices. As such, it had more than its fair share of problems, many of which, now that they're better understood, could probably be dealt with in advance for new projects. Other problems, we feel, are high risk regardless of whether they are well understood or not.

Ultimately, was C3 an "acceptable way of failing"? A short page on the Wiki site discusses the opposite: an "unacceptable way of failing." This page suggests that the following are unacceptable ways of failing:[35]

- Lack of good common sense

- Lack of commitment from either management or workers

- Lack of communication

It's worth keeping these items in mind when you read through the problems that the C3 project experienced, which we summarize in the following sections.

Too Tough for the On-site Customer

As if schedule overrun wasn't bad enough, another key problem that afflicted C3 was the project's overreliance on the on-site customer. This is something that can affect any XP project, because the on-site customer is often a single person over whom the developers have no control, but whose consistently high-quality contribution to the project is a vital factor in its success.

We discuss the on-site customer in Chapter 5.

Later in the project, there were problems with their new, "very bright and dedicated" customer not communicating very much with the so-called gold owner (the people at Chrysler who held the purse strings), which leads us neatly to the next problem.

---

35. See http://www.c2.com/cgi/wiki?AnUnacceptableWayOfFailing.

Too Many Cooks

The C3 project had two customers: the *goal donor* (the on-site customer who contributed the requirements) and the *gold owner*[36] (the project sponsor, who wasn't directly involved in the project). This is probably true of most, if not all, projects: The team has more than one master. This also highlights a classic problem with XP: The customer speaks with more than one voice.

It's likely, and somewhat ironic given XP's emphasis on having an on-site customer, that the project sponsor can normally be thought of as the "real" customer, the one who must be kept happy at all costs. If the project is going in a direction that the real customer isn't happy with, the project stands a heavy risk of being cancelled. This is exactly what happened to C3.

> We suggest some ways to get around the "too many cooks" problem in Chapter 7.

Not Incremental Enough

A point made by Ron Jeffries concerning C3 was this:

> *"One of C3's possibly-not-minor problems was that we did NOT release the payroll incrementally because no one could see how to do half a population. That was IMO a mistake."*[37]

It's generally accepted that small, frequent releases are one of XP's strengths—in fact, they're a vital part of an XP project's success, because without early user feedback, the project's functionality might deviate considerably from what the end user really needs the system to do.

The problem mentioned by Jeffries highlights the fact that "real-world" circumstances often get in the way of the process's ideals. The C3 team would have *liked* to keep the releases small and frequent, as recommended by XP, but it couldn't, because in reality it was too difficult.

---

36. See the definitions of GoldOwner and GoalDonor at http://c2.com/cgi/wiki?GoldOwner. Notably, this page states that "when the GoldOwner and GoalDonor do not have consensus, the project is usually doomed."

37. Ron Jeffries posting to OTUG (http://www.rational.com), subject: "Schedule is the customer's problem!" October 23, 2000.

Developers Strayed from the Path

On the Wiki site, Ron Jeffries wrote:

> *"Don is right to have confidence in the C3 folks, whom he knows. However, as I mentioned elsewhere, we have recently found it necessary to have a revival meeting to recommit to our beliefs, because we had strayed fairly far from them. I'm quite concerned—the whole team is—about what let us get off track so far with no alarms going off. And in this case, I was actually here. So much for the theory that I'm indispensible [sic]."*[38]

The argument surrounds the question, is XP a high-discipline methodology? The answer seems to be that it is, because if you stray even a little bit from the XP practices, your project is more likely to fail. This is borne out by numerous newsgroup postings by the Extremos.

Summary

In this chapter, we examined the beginnings of XP. Because XP was mostly hatched from the C3 project, we set out to describe C3 in detail. We did this using sources that are freely available on the Internet. We supplied as many references as we could, and we invite readers to do their own detective work in addition to this and, of course, to draw their own conclusions. The story that unfolds is quite fascinating to track down and piece together, if only because *so much* has been said and written about C3, and so much of what has been said and written about it is contradictory.

Later in the book (in various chapters), we suggest what we think could have been done to prevent C3's failure (sort of "Okay, kids what have we learned here today?") Of course, to do this we have the luxury of hindsight, but then if we've got it, we may as well flaunt it, right?

In conclusion, much could have been done to prevent the failure of C3. The remedies we propose, however, would result in a software process that just isn't XP. The lessons learned from this project are more relevant than ever today, because the same XP practices that caused its failure are still being actively promoted and adopted in projects all around the world. A whole new generation of software developers is about to get its fingers burned.

---

38. Ron Jeffries posting to the C2 Wiki page High Discipline Methodology, http://www.c2.com/cgi/wiki?HighDisciplineMethodology.

CHAPTER 3

The Case Against XP

Eight Builds a Week
(Sing to the tune of "Eight Days a Week" by The Beatles)

Livin' in a timebox
Guess you know it's rough
Gotta build every day, babe
Even half-baked stuff

Build it, ship it
Build it, ship it

Ain't got time for design, babe
Eight builds a week

Build it every day, babe
Build it right on time
One thing I can say, babe
No time for design

Refactor it, test it
Build it, ship it
Ain't got time for design, babe
Eight builds a week

Well, so far we've talked a lot about the dangers of XP, but we haven't yet described exactly why XP is more fragile than agile. Now it's time to put our money where our mouths are! To do this we use the metaphor of a circle of snakes. Then in later chapters, we describe each of these "snakes" in more detail.

A Self-Referential Safety Net (Circle of Snakes)

"Any one practice doesn't stand well on its own (with the possible exception of testing). They require the other practices to keep them in balance."[1]

—Kent Beck

---

1. Kent Beck, *Extreme Programming Explained: Embrace Change* (New York, NY: Addison-Wesley, 2000), p. 69.

"Well, from my experience, most teams that say they're doing XP don't actually do the practices."[2]

—Alistair Cockburn

"Houston, we have a problem."[3]

—Jim Lovell

Cockburn's comment isn't just an off-the-wall quip about XP: He discusses this particular concern in several other forums. For example, he also describes XP as a "high discipline" methodology—it takes a lot of sustained effort to adhere to XP's practices.[4] This is a fundamental problem with XP, combined with the methodology's fragile nature.

XP is a symbiotic process—that is, you really need to do all of XP or none at all. There's no in-between (unless you perform some very careful and deliberate tailoring). The theory is that each of these individually flawed practices reinforces each other to produce something stronger. Unfortunately, this can also work in the other direction: Stop doing one and the chain unravels. In the real world it proves difficult to adhere to the XP practices for the duration of an entire project.

From Symbiosis to Symbolism

The XP methodology is rife with symbolism that illustrates and reinforces its symbiosis in various ways. For example, XP is often described in terms of fear and courage.

We explore the fear and courage aspect of XP in the section "Fear" in Chapter 4.

And in *Extreme Programming Installed*, Ron Jeffries gives XP a distinctly New Age nuance:

"Steering a project to success all comes down to what we call the 'circle of life.'"[5]

Dreamy, baby.

---

2. Alistair Cockburn posting to the C2 Wiki page XP and the CMM, `http://c2.com/cgi/wiki?XpAndTheCmm`.

3. Jim Lovell, Captain of Apollo 13, April 13, 1970.

4. See `http://www.c2.com/cgi/wiki?HighDisciplineMethodology`.

5. Ron Jeffries, Ann Anderson, and Chet Hendrickson, *Extreme Programming Installed* (New York, NY: Addison-Wesley, 2000), p. 14.

The tightly meshed nature of the XP practices also enables impressive-looking charts and metaphors that show the many ways in which the XP practices interrelate and rely upon each other. Just like too much coupling in a software design, we'll soon see that too much coupling between required practices in a software process can lead to trouble as well.

A prime example is the Extreme Programming Enabling Chart (http://c2.com/cgi/wiki?ExtremeProgrammingEnablingChart), which uses a honeycomb of adjacent hexagons to demonstrate the way in which specific XP practices and ideals combine to enable some other XP practices, ideals, and benefits. It's worth a look, if only because the chart itself is an exercise in ingenuity. It's obvious that the person who produced this chart spent a lot of time on it and is very proud of it. However, this chart, which is really intended to show how XP's practices combine to produce various benefits, also shows exactly how tightly coupled and overly dependent XP's practices are on each other.

Our favorite example by far, though, is William Wake's XP Programmer's Cube (http://xp123.com/xplor/xp0006/index.shtml—if you look at only one URL of all the references we give you in this book, make it this one!). Each face of the cube shows an XP practice, with an arrow pointing to an adjacent face. The three-dimensional nature of the cube demonstrates how each XP practice interrelates with the others. The best part of the cube is the "Integrate or Toss" side—in other words, go home every day at 5:00 PM, and if you have incomplete work at that time, simply toss it away. Wake describes this as "going home clean." (The Web page containing the XP Programmer's Cube also forms the basis of Chapter 9 of *Extreme Programming Explored*—so the XP cube is an "official" artifact of XP, not just something cooked up by a rabid fan.)

> **Child:** *"What did you do today, Daddy?"*
> **Father:** *"I tossed out my code and went home clean. And tomorrow I intend to pair program and stare at someone else typing."*

The theory behind "going home clean" is that when the programmer rewrites the code the next day, the code will be clearer and better structured—primarily because some additional thought process has now gone into the design of the code, and tossing it away and rewriting it allows the programmer to rewrite it to the better design, unfettered by having to refactor the crufty old version from yesterday. Curiously enough, this is the same effect that we get from spending time on an up-front design.

> *We describe the much more efficient and less error-prone process of up-front design and early prototyping in Chapter 12.*

The practice of "going home clean" is also described by Kent Beck in *Extreme Programming Explained*:

> *"If the end of the day is coming and the code is a little out of control, toss it. Maybe save the test cases, if you like the interface you've designed, but maybe not. Maybe just start over from scratch."*[6]

We like this idea so much that, well, it makes us feel like a song:

Yesterday (I refactored Half My Code Away)
Sing to the tune of "Yesterday" by The Beatles

Yesterday
I refactored half my code away
I think I'll do it again today
Oh I had fun on yesterday

Suddenly
When I told my client change was free
They changed all the stories they told me
My requirements change so frequently

I tried to integrate my new code
But there's no way
I could get it done by five
So I threw it all awaaaaaaaaaaaaaaaay

Yesterday

Yep, we like coding *so* much that we're happy to toss the code we wrote today and rewrite it first thing in the morning. Don't click the Save button. Nope. That wouldn't be extreme enough. Rewrite it from scratch. This is even more extreme than refactoring. When you refactor, you (in theory) improve the structure of the code. This is even better! You and your pair just rewrite the *same* code. Wow! It's inspired! Forget "oral documentation"—idiocy has been raised to new and greater heights. Oh heck, it just makes us feel like singing again.

I'm Rewriting Code That I Wrote Yesterday
(To the tune of "I Love You More Today Than Yesterday" by Spiral Starecase)

I'm rewriting code that I wrote yesterday
And I'll refactor tomorrow
I'm rewriting code that I wrote yesterday
And darling I'll refactor it tomorrow

---

6.   Kent Beck, op. cit., p. 33.

Every day's a new day
When I code with you
Every time I unit test my mind starts to wander
And if all my dreams come true
I'll rewrite all my code with you

Ohhhhhhh
I'm rewriting code that I wrote yesterday
And I'll refactor tomorrow

 On a closely related musical topic, if you liked these songs you might also like "Software Is Never Done" at the beginning of Chapter 11.

But we digress. As described earlier, XP is a symbiotic process with tightly coupled, interdependent practices. This *should* make XP a robust process well suited to difficult projects (because in theory the practices strengthen each other), but because the practices are difficult to follow, the opposite happens. To illustrate this, and given the preceding symbolism, we feel justified in introducing some lighthearted symbolism of our own.

Circle of Life or Circle of Snakes?

The tightly meshed nature of XP's practices and activities makes them like a ring of poisonous snakes, daisy-chained together. All it takes is for one of the snakes to wriggle loose, and you've got a very angry, poisonous serpent heading your way. What happens next depends on the snake and to an extent on how good you are at damage control.

To quote Kent Beck again:

"Each of the practices still has the same weaknesses as before, but what if those weaknesses were now made up for by the strengths of other practices? We might be able to get away with doing things simply."[7]

The latter sentiment is admirable, although it could be argued that software development done properly is simple enough already. However, the real problem behind this approach is that XP becomes a high-risk proposition. What happens if an XP team makes even a minor digression from the sacred practices? Well, you're probably in trouble, because each practice only "works" when supported by some other practice; in effect, the XP practices are like a house of cards or a ring of snakes.

---

7.   Kent Beck, op. cit., p. 63.

Each snake, or XP rule, can be made safe only by daisy-chaining it to the next snake, and so on:

 **No detailed written requirements** means the project leaps underway without any formalized requirements (just some user stories handwritten on small cards) and without a particularly solid idea of where it's going to end up. This is a likely scenario because XP is aimed at "risky projects with dynamic requirements"[8] (for instance, converting legacy payroll systems to be Y2K compliant). Due to XP's promises, such a project will likely go ahead, whereas in reality land, the brakes should be slammed on and the project examined to find out how its risks can be reduced before any real expense is committed. Nevertheless, vague and sporadic (sorry, *dynamic*) requirements[9] are handled by designing as you go along: emergent design.

 **Emergent design** means that very little time is spent designing the system before coding begins (i.e., there is no BDUF). The overall design and architecture will morph many times in the course of the project. But the lack of significant up-front design is considered "safe" because the code is being constantly refactored.

 **Constant refactoring** (i.e., constant tweaking and simplifying of your design) creates an unnecessary overhead. Outside the XP world, *occasional refactoring* is welcome, as it is useful to check and improve ("defluff") your design. *Constant refactoring*, however, makes no sense, because plenty of structured thought and discussion will have already gone into getting the design right. In fact, constant refactoring makes sense only in the XP world, where the design is made up as you go along; hence, refactoring is necessary to combat "emergent entropy."

Constant refactoring is time consuming and involves rewriting existing code that was previously thought to be finished. It could also potentially introduce lots of bugs, as dependent code is broken when you make small insidious changes to your design, but it's considered safe because of extensive unit testing.

 We introduce emergent entropy in Chapter 11. Also see the sidebar "Constantly Fighting Emergent Entropy" in Chapter 13.

8.　See http://www.extremeprogramming.org.

9.　We discuss some ways of dealing with vague requirements in a non-XP context in Chapters 10 and 15.

 **Unit tests** are useful in everyday coding (not just in XP). However, as a safety net for test-first design and constant refactoring, they leave a critical area uncovered: design correctness. The problem is that unit tests catch certain types of code-level bugs, but they don't catch "wrongness" of a design. Design errors really need a human to be involved—ideally, a full-time person to sit beside you and behave like a design unit tester. Luckily, XP has just such a safety net: the pair programmer.

 **Pair programming** enables the programmers to help each other to stumble and fumble through the dark tunnels of scary Castle Complexity. Rotating the pairs frequently prevents them from becoming stale and helps to increase code familiarity. However, accountability becomes a problem because each programmer ends up working on several different parts of the system in a day. As usual, XP has an answer for this: *Nobody* is accountable! In other words, everyone "owns" the code as a collective.

 **Collective ownership** is a double-edged snake. On one hand, if everyone is responsible for the entire codebase, then crufty code does not stay crufty for long: Someone will find it and refactor it. On the other hand, collective ownership also means that really, no one is responsible for anything. There's no direct accountability besides the collective team being responsible. The problem of a pair jumping in and changing any piece of code could also be a problem and may result in "endless refactoring," where a design is being pulled in two different directions by different programmer pairs. But without a detailed specification of any sort, the code being produced would become increasingly distant from what the customer really wants. So XP gives the team a walking, talking, mind-changing spec, empowered to make snap decisions that can change the course of the whole project: the on-site customer representative.

 Having an **on-site customer representative** is risky for a number of reasons, not least that he or she is bound to be pretty junior. Is the customer really going to spare a senior decision-maker for an entire year? (How about for 4 years—after all, it's an open-ended variable scope contract, right?) Another, probably more important, reason is that the XP customer role is inherently challenging and therefore stressful. As we saw in Chapter 2, it is unlikely that the on-site customer representative will survive the entire project, and this is the person who holds the detailed requirements in his or her head.

Regardless, the customer representative "becomes" the formalized requirements spec. The presence of the customer on-site also means that the project scope can (and is likely to) change throughout the project. This would be nearly impossible to accurately plan in any detail. But this doesn't matter because planning is just a game anyway. Not to mention that keeping the requirements up-to-date at this rate of change could become a real nightmare. Luckily, XP tells us that we don't need to write the requirements down in any permanent or detailed form.

Also see the section "On-site Customer: The Old Testament" in Chapter 5.

Having **no detailed written requirements** is dangerous because . . . and we're back at the start of the loop. ("There's a hole in my bucket . . .")

We cover the preceding "snakes" in more detail in the remainder of the book.

Voice of eXPerience: Let One Snake Loose, And . . .

This description of an XP project gone badly wrong was given to us by an XPer who understandably wishes to remain anonymous. It's a shining example of XP hitting the mainstream. The team wanted to do all of XP but were prevented from performing all of the practices because management got involved and selectively chose the practices to perform on a spurious economic basis (i.e., "Don't do refactoring, it's rework. Do this new work instead."). The result was, as you can imagine, a mess. We would point out that this is quite an extreme example, but based on information from the various XPers we've spoken to, the situation doesn't appear to be atypical. Our own comments are added in italics.

The team consisted of about 10 programmers, 5 DBAs/admins, plus a team of 15 analysts. Staff turnover on the project was quite high (particularly among the contractors).

Actually, the most interesting thing was how little of XP that we were doing, even though the company describes itself as an XP shop. The prevailing attitude was, "We're doing XP, so don't do any of that up-front design stuff. Just code, code, code. We can refactor it later." Later (where most of the lunacy was driven by management) the attitude was, "Refactor? No, no time for that. We've got all these new features to add!"

This brings up the issue that refactoring doesn't get its own story card; it's just supposed to happen "all the time" as a concurrent process. But in companies where time is scarce, refactoring of existing code may be seen as a luxury.

The codebase was like a small city: huge, sprawling, and unfeasibly complex, with lots and lots of duplication. Sometimes, uncovering buried subsystems was like discovering telephone lines or sewers, then three different sewers because the companies were competing.

This is hardly "once and only once,"[10] but it's a telltale sign of a project that has been allowed to evolve with no up-front design and no time spent on refactoring.

We deviated from XP in other ways out of necessity. We stored user stories electronically because there were too many people to share a single stack of cards. Even a team of two people would find this a problem. Also, the management couldn't justify optional scope contracts—we needed to be able to say, "Yes, we're going to produce this by this date." We also didn't have a "real" on-site customer, but we did have a team of analysts in the same building.

(Luckily, XP has shifted its goalposts to make the last one "real" XP. Goal by default!)

The upshot is that most of the XP practices just can't be justified individually, and that's what happens—XP rarely appears to be accepted as a "whole." It gets adopted piece by piece.

One particular team member championed the cause of unit testing. When she went on holiday, the rest of the team stopped unit testing for a short while (about a week), and it was really noticeable that the code quality suffered almost immediately—suddenly a lot more defects were springing up. Even though we weren't doing much refactoring, the unit tests were still necessary for regression testing as new functionality was being added.

Further discussion revealed that the reason so many defects were springing up was because the code was so badly factored. The unit tests were just about keeping the snakes at bay, but the code seriously needed to be cleaned up.

We also practiced collective ownership. This caused the problem that there was no accountability—new contractors joining the team consistently said, "[Insert expletive here], who wrote this code?" In answer, all the programmers could do was shrug their shoulders, because nobody knew the answer—no one to fire.

So there wasn't much actual XP going on—just enough of it to cause a big stinky mess. And the more we look into this, the more it seems that that's how XP gets adopted in the real world. Introduce the risky, hype-inflated practices first (the ones that give management the advertised "benefits"), and then plan to introduce the other practices later at some stage maybe, if there's time.

And, it seems that XP is especially prone to this failure mechanism precisely because these risky, hype-inflated practices appeal, in many cases, to the wrong types of individuals, including cowboy coders and pointy-haired managers who should know better, but often don't.

Letting the Snakes Unravel

XP projects are difficult, more so because the practices are so interdependent. The XP authors appear keen to admit this fact. For example, according to Ron Jeffries,

---

10. See http://www.c2.com/cgi/wiki?OnceAndOnlyOnce.

"I've observed that when C3 goes off-process, productivity drops substantially. This is consistent with our claim that XP is synergistic."[11]

It takes a lot of discipline to keep an XP project on track. Synergistic? Much like knife juggling, it takes a lot of discipline to keep practicing all of the practices all at once, consistently, throughout the many increments of your project. Lose your concentration for just a minute and the tangle of snakes could unravel. If that happens, productivity is likely to drop considerably.

The question is, to what extent can you relax before one of the snakes seizes this opportunity to wriggle loose? The answer depends on which snake wriggled loose.

What If Your Team Has Stopped Writing Unit Tests?

If your team has stopped writing unit tests but is still refactoring away every day, then this will quickly cause problems. Unit tests are a tool for *automated regression testing*—that is, testing that a change you've just made didn't break the existing codebase. By changing the design of existing code, it's pretty much impossible to know whether you've broken any dependent code without testing it. Without a written design and architecture model to trace dependencies between code modules, you also might not be aware exactly what code calls the module that you're changing. So making these changes without unit tests is virtually suicidal.

How about if a programmer just skips a few unit tests? Say, for example, it's 4:30 PM and you don't want to toss all the code you've been working on so you can "go home clean" . . . so you're hurrying to get it integrated . . . you can skip just a couple of unit tests, right? Sure, you can. Then the problem is more subtle, but it would hopefully be discovered before any real damage is done.

An effect observed in XP projects is that "test-infected" programmers tend to reach homeostasis with their unit tests. They begin by writing too many tests, and then eventually they get lazy, writing fewer and fewer, until the day they notice a bug slipped by. At that point they hike up the number of tests again.

What If Your Team Is No Longer Refactoring?

If your team is no longer refactoring but is also not spending any time producing a design before coding, then the resultant codebase will almost certainly be

---

11. Ron Jeffries posting to the C2 Wiki page All Of Xp, `http://c2.com/cgi/wiki?AllOfXp`.

a botch job of horrific spaghetti code cobbled together with duct tape. Have you *seen* spaghetti cobbled together with duct tape?

How about if the team is still refactoring a bit but has slackened off because, after all, keeping on refactoring code that the team has already proven to work might become a bit tedious (even for the most rabid of code-sniffers) after, say, a year? What if the team is still refactoring, but not ruthlessly enough to really bash the design into shape? This problem is more insidious than the unit test problem, because failure in this area is more difficult to detect. Bad design is, initially at least, a subjective thing—that is, until design errors come back to bite you. This usually won't happen until you need to extend the code with new functionality, or when the current increment is released and the customer immediately complains that the program is too flaky, or too slow, or (worst case) crashes a lot under real-world conditions. This sort of problem can, luckily, also be caught early with small, frequent releases; that is, the customer gets to see bugs earlier.

. . . but see the "What If Those Small, Frequent Releases Get Less and Less Frequent?" section later in this chapter.

The Refactorer's Responsibility

Normally it is the refactorer's responsibility to change all the code that uses the interface that he has changed; therefore, all integrated code must be fully working. However, this does have the side effect (as we discuss in the section "What If Programmers Take Ownership of Code?") that code that was previously thought to be completed suddenly needs to be rewritten, possibly even redesigned, because a separate part of the system has been refactored. As we discussed earlier, many of the XP refactorings involve interface changes, so this is quite a high risk.

Also see the next sidebar, "The Snake That Got Away."

The risk of broken interfaces, or interfaces whose semantics may have changed, is mitigated to an extent with extensive unit tests that cover the entire system in exhaustive detail. As long as the programmer runs *all* the tests, not just the tests for the module he has changed, then the risk is significantly reduced. This is, of course, assuming that the team actually is writing unit tests in sufficiently large numbers and running them regularly. If one snake breaks free, the next one is close on its tail.

Another problem is that none of these practices is free; they all take time. It takes time for the programmers to write the tests, to refactor some code, to discover that a refactoring broke some code elsewhere, to check out the broken code and fix it, to test the fix, and so on.

For a "strange but true" story about just how time consuming refactoring can be from somebody who has been there and done that, check out the "Voice of eXPerience: YAGNI 16 Tests" sidebar in Chapter 8.

The Snake That Got Away

During refactoring, the risk of having to totally *redesign* affected external code is reduced by concentrating on modular design, once and only once (OAOO) and so on. Keeping code modular reduces the amount to which one module affects another module if its internals are changed. In XP, this is achieved through emergent design.

We cover emergent design in Chapter 12.

This does mean, though, that there's actually another slippery snake here to keep at bay. If attention to modular design slips, refactoring becomes more difficult, which in turn makes modular design more difficult to achieve, and so on. If the design becomes steadily more crufty, XP's emergent design process becomes very difficult to follow.

XP's test-first/refactoring approach combined with collective ownership relies heavily on continuous integration to keep the codebase from diverging. However . . .

What If Continuous Integration Becomes Occasional Integration?

XP's recommendation is to integrate the source code as often as possible—that is, to check working code into the version-control system and do a complete build of the overall system, and then run the unit tests to ensure that all the disparate pieces fit together properly. There's no doubt that a daily integration build is a beneficial aspect to any project, although XP recommends taking this even further, even integrating once per hour. If the team forgets to do this, I doubt you'll see a detrimental effect. However, if the integration rate drops below once per day, then you might well start to see problems.

This is actually true of any project (XP or otherwise): If programmers have different builds on each PC, getting them all to fit together can prove more time consuming than writing the code in the first place.

This is even more the case in an XP project, where both the codebase and the design are evolving at a fast rate. Many of the refactorings described in Martin Fowler's *Refactoring*[12] involve interface changes. If an interface is refactored on one PC, it's bound to break code on someone else's PC. This may not be discovered until the code is integrated. This problem will be checked to an extent by compilation errors and also by unit tests (which a lot of XP practices rely on). However, compile errors and unit tests don't always catch code divergence early, because the unit tests you're running are the ones that were written for the version of the code that you have on *your* PC. Therefore, XP requires continuous integration to make sure everyone is refactoring the most up-to-date code. Without it, you quickly end up with ad-hoc versions on different PCs that can become a nightmare to stitch back together.

Writing client code that works one day but breaks the following day because the interfaces changed can also be frustrating, especially when the client programmer simply finds out (rather than being told in advance). So team morale can take a pounding when rapid refactoring is taking place and the programmers aren't integrating their code often enough.

In a non-XP project, code divergence is still a problem, but much less so. Because the design is more stable, refactoring isn't taking place across the whole project at such a breakneck pace, therefore code divergence has less of an impact when it happens. It's definitely still worth doing that daily integration build, though!

What If Those Small, Frequent Releases Get Less and Less Frequent?

If the project has started in earnest with small releases and short iterations, releasing functionality every couple of weeks to a gleeful customer, what happens if the release dates start to slip? (Throwing a bunch of work away at 5:00 PM every day *could* cause this to happen, by the way.)

It's a likely scenario that as the project gets older, the programmers may become tired of retreading old ground and will start refactoring less. As the code becomes harder to change, gradually fewer and fewer stories will be fulfilled in each iteration, therefore releases will be made less often (i.e., the project velocity will slow down). The extent to which this problem will bite you depends on

---

12. Martin Fowler with Kent Beck, John Brant, William Opdyke, and Don Roberts, *Refactoring: Improving the Design of Existing Code* (New York, NY: Addison-Wesley, 1999).

which other snakes have already escaped and are hiding beneath the furniture. Small, frequent releases give us early feedback, which in turn catches a lot of other issues early. If the releases become too big and/or infrequent, then the snakes will continue to prowl the office undetected, sneakily snarling the project.

Similarly, as the project progresses and people become too "comfortable," the iteration lengths might start to increase. An XP team that is switched on to what it is doing will regard this as a big deal, because without fixed iteration lengths it becomes much more difficult to accurately measure the team's progress over time.

What If the Programmers Stop Pairing Up?

What if the programmers stop pairing up? As we saw in Chapter 1, Ron Jeffries sees pair programming as a guideline, an ideal to aspire toward (although other Extremo authors describe pair programming as an unbreakable golden rule). Ironically perhaps, it is not code quality that is likely to suffer directly from a lack of pair programming, but shared knowledge of the project design. Knowledge sharing is one of the primary benefits of pair programming and is one of the reasons XPers feel that they can go for so long without documenting their designs in any detailed form besides source code. If the programmers forget to pair up and, equally important, they do not regularly switch pairs and rotate between tasks, then this communal knowledge no longer flows. This is a real boa constrictor of a problem.

We return to this particular snake in the "Pair Programming Illuminated" section in Chapter 6.

The extent to which the damage can be limited depends on how tightly knit the team happens to be. If the team members regularly communicate over design issues, are frequently seen to be sketching lines and boxes on whiteboards, and so forth, then the problem should be fairly limited. A worst-case scenario, however, is if there's no communication between the programmers. No one talks to anybody else except about why we don't yet have flying cars, about funny MPEGs of elderly ladies kicking small children, and about how to set up the company foosball league. Project? What project?

In such cases, the problem is more deeply rooted than simply forgetting to pair program. However, this is also the sort of situation where writing things down in detail helps even more than usual.

What If the Programmers Don't All Fit into One Room?

The colocated team is a primary tenet of XP. Without it, you would need a major readjustment of the other XP practices. The on-site customer wouldn't be able to give 100% of her time to all teams, unless she's really a time-and-space-shifting lizard creature from the Ninth Dimension (which is unlikely but not entirely unreasonable).

To enable programmers to work in more than one room (or on different premises, or, taken to an extreme, in different time zones), the requirements would need to be recorded in a more permanent and shareable form than hand-scribbled story cards because teams in both rooms will need to refer to them (for example, to avoid writing overlapping or incompatible code if the teams are working on similar user stories[13]). In addition, design decisions can no longer readily be shared between teams, unless they do something radical like place all their design documents on a project intranet.[14] Of course, this also means that they would have to actually write some design documents and regularly keep them up-to-date as the design evolves. This would be unworkable, unless they also schedule some time to do more prototyping and up-front design, so that the design can first be allowed to stabilize a little bit.

So, surprisingly, the simple (and quite likely) scenario of putting teams in more than one room means that we instantly lose the benefits of emergent design, on-site customer, transient story cards, and oral documentation. In fact, for the reasons described, each of these practices suddenly becomes rather risky.

By "patching" each of these practices to reduce its risk, we can end up with a software process that is actually a lot more realistic. The refactored process that emerges involves a greater degree of up-front design, early prototyping, design documents, and electronically stored requirements (whether as use cases or user stories, or "thou shalt/thou shalt not" numbered requirements).

We explore this refactored process further in Chapter 15.

---

13. This assumes that somebody *cares* if you're writing overlapping or incompatible code.

14. Some XP teams install and use their own Wiki (see
    http://c2.com/cgi/wiki?RunningYourOwnWikiFaq) for this purpose.

What If Programmers Take Ownership of Code?

At the start of an XP project, each of the XP practices is carried out in earnest. This includes *collective* ownership, the principle that no one programmer has responsibility for any area of the project. The opposite approach is *individual* ownership, where each programmer takes responsibility for the code that he wrote.

The industry appears to be divided over these two approaches. Each has its benefits and its pitfalls. In an XP project, however, you really do need to use collective ownership, so that the other XP practices stand a dog's chance in a cattery of working.

Assimilating the Team into the Collective

Just for fun, we did a little research on the subject of collectivism, outside of an XP context. It came from Marxist "power to the proletariat" sociopolitical theory (more on Marxism later). Here are a couple of interesting quotes that we found:

> *"Since the supreme aim of collectivism is the abolition of that capitalistic regime which enables one man or one corporation arbitrarily to exploit the labour and the necessities of many men, it obviously does not—in theory at least—imply equal compensation for all individuals, nor the destruction of individual initiative, nor the establishment of a bureaucratic despotism."*[15]

> *"Collectivism holds that the individual is not an end to himself, but is only a tool to serve the ends of the group."*[16]

Is XP similarly a Borg-like process? The second quote appears to concur with Robert C. Martin's "preferences and comfort" quote at the start of Chapter 6.

---

15. Definition from *The Catholic Encyclopedia, Volume IV*, http://www.newadvent.org/cathen/04106a.htm.
16. Definition from Capitalism.org, http://www.capitalism.org/faq/collectivism.htm.

At the root of collectivism is the belief that a collective isn't just a group of individuals, but a single entity. The individuals become secondary to the collective. This could explain why many people see XP as being somehow "cult-like."

> *"Collectivism is a form of anthropomorphism. It attempts to see a group of individuals as having a single identity similar to a person. The collective is claimed to have ideas, and can think. It has purpose, and it acts to achieve goals. It even has a personality, called culture. It claims to have moral rules the collective should follow. It claims to have collective rights, as well."*[17]

Ask not what XP can do for your project, ask what your project can do for XP.

On the other hand, *individual* ownership tends to involve specialization of particular areas of code and of particular technologies. Of course, it's human nature to specialize, to carve out a niche and cling to it like a territorial beaver. What if an individual member of the team begins to take ownership over her areas of code? In XP, this is "guarded" against by pair programming. When two people have "bashed out" a piece of code between them, it's less likely that one of them will become emotionally attached to the code ("I wrote that, hands off!"). So individual ownership might only begin to manifest if pair programming has also begun to slip. Let one snake escape and the next one is close on its tail.

Individual ownership can actually be a good thing because it creates accountability. It also prevents average (or worse) programmers from meddling with perfectly okay code. However, in the XP world, individual ownership would cause friction between team members, because there would be a constant fight to keep refactor-happy coders off your base.

On the other hand, collective ownership can, under certain circumstances, have a positive (and appropriately humbling) effect because it forces programmers not to cling emotionally to their code or to take offense if they see someone turning their precious algorithm into something better. This could, however, prove quite frustrating for highly skilled programmers who really do know better than their average colleagues. If you're the one experienced programmer on a team of junior coders, seeing your well-written code get torn apart over time in

17. Definition from Importance Of Philosophy.com, http://www.importanceofphilosophy.com/ Evil_Collectivism.html.

a relentless display of entropy could drive you to despair. Cue countless confrontations to prevent your code from being rewritten unnecessarily. To top it all, the battle is never won. Come tomorrow, the code that you defended today might have been refactored into an inept programmer's wet dream. Then comes the cry, "Okay, who rewrote my code *this time?*"

We can imagine this amusing scenario as follows:

Bang! Bang! I Think We'll Refactor
(Sing to the tune of "Maxwell's Silver Hammer" by The Beatles)

A pair named Fred and Tim
Checked a bunch of source code in
Then went to the gym

They were very happy with what they'd done . . .
Oh oh oh

They'd been working hard
Burning through the index cards
And their code smelled clean

They forgot that software is never done
No no no

But Ollie and Stan
Had a very different plan
As we will soon see

They thought that they'd have just a little fun
Ho ho ho

And as our boys walked into the gym
Ollie told Stan with a grin
Doot dee doo doo

Bang! Bang! I think we'll refactor that code
That they just wrote
Doot dee doo doo

Bang! Bang! I think we'll refactor
And they won't get a vote
Just ree-factor
Nobody owns their own code

So collective ownership has benefits, but it isn't the panacea for defective code that it might seem. It just isn't for all teams. In non-XP projects, the benefits of collective ownership can be achieved in different ways. For example, individuals can grow bad coding habits if they program in isolation. This is kept in check with tightly knit teams working closely on related areas of code (but not so closely that they're sitting at the same desk), peer reviews, and close mentoring from more experienced developers. Similarly, bad designs are caught out through design reviews and collaborative design sessions.

What If the XP Coach Falls Asleep?

In pretty much all of the degenerate conditions described in this chapter, the responsibility falls to the XP coach to notice that things are deteriorating and to take steps to correct them. This puts a big responsibility on one person, particularly because most of the conditions described would, by their nature, be recurring.

This heavy reliance on having a good, consistently diligent XP coach is a major reason why XP doesn't scale very well to larger projects. How many good, consistently diligent XP coaches can you find to work full-time on this one project? And worse than that, will they always agree 100% on the sometimes ambiguous definitions of the XP practices?

What If the Cost of Change Curve Isn't Flattened?

Finally, we ask what happens if the cost of change curve isn't flattened. This isn't a "practice" as such, but it's the desired net effect of all the XP practices put together.

> We introduced the cost of change curve in the section "The Central Premise of XP" in Chapter 1, and we describe it in more detail in Chapter 13.

If the team deviates from the XP practices, the cost of change curve steepens. What happens then? There is, of course, a knock-on effect: Your project starts to get very expensive, and the gold owner's morale will likely plummet, which has been shown to lead to inexplicable termination of the project. This is the king of all the other snakes, the one to avoid at all costs, and yet it's also the one that will inevitably break loose if the other practices fail even slightly.

As we described in Chapter 1, XP supposedly works because it doesn't cost significantly more to add new features in later than it does to add them in now.

Therefore, all of XP's practices must work flat-out in order to keep the cost of change curve flat. All software is subject to the problem of increasing complexity. As more functionality is added, the design increases in complexity to cope with the new features. This increases the cost of making changes later in a project.

XP counters this with aggressive refactoring in an attempt to keep the design of the software simple.

Without constant, aggressive refactoring, an emergent design will consist mostly of regressive mutations. That is, the design won't evolve into a thing of pure beauty but into a banjo-playing redneck with webbed fingers and crooked eyes.

A lot of other practices and principles must be adhered to 100% without fail in order to keep your design pure and good. If you're gunning for an XP-style emergent design, you'll need constant refactoring; therefore, you'll need unit tests and lots of 'em. You'll also need collective ownership, continuous integration, and pair programmers who are prepared to squeal like a pig if they see a snake on the loose. Is this starting to sound familiar?

So, if even one of XP's practices slips just a little bit, the cost of change increases, and the whole point of XP, the number one purported benefit—the ability to make changes late in a project in an economically effective way—is lost.

In this section we explored the dangers of the XP process "deteriorating" during a project. However, the opposite—putting the process together in the first place—is also problematic.

Putting the Snakes Together: Partial XP

How many snakes does it take to complete a circle? Often, teams that say they're doing XP simply aren't. At best, there may be one or two practices that they aren't using. At worst, they might be omitting all of the "safety net" practices (such as unit testing, pair programming, and collective ownership) but actively employing the "dangerous stunt" practices, such as emergent design or not writing any design documentation.

Refactoring without unit tests is like skydiving without an emergency parachute. It's cheaper, and quicker when packing your gear in the morning, but when you discover too late that your wife has been cutting parts out of your main chute for her patchwork quilt, you'll really wish that you had taken the extra time.

The following quote was posted to the C2 Wiki by "sg":

> *"In the half-dozen projects/places I have tried XP, I have never found anyone willing to adopt the whole thing. I *did* find people interested in trying *one* idea at a time and adding it. For instance, UnitTests. People seem to like UnitTests and will adopt them after being convinced."*[18]

Often, the problem occurs when XP is first being introduced into an organization. Without proper metrics, and hampered by a slightly kooky name, XP can

---

18. "sg" posting to the C2 Wiki Page All Of Xp, http://c2.com/cgi/wiki?AllOfXp.

face an uphill struggle to be accepted. As a result, XP tends to be introduced piece-meal into organizations. The problem then becomes the correct order in which XP must be introduced. Because XP's risk reduction strategy is self-referential, it may be impossible to introduce one or two practices at a time, without accidentally letting a couple of snakes loose around your office.

(Interestingly, about 4 years ago Doug proposed on OTUG[19] that it would be quite an interesting combination to merge the front-end "use case–driven" work he was doing with the back-end coding/testing techniques of XP. He was resolutely rebuffed and informed that all the XP practices had to be used together.)

Our "take" on this is that there just isn't a correct order in which to introduce the XP practices. However, XPers might then accuse us of being defeatist. Just because something is difficult and high-risk doesn't mean you shouldn't attempt it, right? You can find an example of the possible adoption order that you might try here: `http://c2.com/cgi/wiki?ExtremeProgrammingPracticeAdoptionOrder`.

Most commonly, automated testing is introduced first, because this has the most immediate and obvious benefits. As soon as managers see evidence of code quality improving, they will (so the theory goes) be hungry for more. Then budding Extremos start to enthusiastically pull their "tame" snakes out of their bag. This is potentially disastrous, depending on which snake gets pulled out next.

Emergent design is one of the most dangerous practices, because to stand a chance of succeeding, it needs pretty much all of the other XP practices to be in place. However, it's also likely to be one of the first practices to be introduced, because it's the one that many people see as "being" XP. XP is all about evolutionary prototyping, after all. Even if the programmers involved aren't claiming to be doing XP, they may feel that they're improving their process by introducing emergent design. At worst, this could mean simply not doing any up-front design and taking it from there. However, leaping into production coding without spending sufficient time on requirements gathering and designing, and doing it successfully, requires some pretty labor-intensive "safety net" practices, all of which must be performed consistently every day without fail.

The danger could be magnified in organizations where XP is brought in as an excuse to avoid design and documentation. In such cases, we would posit that the circle of snakes is rarely if ever completed.

It may seem unfair to criticize a methodology for failing because people don't follow the instructions on the tin. However, more robust software processes have contingency built-in; that is, if people forget to pair program or the on-site customer is on holiday, the whole circle of snakes doesn't unravel.

To put it another way: In theory you might get a completely daisy-chained circle of snakes, but in practice, you'd better watch your asp.

---

19. See `http://www.rational.com`.

Tailoring a Process to Local Conditions: Why XP Stands on Its Head

As we've shown, XP's practices are too tightly coupled. But the ones that are *most* tightly coupled are also the ones that most need to be adaptable.

The hallmark of a useful software development methodology is that it's eminently adaptable. XP authors often point out that if XP isn't working for you, then you should change XP to fit. This would be good advice if it were really as simple as that, but as we showed in the first part of this chapter, tailoring XP is a potential minefield of poisonous snakes and mixed metaphors.

The situation is made even more difficult by the nature of software projects in general. We'll demonstrate now that, although XP is supposedly adaptable to a wide variety of projects, its authors have got it exactly the wrong way around. When it comes to adaptability, XP stands on its head. And in a pit of snakes, at that!

The Eternal Cat

Here's a little thought experiment: What happens when a strictly logical person and a flagrantly emotional person must sit down together in a meeting room and between them produce a software design?

This is similar to the joke about what happens when you tie a slice of bread, buttered side up, onto the back of a cat and then drop them from a height of about 6 feet. Just as the cat/buttered bread pair will never hit the ground, but will instead spin indefinitely just above the ground, so the logical person and emotional person will likely never reach an agreement over something as complex and prone to individual practices, habits, and opinions as a software design.

As an aside, now try repeating the experiment with not just one pair, but a team of programmers, who must all pair up and between them "evolve" a design over a period of, say, 12 months. Picture a roomful of spinning cats. This is why in *The Mythical Man-Month*, Frederick Brooks recommends the use of a project leader, a chief programmer (or "surgeon") who champions the design and holds the project true to it. Chief programmers are often regarded as control freaks, but a good chief programmer will listen to his team and incorporate their feedback into the design without compromising the overall design vision.

Logical vs. Emotional

The problem is this. There are two opposing sides to software development—the logical and the emotional (see Figure 3-1)—simply because we're dealing with both logical things (computers) and passionate, mostly deeply illogical things (people). These two extremes are present in every single software project, but they rarely sit comfortably together. This is a real dichotomy that has already created an underlying rift in the software community, just barely hidden from view but definitely there, creating tension, sparking off, and heating up arguments between developers over the simplest of discussions. When personalities clash, emotions flare up all too easily.

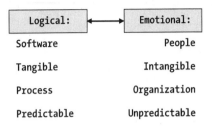

Figure 3-1. The tug of logic versus emotion in every software project

Software projects tend to draw an uneven and uncomfortable line somewhere between the two extremes, the eventual line usually being dictated by the project leaders and the culture of the organization. If anyone in the project doesn't fit into this narrow band, then tough. So in a project that sits too far one way or the other, we risk losing perfectly good staff because they just don't "fit in." This is a real problem. The answer *should* be found in the software development methodologies that we turn to. However, many such methodologies sit rigidly either too far one way or the other—toward the logical and dispassionate, or toward the fuzzy, gooey, warm feeling of a people-oriented process.

In *Agile Software Development*,[20] Alistair Cockburn identifies that no software process will work for all projects in all situations, in all organizations, and all countries. There are just too many local differences, both in culture and in circumstances. Therefore, a good software methodology is one that doesn't dictate (or "prescribe") procedures. Agile methods (and XP in particular) are sold on the basis that they are *nonprescriptive* (i.e., they make no assumptions or stipulations about the precise method that the developers will use to build the software).

What does tend to be overlooked, however, is that there's a core, or "logical," process that *should* be prescribed. This is essentially "how to get from A to B on a good day" (where typically A is the requirements and B is working software).

---

20. Alistair Cockburn, *Agile Software Development* (New York, NY: Addison-Wesley, 2001).

Example of a Logical Process

An example of a logical design process (with much deliberately left out for brevity) is as follows:

1. Iterate between the domain model (analysis-level class model) and the use cases.

2. Use robustness analysis to review the domain model and provide early feedback on its correctness.

3. For each use case, produce a sequence diagram.

4. Use all the above to identify your design-level classes.

5. Then use the sequence diagrams to allocate behaviors to these classes.

6. Then use the class model to write the unit tests and the code.

The organizational aspect (the part that should be tailored) would involve how and where to split the development work into separate iterations (e.g., do we produce the entire analysis model first? The answer depends on both the type of project and the organization).

Visit any large bookstore and you'll see an extensive collection of titles on software design. They mostly offer "off-the-shelf" design processes and techniques that can each be applied in whole to different types of design problems.

The logical process is closer to the logical software end than the emotional people end. The logical process is more about how to *design and build* software than about how to get people to *work together* to design and build software. A well-defined logical process should be applicable to a large number of software projects, regardless of the local conditions (e.g., organizational culture).

Although XP does define the core, logical process to an extent (Release Plan ➤ Iteration Plan ➤ Design ➤ Test ➤ Code ➤ Refactor), it's still a little too high level for the purposes described here. XP does, of course, also describe Test First, YAGNI, OAOO, and so on—but these are guidelines rather than a logical, step-by-step design process.

The further up the scale you go (from logical/software to emotional/people), the more unpredictable and prone to local variations things get. Also, the higher up you go, the less "process oriented" methodologies tend to be. Instead they become more "organization oriented"—that is, they're more to do with organizing people and things (such as the position of office furniture) than to do with prescribed "step 1, step 2" processes.

The parts of the methodology that can be tailored *should* be the organizational aspects, because these are more prone to local variation. These aspects include how to arrange the team, how to plan the project and to what level of detail, iteration size, how often to integrate your code and rebuild the project, and so on. These are all aspects of a software process that will vary according to the local conditions. As such, no process should rely on these practices definitely being followed to the letter (or indeed at all).

Nailing Your Ducks in a Row

Ironically, XP, which is supposedly a nonprescriptive process, prescribes a lot of the organizational aspects, in particular the following:

- Planning (the planning game)

- Whole team (put everyone in one room, including the on-site customer)

- Small releases

- Pair programming

- Continuous integration

- Testing

- Collective ownership

- Sustainable pace

By "prescriptive" we mean that XP requires all of the preceding practices to be performed consistently, without fail, throughout the project. To make matters worse, the practices that are non-negotiable are also the ones that require a significant mind-shift from project managers and customers for XP to be adopted correctly. For example, requiring that the company change the nature of its software contracts from fixed scope, variable date to variable scope, fixed date, as well as requiring that the customer be colocated with the programming team, that the whole team be located in a single room, and that programmers always work in pairs are all potential minefields, depending on the politics of the organization.

The question is, does this actually matter? Are XP projects more likely to fail because they're too inflexible in these organizational areas? The XP literature does state that if parts of XP aren't working locally for your project, then you should change them to fit. However, they give little or no practical guidance as to how to go about tailoring XP. In fact, it's even more difficult than that. As we discussed earlier in this chapter, removing certain key practices from XP causes other parts of the process to fail. For example, emergent design is dependent on constant refactoring, which in turn is dependent on pair programming, continuous integration, testing, collective ownership, and so on.

Because XP's organizational practices are closer to the "emotional" end of a software project, they're the areas most prone to local variation. This means that XP is likely to be unsuited to the local culture or the local organization, or the type of project, because so many of its organizational practices are inflexible.

In Chapter 15 we aim to produce a refactored version of XP that, by requiring less of a political mind-shift and being closer to the way most companies do business, should be more acceptable to a wider range of organizations.

Summary

In this chapter we outlined our basic objections to Extreme Programming as a software development process. We also described why XP is unsuited to the vast majority of software projects.

The problem is twofold:

- XP is too rigid; its component parts are too interdependent. This makes XP a very difficult process to adhere to throughout a project.

- When it comes to tailoring a process to local conditions in an organization, or for a particular type of project, XP gets it exactly reversed. The adaptable part of XP is the logical process, which should be prescribed; the fixed, prescriptive part of XP is its organizational practices, which need to be more easily adaptable than they are.

Despite first appearances, XP is not a jacket made for comfort. It is not a one-size-fits-all stretchy glove that does the job of keeping your hand warm. It is an intricate mechanism of moving parts, each part fragile, but somehow kept together by a complex interplay of forces. All it takes is failure at a single joint, a light hammer blow from outside, and the pieces unravel.

No doubt XP can be a thing of beauty when it works, but it doesn't seem made for this rough-and-tumble world, this world of change. And that's the funny thing—the Extremos embrace change like a long-lost lover, yet this constant change can't help but doom any project. Project X is due in 1 year, but management, due to encouragement from the XP team, spends that year changing its mind. Result: failure. And management is still changing its mind a day before launch.

In the real world it's called making your mind up, having a clue. Yet XP wants to stand all this on its head and encourage ever-changing directions and goals.

In the next chapter we look at XP from a "people" point of view and introduce what we like to call "Extremo culture." Then for pretty much the rest of the book, we examine the circle of snakes in more detail.

Part II

Social Aspects of XP (Mama Don't Let Your Coders Grow Up to Be Cowboys)

CHAPTER 4

Extremo Culture

Just Hack
(Sing to the tune of "Get Back" by The Beatles)

JoJo was a man who really liked to program
But he couldn't do design
He'd start writing Smalltalk early in the morning
'Cause it made him feel just fine

Just hack!
Just hack!
Just hack and whack code all day long!

(Just hack, JoJo)

JoJo's pair Loretta was kind of a loner
Thought more clearly on her own
She would grab the mouse while JoJo wasn't looking
Code when he was on the phone

Just hack!
Just hack!
Refactor if the smell is wrong!

(Just hack, Loretta)

JoJo and Loretta had a disagreement
While refactoring a class
JoJo'd smelled the code a couple times too often
You know it smelled like California grass

Just hack!
Just hack!
Just hack and whack code all day long!

With XP's rise in popularity, a parallel culture has also arisen (we call it *Extremo culture*). You could be forgiven for thinking that this is a counterculture because some of it seems contrary to XP's teachings—except that some of the XP authors seem as immersed in the Extremo culture as their followers. For example, XP teaches us to respect our colleagues and fellow humans, but one or two of the XP authors seem quite active in the popular Extremo sport of "shoot the messenger" (as we explore later in this chapter).

A methodology does not stand alone: It is defined by its proponents. This is probably more true of XP than any other methodology. In this chapter, we examine why this is the case by looking at various aspects of the Extremo culture. These aspects include the pejorative terminology that pervades the XP literature (such as overuse of the word "fear" when discussing software projects) and the tendency of XPers to attack the character of people who are opposed to XP rather than their arguments. We also explain why the dot-com boom and its associated "hack-and-whack" culture were perfectly timed to accelerate XP's popularity.

"XP Is Not About Mindless Hacking!"

The Extremos are quick to point out that XP is not an invitation to hack. So let's get that straight once and for all: XP is *not* about mindless hacking!

It's about jumping straight to code, having breezed over the design, doing the simplest thing that can possibly work, avoiding written documentation like the plague, and fixing up the design later during refactoring.

We think the difference should be clear to everyone.

Why Do XPers Feel That XP Is Not Really Hacking?

When seen up close, the "XP way" is all about discipline. XP practitioners have to be disciplined in order to follow the XP practices to the letter, for the duration of the project. Even the original XP team, whose members described themselves as "the best software team on the face of the Earth" and got book deals, had a lot of trouble sticking to the XP practices for their entire 4-year mission.

More about the original XP team in Chapter 2.

So it takes practice and dedication to be a true XPer. That doesn't sound much like hacking *so* far.

XP also involves lots of good things such as testing and planning. You wouldn't see these highlighted on a hack-and-whack practitioner's resume (actually, come to think of it, what *do* hack-and-whack practitioners put on their resumes?

Hmm . . .). However, as we explore in later chapters, XP also involves some not-so-good things such as not thinking beyond the current iteration.

We discuss in detail why not thinking beyond the current iteration is not such a good approach in Chapters 7, 9, 10, 11, 12, 13 to 15 inclusive, and in fact most of the rest of the book.

In other words, XP involves not designing for future requirements, not writing things down unless the customer explicitly asks for it, and asking the customer to define her requirements in scripted code (as acceptance tests).

Throwing Your Documents to the Lions

As XP becomes more socially acceptable in the mainstream programming world, parts of its Extremo culture are bound to spill over. In particular, the message that we no longer have to document our work is like throwing a tethered goat into a pit of hungry, ill-tempered lions. The hack-and-whack crowd will seize (and have already seized) this excuse to cease documenting their work and to leap into the code without spending time up front at least trying to come up with a decent design (and, of course, writing it down in detail and in a permanent form besides source code).

Although XP is clear about its reasons for not having a high emphasis on documentation (the theory goes that the risk is reduced by other practices, such as collective ownership), the danger is that "no documentation" will resonate with programmers who hate doing documentation. The danger is that in the future, more and more projects (both XP and non-XP) will fail, because all the reasons for documenting your design (and doing this prior to production coding) will have been forgotten about. The industry is in a lot of trouble already, but this aspect of XP really isn't helping.

Why Write the Design Down in Detail Before You Start Coding?

The process of writing a design down is itself a form of review. The process invariably causes programmers to uncover flaws, things that they just wouldn't otherwise have thought about, or just better ways of doing things—and all of this before a line of code has been written. Documenting the design also allows senior engineers to review the design in detail. The documentation acts as a stake in the ground, so decisions made across numerous design meetings aren't misconstrued or forgotten about altogether.

There are even documented ways, methodologies, that explain how to increase the chances of getting your design right first time.

We explore some of these methods in Chapter 8.

With the advent of XP, however, these important methods are in danger of being forgotten, buried beneath the stampeding feet of elated programmers rushing to fling themselves upon the XP shrine and free themselves from the enslaving shackles of up-front design and written documentation. Call us old sticks in the mud, but these days, no one really seems to talk about trying to get the design right first time. Instead, everyone talks about refactoring their existing design—wrongly thinking that they stand no chance of getting it right the first time and therefore shouldn't waste time trying.[1]

From requirements to design, XP appears to be about getting it wrong first, then correcting your mistakes as you go. Of course, you would never set out deliberately to get something wrong. But XP says that it's better not to spend very much time up front trying to get it right. This is why many people see XP as a license to hack.

XP Goes Mainstream

The amount of hype that surrounds XP means it was inevitable that it would be tried out, sooner or later, by a team (we'd guess, many teams) whose programmers couldn't be considered to be "hard-core" XPers—that is, by people who don't study methodologies for a living (or even as an obsessive hobby) or by people who don't hang out on Internet discussion groups and endlessly discuss the

---

1. One of the technical reviewers for this book pointed out that there are studies and maxims like "Plan to throw one away" (Brooks) that oppose this—in other words, that writing code gives deeper insight into the design, hence the second version tends to be much better. This is absolutely true (although Brooks did say "Plan to throw *one* away," not to throw code away each and every day!). The solution, then, is to enhance the design with early prototyping (which we cover in detail in Chapter 12). This speeds up the process, because you gain the insight into the design but without the additional delays associated with production code (e.g., you don't *necessarily* need to pair program or write unit tests for a prototype).

same XP issues.[2] The success of XP in the hands of such non–hard-core developers will be the true test of its viability in the mainstream programming world.

A well-defined methodology will get its point across clearly and be adopted by teams to great effect. The key to an effective software process (at least in the "mainstream" of software development) is that the people who try it shouldn't have to be process experts to understand it. Leave it to the methodology creators to be experts—the rest of us just want to grab a process off the shelf and benefit from its clear and unambiguous wisdom. A process that is absolutely correct in what it teaches will, almost as a direct consequence, be clearly and unambiguously defined, resulting in fewer misunderstandings.

So, if we're to believe that XP *is* correct, clear, and unambiguous, why does it result in so many misunderstandings about what it really teaches?

Smell the Code, Jack
(Sing to the tune of "Hit the Road, Jack" by Ray Charles)

Smell the code, Jack
And don't do design no more no more no more no more
Smell the code, Jack
And don't do design no more . . .

Whoa baby, oh baby my code is so clean
It's the cleanest smellin' code that you've ever seen
I don't need design, figure what the heck
I can just sit back and drink some Becks

(That's right)
Smell the code, Jack
And don't do design no more no more no more no more
Smell the code, Jack
And don't do design no more . . .

XPers Don't Do Design (or Do They?)

An example of the mainstream confusion that surrounds XP is the erroneous message that XPers "don't do design." XP is very clear that it's *not* about "not doing design." It actually involves a lot of design work, just not (we would argue) at the right time or at the right level of abstraction.

---

2. Issues such as "Why can't we base an entire software process around the concept of an on-site customer?" "Because the concept is broken!" "But then C3 would have been a failure, and I saw it reported as a success!" "But C3 *was* a failure!" "Oh."

The message that leaks out of its parallel Extremo culture and into the rest of the programming world, however, is often very different.

Voice of eXPerience: Tales from the Front Line

A couple of months ago, Matt received an e-mail from someone who had read the article "The Case Against Extreme Programming" (http://www.softwarereality.com/ExtremeProgramming.jsp). The e-mail (whose author asked to remain anonymous due to fears of losing his job if certain Extremo zealots found out he had written it) included these comments about XP in the "real world":

"Tales from the front line. Here's what happens in a real XP group:

—lead developers don't pair, yet insist that others do.

—we are packed into a tiny room shoulder to shoulder to foster pairing. In reality, it fosters a stinky noisy room and a headache.

—there are Java classes that are over 9000 lines long.

—business concepts/entities are represented as ArrayLists of ArrayLists of ArrayLists, i.e., Perl style aggregation. You see, in XP there is no design, thus no objects, only ArrayLists.

—every day we have a 'stand up meeting' where we tell the group what we did yesterday, what we will do today, etc. It has a very 'cumbaya' [sic] camp fire atmosphere."

Of course, much of what is described in this e-mail is contrary to what XP teaches. Once again, Doug's favorite quote, "The difference between theory and practice is that in theory there is no difference between theory and practice, but in practice, there is" proves to be true.

For example, properly refactored code would never result in Java classes that are over 9,000 lines long (shudder!) or Perl-style aggregation (horror!). The lead developers should be pairing more than any of the others; they're supposedly the experienced ones, after all, so they should be imparting their knowledge and experience to the junior coders.

We discuss expert-novice pairing and other pair-programming combinations in Chapter 6.

The e-mail captures exactly the sort of thing that really goes on in projects where the teams *think* they're doing XP. They aren't hard-core XPers; they don't have time to read all 20 XP books and absorb their many subtleties. The result is that "Partial XP" must be increasingly common in the mainstream programming world. The core message that XP sends out isn't sufficiently clear and unambiguous to prevent teams from adopting Partial XP (just the parts they understand or think they understand) in an ad-hoc, unplanned manner.

XPers Don't Do Documentation (or Do They?)

Another example of mainstream confusion in XP is its apparent recommendation not to do any documentation. Of course, XP isn't saying not to do *any* documentation, just not to do *unnecessary* documentation.[3] So what's wrong with that? Well, it leaves plenty of room for confusion and misinterpretation by non–hard-core teams who are faithfully trying to adopt XP.

The trouble is that the Extremos' interpretation of "unnecessary" is probably quite different from that of XP newbies. XP regards design documentation as unnecessary because its other practices make up for it. This is probably a bit too subtle for people not well versed in XP thinking. Thus, the erroneous message that spills out of the Extremo culture and into the mainstream is simply "don't do documentation." The more cynical among us (Doug, for instance) find parallels between the "don't do unnecessary documentation" marketing pitch and "you can't smoke until you're 18" cigarette advertising. Squarely targeted at young, slightly rebellious, wanna-be-cool teenagers . . . we mean programmers.

XP in the Mainstream

Another, major risk is that as XP becomes more popular (or at least, as what people *think XP is* becomes more popular), XP will be applied to the type of project for which it just isn't intended. The hype and overselling of XP doesn't help to lessen the confusion. Put simply, XP might be acceptable if it's being used in exactly the intended circumstances (small project, single room, on-site customer) by a team whose members are well versed in the XP ways and who know exactly what they're doing. The advertised XP successes that we've seen are mostly to do with very small-scale projects, so no surprise there. However, the horrific likelihood is that there's a dirty underbelly of unreported XP failures instigated by teams that have been swept up by the hype, but that don't really understand XP.[4]

This is what happens when something goes mainstream. Mainstream people start using it. If something isn't ready for mainstream—in XP's case, if it isn't sufficiently well defined to get its core message across clearly and unambiguously—then it usually sinks without a trace. That is, unless it has a sufficiently

---

3. See http://www.xprogramming.com/xpmag/Misconceptions.htm.

4. As we have progressed through various stages of writing and editing this book, the "horrific likelihood" we originally wrote about has become much more of a certainty. Even as we're getting ready to go to press, we're continuing to receive "Voice of eXPerience" contributions, which you'll see throughout the remainder of this book. Please note that every single one of these "Voice of eXPerience" contributions is a real-world, actual, true story. As one of our correspondents puts it, "The stupidity level exceeds our ability to make this stuff up."

well-oiled hype machine to keep it moving and has caught the mainstream imagination so well that its failures and deficiencies just don't seem to matter.

XP and the Dot-com Boom

At around the time that XP was being introduced (1999 and early 2000), the much-derided dot-com boom was in full frenzy. It's just possible that this was a major factor in XP's sudden rise in popularity. At the time, investment money flowed like water, straight through the fingers of overconfident CTOs wielding outrageous business plans in the faces of starry-eyed venture capitalists. Stressed project managers, late-night hacking sessions, stale pizzas, and bug-infested source code became a cultural de jure, reflected by the emergence of Web sites such as NetSlaves (`http://www.netslaves.com`) in which self-proclaimed IT-workhouse victims described how they were regularly forced to work "all-nighters" and weekends to hit some earth-shattering deadline that could make or break the company. Though the staff generally hated this "unsustainable pace," the prevailing attitude (however erroneous) was that working late was a necessity in order to hit the insane deadlines.

Soon, of course, the boom swiftly turned to gloom, and the cloud of insanity brought on by the promise of a new tech horizon began to dissipate. People had begun to notice that most, in fact *almost all*, of these projects had resulted in "break" rather than "make" for the start-up companies involved. The dot-com generation had engineered a bad name for itself: Dot-commer, thy name be "cowboy."[5]

Most of these failures were due to either the lame, ill-conceived, and badly thought-out nature of the aforementioned business plans[6] or an inadequate software development process (and a butt-kissing staff that should have known better). Usually, there was a combination—a deadly cocktail of problems. Tech start-ups began with a high-level "vision" of what their product or Web site should do, but with very little in the way of concrete requirements. The requirements (i.e., what the product should actually do) would be "fleshed out" as the team went along. The phrase "Internet time" was invented to justify the unrealistic deadlines and ever-changing corporate strategies. Internet time was basically 7 to 1 (i.e., the same as "dog years"). Not coincidentally, most of the companies died like dogs.

---

5. Of course, XP does warn against the "cowboy coder"—for example, see `http://c2.com/cgi/wiki?CowboyCoders`—but this doesn't stop such programmers from being attracted to XP, for the reasons that we state.

6. Which, astoundingly enough, begat lame, ill-conceived, and badly-thought-out software designs, which begat a process—hey wait . . .

Internet Years

Do XPers really use "Internet time" to justify not having a clue? In response to an online article about controlling requirements churn, XP author Ron Jeffries posted this message:

> *"Have internet years been invented where you are? People want to change their minds. People want to start projects before they know everything about what they want. People want to say 'I'll know it when I see it'…"*[7]

It is, of course, useful to be able to move forward with only partial requirements. Sometimes this is unavoidable. However, there's a difference between this and positively encouraging a customer to move forward with only partial requirements, when doing so is avoidable, when it *is* possible to gather and prioritize all the requirements first.

Embracing change is a key aspect of XP that made it such a good fit for dot-com culture.

It was obvious that traditional software development life cycles couldn't cope with such a volatile way of working. The industry, having regressed into a sort of facile, fickle-minded juvenile state, wasn't about to mature and sort out its priorities—so in the meantime something more *agile* was needed.

XP emerged at around the same time. Its origins weren't in the dot-com arena, but in a failed payroll system for Chrysler Corporation.

> *As we explored in Chapter 2, the C3 project was cancelled acrimoniously in February 2000, and later the same year the first XP book,* Extreme Programming Explained, *was published. (Hey, why stop the presses just because the project that begat the book contracts failed dismally?)*

However, XP's appearance and Extremo message were perfectly timed with the cultural forces of the dot-com boom—enough to capture the industry's imagination and gain XP more mind share than it really deserved. Many book deals, a surprise RUP tie-in, and lots of dedicated conventions later, XP continues to gain momentum.

---

7. Ron Jeffries posting to the Software Reality Web site, http://www.softwarereality.com/lifecycle/ tenrules.jsp, August 6, 2001.

Free Pizza!

This story was told to me by a programmer friend who did some work at LastMinute.com (a successful UK-based dot-com start-up specializing in cut-price vacations). The company wasn't doing XP (it's painfully obvious that it wasn't following the sustainable pace and planning game practices), but this story does give some insight into the dot-com mentality:

"When I was at LastMinute, the programmers there bragged about how they had all lost their girlfriends in the first month, and how they programmed into the nights, because they could all get free pizzas. I left in under a month, as they were simply not going to go live in a month, like they believed, like they had promised. They refused to simply stop programming, redefine the schedule with some reality in mind, and work out why they had so many bugs. They eventually went live eight months later."

As a software process, XP was remarkably well suited to the dot-com world. In fact, many of the XP "success stories" involve small-scale Web projects. Many of the dot-com projects (disasters and success stories alike) involved small tech start-up companies with development teams of 5 to 15 programmers and testers, and vague ideas of what they wanted to produce, just that whatever it was should involve a Web site, should provide a service (e.g., Pets By Mail), and should be ready in Internet time. First to market with BrusselsSproutsHomeDelivery.com was all that mattered, regardless of how many people really wanted to buy their sprouts online.

As a culture, XP could have been tailor-made for generation dot-com. Foosball-playing and Nerf gun–toting cowboy programmers love the whole idea of oral documentation, constant snack food and, of course, knocking off at 5:00 PM every day (no more unsustainable pace—besides, working 'til 3:00 AM sucked anyway!). The idea of constant pair programming probably also appeals, young socialites that they are. But especially no up-front design and no documentation. Absolute nirvana for the cowboy coder. Though XP wasn't dependent on the dot-com boom (XP has continued to grow after the crash), both the timing and the way in which dot-com mentality quickly spread to the rest of the computing world were perfect to accelerate XP's acceptance.

In fact, the whole "people process" aspect of XP virtually guaranteed its acceptance in the dot-com culture that still lingers uncomfortably in the post–dot-com world.

XP As a People Process

Agile methods have a much higher emphasis on people than previous methodologies. This is a very good thing: Agile proponents recognize that a large proportion of a project involves people in some way. People are the primary ingredient in any development process. It takes people to do programming, designing, requirements gathering, object modeling, testing (including writing unit tests), and so on.

However, the terminology that accompanies agile methodologies can leave many people cold (particularly techie types, whose personalities lead with logic, perception, and intuition). For such people, the "fluffy" people processes appear, relatively speaking, like a hippie love-in. Most distasteful! Let's all sit down and respect each other? Show compassion for incompetent programmers? *[Sound of logical person spitting feathers.]*

The Hippie Love-in Scale of Agile People Processes

People processes are definitely beneficial because they address a major aspect of software development that has been neglected (partly because of the cultural aspect: Programmers by nature tend to be cold, impassioned, logical beasts. We should know, we fit into this category and we're plum proud of it). Those programmers who get past their natural distaste of the fluffy "people" terminology get to understand better the dynamics of the team that they're working with, and in so doing fine-tune their software process according to the people involved.

But of course, that's really the problem: At the very core of software agility, there's something that a great many programmers must "get over" if they're to accept and benefit from the wisdom that agile methods teach. The height of this particular barrier varies between methodologies—in other words, some methodologies are better than others at getting the point across without turning away their audience.

Scrum, for example, is an agile methodology that's concerned much more with how to manage talented staff than with precisely what the staff should be doing. It makes no allowances for less capable staff; the sentiment is very much that everyone on the team must be pulling his own weight. As with any project, there's no room for freeloaders. Scrum is actually a rather pragmatic methodology, both in its practices and in its relatively "hippie-free" terminology.[8]

By contrast, XP is significantly higher up on the "California hippie love-in" scale. XP has specific practices that allow for the weaknesses of "lesser-abled" programmers. Pair programming (a very people-oriented practice) is one such example. In an XP project, everyone must program in pairs for all production code so that mistakes are caught by the programmer buddy. Another example is collective ownership: No one programmer (or pair) is singularly responsible for any section of code.[9] In fact, programmers are moved around frequently to work on different parts of the project. This has the joint effect of increasing general

---

8. Although, Scrum does have its own language that is mostly derived from Rugby and is admittedly not to everyone's taste.

9. Mr. Cynical reminds us that this also means no accountability when something goes wrong! Now, that would never appeal to a cowboy coder—would it?

awareness of the design (so there are no specialists in the team) and catering to the weaknesses of lesser programmers. Any bugs being introduced by a low-quality programmer will (sooner or later) be discovered and fixed by somebody else.

As we explore in Chapter 3, the prescribed "people process" aspects of XP reduce its applicability to some projects and organizations.

Not everyone will enjoy working under such conditions. Pair programming and collective ownership are both mandatory and pervasive parts of XP. If you introduce XP into your organization, expect there to be *some* cultural differences at best. At worst, expect some programmers to leave (either the project or the company) in disgust.

Of course, some programmers will love the new way of working (especially those whose code is traditionally riddled with bugs). The danger is that, whereas such people should be weeded out of any organization, or at least moved to a nonprogrammer role, an XP project gives them sufficient cover to continue to program. The process shields the people from blame.

Paradoxically, the opposite can also be argued: that XP leads to a tendency to blame the people, not the process.

IfXPIsntWorkingYoureNotDoingXP

For a clue as to why this section title's WordsAreRunTogether, see the section "Big Words Like Constantinople and TerminationCanBeSuccess" later in this chapter.

Luckily, if you're a manager of an ailing project, XP gives you the opportunity to blame the entire team, pretty much:

> *"Extreme Programming sees itself as a 'humanistic discipline of software development'. Project problems are mainly people problems, as Gerald M. Weinberg once pointed out: 'No matter what the problem is, it's always a people problem'. However, it is highly doubtful to solve people problems with a process. If that was possible, you could establish the right process and all problems were solved. This is a false impression Extreme Programming seems to create. Even worse, there are indications that Extreme Programming leads to a tendency to blame the people, not the process."[10]*

---

10. Gerold Keefer, "Extreme Programming Considered Harmful for Reliable Software Development," http://www.stickyminds.com/sitewide.asp?ObjectId=3248&Function=DETAILBROWSE&ObjectType=ART, February 6, 2002.

This can't fairly be blamed on XP itself, but rather on people's interpretation of XP. The problem is that XP is *so* steeped in people practices that if something goes wrong, then it clearly must be the people's fault, not XP. An XP project compensates for the weaknesses of its programmers; therefore managers, initially at least, are much more likely to take a forgiving approach to their staff members, even the incompetent ones. So an XP project kicks off with a small but enthusiastic team that includes one or more incompetent programmers. What happens next? The project fails, having spent months or even years spinning around in refactor land. And so the search for the guilty begins. The programmers are "caught red-handed." With a "low-risk" process like XP, how could the project have possibly failed? It must have been the people! So the team gets unceremoniously fed to the ducks, and XP comes out shining.

So if you're a manager who loves to cover your behind, fully expects your next project to fail, and is looking for a way to come out of it stinking of roses, then why not give XP a try? "I gave them all the snack food they could possibly want . . . I did my bit!"

The indications that XP leads to a tendency to blame the people, not the process, can also be seen in the `comp.software.extreme-programming` newsgroup. When somebody describes a failed XP project, the response is almost invariably along the lines of "You weren't doing such-and-such, therefore you weren't really doing XP. Ergo, XP isn't to blame." You can find a lengthy discussion of this aspect of Extremo culture on the Wiki site at `http://www.c2.com/cgi/wiki?IfXpIsntWorkingYoureNotDoingXp`.

However, it's generally accepted that XP is a high-discipline methodology, meaning that it takes a great amount of consistent effort to keep to the straight and narrow throughout an XP project. If you set someone an impossible task, which she will of course subsequently fail, was the person really to blame for failing?

Similarly (while we're in "unanswered questions" mode), if you set out to use XP on a software project but end up not using some of the practices because they're just too difficult (perhaps in the context of your project), does that count as an XP failure? Or is XP exonerated because the team wasn't performing all of the XP practices? (We leave this one open as a basis for discussion.)

Another danger of XP's own special people-oriented approach is that it becomes too inward focused. That is, the team is busy refactoring, redesigning away, moving between tasks, spending all its time concentrating on how "cool" the code is. The team's only contact with the outside world is the on-site customer, who also spends all his time buried in the project (in the same room as the programmers). A good process needs to encourage the team to look outside the project (by spending sufficient time analyzing the target business environment, the user's actual goals, the real problems behind the customer's stated requirements, and so on). A team that spends all its time looking in really needs to look out.

Taking the People Process to Extremes

A people-oriented approach is definitely a good thing. However, a process that immerses itself too far in the people aspect risks losing sight of the fact that human weakness is a bad thing (in a software project, at least).

For example, XP tells us to spend time writing unit tests for all "important" classes and methods, so the computer can tell us when we get things wrong. XP also tells us to program in pairs to catch each other's mistakes. And XP tells us to keep revisiting and redesigning our code, because we're bound to have got the design wrong.

These safety nets are all great things, but as with most things in life they don't come free. They add time to a project, and that's time that a decent team could put to much better use—for example, designing and writing new code rather than going round in circles in refactor land.

It's a very good idea for a process to try to compensate for human weaknesses, but the XP practices in many ways actually make the problem worse. By eliminating too many of the steps before code, and thereby the ability to review designs before code, we actually reduce our ability to compensate for human error at the design level (a higher level of abstraction than code). So XPers end up refactoring code all day to nudge it onto the next design. Of course, they wouldn't have to spend all day refactoring if they had designed the thing properly in the first place!

Compensating for weak staff is good and beneficial up to a point, but the practices we put in place to do this usually aren't free—and particularly the XP ones aren't. Because of this, we need to draw the line somewhere and say, "Okay, we'll only hire programmers who not only know how to program, but also are *good* at programming, designers who know how to draw and visualize diagrams" and so on. If we do this, then we can free up more time to place safety nets in more appropriate places.

To what extent do we really want to cushion our projects to compensate for substandard programmers? Programming is hard. Don't let anyone tell you otherwise. This very fact riles those who believe that we're all equal, or should be. The requirement for intellectual rigor and capability is in their eyes inherently elitist: "Little Timmy may be slow, but he's got a heart of gold. Put him in QA."

We're all human—we all need safety nets, to an extent, and a process that helps to cushion our day-to-day mistakes is definitely a good thing. However, the next time you watch the Olympics, if you see the championship swimmers splashing about in the water wearing inflatable arm-bands, you'll know that the world is starting to mollycoddle itself just a bit too much.

XP and Snack Food

> *"'There must be food' is a core XP principle, and Chet and I have our dials set to ten on that one."*[11]

Snack food is an important part of Extremo culture, as the following "Voice of eXPerience" section suggests. The "core principle" is that teams find it easier to concentrate when there is plenty of snack food on the table in front of them. We have to wonder whether snacking instructions really have a legitimate place in a software methodology. In fact, it seems that, in XP, snacks are specified more carefully than requirements. Hmm . . .

Voice of eXPerience: Snack Food

This description is from an XPer who wishes to remain anonymous. This is probably the one situation in which you might want to let a couple of XP "snakes" loose.

Thought you might find this interesting. As you know, XP labs are encouraged to have snacks. Well, not surprisingly, we finally have mice. When they found him the little mouse got startled and started bouncing off the walls trying to find a way out, so they let the poor bugger out into the hall to find another stash of XP snacks. Today the building and facilities maintenance group sent out a company-wide e-mail (to all 3,000 or so employees) announcing that we have a serious rodent and bug problem and they are taking care of it. I wonder why?

(My employer doesn't take animals too lightly. A possum managed to shut down the system some time back by chewing through a data wire, in spite of the fact that the data systems are located in an underground bunker.)

Code Hound

(Sing to the tune of "Hound Dog" by Elvis Presley)

You ain't nothin' but a code hound
Smellin' code all the time
You ain't nothin' but a code hound
Smellin' code all the time

Well, the C code smells like whiskey but the Smalltalk smells like wine

---

11. Ron Jeffries, "Adventures in C#: Ship It," http://www.xprogramming.com/xpmag/acsShipIterationOne.htm, August 31, 2002.

You ain't nothin' but a snack hound
Snackin' all the time
You ain't nothin' but a snack hound
Snackin' all the time

If you keep eatin' those donuts you will get a big behind

Better watch out code hound
'Cause you're wasting too much time
Better watch out code hound
'Cause you're wasting too much time

You know if you start snortin' Java you just might lose your mind

Voice of eXPerience: No One Touches His Drink Unless I Say So!

by David Van Der Klauw

My department forced all software developers to do eXtreme Programming in an extremely rigid fashion they called "Vanilla XP." Vanilla XP involved rigid adherence to the 12 XP principles, 7 hours of pair programming per day, no solo programming, and loss of personal desks and PCs.

Criticism and abuse were rampant during the implementation of Vanilla XP. In one ridiculous incident, a team was admonished for taking too long to have coffee and thereafter banned from having coffee before 10:30 AM. Most of that team quit the company soon after.

For our take on snacking and XP, see the section "The XP Society's Annual Picnic" in Chapter 12.

The XP Manifesto: More Cheesy Puffs, Comrade?

The original XP book, *Extreme Programming Explained* by Kent Beck, has been described as a manifesto.[12] It sets out the philosophy and tenets of XP in a relatively high-level and nontechnical way (as compared with most other software methodology books, which usually drill down to the more specific core process). This is an apt description of a process that's more concerned with the way that people work together than with specific design issues.

For more about Beck's plan to change the "social contract" of working, see the section "That's the Customer's Problem" in Chapter 5.

---

12. See http://www.c2.com/cgi/wiki?CritiqueOfXpxec.

It's interesting that Beck's microtome should be described in this way, because in many ways XP represents a political manifesto: a way to increase the power of the "minions," the workers, whilst unloading the real responsibility of the project delivery onto the customer. It's a masterful plan.

> *"Why is XP so much admired? There may be many answers to this, but a key may lie in its radicalism and revolutionary appeal for equality. Programmers work directly with users to specify, design, and test systems, so they answer to no higher authority."[13]*

The Extremos appear to have adopted a Marxist-Leninist role in the industry, of demanding power for the proletariat programmers in their endless struggle with bourgeois management.

We touch on Marxist philosophy again in Chapter 11, albeit in the context of a different Marx.

Power to the Peeps

I was recently interviewing a programmer for a potential contract, and he happened to mention that he had worked on a project in which his team had attempted XP (but found it too difficult for various reasons—in particular, that management wouldn't buy in to the new way of working. Eventually they abandoned the "experiment" [which it quickly became known as], keeping unit tests but not much else).

I asked him what he most liked about XP, and he immediately perked up with, "It empowers the programmers! Puts us on an equal footing with the management. . . ."

XP Terminology

XP is often a bone of contention simply because its recommended practices don't always pair up exactly with the practices' names. Table 4-1 presents some examples. (If you're interested in tracking down the sources for the following items, many of them are quoted back in Chapter 1.)

---

13. Ian Alexander, "Book Review: Extreme Programming Explained," `http://i.f.alexander.users.btopenworld.com/reviews/beck.htm`, October 2000.

Table 4-1. When All You Have Is a Hammer

XP RULE (PRACTICE, VALUE, TEACHING, ETC.)	OBVIOUS OR COMMON INTERPRETATION	WHAT IT REALLY MEANS
The design	A design spec	The code (unit tests)
The architecture	A high-level architecture model	The code (written to a metaphor)
The requirements	A list of requirements	The code (acceptance tests)[14]
Documentation	Text that describes the code	The code ("document" primarily by writing clean code and tests)
Testing	Testing	Writing code[15]
The code	Source code	Production code (and tests)
Customer	Customer	Someone who writes code (acceptance tests)

Thus, on the newsgroups in particular, heated arguments tend to spiral ever faster, because those involved are throwing words and phrases at each other but interpreting them completely differently. Here's a little allegory to illustrate the problem:

Ralph: I don't like cooking. Should we buy an oven?

Alice: That doesn't make sense, Ralph! Besides, we already have an oven.

[Lengthy and highly confusing argument rages for almost an hour.]

Ralph: No, I meant microwave oven all along! You know, like the one Norton just bought! I just meant we should buy one so we don't have to do traditional oven cooking.

Alice: Well, I mean, I guess that's okay, Ralph.

Ralph: Of course, by microwave oven I really meant toaster.

---

14. It could be argued that "the requirements" also include user stories, but user stories are transitory artifacts (i.e., their relevance diminishes once the code has been written). In an XP project, the true test of inclusion of all requirements is the acceptance tests.

15. Writing automated unit tests (code) and acceptance tests (scripted code).

Big Words Like Constantinople and TerminationCanBeSuccess

XP grew up in and around the C2 Wiki Web (see http://www.c2.com/cgi/wiki?ExtremeProgrammingRoadmap). The Wiki is a great idea. It's a way for large and disparate groups of people to collaborate on a single, ever-growing knowledge base, to produce a hyperlinked encyclopedia of their favorite subject. The Wiki's invention is attributed to Ward Cunningham (the "granddaddy" of XP and mentor to Kent Beck).

XP practitioners sometimes set up their own project Wikis to track user stories and acceptance tests. Wikis are also starting to spill out onto non-XP projects, because of their usefulness as a way of easily creating a collaborative web of pages linked by key phrases or buzzwords.

One of the Wiki's strengths also turns out to be one of XP's odd little idiosyncrasies: the mixed-case hyperlinks. To link to another page on the Wiki, you simply run some words together into a single, mixed-case word, such as SpacesNotAllowed or XPersLoveToEatSnackFood. As long as there's another page with the same name, the Wiki system will create a hyperlink to that page. Pretty cool, huh?

One slightly unfortunate result, however, is that XP culture is now littered with mixed-case slang and acronyms that grew out of the Wiki Web. Some common ones are OnceAndOnlyOnce (shortened to OAOO—actually quite a good one—see http://www.c2.com/cgi/wiki?OnceAndOnlyOnce), RefactorMercilessly, YouArentGonnaNeedIt (YAGNI), and DoTheSimplestThingThatCouldPossiblyWork. You will often see that last one shortened to DTSTTCPW—to see this, simply go to http://groups.google.com and search for DTSTTCPW.

You might wonder why this is unfortunate. As with many aspects of XP, this is primarily a "taste" thing. Either you love the XP culture and revel in it, or you find it slightly annoying and at best tolerate it. With XP's increasing amounts of hype and exposure, it's becoming impossible to ignore.

This aspect of the Extremo culture was initially a tool to help differentiate XP from the other software processes that were around at its birth. Therefore, the Wiki words are stronger and less compromising than the message that XP is really trying to promote. This is a prime case of the parallel Extremo culture being a counter-culture to the "real" ivory-tower XP. Ironically, ivory-tower XP is a lot less extreme than the real-world Extremo culture.

For example, phrases such as YouArentGonnaNeedIt (usually shortened to YAGNI) may be used as a cudgel by XP coaches to prevent the programmers from even thinking about designing ahead for something that isn't needed in the current iteration. Thus, the XP coach has to have an arsenal of short, snappy acronyms that he can throw at his team—short, sharp medicine to help make the point quickly.

In some teams, this use of uncompromising phrases and acronyms is a necessary practice to keep the XP programmers strictly to the path. This is because (as we previously explored) XP's guidance runs completely contrary to the very foundations of conventional software wisdom. The result is that certain parts of XP go against the grain of most programmers' preferred way of working (e.g., not thinking ahead in terms of the design, test-first design, and constant pair programming).

It's great that XP encourages people to think for themselves and to question even the XP teachings, but this could potentially be a real pain for an XP coach faced with a real project, real customers, and real deadlines, who just wants to get the next increment out the door. Thus, real-world XP is at odds with XP's teachings (there's that pesky difference between practice and theory again). There's a certain disconnect between XP as seen in the Addison-Wesley series of books and the Extremo counterculture that has arisen as a reaction, a way for the "common programmer" to accept and adopt XP in whatever way he or she can.

It has been suggested that XP is mellowing—it has made the necessary impact to become accepted, respectable even—and now the Extremos can afford to cut back on the hubris. However, as XP continues to go mainstream, the signs are that the Extremo culture is becoming, if anything, even more extreme. YAGNI, BDUF, DTSTTCPW, and OAOO continue to be shouted across the Internet and across the rooms of real-life XP projects. The very idea of designing something in detail before you code it has become open to ridicule. The inmates have stormed the asylum and taken over.

Shooting the Messenger

Criticism of XP can often produce some vitriolic reactions from the Extremos. A brief glance through `comp.software.extreme-programming` uncovers many such examples. These reactions reveal a certain level of insecurity among the XPers: If they weren't so unsure of themselves, they might not be quite so defensive.

A common reaction to somebody saying "I don't like A" is "Oh, so you don't like B or C then?" For example, if you don't like XP, then you must also not like testing, or software agility, or people. Of course, such responses are erroneous and childish at best. We wouldn't describe ourselves as the world's biggest XP fans, but we do generally like people (in fact, some of our best friends are also people). We're also big fans of testing and even software agility. As we've maintained elsewhere, the agile goals of XP are good, it's just the ways that XP goes about achieving those goals that we believe are wrong.

Parts of XP are good, and other parts are bad. However, criticizing one part of XP can produce an extreme reaction because its proponents feel that the whole deal is coming under fire. This makes it easier for them to respond to such criticisms: "A is bad." "But B isn't!"

Why does XP produce this kind of extreme reaction from both its creators and its followers? It could be because what XP teaches is in many ways contrary to the 30 to 40 years of established thinking that has driven the software development world. For example, waterfall and iterative processes, where there are distinct analysis, design, and implementation stages, aren't entirely without merit. It's a good idea to write down your requirements before you design the system, otherwise you don't know what it is you're designing. It's a good idea to design the whole system (or at least a reasonably sized chunk of it—something beyond the current feature you're working on) before you start coding, so that there are no surprises and nothing will need to be rewritten. XP turns all of this on its head. Conventional wisdom gets thrown out of the window.

As we discussed back in Chapter 1, Kent Beck described XP as "a waterfall run through a blender."

Throwing conventional wisdom out of the window is not always such a bad thing—it is good to shake up the establishment every now and again. But it is not *necessarily* always a good thing either. Embracing change—change for the sake of it—tends not to be the best motivation to flip things around. Therefore, there must be a really good reason to go up against conventional wisdom. Those who do risk facing ridicule from the rest of the industry. To be seen to be wrong about one small thing feels like it has much greater gravity than it really does. Every small issue is therefore blown out of proportion. This is even more the case with XP, where all its practices are daisy-chained together in one big, fragile circle of snakes: Prove one item wrong, and the entire argument—the entire methodology—could unravel. Small wonder, then, that XPers are so defensive about their beliefs.

It does seem, however, that it's okay to criticize aspects of XP from within. A quick look through the Wiki Web confirms this: There are pages of point and counterpoint regarding the XP practices—all good, healthy debate that has helped to improve aspects of XP over time. However, by virtue of their location on the Wiki Web, these messages are effectively from XP "insiders." These insiders are arguing because they want to improve certain parts of XP. This contrasts greatly with the sorts of arguments that you see on the newsgroups, whose authors generally divide into two camps: those who are learning XP and naturally question its teachings, and those who are both philosophically and practically opposed to XP and who seek to disprove its practices and theories. It's this latter group that can provoke the most extreme reactions. No one likes to be told that their baby is ugly, and they will likely become quite offended, even in the "face" of overwhelming evidence to support the claim.

So Extremos are often seen to be fanatical about XP. Nary a word shall be spoken against it! The resultant atmosphere is one in which people are afraid to speak out, because the Extremos have honed their adverse reactionary tactics down to a fine art. This atmosphere isn't imaginary. Check out the feedback to the "The Case Against Extreme Programming" article (http://www.softwarereality.com/lifecycle/xp/feedback.jsp, also shown in Figure 4-1) for some examples of people who are uneasy about XP but are even more uneasy about other people finding out this fact. Many of the people who sent these messages asked to be kept anonymous because they were afraid of the repercussions—for example, if their employers discovered that they were anti-XP.

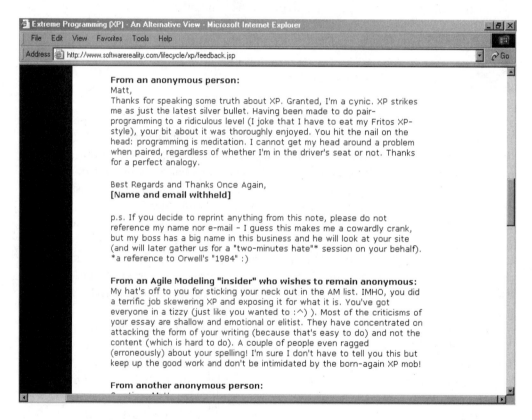

Figure 4-1. Some positive but uneasy feedback

In fact, fear drives (and is driven by) XP in many different ways, as we explore in the next section.

First, though, it's time for something completely different.

The Extremo Inquisition (This May Sound Familiar)

JoJo: Trouble with program.

Customer: Oh no—what kind of trouble?

JoJo: One on't objects gone owt askew with NullPointerException at line 147.

Customer: Pardon?

JoJo: One on't objects gone owt askew with NullPointerException at line 147.

Customer: I don't understand what you're saying.

JoJo: *[Slightly irritated and with exaggeratedly clear accent]* One of the objects has gone out askew with a Null Pointer Exception at line number one hundred and forty-seven.

Customer: Well, what on earth does that mean?

JoJo: *I* don't know—Uncle Joe (the XP coach) just told me to come over here and say that there was trouble with the program, that's all. I didn't expect a kind of extreme inquisition.

[JARRING CHORD]

[The door flies open and Cardinal Becht of Spain enters, flanked by two junior cardinals. Cardinal Geoffrey has goggles pushed over his forehead. Cardinal Henrik is just Cardinal Henrik.]

Becht: *Nobody* expects the Extremo Inquisition! Our chief weapon is courage . . . courage and testing . . . testing and courage . . . courage and testing . . . Our two weapons are courage and testing . . . and ruthless refactoring . . . Our *three* weapons are courage, testing, ruthless refactoring . . . and an almost fanatical devotion to snack food . . . Our *four* . . . no . . . *Amongst* our weapons . . . Amongst our weaponry . . . are such elements as courage, unit tests . . . I'll come in again.

[The Inquisition exits.]

JoJo: I didn't expect a kind of extreme inquisition.

[JARRING CHORD]

[The cardinals burst in.]

Becht: *Nobody* expects the Extremo Inquisition! Amongst our weaponry are such diverse elements as courage, testing, ruthless refactoring, an almost fanatical devotion to snack food, and nice red uniforms—oh damn! *[To Cardinal Geoffrey]* I can't say it—you'll have to say it.

Geoffrey: What?

Becht: You'll have to say the bit about "Our chief weapons are . . ."

Geoffrey: *[Rather horrified]* I couldn't do that. . . .

[Becht bundles the cardinals outside again.]

JoJo: I didn't expect a kind of extreme inquisition.

[JARRING CHORD]

[The cardinals enter.]

Geoffrey: Er . . . Nobody . . . um . . .

Becht: Expects . . .

Geoffrey: Expects . . . Nobody expects the . . . um . . . the Extremo . . . um . . .

Becht: Inquisition.

Geoffrey: I know, I know! Nobody expects the Extremo Inquisition. In fact, those who do expect—

Becht: Our chief weapons are . . .

Geoffrey: Our chief weapons are . . . um . . . er . . .

Becht: Testing . . .

Geoffrey: Testing and—

Becht: Okay, stop. Stop. Stop there—stop there. Stop. Phew! Ah! Our chief weapons are testing . . . blah blah blah. Cardinal, read the charges.

Henrik: *[To JoJo]* You are accused of heresy on three counts—heresy by design, heresy by framework, heresy by coding alone, and heresy by forgetting to unit test your code—*four* counts. Do you confess?

JoJo: I don't understand what I'm accused of.

Becht: Hah! Then we'll make you understand! Henrik! Fetch . . . *the programmer's cube!*

Fear

Fear. This emotive word is often used by XPers (both the authors and the practitioners). They use the word to define the XP development process and to justify why other people seem to prefer different approaches to software development.

A courageous and all-encompassing claim made in the "Fear" chapter in *Planning Extreme Programming* is this:

> *"Unacknowledged Fear Is the Source of All Software Project Failures"*

This is one of those catchall statements that people seem to love so much, but that tend to be false because they have oversimplified beyond reason. There's a very common desire to make claim to having the answer. It gives one a unique buzz, that "*Eureka!*" feeling.

"The love of money is the root of all evil." That'll explain serial killers just fine then. People love to simplify the world, or try to. It makes them feel safe and sound wise.

A nice payoff. And if something doesn't fit their homespun wisdom, they'll just play games with the dictionary, shoehorning one word into another until it does.

Fear = Doubt = Unknown = Dark = Bed-wetting

Or, to quote Chet Hendrickson reciting a C3 "war story,"

> *"This lack of knowledge caused us to become afraid . . . and as we know, 'Fear leads to anger. Anger leads to Hate. Hate leads to suffering.'"*[16]

Nevertheless, it's an interesting hypothesis, that every software project that has ever failed comes down to one thing: fear. Is fear, then, a fundamental universal source? Is it right up there with light, astrology, and life itself as a binding element that governs us all, and from which nobody can escape? Or does it apply merely to software projects?

Fear and the Extremo Culture

The aura of fear has grown up around Extremo culture, so that many people who disagree with XP's teachings are simply afraid to speak out. Those who do often do so apologetically for fear of the possible repercussions. For example, *Application Development Advisor* magazine ran a short article that criticized XP. Its introduction ran as follows:

> *"This month, Angry Young Man Gary Barnett is stepping on the toes of some dangerous people—the devotees of the eXtreme Programming cult. Incoming . . ."*[17]

Their concern was not entirely unfounded. Following its publication, the article "The Case Against Extreme Programming" was publicly flamed by pro-XPers but privately lauded by developers who wished to be kept anonymous. A couple of developers, who were working on different XP projects at the time, were afraid of damaging their career prospects should their employers or coworkers "discover" that they were anti-XP subversives.

We've never before heard of a software methodology that promotes this level of fear and distrust. This is hardly a healthy situation.

---

16. Ron Jeffries, Ann Anderson, and Chet Hendrickson, *Extreme Programming Installed* (New York, NY: Addison-Wesley, 2000), p. 197.

17. Gary Barnett, "XP – it's about 'How', not 'Tao'," http://www.appdevadvisor.co.uk/Downloads/ada6_2/AngryMan6_2.pdf, March 2002.

Fear and the Extremos

Chet Hendrickson (an XP coauthor who was also involved in the C3 project) wrote an article on XProgramming.com that included a section titled "Fear Is the Mind Killer."

We quote from "Fear Is the Mind Killer" back in the section "Doin' the Simplest Thing That Can Possibly Work" in Chapter 2.

The "f" word is, of course, used liberally in XP because it's the antithesis of courage, which is one of the four XP values. For many, however, the usage comes across as an openly contemptuous goading of people who don't agree with the XP practices. If you don't like XP, it must be because you're *afraid* of what it offers.

Remember being called "scaredy-cat" back in elementary school? (Or was that just us?) It isn't really that different. It's pure emotional rhetoric, not entirely appropriate for defining a software development process.

Not long after Matt uploaded the first version of "The Case Against Extreme Programming" article onto his Web site, Ron Jeffries (in a rebuttal placed on the Agile Modeling mailing list[18]) suggested that "the author fears change and wants to suppress it." Then he added, "He's afraid of integration." Why *fears*? Why not "is wary of change," "prefers a changeless approach," "approaches change with caution"?

It wouldn't be nearly as emotive. When "discussing" criticism of XP, XPers frequently shoot the messenger. Take a look at some of the discussions on `comp.software.extreme-programming` to see what we mean.

In *Planning Extreme Programming*, the very existence of a software process is justified in terms of fear of the customers and developers:

"Why do we need a software process? For the same reason that we need laws, governments, and taxes: fear."[19]

The theory is that in order to develop effectively, you must acknowledge your fear of what may go wrong. The chapter goes on to give a "bill of rights" for customers and developers, where each right is intended to resolve the individual's respective fears. We could argue that, technically speaking at least, these are

---

18. See `http://www.topica.com/lists/agilemodeling`.

19. Kent Beck and Martin Fowler, *Planning Extreme Programming* (New York, NY: Addison-Wesley, 2000), p. 7 (from Chapter 2, "Fear").

privileges, not rights—unless the rights are all bound in an ironclad contract (which is contrary to XP anyway; see Chapter 11).

From the same chapter in *Planning Extreme Programming*:

> *"We huddle in fear behind fortress walls, building them ever stronger, adding ever more weight to the development processes we have adopted. We continually add cannonades and battlements, documents and reviews, procedures and sign-offs, moats with crocodiles, torture chambers, and huge pots of boiling oil. But when our fears are acknowledged and our rights are accepted, then we can be courageous."*[20]

This suggests that normal contingency and risk-reduction practices such as documentation, reviews, procedures, and sign-offs are simply things we do to prevent ourselves from being scared. Contingency in this sense is a security blanket that we clutch tightly to ourselves in a desperate effort to prevent the big bad monster from emerging from beneath the bed, as it does each night, to do scary things like make our projects late. Damn those monsters.

Put another way, these practices are simply there to CYA[21]—so that when your manager or customer (who are both equally scared, by the way) asks for reassurance that his security blanket is in place, you can demonstrate (with a slightly shaky voice) that it is. The monsters are locked out . . . for now.

On OTUG, Robert C. Martin suggested that what most of us regard as reasonable procedure—writing down specifications—is regarded as CYA by everyone, not just XP proponents. The following response was given by Doug (in a sort of Wiki parody):

"Really? I guess I must be nobody then, because I regard WritingRequirementsDown to be fundamentally important to DeliveringSoftwareOnSchedule.

On the other hand, I regard NeverWriteAnythingDown as fundamentally important to the philosophy of TheyCan'tClaimI'mResponsible. And the repeated declarations that the cancellation of the C3 project had NothingToDoWithUs is one of the most classic cases of TheyCan'tClaimI'mResponsible that I've ever seen.

---

20. Ibid., p. 9.
21. Cover your a**.

"WritingRequirementsDown is also fundamentally important when it comes to DoingAGoodDesignBeforeCode, and allows for WritingDesignSpecsDown, which is really useful for making ReviewableDesignsBeforeCodingStarts. This, in turn, leads to RemovingDefectsBeforeCode, and GoodCleanArchitecture, (that is, GettingTheOriginalFactoringPrettyCloseBeforeCode) which means you can spend LessTimeRefactoringAndRerunningTests which, of course explains why it's all helpful in DeliveringSoftwareOnSchedule."[22]

It All Depends on the *Fear*

"Our pink slips are here!" Loretta shouted excitedly, bursting into the room.

"That's not really a good thing," JoJo pointed out, from where he sat sprawled in front of his PC, idly clicking through "advocacy" threads on Google Groups. He couldn't do any real work because, until Loretta burst in, he had been the only person in the room.

"Actually, they're not here as such," retracted Loretta. "I just overheard a comment from one of the 'rumor radiators' downstairs."

"So the project's a failure, then?" JoJo murmured disconsolately. "It's being cancelled?"

"We don't know that," Loretta replied, pulling up a chair. "Not for sure. Not yet. It all depends on the *Fear*."

"The what?" choked JoJo.

"You know, the Fear. Every project that fails, fails because of fear," Loretta replied.

"But our project died because we blew the entire budget on snack food, team bonding events, and endless refactoring!" exclaimed JoJo.

"Aha, no," Loretta countered, "the management was *afraid* to give us more money."

"Well . . ." JoJo responded. He was torn between the natural urge to argue and the instilled value of respecting Loretta's opinion. "But surely, the project was simply failing to deliver what it had promised!" he blurted finally.

"Aha," Loretta replied sagely, "the management was afraid of being seen as failures and not the devil-may-care OO pioneers that *we* turned out to be."

Was Fear the Cause of C3's Failure?

At the start of this section, we discussed Kent Beck's statement that unacknowledged fear is the source of all software project failures. To investigate this, let's take a case study of a known failed software project. Off the top of our heads . . . C3? Let's examine whether C3's failure could be attributed to unacknowledged fear.

---

22. Doug Rosenberg posting to OTUG (http://www.rational.com), subject: "CYA," October 11, 2000.

There are, of course, several different versions of why C3 failed (or *didn't fail*, depending on the version in question). Let's examine each of these in turn,[23] in the context of XP's fear "antivalue":

- **It was cancelled inexplicably.** This explanation leaves the door of speculation wide open to all sorts of fearsome monsters. My favorite theory is that some form of morbid spiritual force, or dark angel, drifted into the C3 pair-programming room, looked around, then made a beeline for the higher management at Chrysler and inflicted terrible fear into their minds, causing them to cancel the project immediately. We can't escape this force that is known as *fear*. It's inexplicable. Of course, we're just hypothesizing here.

- **The goal donor (the on-site customer) and the gold owner (the real customer) didn't agree.** This explanation is a bit more concrete. There was a gradual shift in emphasis of the project over its many years of meandering and refactoring. When the XP coach left the project, the goal donor and gold owner began to talk to each other less and less, so that eventually there was a whopping disparity between what the goal donor was creating and what the gold owner was prepared to hand over yet another purse of gold for. Perhaps they weren't talking because they were afraid of each other? Or was the goal donor afraid of what the gold owner would think if she knew what the team was up to?

- **The management had forgotten about the project and suddenly remembered to cancel it.** Oops. Last one out switch off the lights. Better yet, leave the lights on. The darkness is a bit scary.

- **When the project missed its Y2K deadline and the mainframes didn't die anyway, it got cancelled.** Definitely not a failure, though. Perhaps the fear thing here was to do with management's fear of how much more money would be wasted if they continued to plough hard cash and resources into a project that was already massively behind schedule and over budget.

- **None of this really matters because it was just a research project anyway.** Um, ya. Not really anything to do with fear, though.

---

23. Each "version" of C3's untimely demise can be found on the Web (e.g., on the C2 Wiki); most of these are also described in Chapter 2. We're leaving it as an exercise for the reader to hunt them down—sort of an Easter egg hunt for the morbidly curious.

- **We stopped providing value to the customer.** To quote Chet Hendrickson:

"With all that being said, what really happened at C3? I don't think that there is one simple answer to that question. The best answer is that we stopped providing value to our customer. Elsewhere on this page the bifurcation of our customer is discussed. The fact that we had two customers, with differing goals, means that we violated the principle of a single on-site customer. Let this be a lesson to you! Your customer must speak with one voice and if that is not the case you will suffer."[24]

This seems like a plausible explanation—the customer got bifurcated—but was it due to unacknowledged fear? Doesn't seem like it.

We discuss customer bifurcation in more detail in Chapter 5.

- **Early cancellation isn't really failure—in fact, termination can be success.**[25] Because the schedule doesn't exist per se, and a software project is never done. Well, if the project didn't really "fail," then fear can't have been a factor, right?

Is XP Itself Driven by Fear?

"All methodologies are based on fear. You try to set up habits that prevent your fears from becoming reality. XP is no different in this respect from any other methodology...."[26]

In *Extreme Programming Explained*, Kent Beck describes the fears that drove his design of XP (fears such as "Doing work that doesn't matter" and "Making business decisions badly").

In addition to these, we've discovered that XP as a software development process is driven by fear at a number of different levels. The fears we've identified so far include the following:

- Fear of up-front design
- Fear of detailed written requirements
- Fear of documentation
- Fear of accountability
- Fear of coding alone

---

24. See http://c2.com/cgi/wiki?CthreeProjectTerminated.

25. See http://www.c2.com/cgi/wiki?TerminationCanBeSuccess and the linked pages nearby.

26. Kent Beck, *Extreme Programming Explained: Embrace Change* (New York, NY: Addison-Wesley, 2000), p. 165.

If You're Not Doing XP, Then You Must Be Afraid

Was VCAPS (another XP project from around the same time as C3) the victim of unacknowledged fear? The project was cancelled because it was replaced by another system, already under development in the same organization, that rendered VCAPS obsolete before it was finished.

Speaking as outside observers, we feel that VCAPS would have benefited from some more stringent up-front analysis work. This would have helped to establish whether or not the project was safe from cancellation due to external factors.

 We discuss the type of analysis work that would have benefited both VCAPS and C3 in the section "Programming Without a Safety Net" in Chapter 8.

So it seems more likely that unacknowledged fear was not, strictly speaking, the root cause of VCAPS's failure. It was, instead, a much more insidious beast: *unrealized* fear. The lack of fear. Bold, earnest, enthusiastic, naïve, youthful courage.

As for C3, the root cause was similar. The team members were so busy looking inward on their project, refactoring to their heart's content, and making the code technically pristine that they forgot to *look out*. They forgot to think the unthinkable, to be afraid of what might happen if they don't bolster their process with some suitable layers of contingency.

 We give some examples of contingency in the section "How to Be Agile Without Being Fragile" in Chapter 15.

So generally, the XP discussion of fear as the antivalue of courage isn't without merit. It's what you do with the fear that counts. In *Planning Extreme Programming*, the implication is clear: Be totally driven by fear and you will end up putting too many safety nets in place. There is a trade-off, a balancing act between the gravity of the project (i.e., how hard it will fall, how much money will be wasted, whether real lives will be put at risk should something go wrong) and the amount of process overhead that is put in place to protect against things that might go wrong.

Still, though, this is not really being *afraid*. Fear suggests scary monsters (to us, at least). Cautious, yes. Heavy on the forethought, prudent, sangfroidally challenged. But afraid? Mmm, not really. Would you say that you are *afraid* of a software project?

This is where XP becomes a potential catalyst for a big cultural split in the software engineering world. Some people just don't like the pejorative terminology that overflows from XP. Other people love it or at least see nothing wrong with it. Possibly, this is why XP is so often the subject of heated debates. It's a subtle cause, but it's just possible that XP is rubbing some people the wrong way, and the people that are being "rubbed" are in turn rubbing the XPers in return, without really understanding why. In turn, XPers suggest that if you're not doing XP, then you must be afraid.

Summary

In this chapter, we looked at the ways in which the Extremo culture has affected not just XP but the rest of the industry. We also looked at the rise of XP in the context of the dot-com boom, which was busy rising at the same time. We then looked at the "people process" aspect of XP, and how it differs from the "people-oriented" emphasis of other agile methods.

Finally, we examined the Extremos' habit of describing software projects in terms of fear, and (just for fun) we compared Kent Beck's comment about unacknowledged fear being the cause of all software project failures with the various conflicting versions of C3's demise.

Next we look at an aspect of XP that many people see as its biggest single point of failure (and whose definition seems to keep changing): the on-site customer.

CHAPTER 5

The On-site Customer

Schedule Is the Customer's Problem (The Man with Kaleidoscope Eyes)
(Sing to the tune of "Lucy in the Sky with Diamonds" by The Beatles)

Picture a waterfall run through a blender
With each iteration so tiny in size
Somebody tells you that change is not costly
The man with kaleidoscope eyes

Endless refactoring day after day
While deadlines are slipping away
Suddenly there comes a saying that makes it okay

Schedule is the customer's problem
Schedule is the customer's problem
Schedule is the customer's problem

Ahhhhhhhhhhhhhhhhh

 "Once you accept that scope is variable then suddenly the project is no longer about getting 'done'. Rather its [sic] about developing at a certain velocity. And once you establish a velocity then the schedule becomes the customer's problem."[1]

—Robert C. Martin

Back in Chapter 1, we discussed briefly how the XP "customer" role has evolved from a single "actual" on-site customer to a large team of customers. In this chapter, we look at both of these options (or, as we call them, the Old and New Testaments). We also question the sanity of replacing specifications with co-located customer teams that must "speak with a single voice" if the project is to avoid doom.

Currently it looks as if the on-site customer role has become a "pick-and-mix" part of XP—just dial up how many customers you want and hope that the

---

1. Robert C. Martin posting to OTUG (http://www.rational.com), subject: "Scope Creep," October 11, 2000.

rest of XP fits. At this time XP has little or no guidance regarding how its other practices should be modified to fit each of the customer models.

But first, we examine how XP offloads responsibility for many of the "not fun" parts of software development from the programmers to the customer(s).

That's the Customer's Problem

 "I cannot agree that XP is 'just part of the growth of software development best practices'. It is a change in the social contract of working uncertainly on technology of uncertain value. The role of technologists, business people, and managers change under XP. If this isn't your experience of XP, I'd love to swap stories with you."[2]

—Kent Beck

A major weakness in XP is the continuous delegation of responsibility for minor items like requirements management and project schedule away from the programming team and onto the customer. So the (overloaded) on-site customer becomes a single point of failure, while the programmers just keep on refactoring away and go home at 5:00 PM every day.

In *Agile Software Development*, Alistair Cockburn describes a degenerate scenario (in a "hostile XP" environment) in which the customers are not quite sure what they want, but the programmers insist, "Tell us what to build!"

> *"The programmers escape the pressure of the situation by shifting the burden over to the customers (which they are allowed to do). The customers experience the situation as unsettling: There is little time to reflect, examine, experiment, and sort out options."[3]*

Just how much burden gets shifted onto the customer in XP? Here's a list from the XP2001 workshop report "Customer Involvement in Extreme Programming":

---

2. Kent Beck posting to the newsgroup `comp.software.extreme-programming`, subject: "XP/agile disservice to the industry: an example," September 14, 2001.

3. Alistair Cockburn, *Agile Software Development* (New York, NY: Addison-Wesley, 2001), p. 103.

"...extreme programming (XP) insists on an on-site customer, who has many different tasks:

"Understanding customer wishes, maintaining regular contact with end users, and balancing their potentially conflicting interests.

"Talking to developers, clarifying feature requests when needed, and understanding some of the developer's technical concerns.

"Specifying functional tests for user stories, and verifying that these tests run correctly.

"Participating in the planning of iterations and releases.

"Maintaining good contact with management, explaining progress, and justifying the time spent with the development team.

"... Being a customer requires a number of skills that are independent of the application domain. These include balancing potentially conflicting end-user needs, experience in requirements gathering, reporting to upper management, controlling the budget, and checking for forgotten requirements."[4]

Damn! That's a load. Notice how all of this hard work has been offloaded from the development team and its manager to the customer (see Figure 5-1). The programmers are free to refactor, eat snack food, and go home "clean" every day at 5:00 PM. All this and they don't have to document their work either, or do any up-front design! Whee! Thanks, Kent!

---

4. Arie van Deursen, "Customer Involvement in Extreme Programming, XP2001 Workshop Report," http://www.cwi.nl/~arie/wci2001/wci-report.pdf, May 2001, pp. 1–2.

Figure 5-1. Schedule is the customer's problem. Requirements are the customer's problem. The customer seems to have lots of problems.

The Customer's a Beast of Burden
(Sing to the tune of "Beast of Burden" by the Rolling Stones)

The customer's a beast of burden
Ain't got no specs
So nothin's certain
Everything is done from memory

The customer's a beast of burden
He's bifurcated
The project's hurtin'
He didn't speak with a single voice to me

Ain't it hard enough
Ain't it tough enough
Ain't it late enough
And you still think that change is free?

It's pretty pretty pretty pretty pretty pretty strange
Really pretty pretty pretty pretty strange
Can't you see what happened on C3?

The customer's a beast of burden
We leave at five
But he's still workin'
He always writes all the acceptance tests for me

The customer's a beast of burden
We code in pairs
Don't feel like workin'
The schedule
Doesn't mean much to me

Ain't it hard enough
Ain't it tough enough
Ain't it late enough
And you still think that change is free?

It's pretty pretty pretty pretty pretty pretty strange
Really pretty pretty pretty pretty strange
The customer's really got it tough with XP

The customer's a beast of burden . . .

On-site Customer: The Old Testament

In the initial wave of Extremo literature, the on-site customer was a single individual, a walking, talking replacement for a requirements spec who lived in the coding room with the programmers for an indefinite amount of time. And on-site customer couldn't be just anyone. Nope, you needed the "real expert," and for an indefinite period of time, because in XP SoftwareIsNeverDone.

 We discuss why "software is never done" in XP in Chapter 11.

Of course, some people have thought for years that relying on a single on-site customer was lunacy, but until recently this policy has been defended vigorously by the Extremos.

Here are some possible failure modes:

- The goal donor and the gold owner don't agree (but remember, as we discovered in Chapter 2, "TerminationCanBeSuccess").

- The on-site customer gets sick and can't work for 2 weeks, goes on vacation (time for ping-pong![5]), quits, etc.

- The on-site customer can't remember exactly because the user story details aren't written down—at least not until the executable acceptance tests are written (see Chapter 10).

- The on-site customer is inconsistent and tells different things to different people.

- The on-site customer doesn't know everything he needs to and fakes it (after all, the pressure is always on to make snap decisions and keep moving the project forward).

Problems with the "Old Testament" On-site Customer

The theory behind an on-site customer is a little idealistic: The customer (i.e., the domain expert) is empowered to make day-to-day decisions for the project. She then relocates to your office and mixes with the programmers every day for the duration of the project.

The problems with having an on-site customer are as follows:

- The on-site customer is the single biggest point of failure in an XP project. In traditional project setups, external forces (those outside the team's control) are usually counted as the highest risk. This is something that a modern software process should aim to cushion. XP, however, exacerbates the problem by focusing the entire project, for its entire life cycle, around the biggest external force: the customer.

- It's unlikely that you'll get the real decision-maker for the duration of an 18-month project. The on-site representative will more than likely be a proxy for the real customer.

---

5. Of course, XP doesn't actually say, "While the cat's away, the mice should play ping-pong," but if the customer is the programmers' sole source of details for their user stories, what else are they going to do for those 2 weeks?

- The so-called domain expert might not be such an expert, especially if he is freely available for the full project (which may span several years). This isn't really an XP issue, because the same problem would affect any project—if you can't get the information you need from the customer, then you're in trouble. However . . .

- . . . when analyzing a project's requirements, it's much better for the analyst to spend time *up front* discussing the project requirements with as many customer representatives as she can. If one person doesn't have the required information, then the analyst can ask somebody else for it. She can get down into the trenches and find out the real problems that need to be solved from the people who will actually be using the system. Then she can define business processes, extract use cases from these processes, and take the customer through them, making sure that the customer understands what he's getting and why (and all of this before time has been spent producing production code, which the customer may then decide, upon seeing it, that he doesn't want after all).

  Even better, the customer (the *real* customer, that is) will be telling the analyst what he wants; the analyst just needs to establish why and help the customer to redefine what he wants, if need be. Note that XP does create a lot of useful one-on-one time between the customer and team, but the key here is that much of this can be achieved more effectively prior to coding.

- If the programming team members (or the business analysts) find that they need more information, there's nothing stopping one or more of them returning to the customer site and talking to the customer again. In our experience, we've found that customers appreciate this sort of diligence and are keen to help fill in any gaps in the information that has already been gathered. Of course, depending on what's needed from the customer, a simple e-mail or phone call is often enough. This also means that the team isn't restricted to just one customer representative; it's possible to pick up the phone and speak to the person who is most likely to have the required information.

On the other hand, if the customer has gone to the trouble and expense of allocating a full-time staff member and relocating her to the programming team's site, the customer will wonder why the team is bothering him.[6] The on-site customer should be the person responsible for gathering all required information, from the various departments, as and when the information is required (i.e., on a "just-in-time" basis). In other words, the on-site customer must learn to be a software analyst as well as a "normal" customer.

- There's always a risk that the on-site customer will become polluted with technical issues and will start to make business decisions based on the recommendations of the programmers.

- Assuming that the team isn't operating at the same location as the customer's business, having a customer proxy means that you're removed from the political machinations of the real customer's workers. This may seem to be an advantage, but it also removes some of what you gain when you're actually at the customer site, being a consultant. By visiting the customer site, it's possible to establish firsthand whether certain aspects of the proposed new system will be accepted.

  Specific examples of questions that may be answered very easily on-site (but which an isolated on-site customer is more likely to miss) include the following: Will the new "Executive Dashboard" product actually be used? Are the workers sufficiently receptive to keep feeding it new data to keep the system relevant? Is there corporate buy-in, or are internal politics likely to cause problems?

XP's answer to all these problems is that the customer role is "a difficult one." As Kent Beck writes in *Extreme Programming Explained*:

"Being an XP customer is not easy. There are skills you have to learn, like writing good stories, and an attitude that will make you successful. Most of all, though, you have to become comfortable influencing a project without being able to control it."[7]

---

6. This isn't necessarily a problem, but it can become a problem if the single on-site customer isn't up to the job (e.g., if the customer doesn't understand the business sufficiently well). If the team increasingly needs to gather information from outside the room (bypassing the on-site customer), this is a good sign that the on-site customer "snake" is starting to slip.

7. Kent Beck, *Extreme Programming Explained: Embrace Change* (New York, NY: Addison-Wesley, 2000), p. 143.

So, the customer is "responsible" but the programmers are "in control." Hey, sounds like fun, where can we sign up?

Did Problems with the On-site Customer Help Kill C3?

Well, we know by now that fear is the source of *all* project failures, but here's what the XP2001 workshop report "Customer Involvement in Extreme Programming" had to say about it:

> "Ron Jeffries (who considers himself 'the most extreme of the three extremos') reported on the role of the on site customer in the well-known Chrysler Comprehensive Compensation (C3) project, In this very first XP project, two full payrolls were developed for Chrysler. The project began with approximately 145 large user stories, with a total estimated duration of one year.

> "The on-site customer in this project had a vision of the perfect system she wanted to develop. She was able to provide user stories that were easy to estimate. Moreover, she was with the development team everyday [sic], answering any business question the developers had.

> "Half way [sic] the project, several things changed, which eventually led to the project being cancelled. One of the changes was the replacement of the on site customer, showing that the actual way in which the customer is involved is one of the key success factors in an XP project. The new on-site customer was present most of the time, just like the previous on-site customer, and available to the development team for questions. Unfortunately, the requirements and user stories were not as crisp as they were before."[8]

As we can see, simply changing the on-site customer—one person—led to problems of project-destroying proportions. Most businesses would regard this single potential point of failure as being an unacceptably high risk.

Warning: Being an XP On-site Customer May Be Hazardous to Your Health!

Another problem with the on-site customer role, which directly affected C3, is simply that the role is difficult and stressful. While XPers generally talk about XP projects being "fun" to work on, the customer has a much harder time of it.

For the ACM Conference on Object-Oriented Programming, Systems, Languages, and Applications (OOPSLA) 2001, XP author and C3 participant Chet

---

8. Arie van Deursen, op. cit., pp. 1–2.

Hendrickson wrote an open and frank article titled "Will Extreme Programming kill your customer?" In this article, Chet discusses C3's first on-site customer, Marie, who was the supervisor of monthly and biweekly payroll for Chrysler's Corporate Disbursements Department. On C3, Marie was responsible for writing and prioritizing all the user stories, questioning the programmers' estimates, and approving all the acceptance tests (plus, to quote Chet, "a hundred other things that we eventually took for granted").

A few months after the launch of C3's first phase, Marie developed stress-related health problems and wisely transferred to a less stressful position. Her replacement customer was "a very bright and dedicated man." Despite this, it was soon discovered that the replacement customer just couldn't fill his predecessor's shoes:

> *"All we did know was that the job had been too much for the only person we had ever seen actually do it.*

> *"This leaves us with two questions. The first, 'How do you train an XP customer?' is beyond the scope of this discussion. The second, 'Can you do everything that is required to be an XP customer and remain healthy?' is the largest human issue surrounding Extreme Programming."*[9]

And now for something completely different . . .

The Extremo Inquisition, Round 2

A team of seven programmers, who had previously been tailoring RUP for their projects, decides to try out XP.

Billy: Right, we've read all 20 XP books, scoured the newsgroups, entered into a personal tête-à-tête with Cardinal Geoffrey, and cut off one of our fingers as Becht tells us to do in his book sequel *Extreme Programming 15: The Cunning Plan, This Time There's Gore.* I think we're about ready to get started.

Mrs. Potts: I still think he didn't really mean for people to do that.

Milia: Wait! I believe we may have forgotten one thing, Billy. Can you think what it is?

Billy: *I* don't know! I just wanted to use XP because I hear you can get coding straightaway with it. I didn't expect a kind of extreme inquisition.

[JARRING CHORD]

[The door flies open and Cardinal Becht of Spain enters, flanked as usual by his junior cardinals, Cardinals Geoffrey and Henrik.]

---

9. Chet Hendrickson, "Will Extreme Programming kill your customer?" http://www.coldewey.com/publikationen/conferences/oopsla2001/agileWorkshop/hendrickson.html, September 2001.

Becht: *Nobody* expects the Extremo Inquisition! Our chief weapon is fear—fear and snacks, especially those tasty little biscuits with the crumbly toppings . . . Hang on, I'll come in again.

[The Inquisition exits.]

Billy: I didn't expect a kind of extreme inquisition.

[JARRING CHORD]

[The cardinals burst in.]

Becht: *Nobody* expects the Extremo Inquisition! Our three chief weapons are fear . . . tasty snacks . . . *and* . . . a single dedicated on-site customer who codes acceptance tests and speaks with a single voice! *[Blathers on about the virtues of oral communication as opposed to written specs.]*

Henrik: *[Sotto voce]* Wait, sir, the customer got bifurcated last week.

Geoffrey: But surely that means we're going to need a pair of customers!

Becht: *[Deeply frustrated]* Damn! I'll start again . . . *Amongst* our weaponry are such diverse elements as . . . fear, or is that courage? Tasty snack treats . . . and . . . *two* dedicated on-site customers who code acceptance tests, speak with a single voice, manage the schedule, and—

Geoffrey: Hey, wait, let's turn the dial all the way up to ten and bring in a whole squadron of customers!

Becht: Good idea. Amongst our weaponry are . . . *ten* on-site customers who provide snack food, speak with a single voice, code acceptance tests. . . . Now, let's see. *Henrik!* Sit this rag-tag team in some comfy chairs and feed them snack food . . . and . . . *fizzy cola!*

[Dramatic organ music plays . . . lights flash . . . scene fades to darkness, to faces of puzzled-looking programmers.]

On-site Customer: The New Testament

In the foreword to *Questioning Extreme Programming*, Kent Beck now acknowledges that the whole single on-site customer thing was "an error of early XP thinking," and that we should now expect to see customer teams "equal to or larger in size than the programming team."[10]

This is somewhat problematic because many of the other XP tenets (e.g., reliance on oral communication and keeping the whole team in a single room) are predicated on the assumption that the customer is a single person (or at least speaks unambiguously, consistently, and always with a single voice). Ergo,

---

10. Pete McBreen, *Questioning Extreme Programming* (New York, NY: Addison-Wesley, 2002), p. xvi.

many of these other XP tenets are based on a fundamentally flawed argument! (We don't want to say we told you so, but . . .)

According to this New Testament theory, it doesn't matter how many customers we've got, it only matters that they "speak with a single voice." We'd like to make this observation: If we define the customer team as being equal to or bigger than the programming team, we end up with a team that has *doubled in size*.

Here are a few questions that occur to us:

- What does doubling the size of the team do to the project budget? (That's the gold owner's problem.)

- What does doubling the size of the team do with regard to exclusively relying on oral communication? (But he said . . .)

- What does doubling the size of the team do to the size of the room? (Madison Square Garden might be available.)

- What does doubling the size of the team do with regard to having the customer speak with a single voice? (Tower of Babel, anyone?)

- What is the likelihood that our no-up-front-design Extremo friends have considered the ramifications of any of this? (When the problem surfaces, the answer will arise. It's a Zen thing.)

- Why is this better than writing specifications? (What's a specification, daddy?)

What Can We Expect from XP Customer Teams?

To answer this question, let's go back to the XP2001 workshop report "Customer Involvement in Extreme Programming" one more time, referring to a project called DocGen:

"A first observation during this project was that it involved not just one customer, but with many different ones. These include the end user (and even he comes in many categories), the system maintainers, and management, as well as the marketing people and the developers responsible for implementing particular customizations. Making these 'speak with one voice' involved a lot of creativity during the project.

"Another observation was that the project requirements changed frequently. This was partly due to the fact that new people were brought into the project, bringing new requirements. Another reason was that in several cases the people involved in the project easily changed their minds. XP in itself is capable of implementing non-stable requirements. However, the resulting system may be an incoherent collection of features, ultimately leading to project failure.

"Furthermore, technology and potential customers experienced a significant semantic gap when trying to talk to each other. In the DocGen case, the developers had a compiler construction background, whereas the end users came from a mainframe background.

"This difference was amplified by the fact that neither the developers nor the customers considered talking to each other as their 'real job,' easily considering time invested in talking to each other as wasted."[11]

The problems described here are typically solved by introducing a specific role, the analyst, as distinct from the programmers. The analyst is experienced in his field of work and knows exactly how to bridge semantic gaps between the IT and business worlds. A team of analysts, of course, is even better. The "one voice" comes from writing all the details into a central document that gets sign-off from everyone who should sign off.

Although XP has now recognized the need for a proper analyst (or team of analysts), its practices are still predicated around the assumption that there's one on-site customer (goal donor) who provides story details to the programmers in the form of conversations. As we can see from the description of the DocGen project, this development (the introduction of a *team* of customers) didn't really help. In fact, if anything it added to the confusion. For example, the programmers had to use "a lot of creativity" in order to make myriad customers "speak with one voice." Surely, the simple addition of a detailed requirements spec would have achieved this and therefore saved a lot of time and effort.

The problem of new customers joining the project and bringing with them new user stories (and the problem of people in the project simply changing their minds) could also have been mitigated through the creation of a proper requirements spec—particularly if the spec provided traceability back to the original set of project goals, assuming the team had spent time up front thinking about these and writing them down. If people see in writing what has already been agreed upon, then they're more likely to pause and think about whether their exciting new requirements are really going to add true value to the project (i.e., whether the new requirements will help to achieve the original set of goals).

---

11. Arie van Deursen, op. cit., pp. 2–3.

Similarly, when people take the time to write the requirements down in detail, this causes them to pause and think about whether the time spent implementing each requirement is justifiable after all. This also helps immensely in prioritizing requirements for each iteration.

Tracing requirements (tasks, or use cases) back to a high-level set of project goals can also help the team to manage change (rather than actively embrace change). See the "Oral Documentation Defanged" sidebar at the end of Chapter 7 and the "Taking a Goal-Driven Approach" sidebar in Chapter 15.

Too Many Cooks

Most, if not all, projects have more than one master (see Figure 2-6, back in Chapter 2). Even the first XP project, C3, had essentially two customers: the goal donor (the on-site customer who contributed the requirements) and the gold owner (the project sponsor, who wasn't directly involved in the project). This highlights the classic problem with XP that we keep seeing: The customer speaks with more than one voice.

It's likely, and somewhat ironic given XP's emphasis on having an on-site customer, that the project sponsor can normally be thought of as the "real" customer, the one who must be kept happy at all costs. However, the project sponsor is also the person who will almost always be off-site. If the project is going in a direction that this person isn't happy with, the project stands a heavy risk of being cancelled. This is evidently what happened to C3.

We revisit the "too many cooks" issue in Chapter 7 in the sidebar "Did Oral Documentation Kill C3?"

And What About Those Acceptance Tests?

Acceptance tests are the customer's responsibility, and remember that in XP there are no test specifications, only test code. So don't be surprised if the customer has to write code!

Oh, come on, we're making this up, right? Nobody expects customers to write code, do they? Consider these statements from Chapter 5 of *Extreme Programming Installed*:

"The customer responsibility is to provide those acceptance tests as part of each iteration.... There are many different ways to implement the acceptance testing on your project, and the programmers will pick one.

"Programmers, you have the right to know what is needed. Insist on this right in the form of automated functional tests."[12]

(Rhetorical question: If the customers are already crackerjack programmers, why are they hiring the programming team?)

The arrangement is also described in *Extreme Programming Explained*:

"You will have to learn to write functional tests [acceptance tests].... Some teams may even assign you technical help for choosing, writing, and running the tests. Your goal is to write tests that let you say, 'Well, if these run, then I'm confident that the system will run.'"[13]

Depending on the skill and mind-set of your customer, she may not be able to conceive a systematic test, or understand a test once it has been written, or understand how the written code conforms to the idea she has in mind.

It's worth mentioning that customer test frameworks such as Fit and Fitnesse are starting to be introduced, so, in theory, this is becoming less of a problem. In practice, however, there's still a fundamental leap between stating a requirement in plain English ("I want the user to be able to define a new city") and stating it in executable form, such as the following:[14]

```
fit.ActionFixture
start eg.net.Simulator
check nodes 0
press new city
enter name Portland
```

No Safety Net

 What happens if the customer (or customer team) has a glitch?
This is likely, given that it's unlikely the customer will have received any training on how to be a well-behaved on-site customer (apart from being handed the "white book" and being asked to read it on the train to the programmers' office).

---

12. Ron Jeffries, Ann Anderson, and Chet Hendrickson, *Extreme Programming Installed* (New York, NY: Addison-Wesley, 2000), p. 32.

13. Kent Beck, *Extreme Programming Explained*, op. cit., p. 143.

14. See http://fit.c2.com/wiki.cgi?NetworkExample.

Here's a discussion we found on `comp.software.extreme-programming`:

"There are so many ways that the Customer can screw up an XP project. And there is no mechanism for:

1) Managing the Customer

2) Ensuring the Customer checks in and has clearance with his Management

3) Ensuring the Customer is correct, even if he means to be. and most importantly

4) Ensuring The Customer's mistakes don't hose the project

5) No Cover Your A$$ paper trail

"Consider: Everybody's job depends on the customer (1 person) getting it right. If that in house guy does a bad job, YOU take the fall, and so does your team. That is a very high risk methodology that is out there."[15]

But, you ask, what could possibly be done to prevent this sort of thing? Well, here's how it's usually done.

Developers elicit requirements from the customer(s). Then they write these requirements down in a specification. The specification is reviewed by the development team members internally until they think they've got it pretty close to right, and then it's reviewed not only with the customer folks who provided the initial input but also with other project stakeholders. Because the specification is a document, it can be e-mailed out to people who are not colocated with the development team. After the specification is reviewed, the gold owner signs-off on it. Developers have access to the specification whenever they need it. After the system is built, the QA folks can compare the delivered system to the specification and determine whether or not the developers met the requirements. And the development team is *accountable* for making sure it meets the requirements.

Thousands upon thousands of projects have used these techniques. They're not perfect, they're not extreme, and they don't absolve the programmers of all responsibility, but they are intended to eliminate the "single point of failure."

---

15. Jordan Bortz posting to the newsgroup `comp.software.extreme-programming`, subject: "C3 as XP Poster child," January 6, 2002.

The Trouble with Customers Is . . .

The trouble with on-site customers done the XP way is that if the on-site customer is a single person, she becomes a single point of failure in an incredibly difficult, stressful, high-profile position of great responsibility.

If the on-site customer is really a team of analysts, then confusion reigns because it's difficult to get everyone on the team to speak with a single voice and not enough detail gets written down. Too much potentially architecture-changing detail is left to "promises for future conversations"—but with whom?

The On-site Customer Defanged

If you have access to a single on-site customer who really understands the system requirements, go for it—the arrangement can prove invaluable in clarifying ambiguous requirements and providing early feedback.

However, don't make the mistake of using the on-site customer as a regular source of new requirements. There's no substitute for requirements that get written down in detail and signed-off in unison by the project's many masters. If project sign-off can't be achieved, then this is a major risk that has just been identified early on, rather than being left to fester, resulting possibly in a sudden "inexplicable" project cancellation sometime later.

If a team of analysts is providing the requirements, make sure the analysts write the requirements down in detail (not just in "sketch" form as promises for future conversations between the programmers and the analysts).

Also, don't assume that because a customer understands the system requirements she is skilled at project management and quality assurance and should be given responsibility for budget, schedule, and acceptance testing.

Also see the sidebar "Oral Documentation Defanged" at the end of Chapter 7.

Summary

In XP, the customer is the catch-bucket for anything the programmers don't want to do. The programming team is absolved from responsibility for performance to schedule, performance to budget, etc. The customer is the catch-bucket for shortcomings in the XP process itself. Wherever the process is weak, more responsibility gets dumped on the customer. Dumping all the responsibility for schedules, budgets, requirements, and acceptance testing on the customer removes accountability from the programmers.

So when an XP project fails, the programming team is going to be blameless and guiltless. After all, it's the customer's problem, right? You'd better believe it.

Having a single on-site customer may be stressful for the person who has that job and may make that person more prone to making errors. It seems to have dawned on the Extremos now that a single individual as the customer is inadequate, and so now we've got teams of customers. But many of the other tenets of XP (e.g., detailed written requirements replaced by one-line story cards, emergent design, oral documentation, etc.) are based on the concept of one customer being in the room with the programmers all the time.

The customer (or customer team) can be a single point source of failure on XP projects. If the (single) customer drops the ball, bang, you're dead. If the customer team does not "speak with a single voice," you're just as dead. There is no safety net. XP asserts that specifications are unnecessary and that writing specifications is, in essence, an act of cowardice. Yet the Extremos completely fail to account for the project failure modes that specifications are intended to prevent. This is justified by repeating fun statements like "Fear is the mind killer."

CHAPTER 6

Pair Programming (Dear Uncle Joe, My Pair Programmer Has Halitosis)

Your Pair Will Hold Your Hand
(Sing to the tune of "I Want to Hold Your Hand" by The Beatles)

When you're coding something
That you don't understand

You don't
Have to worry

Your pair will hold your hand
Your pair will hold your hand
Your pair will hold your hand

And when you're coding you feel happy inside
The joy of coding is just one you can't hide

People say
We need requirements
They always make a fuss
We think
That requirements
Should be in C Plus Plus
Should be in C Plus Plus

And when you're coding you feel happy inside
The joy of coding is just one you can't hide

When you're unit testing
And you find a bug
You don't have to feel bad
Your pair will give you a hug

Your pair will give you a hug
And when you're coding you feel happy inside
The joy of coding is just one you can't hide

"The only constraint that XP puts on you is that any production code has be [sic] *written by a pair.* Your preferences and comfort do not supercede the delivery of quality to the project, or your parcitipation *[sic]* in the team."[1]

—Robert C. Martin

"In reality, it fosters a stinky noisy room and a headache."[2]
—Anonymous XPer

"I think maybe concentration is the enemy. Seriously. If you're working on something that is so complex that you actually need to concentrate, there's too much chance that it's too hard."[3]

—Ron Jeffries

Pair programming is one of the most controversial aspects of XP, and it presents some of the most amusing scenarios, some of which have even appeared in the Dilbert comic strip.[4] In this chapter we examine some of the claims that have been made about this practice, including those from Laurie Williams' book *Pair Programming Illuminated.* We also share with you some eye-opening real-world "eXPeriences" from our correspondents "in the field."

---

1. Robert C. Martin posting to the newsgroup `comp.object`, subject: "Pair Programming—Yuck!" October 28, 2001.

2. Anonymous XPer, see the "Voice of eXPerience: Tales from the Front Line" sidebar in Chapter 4.

3. Ron Jeffries, posting to the C2 Wiki page "Pair Programming Ergonomics," `http://c2.com/cgi-bin/wiki?PairProgrammingErgonomics`.

4. See `http://www.dilbert.com`.

Pair Programming Basics

The basic idea behind pair programming is that two heads are better than one—that a pair of programmers working together will produce a higher quality product than a single programmer. So, for production code, XP mandates that everyone on the team program in pairs. Pairing up is an effective way of catching errors and identifying ways to further simplify the code. To facilitate collective ownership of the code, XP encourages people to move around and switch partners frequently. It's kind of like square dancing: "Change your partner!" every couple of hours. And, of course, in XP all the pair programming goes on in a single room.

On the surface, pair programming sounds like a great idea. It's been well known since the ancient days of punched cards that having another programmer look at your code can help to catch bugs. In some circumstances it can undoubtedly work tremendously well. Just as obviously, you've got two programmers doing the work that one programmer was previously doing if everybody has to pair program. Some research studies claim there is no significant decrease in productivity (as we discuss later in this chapter).

Problems with pair programming can arise because of several factors, including

- Social dynamics

- Lack of privacy

- Lack of "quiet thinking time"

- Ergonomic issues

Pair programming is necessary in XP because it compensates for a couple of practices that XP shuns: up-front design and permanent design documentation. Coding in pairs can be seen as a compensatory practice that theoretically makes up for the fact that the programmers are (courageously) making up the design as they write the code.

There is certainly no problem with people working in pairs if they want to work that way. So it makes no sense to prohibit pair programming. However, changing it from a voluntary practice to a mandatory one makes quite a difference.

People You'd Least Like to Pair With (No. 48)

Pair programming is definitely not for everybody, as Doug relates here.

Having a number of years of programming experience, I place a pretty high value on peace, quiet, and space to think in. According to a study from IBM's Santa Teresa Laboratory,[5] putting programmers in private offices with doors that closed instead of cubicles resulted in a huge boost to productivity. So the idea of all the programmers in a big, noisy room seems like it would be a huge detriment to productivity. It would figure to drive many people nuts.

I've also worked with some incredibly talented programmers who would have been awful to pair with. One who comes to mind is hypoglycemic and has a tendency to get upset very easily when his blood sugar drops. He's a brilliant programmer who produces prodigious amounts of code that's always efficient and well structured. He and I worked very well together but I would never dream of sharing a desk and a keyboard with him. And I'd resist any process that wouldn't allow me, as a manager, to make use of his skills. So I would never mandate pair programming.

I Can't Code Alone . . . 'Cause I Need My Pair
(Sing to the tune of "Ticket to Ride" by The Beatles)

I guess I'd better go home
It's time to go play, yeah
That pair programmer I had
Called in sick today, yeah

I can't code alone
'Cause I've tried
Gotta have my pair by my side

I can't really write any code
'Cause I need my pair
'Cause I need my pair

When I'm refactoring code
He always sits right, always sits right by me
When we're runnin' our unit tests
He always sits right, always sits right by me

I can't code alone
'Cause I've tried
Gotta have my pair by my side

I can't really write any code
'Cause I need my pair
'Cause I need my pair

---

5. Gerald M. McCue, "IBM's Santa Teresa Laboratory—Architectural design for program development," *IBM Systems Journal* (http://www.research.ibm.com/journal/sj/171/ibmsj1701C.pdf), vol. 17, no. 1, 1978.

There's a Study That Proves My Point!

Proponents of pair programming often describe the "body of evidence" that surrounds pair programming's touted benefits. The most commonly cited study[6] was carried out by Laurie Williams, who also happens to be the coauthor of *Pair Programming Illuminated* and a contributor to PairProgramming.com (http://pairprogramming.com). The study is also described (and referred to repeatedly) in *Pair Programming Illuminated*.

The basic finding behind the study is that pair programming increases code quality by 15% but takes on average 15% longer. The conclusion then is that in exchange for a small drop in productivity, code quality is increased, which in turn saves time and money in later stages of the project.

The problem with this particular study, apart from the fact that it wasn't an independently run test, is that it was conducted in a university, using students rather than experienced professional programmers. Thus, the study is really only an examination of novice-novice pairing, which is actually the most unlikely and least desirable of combinations (we discuss programmer pairing combinations later in this chapter).

The pair programmers' performance was compared with the performance of some solo programmers who also were students (therefore also novices). This raises the issue that the comparison wasn't a fair one. In a real project, "solo" programmers don't really code alone; they're part of a team. Typically, designs are reviewed by senior engineers who sign off on them, prototypes are written quickly to get the design right before the production version is attempted, team leaders monitor their team closely (particularly the novice programmers), and so on. All these practices help to increase both productivity and code quality, yet none was taken into account.

The result is that Williams' study is academic at best; it isn't a true comparison of pair programming versus software development in the real world. And yet, as we mentioned, it's the most commonly cited "proof" that pair programming works.

In the next "Voice of eXPerience" sidebar we get one programmer's perspective, straight from the source.

---

6. Alistair Cockburn and Laurie Williams, "The Costs and Benefits of Pair Programming," http://collaboration.csc.ncsu.edu/laurie/Papers/XPSardinia.PDF, 2002.

Voice of eXPerience: Pair Programming Social Dynamics

by "Rich Camden"

As in other VoXP segments, the reality of what happens to an XP team is often quite different from what XP preaches in theory. For example, XP recommends that the coach also pair programs (i.e., the coach doesn't get "special privileges" above the rest of the team). However, this description from Rich Camden is a good example of what can happen to an XP project when the human factor also plays a part.

The story you're about to read is true. Only the name of the author has been changed to protect the innocent.

Pair programming is the worst of the XP tenets. To recommend pair programming across the board for all developers involved in XP is to not understand the people/personality side of programming. Yes, there are those who will benefit from having another programmer constantly assisting and reviewing their work. But there are many more who will feel uncomfortable and restrained with another programmer watching everything they do.

Unfortunately, this tenet above all others tends to dampen creativity in XP. Many of the best programming gems come after you absorb yourself in a problem and do much deep thinking. This doesn't occur when you have another programmer sitting at the same keyboard.

The strangest part of XP for me is the social dynamics that occur as a result of making many people do things that feel unnatural or make them uncomfortable. In my experience, XP was a mandate from management, not a grassroots developer movement. In a rather short period of time, projects were shifted from comfortable cubicles to small rooms packed with workstations, tables, and people. It looks a lot like a call center, with developers shoulder to shoulder.

I joined my team after the change to XP had occurred. When I first joined the team, I was most interested in pairing and how it worked in real life. I read comments and articles on pairing at PairProgramming.com and at the C2 Wiki pages to prepare myself. I wasn't entirely negative to the idea. Unfortunately, what I read didn't prepare me for what was in store for me.

Joining the Team

On my first day of joining the team, I imagined that an enthusiastic XP developer would volunteer to pair with me and show me the ropes. It seemed that one of the team leads or coaches would be the best person. Instead, I was asked to simply watch the team and get my workstation prepared for development.

As I watched the team, I quickly realized that nobody was enthusiastic about pairing, including the team leads. During the stand-up meeting, developers were asked with whom they were going to pair. Now it seems quite impossible that they would know this until they could surmise who wasn't busy and then ask them to pair. Thus, in most cases the coach would assign pairs. I can't claim to know what people were thinking, but the looks on their faces didn't seem to say, "Oh, boy, I get to pair with ___ today!"

Right of Association

I watched each developer closely to understand the dynamics of the team I was joining. There were two team leads: the coach and the person acting as the customer representative. The coach never paired. This seemed to set the precedent that pairing was indeed undesirable, and if you were lucky enough to be a coach, you didn't have to do it. The second team lead was actively developing but rarely paired either. Again, this seemed to enforce the idea that if you had seniority and were doing important work, you didn't need to pair. This doesn't surprise me at all. Nobody wants someone looking over his shoulder day in and day out. What amazed me, however, was that the same people were actively encouraging the team to pair in classic "do as I say, not as I do" fashion.

That's not to say there was no pairing at all. When assigned a pair, developers would act in good faith and perform their job. The developers that I witnessed pairing normally had a buddy that they tended to prefer to pair with. Again, I wasn't surprised. People associate more with people they work well with.

The ability to choose associates (the right of association) is one of the keys to success. Any successful person uses this fact to her advantage. Forced association only ends in frustration and mediocrity. But even "pairing buddies" weren't actively engaged in pairing as described at PairProgramming.com. What tends to evolve is an arrangement where the two developers agree to work together to beat the system. Essentially, the unspoken agreement goes like this: "I'll work for a while and you daydream, then tomorrow you can type and I'll daydream."

Another interesting anomaly I noticed was that my pairs would always control the keyboard. Never in 5 months did it happen that my pair volunteered to have me type. Of course, if I asserted myself, they would allow me to type, but never did one choose to watch rather than type. The unwritten understanding I gathered was that typing is preferable to watching.

Pairing Fluidity Explained

The partner preferences didn't go unnoticed by the team coaches. As any XP enthusiast will tell you, this is undesirable. A surefire way to solve this would be for each coach to pair with a different person from time to time. Instead, the coaches would break up pairing buddies and assign them using criteria known only to them. This drove me to consider what would cause team members to avoid the fluid pairs approved by XP.

The key to understanding pairing culture is the XP task card. If you aren't familiar with XP, *task cards* describe small tasks that make up larger project goals driven by user stories. A task card has a completion estimate usually between 2 and 8 hours. Once they've finished a task, developers complete the card by writing down who completed the task and how long it took.

It's easy to see that the cards are basically a fine-grained record of exactly what transpires on a project. It takes software development and turns it into a textbook case of micromanagement techniques. Your objective is then to complete as many cards as possible with your name on them. This trumps the more productive desire to see the project succeed.

Your choices are then to either partner with someone you trust as a good developer or attempt to finish tasks individually. As you've already seen, this natural desire to partner is discouraged in XP. Thus, you're at a disadvantage if you're paired with an undesirable partner.

Who would make an undesirable partner? Someone new to the project would definitely slow you down. Every single module would require some explanation, not to mention a description of the business processes behind the application. This explained why my teammates were so reluctant to show me the ropes when I'd just joined the project. They'd most likely have to spend most of their time explaining the whys and hows of what they were doing, unless we had an unwritten pairing agreement, which only happens after some rapport has been built up over time.

It also explains the lack of fluidity in pairs. There's no advantage or benefit to the individual besides deflecting the constant berating of your coach that you should pair more often (which begs the question, if pairing is so great, why don't they do it too?). It's a classic catch-22. You're damned if you do and damned if you don't.

A Metaphor for Molecular Expansion

XP enthusiasts love metaphors. I find pairing to be a great metaphor for the physical characteristics of air molecules. Boyle's Law states: *If the temperature remains constant, the volume of a given mass of gas is inversely proportional to the absolute pressure.* For most of us, that's pretty clear, but I'll elaborate for the benefit of any XP proponents who might be reading. Boyle's Law tells us that if pressure is reduced, air molecules move apart, occupying more space per molecule.

That's exactly what happens in an XP lab. Let's face it, people enjoy personal space. To deny that is to deny common sense. People can be forced into close contact for periods of time, but when the necessity (pressure) to be in close contact is reduced, they'll spread out. A "we need to pair more" scolding from the coach is the pressure. (Note: Real-life XP consists of daily scolding and self-flagellation in the form of "We aren't doing enough of ___.")

A curious VP stopping by the lab is added pressure. The threat of finding yourself without a job if you don't pair is *tremendous* pressure. It's interesting to see pairs form under pressure. It's even more interesting when people "pretend" to pair. One way developers achieve this is by sitting quite close together. From a distance, it's impossible to tell if they're working together or they're just two people sitting really close together. Either way, it looks ridiculous. Two people hunched over, attempting to make an interface specifically designed for an individual work is a visual oxymoron. Without a doubt, there's going to be an increase in neck and back problems in the developer community.

But what's even more amusing is what happens when the pressure is released. This may be in the form of a coach being in a meeting or perhaps on vacation. It could also be as a result of being very early or late in the day, or on a weekend. When the pressure is reduced, the developers, just like air molecules, adjust to a more natural distance. This natural distance consists of developers working at their own workstations. If fewer people are present than normal, developers will naturally choose a position one or two chairs down from the next person.

Peer Pressure and the Silence Factor

By far the most striking characteristic of developers in the XP lab is their inability to admit (or resistance to admitting) that they hate to pair. If they were to admit that they dislike pairing, they would go through a very unpleasant ostracizing process. The reason is that the worst thing that can happen to an XP developer is for someone to find out that he has a few disagreements with the process. I've never experienced fear like I do now on any project I've ever been on. This is key to understanding the XP world.

In a traditional environment, you would be able to say with impunity, "I hate writing documentation." Contrast this to the XP world, where dissention is fatal. Even though XP proponents make a big deal about the ability to change the process, a few processes are nonnegotiable, pairing being one of them. Quite literally, the words of the prophets are written on the lab walls: "Pair up!" Or more precisely, all production code must be written in pairs. I now know methodology can become dogma to the extent of a religion.

> *Don't code, don't code, don't code so close to me . . .*
> *Pleeease don't code so close to me . . .*

Wishing for the Sound of Silence

Why on earth would someone writing code want a quiet place to think? An experienced consultant expresses it this way:

> *"Pair programming appeals to fresh-faced young programmers who want to bond a little too much, people who spend too much time 'being just mad mate', running around being zany, mistaking this for creativity. The best programmers I know want silence, as they are having 'hard thoughts'. They achieve their magic by 'thinking about the problem', not playing around waiting for the gods of creativity to give them a bolt from the blue, whilst they play Kerplunk and talk about why Postman Pat is so cool."*[7]

Of course, Ron Jeffries' thoughts on the topic are somewhat different and bear repeating:

---

7. Dino Fancellu, e-mail to author, January 5, 2003.

"I think maybe concentration is the enemy. Seriously. If you're working on something that is so complex that you actually need to concentrate, there's too much chance that it's too hard."[8]

Jeffries' comment reveals a lot about the Extremo mind-set: A roomful of noisy people working on bite-sized chunks of code is preferable to an environment that is more conducive to hard thinking and elegant designs that take all the project's requirements into account. In XP, it appears that everyone on the team must conform to this form of organization. There is no flexibility.

Conversely, other processes besides XP do at least offer some form of organizational flexibility, as we discuss in Chapter 3.

Another consultant puts it this way:

"Pair programming will always be a problem in a society of individualists (particularly of the American strain). Most of us are willing to share (i.e., peer review) but we do not want to show our 'stuff' until it is ready. It is just human nature. Dealing with a mentor is a bit different. Most of us are willing to use a mentor for suggestion and help, but we do not even want our mentor to sit on our shoulder all day long. Let the mentor help others, too."[9]

It's a Work of Love, Enforced by Coercive Means

Extremos can take their commitment to pair programming pretty seriously. Consider this from the Wiki Web:

---

8. Ron Jeffries, posting to the C2 Wiki page "Pair Programming Ergonomics," http://c2.com/cgi-bin/wiki?PairProgrammingErgonomics.

9. Gary A. Ham, e-mail to author, March 3, 2003.

> *"TheCoach needs to keep individuals on track with respect to the development paradigm: eXtreme Programming. This is a work of love. If you don't respect others, you're not doing it right. TheCoach get [sic] his respect to show through for people who try hard to do the right thing.*
>
> *"TheCoach may need to use coercive means to corral the determined individualist back into the group. Ultimately, TheCoach must ask such an individual to leave, where no supportive contribution to group goals can be made by the individual."*[10]

Uh huh. Pair programming isn't everything, it's the only thing. Or to borrow from Diana Ross:

> *Force—in the naaaaame of love. Pair up or you'll get fired. Think it o-over.*

The Adventures of Uncle Joe and Jack the Siberian Code Hound

One day, "Uncle Joe" Steele, the XP coach, and Jack, his Siberian code hound, were walking through the coding room when Jack started barking and growling at Loretta. Poor Loretta was inadvertently programming by herself for a moment because JoJo had gone to the men's room.

"Nyet, Jack!" barked Uncle Joe, to keep Jack from attacking Loretta after she quickly explained that JoJo would be right back. Just then JoJo walked in and Jack (seeing that Loretta was properly paired up) calmed down and began wagging his tail.

"Nice sweatshirt, Uncle Joe," commented JoJo. "I didn't know you went to Georgia Tech."

"*Da!*" replied Uncle Joe. "Whoops—what'd I say? I mean, that's right. Georgia's always on my mind. Kind of like an old sweet song. Smell the code, Jack!"

Jack put his paws up on JoJo's desk and started sniffing at the keyboard. He sniffed and panted intently, then barked three times, put his paws back on the floor, and furiously chased his tail around in a circle.

"See, Loretta," said JoJo. "I told you we need to refactor that state tax computation."

Loretta was not at all pleased (she had already written the tax computation three times and it passed all the unit tests each time), but she didn't want to say anything in front of Uncle Joe and Jack. "I guess you're right," said Loretta. "I'll refactor it again."

---

10. See `http://c2.com/cgi-bin/wiki?TheCoach`.

"Good work, Jack!" said Uncle Joe with a smile. Jack wagged his tail happily, and the coach and his code hound moved on to the snack area to find a treat for Jack.

As soon as Uncle Joe was safely across the room, JoJo removed his folded-up newspaper from under his chair and resumed working his crossword puzzle, while Loretta tried to figure out how to make the tax computation smell better.

"Hey, Loretta," said JoJo, "what's a five-letter word for 'deception'?"

Loretta paused, thought for a moment, and said, "Do you know what any of the letters are?"

"It starts with 'FR,'" said JoJo, "and it ends with 'UD.'"

Loretta glanced at the copy of *Pair Programming: The SuperEgo and Its Effect on Human Sexuality*, which she kept handy for when JoJo was coding, and said, "It must be Freud. Although I can't quite see where they came up with that definition from."

"Thanks," said JoJo, moving on to his next clue.

Chapter 8 contains more adventures of Uncle Joe and his fearful band.

Voice of eXPerience: Pair Programming Ergonomics

This description was given to us by an anonymous XPer who has some practical reasons for disliking pair programming. (The ergonomic aspect of pair programming, where each pair is "crouched over squinting at a computer screen," can be seen in the photographs of the C3 team at `http://www.xprogramming.com/xpmag/c3space.htm` *and also in* Extreme Programming Installed *on page 78.)*

I've just joined a project using XP. I really wished I had some critical information before jumping in. The pair programming is mind numbing. With this XP stuff, software development is no longer a professional occupation, it's just another type of assembly-line work. We're herded into a small room like telemarketers. (Actually, I bet telemarketers have a better work environment.)

Something that nobody seems to have pointed out is that with pairing, you can't adjust the work chair, monitor, and keyboard to a suitable position. Everybody is crouched over, squinting at a computer screen. The keyboard trays were removed to allow more room for pairing. Another irony is that on my daily walk to the "lab," I pass numerous empty offices and cubes, and several assistants with huge work areas. I'm afraid that in a few years, software development will no longer be considered a "profession."

Productivity: numProgrammers/2 == numProgrammers? Right?

In a white paper on pair programming, Alistair Cockburn and Laurie Williams write:

"The affordability of pair programming is a key issue. If it is much more expensive, managers simply will not permit it. Skeptics assume that incorporating pair programming will double code development expenses and critical manpower needs."[11]

This is a common argument against pair programming: Surely with two people sitting at one computer, concentrating on one program, only half as much work would get done. The usual response is that pair programming actually increases productivity in the long run because the code is of a higher quality; in other words, eventually just as much code gets written (or, to be more precise, eventually the same amount of functionality gets implemented—if it's of higher quality, then it will probably involve fewer lines of code). We've found that doing some detailed up-front design before coding allows even solitary programmers to produce very high-quality work!

This is one area that we see a circular argument in XP emerge. In *Extreme Programming Explained*, continuous integration is justified in part by the fact that because the team is programming in pairs, there are half as many streams of changes to integrate[12]—in other words, half as much code is being produced.

Coder's Little Helper
(Sing to the tune of "Mother's Little Helper" by the Rolling Stones)

What a drag it is smelling code

Things are different today
Since my pair has gone away
And the new one comes to work when he is fried

And those onions that he ate
Make me want to leave the state

I go running for the shelter
Of the coder's little helper
And it helps me through the day
Until I can get away

Breath mints pleeeeease
Take four of these
Go to the store
And buy some more

What a drag it is smelling code . . .

---

11. Alistair Cockburn and Laurie Williams, op. cit., p. 3.

12. Kent Beck, *Extreme Programming Explained: Embrace Change* (New York, NY: Addison-Wesley, 2000), p. 68.

Voice of eXPerience: Overuse of Pair Programming

by David Van Der Klauw

I believe that overuse of pair programming is a major flaw in XP.

Before I comment on pair programming (pairing), I want to make the point that it is a complex issue, not a Boolean variable to be decided Yes or No, Right or Wrong.

Pairing is a lot like marriage in the types of questions and answers that arise. Imagine the reaction I would get if I made a few general comments about the benefits of marriage and then insisted that every person should be married and that CompanyXYZ should employ only married people. There would be outrage. Yet this is exactly how the complex issue of pairing is approached by many people.

Learning by Pairing

Remember a lesson at school or university. The teacher gives a general introduction of the topic, works one or two examples on the board, and then gives you some problems to attempt by yourself. You consult the board and/or your textbook, and then attempt the questions. Should you have trouble, the teacher is there to help.

Imagine how silly it would be if instead of all this, the teacher just sat beside you and you both commenced working on the problems together. Whenever your writing slowed, the teacher told you what to write, and when you were confused, the teacher took your book and completed the problem instead of letting you think it through and work it out yourself.

This is exactly what we do with our pairing.

To me, the worst aspect of pairing is that it prevents me from stopping, investigating, and learning at my own pace when the need arises. When I am pairing, I have the responsibility not to waste the time of or bore my partner as I investigate something. As a result, I will often skip the opportunity of learning or investigating. Pairing raises the cost of learning and wastes many opportunities for investigation and improvement of my skills and the product.

Let Them Eat Cake

Is pairing better than working alone?

It is better in the same way that cake is better than bread, wine is better than water, and meat is better than vegetables. It is better in the right circumstances, but it is definitely not better for all circumstances.

How Much Meat Do We Need?

I tried to find an analogy to show how much pairing we should do. The best I could find is meat versus vegetables.

Vegetarians eat vegetables and do not eat meat. Without debating that topic, let's agree that while it's possible to get everything your body needs from vegetables, it's difficult. Most vegetarians will freely admit this. Therefore, a lazy vegetarian who neglects to monitor her diet would be better off eating some meat.

I've made a graph showing the health of such a lazy vegetarian as she replaces vegetables with meat.

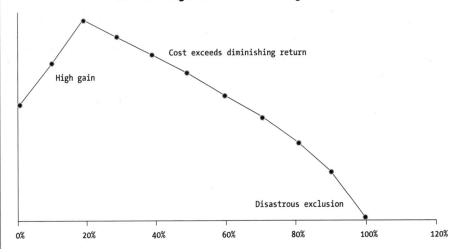

Meat vs. Vegetables: The Shocking Truth

The "High gain" area is where the meat is providing the vital trace elements, iron and protein that the body was previously deprived of.

The "Cost exceeds diminishing return" area is where the high percentage of meat increases the amount of fat and free radicals, while not providing any further health benefit.

The "Disastrous exclusion area" is where the 100% meat diet causes severe problems due to the total absence of certain vitamins and fiber that come only from vegetables.

The Pairing Graph

Now I have made a graph showing the productivity of programmers who replace solitary programming with pairing (the figures shown here are purely illustrative).

The "High gain" area is where the programmers pick up those vital tips and knowledge that can only be learned from watching another programmer in action. As solitary programmers, they were deprived of these.

The "Cost exceeds diminishing return" area is where the high percentage of pairing increases the time taken, frustration, and so forth, while not providing any further benefit to the tasks.

The "Disastrous exclusion" area is where the 100% pairing causes severe problems due to the total absence of certain learning and experience that comes from only solitary programming and study.

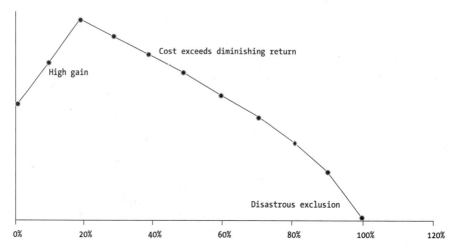

How Much Pairing?

I recommend that the pairing level be adjusted to its optimum. How so? Well, I don't have a crystal ball to tell me the perfect levels, so I suggest a method that can be used.

Regularly ask the programmers if they want more or less pairing. Adjust the level a little bit at a time by majority vote, until half want more and half want less. Once this point is reached, consider whether the pairing level can be further adjusted on an individual person and/or task basis.

Two Minds Are Better Than One

Two minds are better than one. But then again, a chain is only as strong as its weakest link, a train is only as fast as its slowest carriage, and too many cooks spoil the broth. Which adage applies to pairing?

No one will argue that in many situations two minds are better than one. Therefore, all CompanyXYZ programming should be done in pairs if we make a few further assumptions:

- Putting two people in front of one computer automatically makes their minds work together effectively.

- CompanyXYZ is happy to pay twice as much to get the better result.

- Programmers enjoy pairing and won't leave CompanyXYZ for an alternative arrangement.

Is the Cost Justified?

When the value of pairing is questioned, its supporters will often point out one case in which a partner was helpful. They use this as proof that all coding should be done in pairs.

This is a classic case of the one-size-fits-all flaw. I've paired now for more than 6 months. I've had times when my partner taught me stuff, helped increase my speed, and found bugs I missed, and I've had a few good chats and great fun on some days. That's not good enough.

It's necessary to do a proper cost-benefit analysis of the practice of pairing. For something to be justified, it isn't good enough to find one benefit. Benefits must exceed costs and there must be no better alternative.

Don't ask

- Can a partner ever be of any value?

Do ask

- Is a partner of sufficient value to justify the cost?

- Does the partner cause additional problems?

To pay off, pair programming must deliver the average task in half the time it would take a solitary programmer to deliver the task to the same quality. My experience indicates that this order of speed increase isn't occurring. In fact, I think many tasks take much longer.

XP proponents will come back with two arguments:

- Sometimes the quality of work of a pair of programmers is higher than is achievable by a single programmer.

- Occasionally, a pair of programmers will rapidly solve a problem that a solitary programmer would be stuck on.

Rather than dispute these claims, I'll concentrate on the impact of the far more frequent occurrence where the pair doesn't get the task done faster and, in effect, takes twice the hours required for the job.

When you invest money, a sobering fact is that to break even after a loss, the percentage gain you need is greater than the percentage loss taken. For example, a 10% loss needs an 11% gain to take you back to even, a 20% loss needs a 25% gain, and a 50% loss needs a 100% gain. It turns out that these mathematics apply to XP's pairing with equally alarming results.

Consider the case where a pair is normally taking 1 hour to do tasks that take a single programmer 2 hours. In this case, a pair is as effective as a single programmer.

Now consider a situation in which the pair fails to work faster on just one task and instead takes the full 2 hours. In this case, to catch up the pair would have to work at twice their normal rate for the next two tasks. That's right, after taking as long as a single programmer on just one task, the pair would need to work at four times the speed of the single programmer for the next two tasks just to catch up.

You do the math if you don't believe me.

I believe that in the real world, a pair will often take as long as a single programmer to do a task. They may occasionally work faster, the quality of their work may even be higher, and they may avoid getting stuck occasionally. But on balance, the frequent slowness will overwhelm these benefits, as the mathematics shows.

Three's a Crowd

If two minds are better than one, are three minds better than two? If it makes sense to place two people on one computer, then why not turn up the volume, take it to an extreme, and place three or four people on one computer?

Don't laugh this off—it's a very important question. The defense of pairing relies on certain hard-to-prove claims about better quality, knowledge sharing, and collaboration. All of these claims support tripling and quadrupling in addition to pairing.

When I asked *[our XP coach]*, he told me that any more than two people results in slower communication and decision making because there's more than one channel of communication. I find this answer to be unconvincing. Surely, the fastest communication and decision making occurs within the brain of a solitary programmer.

When it comes to programming, I think two is a crowd.

Laborer or Artist?

In my analysis of pairing, I thought about all kinds of work where people worked as a pair. Police officers and airline pilots pair for safety and backup. Laborers pair for greater lifting power.

People in creative professions don't pair. Remember, too many cooks spoil the broth. Can you imagine two painters creating a masterpiece by taking turns with the brush?

Most professions don't pair simply because the cost isn't justified. Bus drivers, taxi drivers, bank tellers, judges, teachers, and most workers in other professions do the job with the smallest unit that can do the job: one person.

Is a programming job more like the jobs that justify pairing or is it more like the jobs that don't justify pairing? I think programming is more like the jobs that don't justify pairing or aren't suited to pairing.

Who Likes Pairing?

Forced 100% pairing is like a forced marriage. It might work out, but it would surely be better if it was voluntary and stood on its own merits.

Ideally, the forced pair would be ideal at pairing and would work ideally together. In the real world, however, things are a bit different. In the next few paragraphs, I make a few generalizations that I've placed in italics. These aren't absolute truths, but they're generally true.

When pairing a bossy and quiet person, the bossy person will tend to dominate the quiet person. It's likely the quiet person will dislike pairing, whereas the bossy person will probably like the extra power he has. *Bossy people like pairing, quiet people do not.*

When pairing an expert with a novice, the novice will tend to slow down the expert and the expert will tend to teach the novice. The novice will probably enjoy this arrangement, while the expert will probably not. *Novices like pairing, experts do not.*

When pairing a high achiever with a low achiever, the high achiever will get less done and will no longer be able to take credit for the high achievement. The low achiever, however, will get more done and will be able to take partial credit for the work, as well as avoid the criticism and responsibility for her previous poor results. *Low achievers like pairing, high achievers do not.*

Although my statements are only generalizations, if they're correct they tend to suggest that if 100% forced pairing was brought into a company, *quiet, high-achieving experts would dislike pairing and leave the company, while bossy, low-achieving novices would like pairing and stay.*

I didn't write this section to insult any particular person or to infer characteristics to someone who likes pairing. I wrote it simply to provoke thought.

Stick to the Task

XP claims that when programming alone, programmers tend to take experimental detours rather than sticking strictly to the task. XP claims this is a serious problem and "solves" it by pair programming, with strict estimation and tracking of time taken.

I have something very important to say about this. I believe that the experimental detours are good. They are vital learning that most programmers need. Think about it: Why do so many programmers do it? It's because it comes naturally. Do programmers naturally do a stupid thing, or do they naturally do a sensible thing?

When is the best time to investigate something that you don't understand fully? When you come across a task that might benefit from it, when the task is right there fresh in your mind.

Under XP, you should make a note of the possible spike, complete your task, and then discuss the possible spike with your team, write it up on the board as a spike, and do it. If something good comes from it, you discuss it with the team and customer, and then write a test for it and include it in the production code (working as a pair, of course). Is it any wonder that these investigations never get done under XP?

What happens if you just have a nagging thought that a really useful function or object lies just around the corner? How do you explain that to the team and get permission to do it?

Now that I've suggested that experimental detours are good, I know what the XP proponents will argue. They will ask how you stop a programmer from spending all of her time on useless detours. Self-discipline and common sense are the answers.

If you've just spent half a day on an unfruitful detour, then it makes sense to stick strictly to your tasks for the next day or two so that you have something to show for your effort.

An unproductive programmer, whether prone to detours or otherwise, will be obvious from the lack of output in the long run. Similarly, the high productivity of a creative, detour-taking programmer will also be obvious in the long run, even if the odd day is wasted on a detour.

Pair Programming Illuminated

The book *Pair Programming Illuminated* (we refer to it as *PPI* for the rest of this section) by Laurie Williams and Robert Kessler, not surprisingly given its title, pitches the case for pair programming. However, it also discusses quite openly some of the problems typically encountered by pair programming teams. We focus on some of those problems in this section and examine how they may affect an XP project as a whole.

Problems with Pairing Different Categories of Programmer

PPI divides programmers into different categories and then discusses the effects of the various combinations thereof. The programmer categories are novice, average, expert, introvert, and extrovert. The pairing combinations discussed in *PPI*, with a chapter dedicated to each, are as follows:

- Expert-expert

- Expert-average

- Expert-novice

- Novice-novice

- Extrovert-extrovert

- Extrovert-introvert

- Introvert-introvert

Because pairs are meant to rotate frequently, these various combinations will resurface often in a team of mixed abilities. Thus, in small teams (which is likely, given an XP project), it would be difficult to keep "problem pairs" apart.

"Go Make Me a Cup of Tea" Syndrome

What happens if you pair up a newbie programmer with an expert? This is described in *PPI* as "expert-novice pairing." The intention of such a pairing would be to "get the easier job done well, while training a novice programmer."

The challenge of such a pairing is primarily that the expert must take on a tutoring role and must maintain extreme patience throughout. If the expert coder slips, then the result is a "watch while I type" session (also known as "go make me a cup of tea while I finish this program" syndrome[13]), in which the novice remains passive throughout and the expert is effectively solo-coding.

Despite this, there are distinct advantages to expert-novice pairing. In fact, it's probably the one pairing combination that's worth mandating, as long as the novice is willing and able to learn and the expert is prepared to give up a portion of her day to teach rather than code in full-flow. This combination is certainly better than novice-novice pairing, which even Ron Jeffries thinks is a bad idea.[14]

Laurel and Hardy Take Up Pair Programming

The intent of a novice-novice pairing combination is described in *PPI* as follows:

> *"To produce production code in a relatively noncomplex area of the project, giving valuable experience to both programmers in the process."*[15]

If you're considering such a pairing, it's important to ask yourself which part of your project is unimportant enough that you can afford to unleash two complete novices, unsupervised, on it.

"Unsupervised" is actually the key. Two novices, unsupervised, would likely produce code that isn't exactly production quality. Luckily, *PPI* has the answer:

> *"There must be a coach, instructor, or mentor available to answer questions and also to help guide the pair. . . . We feel very strongly about the need for a coach. If you are unwilling to assign the mentoring task to some expert, then you need to understand the limitations of the asset being produced by the pair."*[16]

In XP, this responsibility would fall into the lap of the person (or people) performing the coach role.

As with the other pairing combinations, pairs rotate so frequently that in a team of mixed abilities, the novice-novice pairing could happen quite often. Therefore, novice-novice pairing isn't something that can easily be controlled:

---

13. Matt Stephens and Doug Rosenberg, *Extreme Programming Refactored: The Case Against XP* (Berkeley, CA: Apress, 2003), Chapter 6, "Pair Programming."

14. Laurie Williams and Robert Kessler, *Pair Programming Illuminated* (New York, NY: Addison-Wesley, 2002), p. 120.

15. Ibid., p. 118.

16. Ibid., p. 119.

It just happens, almost by accident, several times a week. The coach must be fully aware of the fact that two novices are currently pairing at any time, and the coach must be available to guide them and correct their mistakes. In practice, to combat the proverbial blind leading the blind, there's a risk that the coach may become fully occupied with mentoring one particular pair anytime two novices pair up.

Carrying Your Pair

Similar but less extreme problems occur with expert-average pairing. *PPI* describes three situations where the authors feel that expert-average pairing is a problem. The first is that the average programmer truly is average (i.e., the average programmer is likely to stay that way and will never really progress). The second is when the average programmer doesn't interact enough with the expert. The third is when the average programmer doesn't seem to "get it" and keeps asking the same question over and over:

> *"This can leave the expert frustrated and can reduce the ability of the pair to complete the task."*[17]

And the Winner Is . . .

Aside from the longer-term learning benefits, it seems that the most beneficial form of pairing is with two programmers of roughly the same ability. It's more likely that the pair will be on the same wavelength and will spend less time disagreeing over things that probably don't matter that much.

Unfortunately, when you consider that 50% of all programmers are below average, it becomes obvious that mixed-ability pairing is likely to be the norm. This highlights the problem that teams of mixed abilities are almost unavoidable. Pair programming makes the issue unavoidable by forcing these people to code together on the same program. In a non–pair-programming project, the problem is handled effectively through other more natural practices, such as team leading, code and design reviews, *occasional* (voluntary) pair programming, mentoring, design documents, and so on.

With almost all of the problems described in this section, it's up to the coach to catch and deal with them as promptly as possible. This places a lot of responsibility on the coach (almost as much as the on-site customer!).

---

17. Ibid., p. 108.

Design Documents Reduce Reliance on Pair Programming

Design documents provide a record of design decisions. This makes them particularly helpful for novice programmers to explore the thinking behind the design, as described by the more experienced senior programmers.

If the team is becoming lost in a sea of changed minds and refactorings, the design document often helps to remind the team members of why they originally decided to do something in a particular way. There's usually a pretty good reason.

We discuss the role of documentation in software projects (and how it can lessen the need for pair programming) in Chapter 7.

And More Problems

Chapter 7 of *PPI* (titled "Problems, Problems") discusses several problems with pair programming. We briefly discuss some of these problems here. Although the authors of *PPI* do offer some practical advice to overcome or help prevent these problems, the proposed solutions either result in high maintenance or rely idealistically on the programmers being constantly aware of all the problems (with advice such as "Just proceed a bit more cautiously").

One problem is that of rushing. Because pairs rotate often, they might rush to finish a task before it's time to separate. The advice given in Chapter 7 of *PPI* is as follows:

> "If a task must roll over to another pairing session, the task must roll over to another pairing session! Slow down, and do it right together."[18]

The coach would need to be particularly vigilant to spot this problem recurring, because pairs rotate so often. If the problem happens a lot, it may be because the tasks are too big (another direct consequence—evidence of the circle of snakes unraveling. To counter this, the team may need to spend more time planning or designing, or change its process for estimating stories or tasks).

Another problem, which we suspect would particularly manifest in teams that publicly laud themselves as "the best team on the face of the Earth," is that of overconfidence:

---

18. Ibid., p. 61.

"There may be a feeling that a pair can do no wrong. If you're working together, you might convince yourself that whatever you do together must be right. Remain cautious and careful!"[19]

The problem of overconfidence would need to be watched for carefully by the coach, who should be aware of this type of problem. She would then need to be able to watch out for the telltale signs and be prepared to act on them when she catches pairs reassuring each other into writing bad code. "Well, I suppose it will do for now—we can refactor it later!" is the typical start of a slippery slope.

Another problem is that it's human nature for people to want to be in control, at least of their immediate surroundings:

"New folks should specifically be paired with mentoring types, lest they feel unwelcome or frustrated in the hands of a partner who wants to make only personal progress. This mentor must also give up control and allow the less skilled team member to drive most of the time. When the mentor is directing most of the activity, it's better for the trainee to be typing and not just listening. The student might not be assertive enough to ask for the keyboard."[20]

This is, of course, an idealistic approach. As we discovered in Rich Camden's "Voice of eXPerience" account earlier, being in control of the keyboard is the preferred option for most people. Rich wasn't offered the keyboard once in 5 months (that's not to say that he didn't get to type, but no one actually *offered* to relinquish control). If the other person doesn't speak up, he's not going to be offered the keyboard. As the previous quote suggests, this is particularly a problem with inexperienced programmers being allocated an experienced partner. Everybody likes to be the driver, to be in control.

Watch Out, There's a Snake Under the Desk!

The problems we just described must all be watched for and quickly fixed before they lead to other problems. This is a lot of problems associated with one XP practice, all waiting to slip and catch the unwary coach, who must be especially vigilant.

Pair programming should be a beneficial practice, but its problems are much more acute because (as we discussed in Chapter 3) so much else in XP relies so heavily on its correct and consistent execution throughout the project.

---

19. Ibid., p. 60.
20. Ibid., p. 61.

We examine why pair programming's problems are particularly dangerous in XP in Chapter 3.

A Pair of Fangs

The pair programming "snake" isn't just about whether the team stops pair programming. It's also about

- Preventing individuals from "hogging" the keyboard

- Mitigating problems when ill-matched programmers repeatedly pair up

- Tackling conflicting social dynamics that might impair your pair programming experience

- Keeping tasks short enough to complete in one session to prevent rushing

- Identifying and somehow dealing with overconfidence of "experienced" pairs

And it's about the coach remaining super-vigilant throughout the project. If any one of these risks manifests, the circle of snakes is yet again in danger of unraveling.

And, of course, if one programmer gets a cold, everybody gets a cold!

More about pair programming and the common cold in the "Camp Regretestskiy" sidebar in Chapter 8.

Pair Programming Defanged

The beneficial aspects of pair programming (improved code-level design, knowledge sharing via improved communication, sense of team spirit, and so forth) can be achieved without the negative aspects (high-maintenance practice, potential for incompatible pairing that surfaces every time the pairs rotate, "overkill" for simple tasks, and so forth) by not mandating its use, but instead encouraging that programmers simply pair up for complex tasks.

This can be achieved by following a process that doesn't rely heavily on pair programming. By spending more time on up-front design—and by making this a team process (which XP does to an extent through the use of collaborative design sessions)—most of the key design decisions will have been made by the time the team begins writing production code.

Written documentation (possibly in the form of a project Wiki) also lessens the need for pair programming and colocated teams.

We cover XP's approach to documentation in Chapter 7.

Summary

Pair programming, like many of the other XP practices, appears different in theory and practice. Pair programming as a voluntary activity should be encouraged, when appropriate.

It's important, however, to not lose sight of the fact that programmers need peace, quiet, and space in which to think and concentrate, despite Ron Jeffries' claim to the contrary. The social aspects of pair programming can be very difficult. And, when you add it all up, you're still taking two programmers to produce what a single programmer would under normal circumstances.

CHAPTER 7

Oral Documentation (Oxymoronic, or Just Plain Moronic?)

Talkin' About Documentation
(Sing to the tune of "My Generation" by The Who)

We don't need to write it down
Talkin' 'bout documentation

'Cause we switch our pairs around
Talkin' 'bout documentation

We are always feelin' fine
We don't do documentation
Don't document and don't design
We don't do documentation

Cowboy coders come on in
We don't do documentation!
We're always coding with a grin
We don't do documentation!

It's the latest agile sensation . . .
Just write code, skip documentation

No documentation
No documentation, baby

"XPers are not afraid of oral documentation."[1]
—Robert C. Martin

---

1. Mark Collins-Cope, "Interview with Robert C. Martin," ObjectiveView (http://www.ratio.co.uk/ov4.pdf), p. 36.

"I felt that it seriously impacted my ability to quickly come up to speed on the project when I joined them. There were literally no documents or diagrams that I could look at to understand the implementation at a high level. I was immediately pointed to the code . . ."[2]

—Timothy Fisher

Documentation in XP is one of its more controversial subjects. XPers claim repeatedly that they actually create lots of documentation; perplexed observers notice that most of this "documentation" is either source code, is written on informal (often physical) media such as pieces of cardboard, or is based in an organic "project Wiki" that evolves along with the architecture.

For this reason, the arguments regarding documentation in XP tend to be paradoxical and confusing. Our favorite retort, though, is that XP has documentation in the form of spoken conversations.

"But I Thought You Said . . ."

Pretty much all software projects deal mainly with two types of documentation: requirements and design. Both types are handled very differently (particularly so in XP projects). It is this difference that seems to cause some of the more heated arguments about documentation in XP, because each person is arguing with an implied document type swimming around in his or her head:

Ralph: XP has very little (design) documentation.

Alice: Nonsense! XP can have very detailed (requirements) documents.

Ralph: *[Grows angry, holds out his fist]* You wanna go to the *moon,* Alice? You wouldn't need no (design) document for that.

Alice: But we have lots of (requirements) documents! (They're just not written down . . .)

As you can see, this confusion can lead to some pretty scary scenarios. Therefore, it's useful to distinguish between the two types of documentation in a little more detail.

---

2. See the "Voice of eXPerience: Oral Documentation" sidebar later in this chapter.

Requirements Documentation

Requirements documentation in XP is not *necessarily* that different from "traditional" requirements documentation. A lot depends, however, on how you interpret XP's teachings in this regard, because so much of this area is optional. The basic message appears to be (to sum up the 20 XP books and various Extremo Web sites): *Do as much or as little requirements documentation as you feel is necessary, but personally we do as little as we can.*

It's worth briefly comparing XP requirements (user stories and so forth) with requirements documentation in non-XP projects.

Requirements Documentation in XP Projects

"We combine a focus on verbal communication with automated tests to communicate requirements. The result is much lower need for written requirements within the team."[3]

In XP, the requirements are captured as one- or two-sentence *user stories* (handwritten on story cards), resulting from conversations with the customer. The user stories are "promises for future conversations" (i.e., they are only the first step in a two-step process). These future conversations take place during the iteration in which the user story will be implemented.

Additional documentation can also be attached to each user story to describe the requirements in more detail. If the customer requires extra documentation, it must first be written, scheduled, and tasked as a user story.

An XPer who posted a message to the Software Reality XP forum made this comment about requirements in XP:

> *"Most XP teams do have some written requirements, and they are usually fairly detailed. What they typically are not is: comprehensive, formal, subject to change control procedures."[4]*

---

3. Ron Jeffries, "Essential XP: Documentation," http://www.xprogramming.com/xpmag/expDocumentationInXP.htm, November 21, 2001.

4. Keith Braithwaite posting to http://www.softwarereality.com/lifecycle/xp/forum.jsp, February 8, 2003.

If you're an XP customer, this should worry you. You can, of course, request more permanent documentation (via the magic of stories), and request that it be put through change control. But (and this is a *big* but), you have to *know* that you need to ask for this explicitly. You might be used to other projects in which requirements documents (and reviewable design documents) just sort of happened. When you're working with an XP project, somebody might tell you, but then again they might not, because the XPer mind-set is to produce only the documentation that is asked for.

Requirements Documentation in Non-XP Projects

Requirements in non-XP projects (certainly the projects we've worked on) tend to be documented as "bulletproof" specifications, with numbered requirements describing what the system is intended to achieve from the customer's point of view.

We compare requirements with user stories in Chapter 10.

Producing such a specification usually involves some in-depth analysis of the problem that drives each requirement and, in turn, the root cause behind each problem.

To produce a specification this detailed for an entire project takes a lot of effort, but it's worth it because many problems that would not have been discovered until later when a lot of code had been written are identified and highlighted early on.

To get around the "waterfall"[5] effect (where the programmers are waiting around for months on end for the requirements to be completed), some initial analysis is carried out that divides the project into smaller, logical subsystems. Requirements for each of these subsystems can then be fleshed out in more detail and in parallel.

If a particular subsystem isn't scheduled to begin for a long time (e.g., an entire year), then detailed requirements analysis for that subsystem may also be pushed back closer to the time. This makes sense, because the requirements might change in the meantime.

---

5. The waterfall model was formalized in 1970 in a paper by Winston W. Royce called "Managing the Development of Large Software Systems: Concepts and Techniques." Although Royce didn't actually use the word "waterfall" in this paper (and he certainly wasn't describing the rigid, failure-prone process of "A flows into B flows into C, no exceptions" that most people associate with the term "waterfall"), he is nevertheless generally attributed as the "inventor" of the waterfall model.

Did Oral Documentation Kill C3?

As we mentioned in Chapter 2, a major contributing factor to the demise of the C3 project was the fact that the on-site customer (the goal donor) was headed in a different direction goal-wise from the project sponsor (the gold owner).

The normal method of getting around this "fundamental problem" is to write the requirements down in a *specification*. (Anyone remember specifications? We have to confess, it feels just a little eerie having to write this paragraph. Countless systems have been built using specifications. Really!) The specification is then agreed upon and signed off by all those people involved in the project who could be considered to be a "customer" (i.e., the project stakeholders). This would definitely include the project sponsor.

The written specification is signed off in anticipation, before the next iteration begins, so that there are no outstanding disagreements (e.g., between a local goal donor and a remote gold owner) on what goes in.

This sign-off procedure reduces the on-site customer's role from ad hoc specifier of new requirements to a less demanding role. In this role, the on-site customer (or the team of on-site customers) is simply there to clarify issues, clear up any confusion surrounding the requirements, and provide early feedback on the software produced during and at the end of each iteration.

If the customer does identify a need to change the requirements, a process of change and sign-off with the project sponsor should be followed. Then there is no confusion, just a single, unambiguous state at any time.

The trick is to have a process of change and sign-off that doesn't impact the project timeline (i.e., try not to put change control on the critical path). Of course, this is where an effective project manager comes in, to handle whatever "paperwork" arises. This process shouldn't delay the programmers in any way.

XP gets you halfway to this process with its use of two-line user stories written on pieces of cardboard, but it lets the side down by recommending that these simply be incomplete, transitory artifacts—promises of future conversations with the customer. Requirements need to be more complete than that. They need to show, before the next coding iteration begins, such things as expected behavior of the system, what the system should do when things go wrong or something unexpected happens, and architectural extremes (the maximum number of users, the maximum number of transactions per minute, and so on)—basic things like that.

Design Documentation

Design documentation in XP is more controversial even than requirements documentation in XP. In fact, the rest of this chapter mainly covers design documentation.

It's worth emphasizing that some XPers do create UML models, and they do sketch designs on whiteboards, sometimes before coding. However (as we discuss in the next couple of chapters), the XP design process is based around the concept of *evolutionary design*—that is, the up-front design phase is virtually nonexistent.

Design documentation in XP is also very ad hoc. XP has no guidelines on specifically what types of documents are worth producing and maintaining. The decision is left to the whim of the collective team—whatever it thinks is best. Having said that, XP teams do pride themselves on readable code (including coherent, simple, clean object names and relationships), the intention being that the code itself is a design document.[6] XP has been supplemented by third parties (most notably Scott Ambler with *Agile Modeling*) who provide better guidelines on what to document and maintain in an XP project.

See Chapter 15 for more about supplementing XP with better documentation and modeling techniques.

Documenting for the Future

Extremo author Martin Fowler has this to say on UML and XP:

> *"There are a number of points of incompatibility. Certainly XP de-emphasizes diagrams to a great extent. Although the official position is along the lines of 'use them if they are useful,' there is a strong subtext of 'real XPers don't do diagrams.' This is reinforced by the fact that people like Kent [Beck] aren't at all comfortable with diagrams. Indeed, I've never seen Kent voluntarily draw a software diagram in any fixed notation."[7]*

---

6. However, we have argued elsewhere that "the code is the design" is not a sufficient replacement for design documentation, because proper design documentation is at a higher level of abstraction to the code.

7. Giancarlo Succi, Michele Marchesi, et al., *Extreme Programming Examined* (New York, NY: Addison-Wesley, 2001), Chapter 1, "Is Design Dead?" (written by Martin Fowler). (See also http://www.martinfowler.com/articles/designDead.html.)

Perhaps Kent Beck is averse to diagrams because he has stated on the C2 Wiki that visualizing objects before coding is a dangerous practice and should be stopped (it's a Zen thing).[8]

More about "Zen and the Art of Software Maintenance" in Chapter 16.

Fowler's quote highlights the fact that design "documents" in XP are mostly transitory. This contrasts greatly with the notion of design documents in, say, RUP, which calls items of documentation "artifacts" (which suggests documents that are long-lived and may be dug up several years later). Although this notion may at first seem absurd, the maintenance teams who actually do need to dig up that documentation several years later will offer a prayer of thanks to the previous team members for their forward thinking.

This approach is crystallized by two of the *Agile Modeling* core principles:

- Software is your primary goal.

- Enabling the next effort is your secondary goal.

"Your project can still be considered a failure even when your team delivers a working system to your users—part of fulfilling the needs of your project stakeholders is to ensure that your system is robust enough so that it can be extended over time."[9]

Of course, not having a documented design is often regarded by programmers as good job security. If you're an XP customer or manager, take note!

The following quote is from Ron Jeffries on good old `comp.software.extreme-programming`:

---

8. See `http://c2.com/cgi-bin/wiki?ToAyoungExtremist`.

9. Scott Ambler, *Agile Modeling: Effective Practices for eXtreme Programming and the Unified Process* (New York, NY: John Wiley & Sons, 2002), p. 28.

"Customer says 'Please do these eleven things'. Team says 'We can do any ten this iteration, which ten do you want first?'.

"Customer says 'I want eleven'. Team says 'We can do any ten this iteration, which ten do you want first?'.

"Customer says 'You are idiots, I need eleven'. Team says 'Yes, we are, but we can do any ten this iteration, which ten do you want first?'

"Customer says, 'If you won't do [eleven], I'll get another team'. Team says, 'If you can get a team that knows the system as well as we do, costs as little as we do, and that can do eleven, you should definitely get them. While you work on that, we can do any ten this iteration. Which ten do you want first?'"[10]

What really got to us about this hypothetical conversation (aside from the fact that it stereotypes the customer as an unthinking moron) was the attitude barely hidden behind it. There is an implied "So bite me!" at the end of the team's response. It sums up the XP attitude that the customer can't afford to get rid of the XP team because no one else "knows the system as well as [they] do."

Why doesn't anyone else know the system as well as they do? Because there's no frickin' documentation! Therefore, the XP team calls the shots. The inmates are running the asylum (again[11]). The team is on the snack-laden comfort train all the way to Smugville, at least until its project gets cancelled.

The Code Is the Design!

On XProgramming.com, Ron Jeffries writes this regarding design documentation (as driven by user stories):

---

10. Ron Jeffries posting to the newsgroup `comp.software.extreme-programming`, subject: "Managing Scope," January 30, 2003.

11. See the section "Big Words Like Constantinople and TerminationCanBeSuccess" in Chapter 4. We also discuss Alan Cooper's *The Inmates Are Running the Asylum* in Chapter 15.

"Those conversations will be captured as additional documentation that will be attached to the card, *will be acted out during Class Responsibility Collaborator (CRC) design sessions, and, better yet, as acceptance tests and application code. (Emphasis mine.)"[12]*

So that's official, then: Although the design is acted out during CRC design sessions, it is "documented" as application code. Going by Ron's description, acceptance tests are a murky halfway house between requirements and design.

Because the acceptance tests are modeling the requirements as source code (or scripted code, which from the customer's point of view is essentially the same thing—see Chapter 5), they blur the distinction between requirements and design. This wouldn't be such a bad thing if XP provided a clear route to get from user stories to source code.[13] Unfortunately, this gigantic leap is left as an exercise for the reader. This leap isn't made any easier by the fact that it's now less clear exactly what *is* a requirement versus what is design—because the distinction between them has been blurred.

Voice of eXPerience: Pairing Replaces Documentation

This account was sent to us by an XPer who wishes to remain anonymous.

A tenet of XP is that documentation (such as design diagrams and detailed comments in the code) is unnecessary because since everyone works on all the code, chances are one member of the pair will have worked on any piece of code and will therefore understand it without documentation.

I believe that this lack of documentation is a serious flaw of XP that will affect all except the smallest teams on the shortest projects. The fact is that everyone doesn't work on all the code. If you've got eight on a team—four pairs—you get to see a fraction of the code as it's written. Sure, you'll modify some code and debug through some more, but I think it's fair to say that if the code is well written and works, each team member will never see much of the code. If the project continues over the years, people will leave and new people will join, and the situation will get worse.

Even if you've written the code yourself, it doesn't mean you remember it. I've had to relearn code I wrote months or years before.

My experience suggests that some basic documentation is necessary, and pairing in no way reduces the need for documentation of code and design.

---

12. Ron Jeffries, "Essential XP: Documentation," op. cit.

13. Modern development methodologies typically suffer from a crucial "missing link" between analysis and design—that is, a predictable way of getting from requirements to source code. There is also a common misconception that there is no reliable way of achieving this via a logical process (so why bother trying), as we discuss in Chapter 8.

Just Plain Moronic

In this section, Doug relates some of his own experiences with oral documentation.

A few years ago there was an interview in Ratio Group's e-magazine *ObjectiveView* with "Uncle Bob" Martin (see Figure 7-1). In the interview, Uncle Bob stated, "XPers are not afraid of oral documentation." This is one of my favorite Extremo quotes of all time. It disguises an attitude that I'd sum up as "We're too lazy to document our work" and makes it sound like this is somehow an act of bravery and courage. What a load of crap!

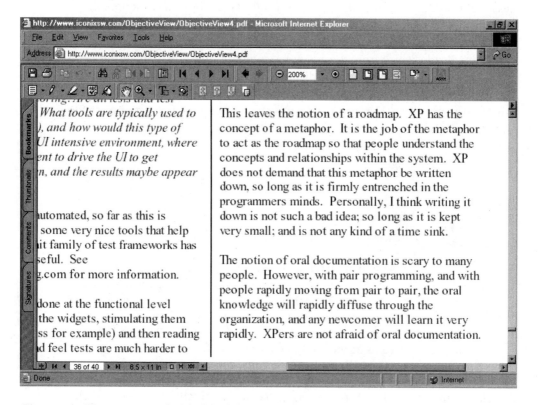

Figure 7-1. XPers are not afraid of oral documentation![14]

I remember exactly when this article came out, because my son Rob was about 10 years old then, and he was sitting in my office after school when he saw me busting a gut laughing at this line. A couple of days later I was driving him to school in the morning when he asked me, "Dad, is oral documentation oxymoronic . . . or is it just plain moronic?" I quoted him in one of my UMLWorld keynote speeches and the whole audience just completely broke up laughing.

---

14. See http://www.ratio.co.uk/ov4.pdf.

Been There, Done That

My first programming job when I graduated college was working in the aerospace industry on some fairly mind-bending software that verified the layout of integrated circuits. This was back in the early 1980s (long before XP bounced on to the scene), and this software was some of the pioneering work in design verification for computer chips (literally the way these layouts were checked previously was to print out a plot of what the circuit would look like on a huge plotter and color in the lines with colored pencils), and the existence of this kind of software helped to enable the current generations of computer chips that we have today.

Just Slightly Ahead of His Time

My boss, Jim (who I mentioned in Chapter 1 as the inventor of the "Samurai debugging" technique), also was a believer in oral documentation. That is to say, he didn't bother doing any. Which was all fine until one day he decided to quit and start his own business. He had written all the original software to verify these chip layouts, and my job was to extend the work he had done to make his ideas work for a much more complex chip fabrication process (we were working on a big contract called Very High Speed Integrated Circuits).

I think Jim was an Extremo 20 years ahead of his time, because he also didn't believe in commenting his code. At least not with any comments that would mean anything to anybody other than himself. There was never a comment about why he had chosen to do something in a particular way. Oh, and he had a great fondness for cryptic acronyms as well.

I learned at a very early age how much fun it is trying to understand what somebody else was thinking when he wrote a particular piece of code and left no clues behind for whoever had to do something with that code later. Of course, because Jim left a whole bunch of undocumented work hanging around, our department was forced to hire him as a consultant so he could explain stuff that was only "documented" in his head. So I had some personal experience in mind when I wrote the next song.

The Long and Winding Thread
(Sing to the tune of "The Long and Winding Road" by The Beatles)

The long and winding thread
Leads me straight
To your code
That you wrote sitting here
A long, long time ago
You thought your code was clear
And then went out the door

Many times I've read your code
And many times I've cried
I wish I had a diagram
Because my brain is fried

But bugs still bring me back
To that same
Piece of code
That you refactored here
Many years before
Then you stopped working here
A long, long time ago

Many times I've read your code
And many times I've cried
I wish I had a diagram
Because my brain is fried

Panel Members Have Lost Touch with Reality

One year at UMLWorld I was on a panel that included Uncle Bob and Martin
Fowler, who were of course arguing that documentation was a waste of time, and
I told the audience the story of Jim and his aversion to documentation and code
comments.

It's amazing how many of the questions from the audience were related to
the lack of documentation. It was obviously of concern to the people attending the
conference. I remember getting my speaker evaluations back from that panel and
seeing one that read, "Panel members, except for Doug, have lost touch with reality."

Don't Bother Me, I'm Busy—Go Watch the Videotape

Documentation doesn't have to be heavyweight, 600-page volumes, though. A few
years later in my programming career I was working on another Very Large Scale
Integration (VLSI) project, this one involving an automatic router for wiring up
chips. I needed to extend this router, which already existed, to do some stuff it
had never been designed to do.

It was a fairly complex piece of software, and it used a data structure called
a *quad-tree.* (The quad-tree is similar to a binary tree, but each node points at
four children instead of two. It's very useful for two-dimensional graphics, such
as maps and integrated circuit layouts.) The quad-tree package had been written
by a less gregarious programmer (I mentioned him in Chapter 6 as being a brilliant programmer with whom I wouldn't have been able to share a keyboard).

This fellow (I'll call him "Bret" because that's his name) didn't want to be
bothered with people asking him questions about how his quad-tree software

worked, so what he had done was to stand up in front of a whiteboard and explain how it worked to a video camera. When I started on the project, he told me to go watch the tape. I did, and I learned how it worked, and I was able to use it very effectively.

It could be argued that this was "oral documentation," but a better term might be "video documentation," because he was recording to something rather more permanent than thin air.

Years later, when I was managing a team of programmers who were building a suite of CASE tools at ICONIX, I needed to get a fairly complex piece of code written. I believe it was a spline package to draw smooth curves through a series of points for our dataflow diagram editor. Which of my two ex-workmates (I would characterize both of them as brilliant programmers) do you think I called? (Hint: Not the one who relied on oral documentation—that is to say, *no* documentation.) I gave Bret the requirements and let him work from home, undisturbed. He produced quite a lovely piece of code—very efficient, well commented, and bug-free.

The point here is that it is really important to leave some nontransient form of explanation of the intention of the designer behind. The form of that explanation can be comments, UML, or videotape. But it has to be nontransient. Some permanent, enduring, nontransient record of the thought process (besides the source code) has to exist, somewhere. Ideally, if you learn to design using tools like UML, the design activity itself leaves the trail of breadcrumbs you need without a lot of extra effort.

And What About the New Programmer Who Gets Hired Midstream?

As we discussed earlier in this chapter, this idea that "documentation isn't necessary until someone outside the team needs to understand what's going on," can all too easily be used as a job security program for the XP team.

Think about it: An unsuspecting manager hires a team of XPers, thinking that the world's most agile process will get her software delivered on schedule. Somewhere along the way she learns that "SoftwareIsNeverDone" and "the schedule does not exist per se." Can she consider replacing the development team? Well, nothing is written down about the design . . . hmm. Obscurity = job security?

See Chapter 11 for a discussion of the slightly surreal Extremo philosophies "SoftwareIsNeverDone" and "the schedule does not exist per se."

Freedom from documentation is almost certainly one of the prime factors in XP's wild popularity among cowboy coders. These are the folks who say they're doing XP, but they aren't pair programming, unit testing, and so on. They're just "bravely" not documenting their work. Which leads us to our next "Voice of eXPerience" section.

Voice of eXPerience: Oral Documentation
by Timothy Fisher

The lack of documentation on our project was a significant issue. I felt that it seriously impacted my ability to quickly come up to speed on the project when I joined the group. There were literally no documents or diagrams that I could look at to understand the implementation at a high level. I was immediately pointed to the code upon asking any questions that I had about the architecture or design.

I hadn't heard the term "oral documentation" before and I can't say that they used "oral documentation." They just tended to believe that no documentation was necessary. They had the mind-set, which I know is common in XP, that the code itself should be all the documentation necessary for the project. There are so many problems with that attitude that I could go on and on about. For one, it provides nothing for the managers and higher-ups to understand the implementation. They certainly aren't going to sit down and go through the code. Although well-written code can serve as good code-level documentation and can be self-describing, it certainly doesn't provide the architectural overview or any insight into the structure and design of the code and code components.

This issue again goes back to what I think is a fundamental flaw in the XP methodology, in that it's an extremely "code-centric" methodology that leaves little room for analysis and design, and certainly no framework that would mandate any design at all. You could complete a project following all of the tenets of XP and end up with zero documentation and no clear overall structure to the design. Although the code may be well written at the class level, and it may be well tested and even apparently successful, over time the flaws in the XP process will begin to show themselves when the maintenance phases begin.

Unit Tests Are Documentation (Yeah, Right)

Unit tests are an integral part of test-first design, which is an integral part of XP. But are unit tests (coupled with the "actual" source code) a sufficient substitute for design documentation? (See Figure 7-2.)

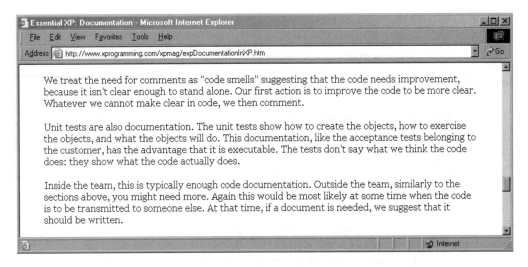

We treat the need for comments as "code smells" suggesting that the code needs improvement, because it isn't clear enough to stand alone. Our first action is to improve the code to be more clear. Whatever we cannot make clear in code, we then comment.

Unit tests are also documentation. The unit tests show how to create the objects, how to exercise the objects, and what the objects will do. This documentation, like the acceptance tests belonging to the customer, has the advantage that it is executable. The tests don't say what we think the code does: they show what the code actually does.

Inside the team, this is typically enough code documentation. Outside the team, similarly to the sections above, you might need more. Again this would be most likely at some time when the code is to be transmitted to someone else. At that time, if a document is needed, we suggest that it should be written.

Figure 7-2. Unit tests are also documentation.[15]

XPers use the design mantra "you aren't gonna need it" (YAGNI). This design mantra drives the theory behind emergent design—that you design and code for the current 2-week iteration and turn a blind eye to any possible future design concerns. In the context of design documentation, you might think that YAGNI is a pretty good reason to avoid writing documents; otherwise, there'd be a lot of documentation to update.

We cover test-first design in the next chapter and emergent design in Chapter 12.

Ironically, however, written statements of intent are much more important in an evolving design because they record the overall direction that the codebase is intended to head in. These documents are written at a higher level of abstraction than the source code (the only "permanent" XP design artifact). Therefore, design documents need additional information to describe the theory behind a particular design. This removes the temptation to add extra comments to the

---

15. Figure 7-2 states that "inside the team, [unit tests] are typically enough code documentation." Well, suppose the team quits, or management isn't happy with the team's performance and wants to replace its members. That's the primary scenario where documentation for somebody outside the team would be required. We see the lack of said documentation as the cause of the "So bite me!" attitude that we discussed earlier in this chapter in the "Documenting for the Future" section.

code or to clutter the source with "code stubs"[16] as placeholders for intended future functionality.

Oral documentation also becomes a cultural epithet for the real thing in the Extremo world. Consider, for example, this quote from XProgramming.com:

> *"It is common for XP teams to have some pictures of the system's design on the wall for extended periods. I observe that these seem to serve more as decoration than as documentation: people don't look at them very often. They ask each other, or they pair program with someone who knows the answer."[17]*

A programmer/contractor friend, Dino Fancellu, e-mailed me his opinion of oral documentation. I've reprinted the e-mail here in full:

> *"Re lack of documentation: This is exactly the opposite of what I do, the teleworker. I can't afford to have endless cozy chitchats about how I feel like coding today.*
>
> *"Everything I do is given to me via email, bounced back and forth, polished, verified, until I'm sure it is what they want, and more importantly, what they need.*
>
> *"I can't abide people telling me to do things on the phone, as I know they will forget, and so will I. I'm only human, and the bigger and more complex the project the more I will forget, the more I will misinterpret.*
>
> *"Even if I get sign off after a thought clearing phone call I'll make sure I get a verifying email. I've worked this way for years, all on successful projects.*
>
> *"XP seems to do little for teleworkers. And don't even get me started on pair programming!"[18]*

More from Dino in the section "Wishing for the Sound of Silence" in Chapter 6.

---

16. XP discourages the practice of adding code stubs for functionality that is not in the current iteration. If the design is evolving, though, there may still be a temptation to add "intention-revealing" code or comments so that programmers in future iterations catch on to the direction that that part of the design is headed in.

17. Ron Jeffries, "Essential XP: Documentation," op. cit.

18. Dino Fancellu, e-mail to author, November 2002.

With some effort, it is possible to "patch" the XP process to allow for distributed teams (such as telecommuters). However, this typically involves significant additional design documentation and a rethink of the way that the on-site customer works—thus, the main benefits of XP are lost.

We discuss the effect of distributed teams on XP in Chapter 14.

Without proper design documentation, avid YAGNIers run the risk of losing sight of their original goal, forgetting why a design was originally being launched in a particular direction. As we discussed in the previous chapter, pair programming is an important XP safety net to prevent this from happening. Another snake threatens to break loose.

UML Won't Write My Code
(Sing to the tune of "Can't Buy Me Love" by The Beatles)

Won't write my code
UML won't write my code
Won't write my code
No, no, no, no

Say you want me to use UML
I say it's a waste of time
I'd rather go by the code smell
'Cause the code is the design
I don't care for UML diagrams
Cause UML won't write my code

Won't write my code
UML won't write my code
Won't write my code
No, no, no, no

You say you want me to document
Well I'll tell you hell no
It's a waste of time to document
I'm not afraid to tell you so
Why the hell would I want to document
When I could be writing code

Just writing code
'Cause it's really all I know
Just writing code
Go, go, go, go

Fangs Is on the Loose Again

Oral documentation can lead to lack of focus, Constant Refactoring After Programming, and software that is never done, because people generally don't remember the same details in exactly the same way. This affects both the design and the requirements.

Also see the section "Embrace Rampant Scope Creep Regularly" in Chapter 11.

The oral documentation "snake" is theoretically kept at bay by pair programming, collective ownership, and colocated teams (including the on-site customer). The theory is that the team collectively knows the design and doesn't have to shout very far across the room in order to communicate it, and the customer knows all 1,000 requirements in detail and carries them around in his gargantuan head. Therefore, the need for permanent documentation is significantly less. That is, until one of the dependent snakes starts to slip.

Oral Documentation Defanged

Many of the problems associated with XP can be solved with the simple introduction of clear, concise, unambiguous documentation (for both requirements and design).

Design documentation is valuable at so many levels (especially when it is produced as a by-product of the design process) because it encourages the team to think the design through in exacting detail.

We discuss how to make detailed design documentation a by-product of the design process in Chapter 8.

This can help prevent endless refactoring (where the project "spins out" into refactoring eddies without really completing very many new requirements—in other words, the project velocity is very low).

XP relies heavily (too heavily, we believe) on osmotic communication (e.g., knowledge sharing via pair programming or overhearing two programmers discussing a design issue) to keep everyone up-to-date on the latest design decisions. Keeping an up-to-date written design lessens this dependence, so that osmotic communication becomes a "nice-to-have" rather than a "must-have-or-we-all-go-off-the-rails."

Written requirements—fleshed out, clarified, and signed off before production coding begins—help immensely in keeping a project focused and on track, working toward a well-defined, unambiguous set of goals.

Ambiguity sinks projects. If a requirement is ambiguous, get clarification and then update the written requirements.

Put the requirements onto a project intranet (even a Wiki) so that everybody has access to them. Start with a definition of the goals of the project, and make sure every requirement can be traced back to at least one of the goals. If a goal changes during the project, change the goal, but treat this as the big deal that it really is. Any requirements that trace back to that goal will probably also need to be revisited to ensure they're still relevant to the project.

Recognizing how many requirements are really based on a particular goal sure helps to keep the project focused. This may be seen as "nonagile" because of the additional documentation required, but in reality it's a way of identifying and *remembering* the true lines of dependency between goals, requirements, and implementation tasks (these lines exist in any project, even XP projects). Pretending they're not there means potentially storing up trouble and spinning a project that's completely lacking in focus.

Summary

Debates concerning documentation in XP tend to confuse requirements documentation with design documentation. XP's approach to requirements documentation is marginally better than its approach to design documentation. However, the transition from requirements to design (via coded or scripted acceptance tests) can be a murky one.

As we discussed in the section "Tailoring a Process to Local Conditions: Why XP Stands on Its Head" in Chapter 3, XP has lots of guidance about how to organize teams that are trying to get from requirements to code, but it offers little guidance in terms of a logical process detailing precisely how to do this. It is possible that this is because XP's design process only really "kicks in" properly once you have existing code.

We cover XP's design process in the next chapter.

Part III

We Don't Write Permanent Specs and Barely Do Any Upfront Design, So . . .

CHAPTER 8

Design After First Testing

Unit Test Writer

(Sing to the tune of "Paperback Writer" by The Beatles)

Don't like UML
Man it's much too hard
Rather scribble some notes on an index card

Hey design is dead
And things couldn't be better
I just got a job
And I'm gonna be a unit test writer
Unit test writer
Unit test writerrrrrrrr

Well, requirements
Are a pain in the neck
Good thing that I found this book by Kent Beck
They're the customer's problem
It says so right here
So I don't care too much
'Cause I'm gonna be a unit test writer
Unit test writer
Unit test writerrrrrrrr

Don't do architecture
Haven't got the urge
Rather just write code and let it emerge
At five PM each day
You know I'm on my way
Schedule's not our job
Man it's fun to be a unit test writer
Unit test writer
Unit test writerrrrrrrr

"There can be no misunderstanding a specification written in the form of executable code."[1]

—Don Wells

"When the acceptance tests are written in high level scripting languages, they are readable by developers and customers alike."[2]

—Robert C. Martin

"Human language is not particularly good at capturing the kind of precision necessary for documenting requirements."[3]

—Robert C. Martin

Well, we've reached the middle of the book. In this chapter we get a bit more serious than usual and look at XP's application of unit testing and its related process, test-first design.

The heart of XP's objection to Big Design Up Front (BDUF) is that it takes longer to maintain a class diagram (and other design documentation) in addition to the code than it does to simply maintain the code, so why maintain the design documentation at all? (Or while we're at it, why spend time up front producing very much design documentation in the first place?)

In this chapter we examine this and other XP attitudes to the process of designing software.

When All You've Got Is a Hammer

In the Extremo mind-set, any justification to avoid up-front design is a good one. This fear of up-front design (FUD) is astoundingly similar to the hack-and-whack mind-set. (Is it starting to be clear yet why XP is popular with the hack-and-whack crowd?)

One of the most popular Extremo justifications for avoiding up-front design is that writing the unit test before writing the code is actually design. In other words, the tests are the design. But, of course, in XP the code is also the design and the tests are also the requirements. So actually everything is code. When all you've got is a hammer, everything looks like a nail.

---

1. Don Wells, "Code the Unit Test First," http://www.extremeprogramming.org/rules/testfirst.html, 2000.

2. Robert C. Martin posting to the newsgroup comp.software.extreme-programming, subject: "Documentation," June 11, 2002.

3. Ibid.

As we've established elsewhere, the Extremos do advocate some up-front design before writing code. The amount varies depending on which Extremo you listen to. Ron Jeffries recommends 10 to 30 minutes at most, after which you should "let the code participate in the design session."[4] Martin Fowler, on the other hand, is less extreme—he suggests a ratio of 20% to 80% (i.e., 20% up-front design followed by 80% refactoring).[5] This is still a lot less than what we feel is a necessary amount of up-front design (for reasons that we go into later in this chapter).

The 20% design/80% refactoring ratio is discussed further in Chapter 12.

We don't have anything against writing the unit tests before writing the code, and we don't deny that this forces a certain level of thinking before the code is written, but we beg to disagree that doing this in any way compensates for not designing your software up front. This is because the design issues being dealt with are at entirely different levels of abstraction. What do we mean by this? Unit tests exercise code at a very atomic level of detail. Up-front design, when done correctly, makes sure that larger design issues have been thought through.

Let's explore this thought in a little more detail. If we grossly oversimplify object-oriented design, we can focus on two questions (we were going to say that there are only two important things about software but decided against it):

- What objects are we going to need?

- How do we distribute the behavior (i.e., set of software operations) across the objects?

Attempting to answer these questions for an entire system all at once would probably lead to a nasty case of analysis paralysis, so we prefer to ask these questions one scenario (loosely speaking, one user story) at a time. We don't consider this Big Design Up Front; we consider this Enough Design Up Front.

We use sequence diagrams to show the allocation of behavior across objects for a scenario, and we use robustness diagrams (in conjunction with a larger-scope domain model) to give us a first guess at which objects will participate in a scenario. The clean allocation of operations to classes you can achieve on a sequence diagram will eliminate the need for a whole bunch of Constant Refactoring After

---

4. Ron Jeffries, Ann Anderson, and Chet Hendrickson, *Extreme Programming Installed* (New York, NY: Addison-Wesley, 2000), p. 70.

5. See http://www.artima.com/intv/flexplex.html.

Programming, because you're going to come a lot closer to getting the design right the first time.

Writing unit tests before coding the methods addresses exactly none of these design issues. A single unit test tends to cover just a small aspect of the design (covering maybe a few methods and one or two classes). Actual up-front design addresses issues on a larger scale: the impact of implementing a given scenario on the overall design.

Extremos tend to want to replace both requirements and designs with code and tests, in somewhat of an interchangeable manner. So in addition to test-first design (or as we prefer to call it, *Design After First Testing*) we also see quotes like the three zingers at the start of this chapter.

So, in essence, the Extremo philosophy here is, "We have unit tests and refactoring, so up-front requirements elicitation, up-front analysis, and up-front design can be conveniently deemphasized (in certain cases, almost dropped altogether)."

Test and Shout
(Sing to the tune of "Twist and Shout" by The Beatles)

You failed a unit test baby
(Failed the test baby)
But do not shout
(Do not shout)
You failed a unit test baby, now
(Failed the test baby)
So go and rip that code out
(Rip that code out)

You know you code so good
(Code so good)
You know you test so fine
(Test so fine)
I'm so glad we're pairing now
(Glad we're pairing)
Instead of doing design
(No design)

Aaaaaaaaaaaaaahhhhhhhh

Before you write some code baby
(Write some code baby)
Test and shout
(Test and shout)
Then rewrite it all over
(Rewrite it over)
That's what XP's all about
(What XP's about)

Aaaaaaaaaaaaaahhhhhhhh

Voice of eXPerience: The Quality Contradiction

by David Van Der Klauw

David provides the following observation on quality in XP (more from him later in this chapter).

XP has a contradiction regarding how it achieves quality.

On one hand, it uses exhaustive testing to guarantee quality. XP states that you should write tests first and write the minimum code needed to pass the tests. If all the tests pass, then by definition the product works.

On the other hand, XP claims that programmers must pair in order to write code of appropriate quality.

The obvious question is, if the testing guarantees quality, then why do you need the pairing for quality?

XP Design Mantra: No BDUF

"What could be more courageous than stopping after a little bit of design, confident that when the time comes, you can add more, when and as needed?"[6]

The XP design mantra of "no BDUF" is perhaps the most important, because it is central to the way in which XP impacts the project life cycle. It removes the water-fall element, and it is what makes XP an incremental process.

The theory is that a small amount of design is produced up front solely for the user story that you're about to implement. Any design documentation produced is purely transient, however (similarly, the *design* is transient because it may get refactored). If the design is written down at all, it doesn't matter if it gets lost or thrown away because it's "stored" in the collective consciousness of the team (at least, that's what the XP authors teach us).

One important aspect is that the programmers are going straight from user story to testing/programming/design, which are all done concurrently. Even up-front design is optional—it's best to do some, but if you don't it doesn't really matter.

This effectively eliminates architectural documents and deemphasizes the up-front design process to the point where it's almost nonexistent.

The replacement is a technique known as *test-first design* (as described at the beginning of this chapter). In fact, this technique, essentially a subset of XP, has been wrapped up in a process called *test-driven development* (TDD). TDD is

---

6. Kent Beck, *Extreme Programming Explained: Embrace Change* (New York, NY: Addison-Wesley, 2000), p.104.

described in Kent Beck's book *Test-Driven Development: By Example*. Given the somewhat controversial nature of XP, separating the test-driven aspects of XP into a stand-alone process with a sensible name was a wise move.

Unit tests aren't specifically an XP thing. You can make extensive use of unit tests without labeling yourself an XPer. In fact, if you retain just one thing from XP, be sure to make it unit tests.

Being able to run your tests and see a green light at the end gives a boost of confidence. You can run your tests before making the change and afterward, to make sure the green light still lights up. Some people claim that this makes programming somehow more satisfying than it already is (as if that were possible).

As ever, there is a note of caution (an entire octave, in fact).

Problems with Unit Testing

There are some known issues with unit testing that can affect its applicability to certain types of projects. In particular, unit testing is not well suited to multithreaded systems or systems that use asynchronous messaging (both system types are increasingly commonplace—almost all modern GUI applications use multithreaded toolkits [e.g., Java Swing] and enterprise platforms such as J2EE make use of asynchronous messaging).

Tests for Asynchronous Messaging and Multithreaded Systems

> *"There certainly are programming tasks that can't be driven solely by tests (or at least, not yet). Security software and concurrency, for example, are two topics where TDD is insufficient to mechanically demonstrate that the goals of the software have been met."*[7]

One of the problems, for example, with the JUnit testing framework is that the test method needs to wait for a synchronous response so that it can do its assertEquals() on the result. You could get around this by maybe adding a callback method that waits for a preset time and then times out, but this is not ideal (not least because it could require modification of the code being tested).

These days, most GUI programs are multithreaded to improve performance and usability. For example, in Java Swing, a dedicated thread (the event dispatch thread) handles processing of GUI events (such as notifying listeners when the user clicks a button or scrolls a window). If the listener code needs to perform

---

7. Kent Beck, *Test-Driven Development: By Example* (New York, NY: Addison-Wesley, 2002), p. xii.

a time-consuming operation (e.g., connect to a remote FTP server), it should create a separate thread to do this so that the GUI does not appear to lock up.

We provide a case study of an agile project targeting Swing in Chapter 15.

Multithreading is essential in GUI applications to keep the user experience a positive one. Does this then mean that GUI applications cannot be unit tested?

Luckily, the problem is not insurmountable. Aggressive use of the Model-View-Controller (MVC) design pattern, for example, means that all the program logic can be kept out of the GUI-related code. The business logic can then be unit-tested independently of the GUI (i.e., the unit tests call the business logic classes directly, bypassing the GUI code).

You can use a similar testing method for non-GUI asynchronous code by moving as much of the logic as possible into synchronous methods that can be invoked directly from your unit tests. Inevitably, however, some code must remain asynchronous (e.g., event listeners).

The situation is improving as more community understanding is gained regarding how best to unit-test asynchronous systems (for example, the book *Java Extreme Programming Cookbook*[8] provides some useful tips on the subject)—although asynchronous and multithreaded systems by their very nature will always be problematic. Therefore, refactoring of such systems ends up being more expensive and is more likely to introduce subtle concurrency-related bugs.

In fact, this category of system very much lends itself to detailed up-front design. Multitasking, concurrent transactions, and so on can be analyzed with design models such as state diagrams. Even with diagrams, it can still be difficult to prove that all the cases have been covered, so it is vital to follow a suitably thorough logical design process that does catch all the cases (or as many of them as possible) to minimize the amount of refactoring that will need to be done later.

Voice of eXPerience: Unit Testing

by Robin Sharp

This short description from Robin of unit testing gone wrong is a sign of what can happen to an XP codebase that isn't being refactored. Although emergent design (without lots of up-front design) isn't exactly our favored approach, it's safe to say that if a team does use emergent design, team members should refactor

---

8. Eric M. Burke and Brian M. Coyner, *Java Extreme Programming Cookbook* (Sebastopol, CA: O'Reilly & Associates, 2003). This is one of the better XP books. It contains lots of practical, hands-on advice that's useful even for non-XPers.

ruthlessly as well. If they don't, then Fangs (the slippery-slope serpent) strikes again. In this particular project, the managers were drawn to XP because they thought that not doing design up front would save them time and money.

The software was too complex to test fully. Our test suite took hours to run. In fact, the tests took so long (about 8 hours) that we often didn't have time to run them all. One of the issues was that tests are supposed to be self-standing. Tests often left the databases dirty. The side effects often caused errors in the code that we had no idea about. So we had to keep rebuilding the database. Continuous GUI testing is also very problematic, and you have to use a tool like WinRunner.

More from Robin in Chapter 9.

Other Problems

Some other downsides of unit tests are as follows:

- Unit tests catch only the bugs that you have anticipated. In XP, programmers are responsible for writing their own tests (which is a good thing), but there will inevitably be errors of omission.

- Not all code can be unit tested (at least not easily). It could, of course, be argued that in this case, the code should be simplified until it *can* be unit tested. As we mentioned in Chapter 3, some teams reach homeostasis, where they swing from doing too few tests to doing too many (and back again) until they reach the optimum level.

- Writing unit tests for every single class to test every aspect of every function is a tall order. By following XP to the letter, you'll likely end up writing one to two times as much test code as functional code. As the late, great Groucho Marx said (while interviewing a woman who had something like 15 kids), "I like my cigar, too, but I take it out of my mouth once in a while!"

- What if there are bugs in the unit tests? Where there is code, there will be bugs. Usually, this turns out not to be a problem—unless you're using a process that *relies* on 100% reliable automated tests. Luckily, XP has the answer:

    "BugsInTheTests don't matter that much."[9]

---

9. Ron Jeffries posting to the C2 Wiki page Bugs In The Tests, `http://c2.com/cgi/wiki?BugsInTheTests`.

- Unit tests are part of the codebase, so when the team refactors, it must refactor the test code too.

- Refactoring occasionally makes some tests obsolete. The team must make an effort to delete or update obsolete tests as the design changes.

- Even with such a large number of unit tests, is *complete testing* possible?

  "If the objective of testing is to prove that a program is free of bugs, then not only would testing be practically impossible, but it would also be theoretically impossible."[10]

  This isn't an argument against unit tests, which are a valuable tool in the quest for the Holy Grail of complete testing. The problem is that in a software process such as XP, which embraces change, it's supposedly okay to go ahead and make changes to the system, because the unit tests will catch any resultant bugs. The tests are useful as a safety net, but they aren't sufficient to form an intrinsic part of the process—in particular to remove the risks associated with Constant Refactoring After Programming. Unfortunately, the illusion exists that running, and rerunning, and rerunning the tests (over and over and over and over again) does remove those risks.

As we discussed earlier, test-first design isn't a replacement for up-front design. A major problem with applying unit testing to a tightly-wound process such as XP is that unit tests don't catch coding errors at a sufficient level of abstraction.

Unit Tests Are Easy—the Customer Gets to Write Those Nasty Acceptance Tests

One of the problems with test-first design (as a replacement for up-front design rather than a useful supplement) is that it doesn't make a concerted effort to anticipate error-prone usage paths. Unit tests are the easy part. Writing a unit test for a method is generally trivial. It passes or fails.

The nasty part of testing, where you have to deal with all the alternative courses of action (exceptional behavior, recovery, security, etc.) is really all defined in the acceptance tests. And guess what—that's the customer's problem in XP. So Kent Beck's "social contract" has been changed in a way that the programmers loudly claim to be test driven, but in fact the hard part of testing has been delegated to the customer.

---

10. Boris Beizer, *Software System Testing and Quality Assurance* (International Thomson Publishing, 1984), p. 12.

For more about Beck's plan to change the "social contract" of working, see the section "That's the Customer's Problem" in Chapter 5.

Voice of eXPerience: Aspects of Testing

by David Van Der Klauw

More insight from David Van Der Klauw. Here he describes the pitfalls of turning the unit-test dial all the way up to ten.

Software testing is an art and a science in itself. Software is sometimes easy to write but often hard to test and impossible to prove. What to do?

XP solves the problem of testing by simply insisting that everything be tested and with a test written before the code. If only life were so simple.

While acknowledging that testing is very important and something that CompanyXYZ *[David's anonymous employer]* has neglected, I believe that XP oversimplifies the difficulty of testing and misallocates testing resources.

Although test-first coding is an interesting concept, I believe that the reality is different from the XP theory. My experience is that many things that can be test-first coded are so simple that a test is unnecessary. On the other hand, many things of moderate or greater complexity cannot be test-first coded. Only after the coding is finished is it possible to envisage the tests. I am not hard-line about this, and I may change my opinion over time.

As to degree of testing, I think XP makes the dangerous simplification of applying the same degree of testing to all areas. My concept of bug finding is something like this: A programmer should find 9/10 bugs before check-in, the automatic tests should find 9/10 remaining bugs before handover to QA, QA should find 9/10 remaining bugs to customers who find 9/10, and 1/10 remains undiscovered. Therefore, the customer sees only 1 in 1,000 bugs.

My belief is that this is good enough quality. Sure, it would be nice if the customer saw zero bugs, but is the customer prepared to wait years longer or pay twice as much for this level of quality? Probably not.

I understand that some people have gone overboard with the tests that they write. Tests have been written for some things (like constructors) that can never fail. Some testing of module internals has been so detailed and extensive that it greatly increases the cost of ever changing the internals of the modules in the future. This is not agile programming.

Rather than obsess about XP's testing simplifications, I suggest to instead do a lot of thinking about how best to test. Spend a reasonable percentage of total time on testing, and test as much as possible for the given time and resources. When a customer finds a problem, add new tests so that no customer will ever see that problem again.

Test what the customer sees first. As those tests fail, add more detailed internal tests to pick up faults that are actually occurring.

Voice of eXPerience: YAGNI 16 Tests

by David Van Der Klauw

One inevitable result of combining the two XP practices of Design After First Testing and Constant Refactoring After Programming"[11] is that you can spend a lot of time writing tests for code that's subsequently thrown away. So you can spend time coding lots of tests that you don't need. It's not analysis paralysis, and some folks might even regard it as fun, but it's certainly an insidious way to pour programmer-hours down the drain.

This never happens on a real XP project, right? Well, David details his real-life experiences with this phenomenon in the following "Voice of eXPerience" segment, and then we "turn the satire dial all the way up to ten" with a piece that we call "Camp Regretestskiy."

Our unit tests were made up of two functions per test. The first function called the second and outputted the name, description, and pass/fail result. The second function simply returned true or false.

The task of our pair was to add unit testing for a new menu condition that would affect eight menu items. My partner, a junior, claimed he knew the code well and jumped straight to some testing code with eight blocks of code like this:

```
Function ShowTestMenuItemA
    TestOutput("TestMenuItemA", "description A", TestMenuItemA())
End
Function TestMenuItemA()
    Return(GetMenuItem("ItemA").visible=true)
End
```

I didn't like it and said that all eight checks should be done in the one function, but I was told that this was the simplest thing possible.

Now our task was to do the simplest thing possible, so my partner duplicated the 8 tests, edited all 16 to cover the new condition, green-screened it, and checked it in. Our highlight at the next stand-up meeting was that "we have added eight new tests." Everyone clapped, but I was not impressed.

Later that week someone discovered that the function tested by our 16 tests was not actually called by the UI in determining menu item visibility. Therefore, the highlight at that stand-up meeting was that they "were able to YAGNI 16 tests." Everyone clapped.

Somehow two XP highlights were a lowlight to me.

---

11. See the section "Emperor's New Code" in the preface for the proper acronyms for these practices.

Camp Regretestskiy

"Uncle Joe" Steele sat at his desk and looked over his to-do list (which was, of course, written on a red index card). "Rewrite history of C3, da!" said Uncle Joe. "C3 was glorious victory of the people. This has now been firmly established in books, magazines, and on newsgroups. Project was glorious success."

"Next, buy borscht. I'll do it on the way home."

"Next, deal with big backlog of regression tests." Uncle Joe looked down at his code hound Jack, who was curled up in a corner of the office and said, "This is a big problem, Jack, and we need to do something about it. All these dewelopers Constantly Refactoring After Programming and continuously integrating are changing our codebase so quickly that 8 hours is not enough time to run all of our tests, and the problem, of course, is made much worse when the dewelopers don't pair up, because there is twice as much new code to test."

"Arf!" agreed Jack.

Uncle Joe pressed a button on his phone and summoned his assistant, Boris Codunov. Boris, a short man with a mustache who was wearing a black suit, walked in and said, "Yes, Fearless Leader, how can I, your humble servant, subjugate myself to the interests of the project today?"

"Codunov, we have a problem," said Uncle Joe. "Our glorious programming team has achieved such an incredible velocity in refactoring the codebase that we can't run our tests quickly enough. And, you know, some of these dewelopers just refuse to pair-program. This makes the problem even worse, as with pair programming there are only half as many streams of changes to integrate. As you know, Jack has been catching more and more dewelopers coding alone instead of pairing recently. But I have devised a brilliant solution that will solve both problems at once!

"You see, Codunov, these disloyal dewelopers need to be taught a lesson. So, we will establish a gulag for regression testing. I have decided to call it Camp Regretestskiy. It will be located in Hackensnack, New Jersey. And you, Codunov, are going to run it for me," said Uncle Joe.

"Hoo-boy," Boris said. "I am honored to be in charge of Camp Regretestskiy. I'll get to work on it right away, Fearless Leader." Boris left the office, stopping to give Jack a pat on the head.

A few days later, JoJo and Loretta were refactoring the state tax computation for the thirty-fifth time when JoJo suddenly started sneezing. "Achoo! Achoo!" sneezed JoJo over and over again. "Bless you," said Loretta after he stopped. "Are you all right?"

"I'm sorry, Loretta," said JoJo, "but I seem to have picked up a nasty cold. I woke up this morning with a terrible hacking cough, and I've been sneezing all day. I would've stayed home but I didn't want you to get in trouble with Uncle Joe for coding alone. But I really don't want you to get sick too, so I think I'd better go home early."

"That's all right, JoJo," said Loretta, secretly relieved. "Why don't you go home and get some rest? You can always refactor the tax computation again next week when you feel better."

"Thanks, Loretta," said JoJo, packing up his briefcase.

Loretta, who liked JoJo but secretly preferred coding alone, got out a spray bottle of disinfectant and began to spray the keyboard and mouse that JoJo had been using. Even though she had been taking vitamin C++ every 15 minutes since JoJo arrived that morning, she could already begin to feel her eyes itch and water.

"I'd like to shoot the person that published the study claiming pair programming increased productivity," muttered Loretta under her breath. "They forgot the chapter on 'Pair Catching a Cold'—how's *that* for a productivity increase? Not only that, but I had this tax computation done a week ago and it passed all the tests 100%, but I seem to be the only one who minds refactoring around in a circle. Luckily, I kept a printout of my sequence diagram from last week." She wiped off the keyboard and settled down to start work.

A few minutes later in Uncle Joe's office, Jack woke up from his nap, barked softly, and lazily chased his tail in a circle three times. Uncle Joe looked up from his e-mail. "Da," he said. "Good boy, Jack. Let's go check if any of our dewelopers are being disloyal. I just got an e-mail from Codunov, and we'll have quite a surprise for them, won't we Jack?"

"Arf," said Jack as he wagged his tail. The coach and his code hound walked down the hall to the coding room.

Just as Jack was waking up from his nap, there was a loud argument underway in the coding room. "I don't care what Uncle Joe says about coding alone," said Ralph. "It says right here in this book that 'there must be food' is a core XP principle. And I . . . am turning the dial all the way up to 20 on this one!"

"From the size of your belt, Ralph, it looks like the dial is a bit past 20—maybe about 54," said Alice.

"One of these days, Alice . . . Pow! Right in the kisser! Now I'm going to the store to get donuts, and *don't* try to stop me!" exclaimed Ralph.

"Only the door can stop you, Ralph—when you can't fit through it anymore!" replied Alice.

"Achoo!" sneezed Loretta. "Bless you," said Ralph over his shoulder as he stormed out of the coding room. "Better take more vitamin C++, Loretta," said Alice as she settled down to continue refactoring the social security withholding calculation.

Just as the elevator doors closed behind Ralph, Uncle Joe and Jack came down the hall toward the coding room. As Jack walked into the room and saw both Loretta and Alice coding alone, the fur under his collar began to stand up. He bared his teeth and started growling and barking. Jack went over to Loretta's desk, grabbed the sequence diagram she was using with his teeth, and then tore it to shreds.

"Help!" cried Loretta. "Please, Uncle Joe, make him stop!"

"Y*b**nna mat! You have been a disloyal deweloper for the final time! Not only are you guilty of coding alone, but you have forgotten the most important rule that we have in this organization. And that is, Never Kode Vit Documentation! N! K! V! D!" yelled Uncle Joe.

Five large men in red T-shirts with the letters *NKVD* emblazoned on the chest ran in. "You called for us, Fearless Leader?" asked Captain Medvedenko, who was an imposing 6'10" tall and weighed about 250 pounds.

"Da," said Uncle Joe. "Take this disloyal deweloper off to Codunov at Camp Regretestskiy!"

Suddenly, Alice, who had been sitting in her chair terrified, sneezed, causing Jack to run over to her desk and start growling ferociously. "Ralph, Ralph!" barked Jack. Alice began to cry.

Uncle Joe turned around and looked at Alice and Ralph's empty chair next to her. "Alice has been disloyal as well! Haven't I told you people that coding alone produces twice as much code and twice as many streams to integrate? Now you'll see what the testing backlog you create looks like! Take her too! At once!"

"Da," said Captain Medvedenko, and he and his squad bundled Loretta and Alice off to Hackensnack.

A few hours later, Loretta and Alice, accompanied by the enormous, hulking Captain Medvedenko, arrived in Hackensnack at the gates of Camp Regretestskiy. Loretta and Alice (who, being at the next desk, had also caught JoJo's cold) were both sneezing profusely.

"I bring you new laborers, Comrade Codunov," Medvedenko said to Boris, who was accompanied by his girlfriend, Natasha. Boris handed Medvedenko a set of handcuffs.

"Thank you, Captain," said Boris. "Please chain their right wrists together for me, then we'll take them down to start coding up tests."

"But Boris, darling, how are they going to code tests with their right hands chained together?" asked Natasha.

Boris replied, "Uncle Joe wants everybody at Camp R to learn to work in pairs . . . and don't forget, Natasha, we are leftists here at Camp R. We do everything with the left hand!"

Medvedenko handcuffed poor Alice and Loretta's right wrists, and, accompanied by Boris and Natasha, walked them down several flights of stairs to a desk in a damp, dimly lit basement room with no windows.

"Achoo!" sneezed Alice, as they were walking down the stairs. The group approached a desk with a computer and a pile of index cards on top of it and two chairs in front of it.

"Here you go!" said Boris, with a grin. "The story cards are waiting for you. Sit down and start coding those tests."

Alice and Loretta struggled to sit in the chairs and still reach the keyboard and mouse with their left hands. "Achoo!" sneezed Alice. "Can you reach the mouse, Loretta?"

"I can type one-handed, but I can't type and move the mouse at the same time," said Loretta.

"If I twist around like this . . . *Achoo!* I think I can just grab it," replied Alice.

"Boris, you are *so* evil," grinned Natasha, as she watched Loretta and Alice crane their necks trying to see the monitor.

"You betcha," replied Boris. "Uncle Joe didn't pick just anybody to run his gulag, you know." Boris and Natasha both broke into peals of gleeful laughter.

Slowly and painfully, Loretta and Alice began to write unit tests for the pile of stories. Just as they began to make a small dent in the pile, three guards wearing NKVD T-shirts walked in carrying big baskets full of index cards. They walked over to Loretta and Alice's desk and began dumping cards onto the pile.

"Stop!" screamed Alice. "We'll never be able to code that many tests!"

Comrade Nikita, the leader of the group, responded, "We will *bury* you in index cards!" He then took off his shoe and banged it on the table for emphasis. Alice and Loretta both began to cry.

As the months passed, Alice and Loretta, working left-handed, continued to churn out the unit tests. Slowly but surely, the stack of unit test printouts on their desk grew ever taller. Poor Alice and Loretta became thinner and thinner, due to the NKVD's "you hack, we snack" policy. They worked 18-hour shifts and longed for the days when they got to go home clean at 5:00 PM every day.

Finally, one day Boris and Natasha came to visit them. "Well, disloyal dewelopers, have you learned your lesson about coding alone?" asked Boris.

"Oh, *yes*, Mr. Codunov," said Loretta and Alice in unison. "We promise we'll never think about coding alone again if you'll just send us back to Uncle Joe," they begged.

Boris looked at Natasha, then got out a key and removed the handcuffs from Alice and Loretta's right wrists. "Call the fire department, Natasha," he said.

"But Boris, darling, there isn't any fire," said Natasha.

"Just do it, Natasha—there will be," grinned Boris, as he looked at the enormous pile of unit test printouts stacked up on the desk.

A few minutes later, Comrade Andrei Griffitsky of the Regretestskiy Fire Department (RFD) walked in, whistling a happy tune and carrying a flamethrower. Griffitsky was accompanied by a small group of men wearing RFD shirts. "You sent for me, Comrade Codunov?" asked Griffitsky.

"Da!" said Boris. "Uncle Joe called me this morning and said that the customer has changed his mind about all the stories, so it's YAGNI for all these tests. You know what to do!"

The RFD squad began to chant, "YAGNI all the tests. YAGNI all the tests. YAGNI all the tests. YAGNI all the tests."

Griffitsky stopped whistling, grinned widely, took out his flamethrower, aimed it at the stack of unit test printouts, and incinerated them in a massive burst of flames. The RFD squad continued to chant, *"YAGNI all the tests. YAGNI all the tests. YAGNI all the tests. YAGNI all the tests."*

"This new flamethrower works even better than using a Molotov cocktail!" said Griffitsky.

Loretta and Alice broke down and began to cry as they watched the results of all their left-handed unit-test coding go up in smoke.

"You see, Natasha, they have learned their lesson. They're ready to go back to Uncle Joe," said Boris. And he handed the women back to Captain Medvedenko for the trip back home.

Programming Without a Safety Net

XP's primary "safety net" is, of course, unit testing (others include pair programming and collective ownership). With such safety nets in place (so the theory goes), it should be sufficient to cut out a lot of process that might otherwise be essential (such as sufficient design up-front and getting sign-off on detailed written specifications). But is this really a safe approach to software development? To put it another way: Should a team really be measuring success by the seat of their pants?

Picture a wartime night gunner who must keep a lookout from a small bunker on top of a remote hill somewhere. If he switches off his nighttime radar, he can save some serious battery power and therefore keep his soup-stove hot for the entire night. If his plan works, and he returns from his watch fully fed and flushed with victory, then this can be viewed as a success (and will probably be recorded as one in the sergeant-major's night-watch log book: *"No raids last night. Night gunner well fed. Another bleeding success!"*). But if there happens to be a nighttime air raid during the well-fed gunner's vigil, he'll be none the wiser until a bomb drops inexplicably into his soup bowl.

The moral of this tale is that it's fine to cut corners and take risks (such as not specifying everything in a bulletproof, legally binding specification), as long as nothing goes wrong. People who do so will claim success. But when something does go wrong, you're in serious trouble. Even the unthinkable—early termination of the project—could happen. Looking ahead can be achieved simply by spending sufficient time on the design before you begin writing production code.

Although XP does include some practices that we should all put into use (in careful moderation), the package as a whole leaves too many factors wide open to the forces of change (which is ironic given XP's "embrace change" motto).

Another analogy would be an American football team (we call it that in England) whose players have discovered that if they remove their helmets, they can run and dodge a bit faster. They might even win some games this way, but most of them will be too concussed to remember.

 ### Fangs Gets His Eyes Tested

Test-first design (or Design After First Testing) focuses on code-level issues with the scope of a single test case or a small group of methods. Although it's not a bad practice, it's dangerous to rely on it as a replacement for up-front design.

Combined with refactoring and emergent design (covered in Chapters 9 and 12), the process represents a myopic approach to software design.

DAFT Defanged

Detailed up-front design modeling and test-first design can be used in conjunction. In fact (as we describe in Chapter 15), they're entirely complementary because they address different levels of design.

Detailed up-front design is seen by XPers as a drawback because it delays "progress." Our experience is that it saves potentially months of additional rework and redesign later. The following advice also sums up the benefits of detailed design:

"During development, encourage developers to go to quite a detailed level in the design. They will hate you for it . . . initially. Well maybe at the end too! But, a few missed parameters can be a real headache. Ensure that your proverbial Channel Tunnel meets in the middle."[12]

It's important to balance this by doing up-front design in *just enough* detail, to recognize when you might be getting bogged down with analysis paralysis, and to use effective design techniques that provide a return on the time invested in them (rather than simply designing for the sake of it).

Summary

Unit testing is without a doubt the best concept to come out of XP. If you retain one thing from XP, make it unit testing.

The following quote from Fred Brooks helps to explain where unit testing can be most valuable:

"Systems program building is an entropy-decreasing process, hence inherently metastable. Program maintenance is an entropy-increasing process, and even its most skillful execution only delays the subsidence of the system into unfixable obsolescence."[13]

Unit testing is essentially a tool for regression testing. Add something to the system or make a change, and run the tests to make sure nothing's broken. As such, unit testing (as a part of the larger refactoring process) is a valuable innovation for the maintenance phase of a product life cycle, where it helps to keep entropy at bay. (Of course, XP puts a product into the maintenance phase very early in its life cycle, which increases its reliance on unit tests.)

---

12. Antony Hirst, "How to Make a Software Project Work," http://www.softwarereality.com/lifecycle/project_succeed.jsp, January 4, 2003.

13. Frederick P. Brooks, Jr., *The Mythical Man-Month, Twentieth Anniversary Edition* (New York, NY: Addison-Wesley, 1995), p. 123.

However, the effectiveness of unit tests is entirely dependent on the development process in which they operate. Test-first design, for example, is no substitute for sufficient up-front design. Used together, on the other hand, up-front design modeling and test-first design can be a very powerful combination—but then that just wouldn't be XP.

Test-first design is fundamentally a part of emergent architecture and design. We cover this aspect of XP in Chapter 12.

Another, vital element of test-first design is, of course, refactoring, which we cover in the next chapter.

CHAPTER 9

Constant Refactoring After Programming (If It Ain't Broke, Fix It Anyway)

Refactor
(Sing to the tune of "She Loves You" by The Beatles)

Refactor, yeah, yeah, yeah
Refactor, yeah, yeah, yeah
Refactor, yeah, yeah, yeah, yeah

You say you wrote some code
And it smells pretty bad
Your pair programming buddy
Is lookin' kinda sad

You just refactor
And then you're having fun
Refactor
Don't worry 'bout getting done

You've coded it ten times
But no one seems to mind
It passes unit tests
But it's never been designed

So just refactor
'Cause it's all about havin' fun
Refactor
'Cause software's never done, oooooooooooooh!

Refactor, yeah, yeah, yeah.
'Cause if your code smells clean your client won't get mad

Doesn't matter when it's done
Or even what it does
'Cause you're doin' XP
And it's the latest buzz

So you refactor
'Cause you know you will be glad
Refactor
And you never will be sad, ooooooooooooooh!

Refactor, yeah, yeah, yeah
Refactor, yeah, yeah, yeah
'Cause if your code smells clean your client won't get mad
'Cause if your code smells clean your client won't get mad
'Cause if your code smells clean your client won't get mad

Yeah, yeah, yeah!
Yeah, yeah, yeah!
Yeah, yeah, yeah, yeah!

Refactoring in XP is based around the premise that you probably won't get all the requirements right up front and you'll probably pick an imperfect design (we discuss each of these premises in Chapter 10 and Chapter 12, respectively). Therefore, why not make up the design as you go along?

Refactoring, as a technique for cleaning up poorly structured code, certainly has its place in our toolkit of useful techniques. However, refactoring, as it's used in XP, is essentially the place where you catch all the design errors that you probably would have found in design if you hadn't skipped over designing up front in the first place.

In this chapter we examine refactoring in XP from a variety of angles.

There's No TIME to Write Down Requirements[1]

Suddenly the white rabbit, whom Alice had encountered earlier, dashed up and began shouting at her. "There's no TIME to write down REQUIREMENTS," said the rabbit, iterating furiously. "And what's more, users never know what they want!"

"Just have them tell you a story, and CODE IT," he said. "They change their minds several times each morning, anyway—the only way to keep up is to refactor the code faster than they can change their minds. Why, we can go through five iterations in the time it takes a typical user to change his mind, you see if we can't!"

"Refactoring?" asked Alice. "I think I've heard of that, somewhere."

"It's the latest thing," said the rabbit. "Everybody's doing it. Design's dead, you know. With enough refactoring, you don't need design. The design figures itself out from the code. Ask the Hatter!" And off he rushed again.

---

1.   Originally presented at UMLWorld as part of Doug's "Alice in Use Case Land" keynote speech. The full text is available at http://www.iconixsw.com/aliceinusecaseland.html.

You Might As Well Say the Code Is the Design

Alice, not knowing what else to do, and feeling somewhat shaky again after hearing about designs figuring themselves out from code, decided to follow the rabbit for a while. On they went, the rabbit pausing every few feet to iterate around in a circle a few times. Eventually the rabbit, rushing ahead at top speed, pulled far enough ahead that Alice couldn't see him anymore.

Alice kept walking, and after a time she came to a clearing where she saw the rabbit, along with a large mouse and a little man wearing a big hat, all working furiously over a table and some chairs. When Alice walked up, all the legs from the table and chairs were sitting in a big pile on the ground. Alice watched as the Hatter, the rabbit, and the dormouse each grabbed four legs from the pile and screwed them into a chair. The problem was that the legs were of different lengths, and Alice watched in fascination as they each finished assembling their chair, turned it over, and sat down. The chairs often tipped over, what with the legs being of different lengths and all, and when this happened they yelled out in unison, "Failed the unit test!"; flipped the chairs back over; and began unscrewing the legs and tossing them back onto the pile.

"What kind of game are you playing?" asked Alice.

"It's not a game, we're refactoring the furniture," replied the Hatter.

"Why don't you read the documentation for assembling the chairs?" asked Alice. "It's sure to specify which legs should go on which chairs."

"It's oral documentation," said the Hatter.

"Oh," said Alice. "You mean you don't have any."

"No," said the Hatter. "Written documentation is for cowards. We can refactor very quickly, so we can be brave enough to let the design figure itself out."

"Oh, yes. The rabbit said I should ask you about that," said Alice. "How can designs figure themselves out from code?"

"You poor, ignorant child," said the Hatter, in quite a condescending tone. "The code *is* the design, don't you see? Perhaps you'd better let the Duchess explain it to you," he said, and resumed refactoring the chairs.

Refactoring Heaven

In essence, much like "sentence first, verdict afterward" from Alice's trial in Wonderland, it's "code first, design afterward" in XP. "Stuff and nonsense! The idea of writing the code first!" seems pretty applicable to us.

Refactoring itself isn't a bad thing, but it does, in our opinion, make a very poor substitute for design. Assuming that the only way or the best way to achieve a clean design is to refactor code is to ignore the benefits of techniques such as UML sequence diagrams. These techniques can be amazingly effective in helping you to come up with a good factoring of your design in the first place. The Extremo mind-set relegates these techniques to the scrap heap, the justification for which seems to be that the Extremos don't know how to use them effectively.

We believe that a more efficient approach is to make a reasonable attempt at doing a good design before jumping into code, and then use refactoring to catch the (hopefully few) design errors that slip through.

There are a few other troubling aspects to the widespread adoption of refactoring as a replacement for design, not the least of which is performance to schedule. Remember that the definition of refactoring involves making no changes to the external behavior of the code. You're just rearranging the internals to make the code smell better.[2] Keep in mind that according to Extremo theory, the code you're refactoring has already passed all of its unit tests and scored 100%. So the code is already "right" in terms of producing the correct results, we're supposed to assume. Yet, even though it ain't broke, we're gonna fix it. And when do we stop fixing it? When it smells good! Yeah! Makes us feel like singing.

A Day in the Code
(Sing to the tune of "A Day in the Life" by The Beatles)

I smelled the code today, oh boy
It smelled of pink champagne and strawberries
An architecture had emerged
And I just had to laugh

He wrote it on an index card
He didn't know that the requirements changed
So when he ran his unit tests
The gold owner became distressed

But we're still
Coding
On

I heard the news today, oh boy
The payroll project had just gone away
The code was really just a mess
But you must remember termination can be success

The hype goes on
And
On

Occasionally we wonder . . . what if the code smells like . . . grapes, but we're sort of looking for a strawberry essence to waft gently into our nostrils when we smell the code? Is refactoring to suit olfactory preference in this fashion considered good practice in our brave new world?

---

2. In XP, "code smell" is shorthand for a coder's intuition of when code is in need of improvement.

Key to making this whole refactor-instead-of-design equation work (well, sort of) is the fact that XP contracts are always variable in scope and schedules are never fixed (not even when there are 76,000 employees who might not receive a paycheck, it would seem). In the XP world, "software is never done" (presumably this is because you can always find another way to rewrite it).

This strange, "bizarro-world" parallel universe where "software is never done," although undoubtedly a blessing to programmers who are getting paid by the hour with no end of the project ever threatening to end the gravy train, is a very foreign concept to the intrepid authors of this book. When on a programming assignment, we've always assumed that our job is to actually get the client's job done, and get it done as soon as possible (within reason). So we invest a little bit of time in up-front design and then do our damnedest to write the software right the first time. And most of the time (astoundingly) we're able to do a pretty good job at this. We're not infallible—once in a while the design might not be as clean as we'd like because we learned something along the way or because a requirement changed on us. When this happens, we're happy to use the refactoring techniques to improve the quality of the code.

Heretical and stodgy as it sounds, we think we should use requirements analysis techniques such as use cases to help us figure out what we're going to build; use design techniques such as sequence diagrams to help us do a good factoring of the design; and then code it, test it, and use refactoring techniques to do further cleanup if necessary. And we should get the freaking software done on schedule.[3]

But the Extremos advise us that we shouldn't invest time in up-front requirements analysis and design. Rather, they say we should code the simplest thing that can possibly work, ask us to believe that turning a blind eye to future requirements and coding the simplest thing that can possibly work with a focus on only the bit we're working on at the moment is somehow different from hacking, and then tell us to plan on refactoring it on pretty much a continuous basis. Small wonder that software is never done in the Extremo universe. "Look, Martha, we've invented a perpetual coding machine."

What we can't understand is why a client would ever knowingly go for this approach. The key word in that sentence being "knowingly." Which pretty much explains why we've written this book, come to think of it.

---

3. Extremos often claim that XP helps to bring software in on schedule because they keep revising the schedule in each iteration—in other words, they have "schedule," but "the schedule" doesn't exist per se. And if the team encourages the customer to embrace scope creep, they can just keep adding features as they go, revising the schedule ad infinitum, until the project gets cancelled. More about this in Chapter 11.

XP Design Mantra: Refactor Mercilessly

This mantra describes the XP practice of constant refactoring. Refactoring, without a doubt, improves the design of existing code, assuming the code was bad in the first place. It takes the approach of many short steps, carefully nudging the code into better shape.

Smelling Better
(Sing to the tune of "Getting Better" by The Beatles)

It's smelling better all the time
Better, better, better

You have to admit the code smells better
It's smelling better all the time
(It couldn't smell much worse)
You have to admit it's smelling better
It's smelling better
On rewrite nine

My code is smelling better all the time

It's smelling better all the time
Better, better, better

I used to design like a fool
But refactoring is so cool
We don't write it down
Just smash it around
And ship it as fast as we can

You have to admit it's smelling better
It's smelling better all the time
(It couldn't smell much worse)
You have to admit it's smelling better
It's smelling better
On rewrite nine

Smelling so much better all the time

In XP, refactoring is also an important method of preventing software entropy from creeping in—that is, preventing the design from becoming more complex as new functionality is added. By applying standard refactoring techniques repeatedly to the code, the code is kept simple and hence easy to extend with new functionality.

When Refactoring Is Useful

Refactoring—used in the right context—is a valuable practice. In particular, refactoring is useful on legacy systems that need to be extended with new functionality. If the new functionality requires a change in design, then refactoring (with a full suite of unit tests) is a safe technique for making the change.[4]

As described in Martin Fowler's book *Refactoring: Improving the Design of Existing Code*, refactoring consists of specific practices and techniques that can be applied to existing code, usually with an aim to reach a certain design pattern. In fact, the book can be thought of as "Design Patterns in Motion." It includes such refactorings as "Substitute Algorithm," "Move Method," "Replace Type Code with Subclasses," and "Decompose Conditional."

The prescribed refactorings in Fowler's book on the subject are pretty much all sensible techniques.[5] In addition, the advice about refactoring first (making the code clearer, simpler, and more malleable) and then optimizing afterward *if* the code needs it is profoundly important for most projects.

Given a project that is in trouble (e.g., collapsing under the weight of its unwieldy codebase), refactoring can have an almost miraculous effect, unraveling code that previously seemed locked forever in its spaghetti-like embrace. That is the sort of situation where merciless refactoring is useful.

Conversely, if your project is starting afresh with a new design, then you should find that it's possible to apply the same sound principles (and the same "Gang of Four" design patterns that Fowler's book espouses) to the new system. It's all common sense, and it all represents good design.

You should also find that refactoring a class model prior to writing code is much faster than refactoring source code, simply because there is less to change. So refactoring can prove to be *very* useful before coding even begins.

Repeated refactoring of particularly badly written code (by applying and fully unit-testing one refactoring at a time) will eventually get you to a nice, clean codebase.

As we just mentioned, refactoring involves cushioning all of your code with unit tests. The tests should be sufficiently comprehensive that you can run them with the confidence that they will catch most problems, even after a small change to the code.

---

4. In fact, XP's practices could have been tailor-made for maintaining legacy systems (possibly because XP aims to put the project into "maintenance mode" as early as possible, as we discuss elsewhere).

5. Except, perhaps, for "Introduce Null Object," in which an object that represents null is introduced so that null values don't need to be given special consideration. This has a very limited application, because the whole point of "null" is that it *is* special, and therefore should be treated differently from non-null values. Introducing objects that represent null could be storing up trouble, allowing special cases to pass through your code unchecked.

Refactoring isn't the most efficient way to design software. A more efficient approach, we've found, is to sketch some lines and boxes, quickly knock together a few throwaway prototypes, and then go with the design that you prefer.[6] However, if you need to fix some badly written code (or even to tidy up some code that isn't too scruffy, if you have the time), then refactoring is the safest— possibly even the quickest (in the long run)—way of doing it.

Note that if you're approaching a body of code because it contains a nefarious bug that needs to be rooted out and crushed, but the code is badly written, then refactoring the code first might seem like a good idea. One of the key principles of refactoring, however, is that you shouldn't make any further changes until all the unit tests pass. If the code contains a known bug, then presumably it's causing a unit test to fail (and if it isn't, a test should be quickly added in so that it *does* fail). At this stage, whether or not to refactor first is really a judgment call. You might just find it easier (and safer) to root out the bug first.

Afterward, you might decide whether to go ahead and refactor the code anyway. This is another judgment call. It depends on if the area of code has been identified as a known "hot spot" for bugs—in which case, spending a little time improving the code will probably save a lot of time later on.

A code hot spot is described in Steve McConnell's book *Rapid Development* as an *error-prone module*:

> *"An error-prone module is a module that's responsible for a disproportionate number of defects. On its IMS project, for example, IBM found that 57 percent of the errors were clumped in 7 percent of the modules."*[7]

Tracking and analyzing defects can help to identify areas of code that would benefit hugely from some heavy refactoring. It's a fair bet that clean, well-designed code will contain fewer defects than hastily designed spaghetti code. So the time spent refactoring error-prone modules produces a better return than refactoring code that is relatively defect-free.

---

6. The key point here being that you design the system in detail, leaving no stone unturned. Taking the right approach (following a logical design process, as we discuss in Chapter 8) can work wonders in uncovering design errors (or preventing them from occurring at all) before any production code has been written.

7. Steve McConnell, *Rapid Development: Taming Wild Software Schedules* (Redmond, WA: Microsoft Press, 1996), p. 72.

When Refactoring Falls Short

> *"We have worked at some of the big refactorings for months or years on running systems. When you have a system and it's in production and you need to add functionality, you'll have a hard time persuading managers that they should stop progress for a couple of months while you tidy up. Instead, you have to make like Hansel and Gretel and nibble around the edges, a little today, a little tomorrow."*[8]

> —Kent Beck and Martin Fowler

So, in other words, not getting the design right early costs big-time later on. Contrast that with this quote from the same source:

> *"With refactoring the emphasis changes. You still do upfront design, but now you don't try to find THE solution. Instead all you want is a reasonable solution. You know that as you build the solution, as you understand more about the problem, you realize that the best solution is different from the one you originally came up with. With refactoring this is not a problem, for it no longer is expensive to make the changes."*[9]

> *This strikes us as circular, to say the least. Refactoring is time consuming and may involve "guerilla tactics" to get it done under the nose of management, who doubtless want you to spend time producing new functionality, yet it is also "not a problem" and "no longer expensive."*[10]

Normally, we view software development as problem ➤ solution. The XP approach appears to be solution ➤ problems.

Now it's time to push the controversy dial up to ten, with this rather vilifying statement: In a software project that is following sound design principles, constant refactoring is the ultimate time-waster. Countless programmer-hours have been lost to perfectionists tinkering away at their finished code, polishing it unnecessarily.

---

8. Martin Fowler, *Refactoring: Improving the Design of Existing Code* (New York, NY: Addison-Wesley, 1999), p. 359.

9. Ibid., p. 67.

10. In fact, suggesting that "it is no longer expensive to make the changes" isn't circular, it's just plain wrong. It's an assertion made without proof—and it's wrong.

Outside the XP world, constant refactoring (as opposed to occasional refactoring, which is useful) just doesn't make sense, because you don't have to support XP's other practices. The Extremos would argue that constant refactoring is necessary because you're "evolving" your design as you go along. So if you begin by producing your design, you don't need to spend all that time constantly refactoring your code.

The Extremo justification for constant refactoring (in the context of emergent design) is that it allows you to get functionality into the hands of the users early. We discuss this further in Chapter 12 (and also in Chapter 15).

Visualize the Smell and You Will Know When to Stop, My Son

The danger (sorry, *one* of the dangers) with constant refactoring is that it's difficult to know exactly when to stop doing it. Depending on which Extremo you listen to, you must either *listen* to the code or *smell* the code. As we discuss in Chapter 16, this is like listening for the sound of one hand clapping.

It's easy to just keep going, because it feels like you're doing good work (even though the project, from an observer's point of view, isn't making any progress)—if you see a better design, then why not go ahead and change the code? Anyone can change anyone else's code because of the XP practice of collective ownership.

Actually Knowing When to Stop

If you see a better design, why wouldn't you change the code to use it? If the code works and has a low (or zero) defect count, and your architecture tells you that this section of code is essentially complete, then there's no need to modify the code any further. It's finished. A detailed architectural model makes it easy to identify dependencies across the overall design, so that we can identify when a piece of code really is complete (i.e., doesn't warrant further refactoring).

If, later on, further defects are discovered in that area of code or additional functionality needs to be designed in, then the code can be revisited—refactored into a better design if needed.

Refactoring should be approached on the basis of necessity—identifying what's needed to complete the project. This strikes us as a more effective way of tackling design and code quality than simply sniffing out code smells and attacking any crufty code that you find (regardless of whether redesigning it will benefit the rest of the project).

Refactorin'

(Sing to the tune of "Taxman" by The Beatles, with apologies to George for the attempt at rhythm guitar in [])

[dumb, dumb, da dumb dumb dumb]
[dumb, dumb, da dumb dumb dumb]

I'm happy as a man can be
My client thinks that change is free
So I'm refactorin'
Yeah, refactorin'

[dumb, dumb, da dumb dumb dumb]
[dumb, dumb, da dumb dumb dumb]

I rewrite my code all day long
First it seems right, then it seems wrong
So I'm refactorin'
Yeah, refactorin'

[dumb, dumb, da dumb dumb dumb]
[dumb, dumb, da dumb dumb dumb]

My project is so very small
That I don't have much work at all
But I'll have a job for years to come
Because software is never done
When you're refactorin'
Yeah, refactorin', yeah

[dumb, dumb, da dumb dumb dumb]
[dumb, dumb, da dumb dumb dumb]
[dumb, dumb, da dumb dumb dumb]
[dumb, dumb, da dumb dumb dumb]

"Subsequent launches of additional pay populations were wanted by top management within a year. The team thought that was possible, though I can't remember why."[11]

---

11. Chet Hendrickson as quoted on the C2 Wiki page Chrysler Comprehensive Compensation,
    http://c2.com/cgi/wiki?ChryslerComprehensiveCompensation.

The temptation is always to keep improving the design, perfecting the code, turning that search function into a class, extracting methods here, combining methods there, and so on. This is a dangerous trap to fall into. Once a piece of code works, leave it well enough alone. It works. Once a piece of code is "fit for purpose," then it's good enough (albeit with the caveat in the next paragraph). Any more time spent on it is time that could be spent elsewhere on the project.

It's possible to take this "good enough" approach because we produced a design up front, and spent time prototyping and thinking about the design before we began coding. Therefore, it's a fairly safe bet that for any part of the system, we'll only need to write the code "once and only once."

Is Up-Front Design Sufficient to Avoid Large Refactorings Later?

As it turns out, detailed up-front design can actually be supplemented rather well with test-first design (in fact, as we mentioned in Chapter 3, Doug proposed this on OTUG[12] about 5 years ago and was summarily rebuffed by the Extremos, so we're making the case again in this book). The resultant combination essentially means more up-front design and less of a dependency on unit testing[13]—not to mention less pair programming and fewer integration issues.

In this section, we examine the Extremo attitude to up-front design and ask, can a detailed up-front design process, performed correctly, provide a good enough design to avoid large amounts of refactoring? (Hint: Yes.)

Is the Code Really the Design?

A mantra you often hear in XP circles is "The code *is* the design!" In other words, documentation is only a snapshot of the design—a collection of instantly out-dated assertions regarding how the program is constructed. The only really up-to-date reflection of the design could possibly be the source code because this is the manifestation of the design; therefore, it *is* the design. This is roughly equivalent to claiming that bricks, pipes, and conduits are actually blueprints because they are the manifestation of the blueprints.

This actually reveals an interesting division of thinking between Extremos and, well, non-Extremos. When most of us talk about "design" we are referring (albeit implicitly) to the design process, and when we talk about "updating the

---

12. Rational's Object Technology User Group, http://www.rational.com/support/usergroups/rose/otug.jsp.
13. Note, that does *not* mean less unit testing—we just rely on them less!

design" we are talking about updating the design documentation. Extremo philosophy, however, is that the "design" is inherent in whatever structure has been produced—although it can't be touched, it's just there, like the ether. Therefore, the code is the design; therefore, because code is the end-product, anything besides code, such as design documentation, is optional.

Should we allow this piece of logic to dictate the amount of design *documentation* that we write and maintain? The following quote is from Alan Cooper (who has taken a relatively "anti-XP" stance in the past):

> *"When the words are fuzzy, the programmers reflexively retreat to the most precise method of articulation available: source code. Although there is nothing more precise than code, there is also nothing more permanent or resistant to change. So the situation frequently crops up where nomenclature confusion causes programmers to begin coding prematurely, and that code becomes the de facto design, regardless of its appropriateness or correctness."[14]*

Hmm . . . maybe the code really *is* the design.

Of course, Cooper is actually describing what happens in a project with inadequate design documentation. If the documentation is no good, we have to rely on the code.

So the argument in XP that we should use the code as the design documentation because the documentation is no good is, frankly, circular.

We also quote Alan Cooper in Chapter 15 regarding Interaction Design (i.e., getting the product design right before coding—a discipline that is sorely missing from XP).

Design documentation gives us something that source code can't: an abstraction of the design, a view from above rather than right down in the gutter. Simply asserting that "the code is the design" isn't enough. There are design idioms, intentions, and strategies that are all essential parts of design and architecture. The source code is just a snapshot of the architectural roadmap at any one time. It is completely lacking an extra dimension, which we would normally see captured in the architecture document.

---

14. Alan Cooper, *The Inmates Are Running the Asylum: Why High Tech Products Drive Us Crazy and How to Restore the Sanity* (Indianapolis, IN: Sams Publishing, 1999), p. 186.

We discuss design documentation in more detail in Chapter 7.

Is Up-Front Design Really a Bad Thing?

Up-front design is synonymous with thinking ahead.

We are not suggesting that the entire design for a large project should be carried out up front to the last detail, waterfall-style, but certainly a high-level technical architecture is essential to start with. Then (as the project is divided up into parallel teams and staged deliveries), more detailed (lower level) designs can be produced up front for each iteration.

Basically, the more up-front design, the better (well, at least until you have "enough"), but there is a trade-off between the benefits and just making some progress with the coding. There is a cutoff point for design, a law of diminishing returns. However, due to its LackOfUpfrontDesign (LOUD), it is a point that XP falls way short of.

In his article "XP Essentials: Emergent Design," Ron Jeffries writes:

> *"There are many well-known modeling and design techniques that can be used to bring about a 'good design'. An incremental process may limit the applicability of these techniques, which are most powerful when applied and committed to 'up front'."*[15]

When you take the time to think a design through and produce a class model, something special happens. The design becomes sane and well thought out, before any code has been written. It is well worth this relatively small investment in time, as the payoff is huge.

What are the benefits of doing an up-front design? Here are some, in no particular order:

- It provides design clarity.

- It provides a breathing space to let ideas gestate and develop before you risk getting bogged down in code.

- It is autodocumenting (the design is also the documentation).[16]

- Teams can move much faster because there is no dependent code yet.

---

15. Ron Jeffries, "Essential XP: Emergent Design," http://www.xprogramming.com/xpmag/expEmergentDesign.htm, October 21, 2001.

16. This is also an XP practice—the source is self-documenting, so design = source code = documentation. When all you've got is a hammer. . . .

- The interfaces are defined early on, which helps teams to work in parallel.

- Changing a class model is much easier than making the same change in code, because the class model is (or *should* be!) abstracted out to show only the detail that is relevant to the design.

- It makes subsequent changes easier (design diagrams give the team a high-level view of the design—for example, a logical view that is separate from specific implementation details).

- Impact analysis is easier, because the design view gives the team a bigger picture of the dependencies between modules.

- It provides a reference point to make sure the code matches the design (i.e., an essential part of testing).

- It forms a contract. A contract sets expectations. You know when you've finished. You know when you'll get paid. You know when it works.

Designing and programming are part of an iterative process. Even with the most well-realized and thought-out design, programming will reveal some areas where the design can be improved or needs to be changed. Thus, we need to go back to the design, make some changes, and then reflect the changes in the code.

More often than not, the process (having discovered a gap in the design) ends up being

1. Code the solution.

2. Update the design retrospectively.

This is partly why XP forgoes design and gets straight to the coding perhaps sooner than it should. The Extremos' reasoning is that it takes longer to maintain a class model (or other design documentation) in addition to the code than simply maintaining the code.

This is a spurious argument, however, as it really doesn't take long to update the design in tandem with the code, especially given the "round-trip" capability of tools such as Together ControlCenter.

 In much the same way that refactoring is a concurrent process in XP, keeping the design documentation up-to-date can also be treated as a concurrent process, albeit with significantly less overhead than refactoring (for starters, typically one person at a time can keep the design documentation up-to-date, whereas in XP the whole team must constantly refactor).

The benefits that you get from a design model also massively outweigh the small overhead involved in maintaining it, especially if you follow some of the *Agile Modeling* principles such as "Model with a Purpose" and "Travel Light."

XP also forgoes up-front design on the basis that the design would be full of gaps anyway, and these are only revealed when you start coding. Sometimes this is the case, but as with many things in life, there are "degrees of." In particular, the extent to which coding reveals gaps in the design depends on how much experience the designer has had with this type of project or the technology being used.

For many projects, the design will follow a well-trodden path. For example, J2EE projects use tried and tested design patterns and often become a "paint-by-numbers" process. Web sites such as TheServerSide.com offer a multitude of "best practice" design patterns that you can pick off the virtual shelf and apply to your own design. With such projects, it is becoming increasingly rare that a new type of wheel needs to be invented every time.

Of course, this is not always the case. There is invariably *some* aspect of a project for which there is a paucity of prior experience. Just the amount varies. In such cases, testing and consolidating the design early through prototyping is essential.

How Much Up-Front Design Is Enough?

The criticism most often associated with up-front design is that the designers quickly get bogged down in design issues. This prevents the team from moving forward—in other words, the team gets a nasty case of *analysis paralysis*. In fact, analysis paralysis (where the team is stuck in neutral, and no code is even in sight of being written) is a key sign that the team is doing *too much* up-front design.

So, how much up-front design is enough? Or, to put the question another way, what's the minimal amount of design that is sufficient to "get it right" while still avoiding analysis paralysis?

Doug has spent a large portion of the last 10 years answering this very question, and he has taken the trouble to write two books that focus on getting through analysis and design without catching a case of analysis paralysis. So we're going to borrow from that work here to answer this question.

Where XP is driven by "stories," the ICONIX Process[17] is driven by "scenarios" (aka use cases). The difference starts there, because a properly written use-case scenario details both the normal and exceptional behavior of the system from the user's perspective. XPers leap into coding for the sunny-day scenario with loud cries of being "test driven" because they're writing unit tests

---

17. Doug Rosenberg and Kendall Scott, *Use Case Driven Object Modeling with UML: A Practical Approach* (New York, NY: Addison-Wesley, 1999).

for the methods they need "right now" while they're coding the simplest thing that can possibly work. In XP it's the customer who gets to worry about the rainy-day scenarios. In the ICONIX Process, the development team needs to take responsibility for making sure that some exceptional bit of behavior doesn't break the system. This is a *huge* difference.

One of the issues with design (either up-front or leap-ahead) is that it's tempting to allocate behaviors to objects (classes) before the objects have been identified. Doing so can (and often does) lead to analysis paralysis, as making these decisions can require careful thought. If the decisions aren't made with careful thought, the result is a bad factoring (allocation of operations to classes) of the design, and the result of this is Constant Refactoring After Programming. The irony is that in leaping ahead to behavior allocation, the intention would obviously have been to get a head start—to go straight to detailed design (or "coding" in XP) and identify objects as you go along. Of course, XP adds fuel to the fire by *encouraging* this approach.

Simply doing some preliminary design work (domain modeling, robustness analysis) is very effective for identifying pretty much all of the objects that the system will use.

So that tells us how to recognize when to do *more* up-front design (in this case, preliminary design) to save time and avoid analysis paralysis. This also gives us the vital clue as to *how to know when we have done **enough** up-front design*. The answer is that we've identified all the classes and all the "important" methods on each class.

In the ICONIX Process, the Critical Design Review (CDR) stage tells us whether or not the design is complete:

> *"Before you commence CDR, you need to make sure that you have sequence diagrams for all of the use cases for which you're going to deliver code in the current release. You can't be sure that you've found all of the responsibilities for each of your objects unless you've drawn sequence diagrams for all of your basic courses and all of your alternate courses for all of your use cases. Taken together, these diagrams form the core of your dynamic model, which should now show the behavior of your system at runtime, including how the system will accomplish that behavior, in great detail."*[18]

This is, of course, a serious amount of design detail, but we're talking here about the final part of the design in a process that streamlines the path from use cases to detailed design and concentrates on getting the design right. Effectively getting this amount of up-front thought in the design, and having that design

---

18. Doug Rosenberg and Kendall Scott, *Applying Use Case Driven Object Modeling With UML* (New York, NY: Addison-Wesley, 2001), p. 108.

reviewed by the senior developers before code, saves *huge* amounts of time-consuming refactoring after you've started coding for this iteration.

The key is to know what parts of the design to concentrate on in detail and, more important, which parts can be safely economized on, so that you aren't storing up trouble for later.

The book *Agile Modeling* also offers useful guidance on the subject, for example (describing the Agile Modeling [AM] core principle "Model with a Purpose"):

> *"If you cannot identify why and for whom you are creating a model, then why are you bothering to work on it at all? Many developers worry about whether their artifacts—such as models, source code, or documents—are detailed enough or if they are too detailed, or similarly if they are sufficiently accurate. What they're not doing is stepping back and asking why they're creating the artifact in the first place and whom are they creating it for."[19]*

> *We provide more advice on the subject in the section "Use Up-Front Design to Enhance Agility" in Chapter 13.*

Refactoring with an Installed User Base

How do you refactor code once the system has an installed user base? Answer: With difficulty (as we explain in this section).

XP makes the correct assumption that we want to get the product into the hands of the users as soon as we possibly can. However, the Extremos' idea of "as soon as possible" is quite different from ours, as this quote from *Extreme Programming Explained* indicates:

> *"Most projects seem to have exactly the opposite strategy. The thinking seems to go, 'As soon as the system is in production, you can no longer make "interesting" changes, so keep the system in development as long as possible.' This is exactly backwards...."[20]*

19. Scott W. Ambler, *Agile Modeling: Effective Practices for eXtreme Programming and the Unified Process* (New York, NY: John Wiley & Sons, 2002), p. 31.

20. Kent Beck, *Extreme Programming Explained: Embrace Change* (New York, NY: Addison-Wesley, 2000), p. 32.

Keeping code in development for as long as possible has its own set of problems (lack of early feedback from the customer and "big-bang delivery" are two of the worst). However, releasing code to the users as soon as possible is really the other extreme, equally undesirable, and brings with it its own particular set of problems. Yet this is what XP tells us to do:

"You are going to have to live with supporting production and developing new functionality simultaneously. Better to get used to juggling production and development sooner rather than later."[21]

All Maintenance, All the Time

The problem with releasing code too early (done the XP way) is that the design is likely to be nowhere near finished. Say the users are given "production-ready" code after just 3 weeks of the project's inception. On the surface, this seems great: The users can get productive straightaway, even though the initial set of functionality is probably quite small. However, the whole point of XP is that the design gets refactored as you go along. The module that was released after the first 3 weeks was designed purely to facilitate the tiny amount of functionality that gets unleashed along with it.

Consider that the final release, in about a year's time, will be a panther (not literally, of course). The first 3-week release would have been little more than a mouse in comparison. There is clearly still a serious amount of design work to be done. In a year's time, it's probable that none of the first 3 weeks' worth of code will still exist in the live system.

 Typical problems with refactoring live code are as follows:

- The product needs to be reinstalled or "patched" (although a "live update" mechanism, such as that offered by NetBeans and other application frameworks, makes this less of a problem).

- The product needs to be regression tested (unit tests should handle this, but the fact that a live system is being regression tested means that the unit tests are being relied upon even more heavily than before—Fangs, the slippery-slope serpent, just got venomous).

- The users may need to be retrained if the user interface (UI) has changed (a likely prospect, because the UI design will be evolving equally as much as the code design). See the next section, "Annoying the Users: Refactoring a Live User Interface."

---

21. Ibid., p. 32. Also see the "sheer thrill" quote in the section "The Perpetual Coding Machine (Embracing Change)" in Chapter 13 of this book.

- The database contains live data, therefore any changes to the database structure involve writing an update script that must be fully tested on a development database and then run on the customer installation. We discuss this shortly, in the section "Really Annoying the Users: Corrupting Their Live Data."

- User manuals and/or help screens (if there are any) may need to be updated.

Are the XP practices really sufficient to refactor live production code from a mouse to a panther, without breaking the user experience or corrupting the data? Possibly, with creativity and perspicacity, and lots of unfailing hard work to keep the snakes from unraveling.

But there is a better way. . . .

 An easier approach is to spend more time up front on the architecture and design (doing both design modeling and prototyping). Try to stabilize the internal design as much as possible before any production code gets released to the customer, and employ a professional interaction designer to spend time with the users to get the UI right from the start. Even a few extra weeks spent doing this can make all the difference. This doesn't mean that the entire design has to be implemented in code before anything gets released. The code can still be developed and released in small increments of 2 to 3 weeks, but the time spent getting the design right up front stabilizes it considerably, so that much less refactoring needs to be done on installed code.

 We discuss this refactored approach in more detail in Chapter 15. Also see Chapter 12 for a discussion of early prototyping versus XP's emergent design approach.

The recent industry spotlight on XP and agile methods has created an emphasis on refactoring existing code: jumping into code without spending enough time getting the design right first, and then fixing it up later. The resultant "common wisdom" that is beginning to emerge is that it isn't possible to get the design right before you begin writing production code. However, nothing could be more wrong. There are tried and trusted logical design processes that have been around for years and that have been proven to work on countless numbers of successful projects.

Annoying the Users: Refactoring a Live User Interface

 Refactoring of the UI isn't something that has really been addressed by the Extremos. In an evolving product, however, the UI design is equally as dynamic and volatile as the code design.

When a new version of a system is delivered, end users frequently complain about the changing UI. The problem is multiplied with an incrementally delivered system, simply because there are so many new versions (one every few weeks). Just when the users get used to doing things one way, everything is moved around to accommodate a change or addition in functionality. For example, a Tools drop-down menu might be added to house the increasing number of system tools that until then were located in various ad hoc parts of the system (which made sense at the time for each individual tool). The trouble is, the users will have grown used to going to those ad hoc parts of the system to achieve their tasks. People are creatures of habit. When it comes to such day-to-day routines as using the computer system at work, they resist change.

UI improvement of the type described should not be avoided if there is a chance to improve the user experience; but the same users that you are trying so hard to please will invariably be annoyed when things change. In fact, continually changing the user interface doesn't just annoy the users, it can also be expensive if it involves retraining or a "settling-in" period as the users grow accustomed to the new layout.

UI refactoring is inevitable and necessary in an evolving system. That's why it pays to at least try to get it right early on, so that the amount of change to the live system's UI is minimal. This means spending a little extra time up-front thinking about the user experience, not just for the tasks that are implemented during the first three weeks, but the sort of tasks they will be performing in six months to a year's time.

We mentioned earlier on (and also revisit in more detail in Chapter 15) that it is well worth employing an experienced interaction designer (i.e., someone who designs user interfaces for a living). Generally, programmers (myself included) are not the best people to design user interfaces, because they think in terms of the solution, not the user's goals. Similarly, users are not the best people to design user interfaces, because they have neither the experience nor the training. Conversely, an interaction designer—a good one, of course—can get the user interface right, because she knows what makes a good user interface, and understands the user's goals probably better than the users. Because the product is essentially driven by its required behavior, getting the interaction design right early on can drastically reduce the amount of *internal* redesign (hence refactoring of code) needed later.

Really Annoying the Users: Corrupting Their Live Data

 Most business applications use a database. However, databases are also a recognized problem area for refactoring.[22] Using emergent design, it's rare that a system will start out with a complete database,

---

22. Martin Fowler, op. cit., p. 63.

with all tables and relationships even identified, let alone fleshed out. The problem is also intensified by XP's emphasis on short (2 to 3 week) iterations.

Refactoring Live Data

As the design evolves, the database design will need to be refactored almost as much as the code design. In XP, the YAGNI principle applies equally to the database design as it does to the code. Therefore, database tables will be added, removed, merged, and separated; relationships will change from one-to-many to one-to-one and back again; constraints will be added and removed; data types will be changed; and enumerated types will be added, extended, and turned into dedicated lookup tables as their complexity increases. It's a process that every database design goes through, until the ideal design for the complete system is reached.

And all of this will be taking place on live data. This is something that the Extremos expect and in fact encourage (see http://martinfowler.com/articles/evodb.html).

This means that for every database change, you'll need to write a script that updates the user's database, migrates data between tables, changes data types, introduces new constraints and "massages" the existing data to fit, and so on. Each script will also need to be thoroughly tested before it's run on the live system. The only way to really prove that the script works is to get hold of a copy of the customer's entire production database, but this isn't always possible (for either technical or political reasons).

And, of course, all users will need to log out while the update script is run. That could mean regular disruption every couple of weeks or so. (Of course, your team could update the system in the middle of the night, but then it breaks the XP rule of going home at 5:00 PM.)

Voice of eXPerience: Refactoring the Database
by Robin Sharp

The following is a description of database refactoring hell.

Database change was constant. We did releases every week, and for most releases, we had at least one migration script to run. The database was never stable enough to refactor as a whole. The whole thing was aggravated by not having an up-front object/relational design scoped for each major release. It was like being forced to make it up as we went along, even though we were capable of producing a better design.

Relational databases demand conformant relational models, and we couldn't deliver that. The DBAs lost confidence in the developers and spent most of their time tuning queries to get any sort of performance.

We also did evolutionary database design. If you changed the database, you had to write a migration script. We each had our own development database. It worked okay-ish, but I guess you would soon run into license issues (i.e., very expensive). Because we each had our own database, we also had CPU issues, which slowed dev performance.

You could maybe get around this by having many database schemas on one server—but again, there would be licensing issues, plus some serious admin issues, I would think.

I would also have liked snapshots of old databases for bug hunting and defect tracking (but some databases got very large and we couldn't simply load old databases up).

In many cases, it's hard to see how you can avoid this.

Shielding the Code from Change

A common problem is when database access code is tightly coupled to the database design. The result is that making changes to the database means making changes to the source code. This is a highly problematic aspect of refactoring an emergent design.

Normally, the solution is to create a layer of abstraction between the code and the database: business objects. These business objects encapsulate the database design, so that the client code doesn't need to care about the structure of the database or implementation details of the database access code. Instead, it just calls the interface of each business object, which exposes database-agnostic methods such as "findCustomersByZipCode".

The code can be further shielded by not basing the object model directly on the database model (as described in the article "Why Data Models Shouldn't Drive Object Models [And Vice Versa]"[23] by Scott Ambler).

Some database changes are more costly than others. For example, simply adding a column or a new table won't affect existing code. However, changing existing metadata (which Fowler describes as "destructive changes"[24]) requires a stringent and time-consuming refactoring process.

Taking the refactoring approach for such a change is definitely less risky than simply making the change without any safety nets, but it's less risky again to concentrate on getting the design right as early as possible (ideally, by following a logical design methodology that guides the programmer into making good design decisions).

---

23. Scott Ambler, "Why Data Models Shouldn't Drive Object Models (And Vice Versa),"
    http://www.agiledata.org/essays/drivingForces.html, 2003.

24. Martin Fowler and Pramod Sadalage, "Evolutionary Database Design,"
    http://martinfowler.com/articles/evodb.html.

Having said that, XP's approach of planning for change is worth keeping in mind. However, we prefer to *manage* change rather than embrace change.

We discuss managing change (over embracing change) further in Chapters 13 and 15.

How Simple Is Simple Enough?

The problem in XP-land is that adding extra layers of code is considered to be extra complication: We are adding unnecessary code "just in case" we need to make a change later on. Having an extra layer of code is not the "simplest thing that could possibly work," and yet paradoxically it *is* the simplest solution to the problem (considering that the problem is not just about here and now, but also about how to keep the code simple in the long term).

Conversely, adding a layer of indirection is sometimes precisely what you don't want to do. A layer of indirection adds value if it ultimately simplifies the code; otherwise, it simply adds complexity without really giving you anything back. One of the keys to effective software design is learning to tell the difference. In this regard, we actually agree with the Extremos: The code should be made as simple as possible and no simpler.

Where we part company, however, is in the Extremo approach of making code as simple as possible for the current 1-week iteration, then redesigning it the following week, and so on.

More about this "emergent design" approach in Chapter 12.

Enter the Fang

The constant refactoring "snake" is driven by these issues:

- Refactoring is *not* inexpensive.

- Refactoring is time consuming.

- Criteria for when to stop refactoring are not well defined.

- Releasing code prematurely to the users puts you in "all maintenance, all the time" mode.

- "If it ain't broke, don't fix it" is still good advice.

- Refactoring of databases is problematic (especially for live databases that must run 24/7).

- Refactoring of UIs on live production software is problematic.

Pretending that refactoring is neither expensive nor time consuming, for example, places greater stress on the other XP practices to perform in order to keep the circle of snakes from unraveling.

LackOfUpfrontDesign (LOUD) leads to Constant Refactoring After Programming, which explains why SoftwareIsNeverDone in XP.

Refactoring Defanged

Knowing when to stop refactoring is critical to keeping the software on schedule. XP recommends looking for areas of problem code and refactoring whenever you see such areas. With a detailed architectural model, however, it's possible to be more selective and only refactor the areas that are still being built or have dependent code still to be built. Tracking defects and identifying defect hot spots in the system can also help to identify which areas need the most refactoring.

We cover management of refactoring in "Embrace Rampant Scope Creep Regularly" in Chapter 11.

Although refactoring is useful, designing the system up front using proven design techniques massively reduces the amount of refactoring that's needed later. Effective requirements elicitation reduces "requirements churn," which in turn reduces the amount of redesign that will be needed.

Hiring a professional interaction designer early in the project can help to reduce the amount of UI refactoring necessary, which in turn reduces the amount of user retraining needed every time a new release goes out the door.

Summary

In this chapter, we looked at refactoring and examined how it is applied in XP. Even outside XP, refactoring is a useful tool. Inside XP, refactoring is an integral part of emergent design.

We explore refactoring as used in emergent design in Chapter 12.

Refactoring by itself is useful for correcting or improving a design, though constant refactoring is expensive. Refactoring a database is even more expensive, because the database tends to drive the entire application (though the code can be shielded to an extent). Recognizing this fact is an important first step toward recognizing the importance of spending extra time trying to get the design right (particularly the database design) up front.

One of the reasons why refactoring and emergent design play such a large part in XP is that the project is designed only for the current iteration. Any attempt to design ahead is met with a cry of "YAGNI!"

In each iteration, the functionality to be added is defined by user stories, which we cover in the next chapter.

CHAPTER 10

User Stories and Acceptance Tests

Code Together
(Sing to the tune of "Come Together" by The Beatles)

You got no requirements
You got no schedules
You got pair programmers
You got lots of Pepsi
You got goal donors tellin' you stories
One thing I can tell you is you can't code in threes
Code together
Right now
With XP

You got ree-factoring
You got unit testing
You got tasty snack food
You got no documentation
You got index cards up to your knees
Go ahead and change that 'cause you know change is free
Code together
Right now
With XP

"XP prefers that requirements be documented in terms of executable acceptance tests. XP prefers that design be documented by the code."[1]

—Robert C. Martin

"If you lose a card, and if the customer does not detect that loss, then the card wasn't very important. If, however, at an interaction planning meeting, the customer says: 'Hay [sic], where's that card about blah, blah, blah', you'll find it easy to recreate."[2]

—Robert C. Martin

User stories are, by their nature, transitory artifacts. They contain very little detail. The true tests of inclusion of a requirement in the production code are the *acceptance tests* (an automated method of "proving with code" that each user story has been implemented).

The stories themselves are simply placeholders—promises for future conversations with the on-site customer. That is to say, they really don't contain a lot of detail (generally just one or two brief sentences). They are memory joggers and a lightweight tool to help with the planning game rather than a specification.

In this chapter we look at user stories and acceptance tests together, because they're really two sides of the same coin.

Round and Round the Story Goes

On the OTUG discussion forum, Robert C. Martin wrote the following:

"XP prefers that requirements be documented in terms of executable acceptance tests. XP prefers that design be documented by the code."[3]

So the code is the design and the tests are the analysis. Therefore, because you're coding and testing the whole time, you are by definition doing analysis and design all along. Circular, but brilliant nonetheless.

1. Robert C. Martin posting to OTUG (http://www.rational.com), subject: "<<include>> or <<extend>> 'Just Say No'," October 5, 2000.
2. Robert C. Martin posting to the newsgroup comp.software.extreme-programming, subject: "The Case against XP," January 31, 2002.
3. Robert C. Martin posting to OTUG, op. cit.

Perhaps XP doesn't go far enough. Catchy slogans and circular reasoning could be used to sell pretty much anything. Here are some we prepared earlier:

- **"The Java bytecode IS the requirements."** Note that they are both concise and executable!

- **"The debugger IS the documentation."** Who needs anything else? All clients should know how to use the debugger.

- **"Do Software Quality Assurance by Smelling the Code."** Oops, that one isn't ours—can't take credit for it.

- **"Rip-up, re-write, re-code, re-test, re-factor, realize its a rat's nest, resign."** Kind of catchy, isn't it?

Tell Me a Story, Daddy

This definition of user stories is given by Ron Jeffries:[4]

> *"A UserStory is a story, told by the user, specifying how the system is supposed to work, written on a card, and of a complexity permitting estimation of how long it will take to implement. The UserStory promises as much subsequent conversation as necessary to fill in the details of what is wanted. The cards themselves are used as tokens in the planning process after assessment of business value and [possibly] risk. The customer prioritizes the stories and schedules them for implementation."*

Therefore, a "good" user story is one that can be estimated, prioritized, implemented, and tested. Often, a single user story must be broken down into smaller stories in order to fulfill these criteria.

User stories in XP double as a form of task list (see Figure 10-1). (In fact, the stories themselves are divided into smaller, piecemeal tasks that are easier to allocate and estimate.) The customer decides which stories will be in the next iteration. Then the programmers sign up for specific tasks, depending on which stories interest them the most, which tasks they feel the most technically able to implement, and so on.

The possible scope of any user story is pretty much wide open. If you can fit it on a story card, then it's a user story. However, to be a "good" user story, it must conform to the criteria that we describe later in this chapter—in particular, it must be testable and estimable (i.e., you should be able to predict how long it would take a programmer to code on an "ideal" day). Thus, a user story may define either functional or nonfunctional requirements (as long as they can be tested).

---

4. Ron Jeffries posting to the C2 Wiki page User Story, http://c2.com/cgi/wiki?UserStory.

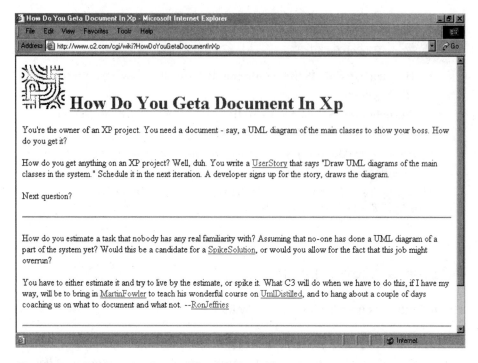

Figure 10-1. User stories form a list of deliverables

On the Extreme Programming discussion group on Yahoo, Ron Jeffries describes the fundamentals of a user story as follows:

> *"Every function that you are going to program needs to be /covered/ by a story. Remember that a story is*
>
> *Card—planning token for estimating and scheduling*
>
> *Conversation—transmission of the understanding of what has to be done for this story*
>
> *Confirmation—customer test showing that the functionality for the story is working"*[5]

In the same message, he adds

> *"The examples in XP Installed are mostly /larger/ than what I would do now. Your stories only need to communicate between you and your customer."*

5. Ron Jeffries posting to the Yahoo group Extreme Programming, http://groups.yahoo.com/group/extremeprogramming/message/68531, subject: "[XP] Stories," January 10, 2003.

This drives home a couple of issues:

- Individual user stories are very, very small. They aren't intended to convey very much themselves; they are memory joggers, nothing more.

- The detail of the user story is in the verbal conversation held with the customer (i.e., it's not written down, except in the acceptance tests).

The quote from Robert C. Martin at the start of this chapter was in response to somebody's suggestion that it might be prudent to use a program to store your user stories, because you *cannot* afford to lose them. Martin's response began, "Yes, you can."

We humbly suggest that this is another risk-increasing aspect of XP. In our projects, it has never been "okay" to lose a requirement or to hope that if it's been forgotten that it wasn't too important. Fingers crossed, eh?

It's safe to say that if your project is for a hospital system that tracks patients' medical records, you wouldn't take this approach. Every user story, every requirement, will have gone in there for a reason. It isn't sufficient to simply say, "Let's hope that none of that stuff we forgot was important." There needs to be a catchment system, some form of contingency, to ensure that nothing is missed, and that if a user story is left out, it's for the right reasons (i.e., the customer decided to leave it out, he didn't simply forget about it).

Another way to phrase this is, *If your project is really important, you wouldn't follow the Extremo advice of it being okay to lose written requirements.*

Symbolic of a Greater Problem

We revisit the "losing a story card" issue several times in this book. You'd be forgiven for wondering why we keep returning to it!

The issue isn't so much with the "dangers" associated with losing a stack of vague, loosely worded story cards—the issue is that this particular practice really sums up the XP attitude to contingency. It's symbolic (if you will) of the cowboy philosophy that's woven throughout XP: It's "okay" to lose story cards because they probably didn't matter. In a similar manner, it's "okay" not to write things down in detail because enough people should be able to remember, it's "okay" not to elicit the requirements in detail because we can just ask the customer as we go along, it's "okay" not to design for the future because we can just change the design when we get there, and so on.

Being Negative

On the C2 Wiki site, there has been some discussion over what really constitutes a user story. For example, can a user story be written in the negative, as follows:

"The importing of invoices shall not corrupt the database."

This example cannot reasonably be "implemented" by a programmer, so it would need to be broken down into more user stories, which are likely to be written in the positive:

"The invoice importation process will include a data validation stage, which prevents incorrect or corrupting data from being written to the database."

"Any data written to the database in multiple writes will use transactions, so that the database is never in an incomplete state."

In the non-XP world, high-level requirements can still be written in the negative ("The user shall not be allowed to cause a system meltdown"), so the customer's actual requirements may still be captured in a style and format that's natural for the customer, without having to translate them into something more suited to developers.

If, in addition, the system functionality is captured as behavioral requirements (aka use cases), then the problem wouldn't arise. It should be possible to implement each and every use case because there's a clear and logical path from use cases to code.

We discuss this logical design process in Chapter 8.

User Stories vs. Use Cases

"Special note on Listening: we do listening in two ways:

UserStories. *(Similar to 'use cases'.) On cards, our customers write stories describing how something is supposed to work. A story might say 'An employee making $10 an hour works four hours of overtime on Friday and two on Sunday. She should receive $60 for the Friday overtime and $40 for Sunday.' We have hundreds of cards describing the product.*

Acceptance Tests. *These are typically single use cases with expected answers provided by the customer."*[6]

—Ron Jeffries

---

6. Ron Jeffries posting to the C2 Wiki page Extreme Programming, http://c2.com/cgi/wiki?ExtremeProgramming.

User stories are often compared with use cases, partly because they have similar names, but ultimately because they're there to achieve the same thing: Define the system requirements in terms of what the users do. However, as we explore in this section, the similarities pretty much end there.

Jeffries' comparison of user stories with use cases is quite erroneous, because use cases represent only behavioral requirements, which is what you'd think a user story would be. Unfortunately, user stories aren't defined that tightly. User stories are vaguely defined as "whatever notes you make on the index card." That can include behavior requirements, functional requirements, and just about anything else you can think of, such as requests for documentation.

Stories are often equated with use cases (even by Mr. Jeffries, as in the previous quote). So let's compare the two (later we compare stories with requirements).

The Use Case

Before we get started comparing user stories with use cases, let's quickly define what a use case is, and then describe how it's used in "use case–driven" development.

A *use case* defines discrete system behavior of value to a particular actor (user role). The best use cases are those written in active voice, in present tense, in terms of user action/system response ("the user does this; the system responds by doing that"), and unambiguously using the terms defined in an accompanying glossary or domain model.

A single project may have hundreds of use cases defined. Because the use case defines external system behavior (as observed by the user), it doesn't make inroads into design. In other words, it defines the "what" of a system (as in, what do we want this system to do?) rather than the "how" (as in, how shall it do it?).

A *use case scenario* is a specific example—an instance of a use case. The *sunny-day* scenario is the normal case: What happens if the user does exactly what is expected and completes the transaction? The *rainy-day* scenarios (of which there are usually many) are variations on the use case (e.g., the user tries to perform a task for which she isn't authorized).

What Is Use Case–Driven Development?

Although it's not our purpose to explain use case–driven development completely in this book (there are already a couple of pretty good books on the topic[7]), it's at least worth explaining to the level of detail that it can be compared to the XP approach.

In use case–driven development, the major steps for designing a scenario are as follows:

1. Write a couple of paragraphs of English that explain the behavior, including both sunny-day and rainy-day (exceptional) usage paths.

2. Identify the objects that will participate in the scenario.

3. Assign responsibility for specific operations to the appropriate classes.

4. Code it.

5. Test it.

In XP, as in use case–driven development, programmers are working on one story (loosely speaking, analogous to a use case scenario—at least it might be, depending on the kind of story you've got). In XP, you'll also identify participating objects and assign responsibility for operations to classes, but you do all this as the code is being written. And in XP, those nasty special cases (exceptional behavior) can be dealt with by saying YAGNI and DTSTTCPW. So it *looks* like you're getting done real fast, initially. But that's because you've swept the problematic stuff under the rug.

For an example of this phenomenon in action, see the section "Generate a Quick Illusion of Success" in Chapter 2.

The programmers write some tests for each operation being coded and then code it. The overall responsibility for making sure all the exceptional conditions from a system usage standpoint are handled in acceptance testing—that is to say, they are pushed off to the customer.

In use case–driven development, the use case text is written in the context of a domain model, which is something like a combination of XP's metaphor and an early stab at a core object model/architecture, focused on the problem domain. And, in use case–driven development, the object model is evolved in the abstract for a group of scenarios (whatever is in your current iteration) in parallel, before

---

7. Doug Rosenberg and Kendall Scott, *Use Case Driven Object Modeling with UML: A Practical Approach* (New York, NY: Addison-Wesley, 1999). Also, Doug Rosenberg and Kendall Scott, *Applying Use Case Driven Object Modeling with UML* (New York, NY: Addison-Wesley, 2001).

the classes are committed to code. And this object model *rigorously* takes into account the need to handle exceptional behavior. And the object model and use case model are *reviewable* by the team before anything is committed to code. This review process can catch oodles of errors that otherwise have to be addressed by Constant Refactoring After Programming.

Note that this minimalist style of use case–driven development is not BDUF. It is design for however many scenarios are in the build that you are working on. And it is done at a very similar granularity to stories—a two-paragraph use case would fit nicely on an index card. It is, however, done within the context of a larger object model, and the use cases are captured in writing, so they are a much more permanent record of what the system has to do than are "orally documented" stories. The advantages are numerous and include the following:

- Unambiguous written understanding of the system behavior.

- Behavior requirements reviewed by the team.

- Evolution of the object model for all scenarios in the current iteration.

- Evolved object model reviewed by the team.

- Clean allocation of behavior (functions to classes).

- Review of behavior allocation by the team before coding.

- No "extra work" to produce documentation, because use case descriptions, class diagrams, and sequence diagrams are the natural work products.

- No big nasty surprises waiting because the exceptional behavior has been overlooked.

- Working with an electronic use case model that can be accessed by the entire team helps to develop a shared sense of the "big picture"—much more effectively, we suggest, than relying on constantly rotating pair programmers. Heck, people could even gain this understanding while sitting at their nice quiet desk in their own office.

Doing the proper amount of up-front design lets us write code "once and only once," and it's entirely feasible for programmers to be successful working alone because *it is much easier to write code to an unambiguous behavior spec within the context of a well-defined object model.*

Use Cases Are More Rigorous Than Stories

The rigor of anticipating rainy-day scenarios is one of the big differentiators between use cases and user stories. *User stories,* which can be pretty much anything you decide to write on a card, combined with YAGNI are very weak. Let's explore this in more detail.

In this quote from the C2 Wiki web, Alistair Cockburn describes user stories as "2-bit use cases":

> *"Think of a User Story as a Use Case at 2 bits of precision. Bit 1 of precision names the goal of the use case, Bit 2 adds the main scenario. Bit 3 adds the failure conditions, Bit 4 adds the failure actions. Bit 5 adds data description of the in/out data. I would put Catalysis at a 6th bit of precision, as they include a model also of the recipient of the message. In the CrystalMethodology family differently founded projects use use cases at different levels of precision. A methodologically light project uses User Stories, a methodologically heavier project uses Use Cases to 4 bits of precision, and Catalysis uses 6 bits of precision."[8]*

A user story, then, is roughly equivalent to a use case scenario (but without the failure conditions or failure actions—the rainy-day scenarios). The difference in rigor between use cases and user stories starts with the anticipation of exceptional usage paths in a well-written use case. The processes of story-driven development in XP and use case–driven development are parallel in some ways but have some very significant differences.

We'd like to suggest that Alistair's third and fourth bits of precision are incredibly important. What are the failure conditions (really, exceptional usage conditions), and how does the system respond to them? Sunny-day scenarios generally account for less than half of the behavior in any software system. Ignoring the rainy-day scenarios is one of the big factors that makes rapid prototyping rapid, and it also accounts for "doing the simplest thing that could possibly work" generating a quick illusion of success in XP projects.

Anticipating Failure Modes: *Not* the Simplest Thing That Could Possibly Work

To a certain degree, acceptance tests help to identify alternative cases by testing as many paths as possible through the system, including errors and failures.

Our feeling is that, although proving useful in other ways, acceptance tests capture the alternative paths in the wrong place. More precisely, the responsibility for catching these errors is shifted from the developers to the customer because

---

8. Alistair Cockburn posting to the C2 Wiki page User Story And Use Case Comparison, http://www.c2.com/cgi/wiki?UserStoryAndUseCaseComparison.

writing the acceptance tests is the customer's problem. So, by leaving the problems to be caught during acceptance testing, if a few slip through, that just means the customer wasn't doing his job! XP and the programmers are "clean." Also, of course, the alternative paths are caught at the test-driven design stage (aka coding), not before. This is an example of how XP blurs the distinction between requirements and design.

It needs to be obvious to everyone involved that all the alternative paths have been identified. The format typically used for automated tests doesn't really qualify. This is, of course, a matter of debate, depending on whether you feel the acceptance tests (even in supposedly "customer-friendly" spreadsheet form) are too technical to be classified as documented behavioral requirements.

User Stories vs. Requirements

Typically, *requirements* are more similar to user stories than are use cases. Use cases tend to flesh out requirements with a description of the system behavior needed to achieve specific requirements. Stories are defined amorphously so that they might resemble use cases, they might resemble requirements, or they might be something entirely different, such as requests for more donuts or requests to produce documentation. (We're sure this is an incredibly popular story, although it might explain why it's deemed okay to lose story cards: Customer writes documentation request story card, programmer doesn't feel like doing documentation and loses story card—no problem!)

We've compared stories with use cases in detail. Let's now compare stories with requirements.

The Requirement

Many a fat book has been written about the software requirement: what it is, what it isn't, what it used to be, what it is now, what it means to you, how big (or small) it is, how to measure it—not to mention all the different types of requirements.

For all the different (and often conflicting) definitions of the requirement, one fact (even in XP) stands tall and consistent: You need them, and lots of 'em (although in XP they aren't exactly defined in great detail, but we'll return to the XP world in just a minute . . .).

Requirements, if you're not doing XP, tend to be written in specifications (sometimes Word documents, sometimes via requirements management tools such as Requisite Pro or DOORS). The specification can then be baselined for specific releases and put within easy reach of everyone who needs to read it (e.g., on the project intranet [9]). The requirements tend to be individually numbered so that they can be tracked and easily referred to. Contrast this with XP, where they are handwritten notes jotted down on cards, which, we are told, it's okay to lose. Each requirement should also be clear, concise, and unambiguous. Writing good requirements isn't difficult; in fact, it's possible to write to a simple formula and end up with requirements that are indeed clear, concise, and unambiguous.[10]

Just as the plant and animal kingdoms are broadly divided, requirements can be divided into functional and nonfunctional requirements. From there, further classification is dependent on the type of project.

In XP (and agile methods in general), an important development is the recognition that not all requirements will be completely identified and detailed correctly right at the start of the project. Well, okay, we've known that has been the case all along, but now it's more acceptable—trendy, even—to embrace the fact, because XP tells us to "embrace change" and to welcome requirements creep even late in the project.

We discuss XP's approach to requirements creep in Chapter 13.

Our real point of concern, though, is that XP takes this whole thing too far, and—by making it socially acceptable to have incomplete requirements—may encourage[11] teams to embark upon the implementation of a project too early, because all the gaps can be filled in later (gaps in the requirements inevitably also mean big gaping holes in the design).

The hype behind XP has also overshadowed the fact that for the most part, it *is* actually possible to define most of your requirements early in the project and to get them pretty much right. A casual glance through the XP literature suggests that the Extremos fundamentally disagree with this premise. The XP philosophy is that spending lots of time analyzing requirements up front can lead to big delays and overdesign. It's strange, though, because our own experience has been that taking this "requirements up front" approach actually helps to bring projects in on time, clearly focused, and with just the right level of design. (We

---

9. A handy tip here is to make sure that everyone on the team has the Web page containing the requirements bookmarked in their Web browser. If they're using Internet Explorer (IE), the bookmark (sorry, Favorite) should be placed in the Links folder so that it's permanently visible on their toolbar.

10. Functional requirements documents are often referred to as *functional specifications.* If you want to know how to write functional specifications properly, refer to this short and pithy article (which also includes a very handy functional specification template) by Dino Fancellu: http://www.softwarereality.com/lifecycle/functionalspec.jsp.

11. Mr. Cynical says, "Absolutely does encourage and in fact ridicules any other approach."

do still advocate breaking a project into small iterations, though, to avoid the "big-bang delivery" problem and to shield the project from the forces of change by delivering working software in smaller increments.)

Agile methods, like any other set of tools, are appropriate to a given situation—the right tools for the right job. XP is often touted as being suited to projects with vague requirements. Vague, however, doesn't always mean that the requirements aren't known by anyone. It may simply be that they are vaguely defined (e.g., in brief one- or two-sentence user stories).

This is another circular argument behind XP. XP is supposedly suited to a project with vague requirements, but the requirements are vague (not written down in detail and agreed upon by all project stakeholders) because you're using XP.

Listening Without Preconceptions

Picture the scene: a gas-lit alley in 1888, with typical London smog swirling ominously around the pedestrians' chattering knees.

A horse-drawn carriage bearing the royal insignia clatters past, the horses' iron-clad hooves creating sparks against the smooth pebbly cobbles. A harassed-looking police constable makes his way on foot to the scene of a nearby murder. He is met by a wild-eyed "painted lady" who demands to know who might have attacked her colleague and whether the attacker is going to strike again anytime soon.

"I need to ask you some questions," the constable says to the woman, who has begun to calm down a little. "First of all, do you have any idea who might have done this?"

The woman pauses and then launches into an emotional tirade about how that should be the constable's job, surely, to find out and tell *her* who did this. Her harsh, uneducated East-End accent ricochets off a nearby railing, the sparks threatening to ignite the smog.

"That's hardly the way it works," the tired-sounding constable explains, and adds (in a completely inappropriate explanation given the situation), "You should think of me as a gestalt being, whose existence is driven only by the information given to me by street creatures such as yourself. I am a being that consists purely of information. I have no state or matter of my own. Now, I can solve this crime given the correct information, but all I do is collate whatever details are given to me—including, one hopes, the name of the killer. I can impose my own rules and behaviors upon the information, deriving and analyzing it using my own training and in the context of other information that other people have given to me. But I cannot add my own information to the mix, for I have none—and if I do have any, then it is my job to ignore it to the best of my abilities, such that I do not carry any misleading preconceptions about this crime or the situation herein, that may lead me erroneously to the wrong decision. Does that make sense to you now, my poor, sweet little street creature?"

The woman nods sagely and says, "I understand now, Constable. It is your job to ask questions, and to listen, and to reach a conclusion based upon the information given to you in the context of your investigation, and nothing else."

"That's right," the constable replies, sounding surprised.

How Are Vague Requirements Handled in a Non-XP Project?

"The UserStory promises as much subsequent conversation as necessary to fill in the details of what is wanted."[12]

In a non-XP project,[13] the whole attitude and approach to vague requirements is very different from an XP project. Partly this is due to the difference in documentation culture. Extremos see nothing inherently bad about the concept of oral documentation; hence, if something isn't written down, that doesn't mean (in their world) that it's vague or missing.

In a non-XP project, a vague requirement—that is, a requirement that hasn't been written down in sufficient detail to be clear and unambiguous—is seen as a danger signal that not enough thought has gone into it and it should be revisited at the earliest instance (particularly if it has already been factored into the project plan). A poorly defined requirement is usually a thinly disguised mass of additional requirements (rather like a warship hiding behind a small sandbank), all of which will impact the project timeline.

If we renounce the concept of fixed deadlines and chant "Software is never done!"[14] then this isn't a problem, but in most projects the management will want to know about this potentially huge delay as soon as possible.

How do you recognize a vague requirement? Well, the Extremos like to talk about "code smells," so (with heavy heart) we talk about requirement smells. Actually, let's not. Let's talk about "characteristics of vague requirements" instead—that's much more palatable!

One characteristic to look out for is the dreaded "for example." It's always good to clarify requirements with a concrete example to illustrate the point, but examples should never be used to actually define the requirement. Examples (of the "e.g." variety) tend to be incomplete lists, which imply any number of unstated requirements. Here's an example to illustrate the point:

---

12. Ron Jeffries posting to the C2 Wiki page User Story, op. cit.

13. There is an implicit assumption here that we are talking about *well-executed* non-XP projects. Our comments wouldn't hold true for bloated, waterfall-style, big-bang delivery projects, for example.

14. We'd like to suggest, if you decide to try this, that shaving your head and dancing on the sidewalk in long orange robes while tapping on tambourines is the most appropriate attire.

1.4.1.3. The product shall provide the ability to connect to different types of server, e.g. FTP, BACS, SAP, JDBC.

With such a requirement, there's no indication of whether the list of server types is complete or whether other types are implied. If some types have yet to be identified and will be added later, this should be stated explicitly.

Implementing each server connection will take additional effort, so each server example should really be a separate requirement that can be individually estimated. Connecting to a JDBC-compliant database would no doubt be pretty easy, but connecting to an unfamiliar server type could involve a steep learning curve.

Vague requirements can also be spotted if they're neither estimable nor provable—that is, it isn't possible to prove that the requirement has been fulfilled (this problem would also show up in XP, because it wouldn't be possible to write an acceptance test for an "unprovable" user story). So to its credit, XP actually does have a mechanism for detecting vague requirements that are neither estimable nor testable. (However, as we discussed earlier in the sidebar "Anticipating Failure Modes: *Not* the Simplest Thing That Could Possibly Work," XP's mechanism for tackling vague requirements isn't quite the same as defining detailed requirements in a customer-friendly language such as English.)

It isn't always the case that requirements are vague simply because they're badly written. Sometimes, a vague requirement is a symptom that the analyst isn't listening to the customer (we mean the real customer in this case) or the end users. Just like the harassed police constable in the sidebar, the information you gather for your project's requirements must be based not on your own preconceptions of what they "probably need," but on the actual information given to you from a variety of sources (and not just the painted ladies).

Similarly, a requirement is sometimes vague because it hasn't been thoroughly investigated. The answer to "What types of server should we connect to?" might be "*I* don't know!" This is the sort of situation that XP (and agile methods in general) attempt to solve. This is one of the agile goals of XP: to reduce the cost of adding new requirements later in the project.

 As we discuss in Chapter 15, it's possible to address and manage change in a more robust way than "simply" applying all the XP practices.

In XP, the user story lacks detail, and intentionally so. Estimating user stories accurately supposedly becomes a "knack" that's honed over the course of the project (so on the last day of the project the team gets *really* good at estimating stories!). The same problems that afflict vague requirements also apply to vague user stories: They can hide entire subsystems—months of work—in a single sentence or in a single "for example." This hidden functionality may be discovered only when it is time to flesh out the story in more detail with the promised conversation with the customer.

In theory this is okay because the project is embracing change. At the point when the required functionality is abruptly identified (to the sound of a collective *"Gulp!"* from around the table), the "new" functionality would be written as new stories and scheduled for a future iteration. This is fine for a project that's embracing change and plum proud of it, but in practice it sure makes a project difficult to plan.

Architecture-Shifting Requirements

It's usually the nonfunctional requirements that end up having the most impact on the architecture. For example, the user story "Must be able to handle up to 3,000 transactions per minute" might not be planned in until much later in the project, after a serious amount of code has been written.

Sometimes, identifying different types of requirement and classifying a set of requirements accordingly can help to establish the level of risk inherent in the project—that is, just how many architecture-shifting nonfunctional requirements are there? A little extra time spent on this can help with prioritization of requirements (or stories) by getting the high-risk requirements out of the way first.

Without this additional piece of analysis work, the customer would almost certainly prioritize the stories in a different order, so it's definitely worth giving her this extra piece of information so she can make the best possible decision.

"Documenting" Requirements As Acceptance Tests

A *requirement* is something that a system has to do. An *acceptance test* can verify whether a requirement is satisfied. And we applaud the effort to verify requirements with tests. But to equate tests with requirements is completely fallacious. Traffic laws exist to govern the behavior of drivers on the road. Police officers (traffic cops) enforce the traffic laws. But the traffic cop isn't the traffic law.

Trying to relate this to software, the first reason that comes to mind that exposes this fallacy is a very simple one: Requirements have to be something that can be understood by nonprogrammers. Customers, goal donors, gold owners, marketing folks—all of these people have to determine the required behavior of the system, and these requirements need to be reviewable by the folks that are responsible for them. XP makes the presumption that customers can write acceptance tests. If your customer works in the marketing department, are you *sure* that's the person you want defining the acceptance tests for the system?

See Chapter 5 for more about the perils of the on-site customer.

Generally, the first cut at defining these requirements isn't going to be correct. This is why they need to be reviewed. Extremo philosophy is that source code is "progress," therefore (having discussed the requirements with the customer and perhaps made a first-pass effort to validate their correctness) we should jump to code whether or not the requirements are known to be correct (in fact, with requirements that are almost guaranteed to be incorrect—for the reasons that we discussed earlier in this chapter). Then we write acceptance tests to verify these incorrect requirements. Then we code the incorrect behavior, show it to the users, refactor everything, and do it again (and again, and again). Lather, rinse, repeat.

Does this make sense? Not to us. Can we eventually converge on an answer this way? Possibly. But it certainly seems like a daft way to go about it. It is, to be blunt, ridiculously difficult. It does, however, explain how a team of programmers could spend 4 years building one-third of a payroll system.

The term "agility" has inherent connotations of "fast." You hear "agile" and you think "fast." But going through the overhead of writing unit tests, writing code, building, and integrating over and over again because the only technique deemed acceptable for improving the quality of requirements is working, released software is anything but fast. When pressed on the subject, Extremos will sometimes back off on claims of "fast" and only claim "constant velocity." For example (we present both of these quotes elsewhere in the book, but they bear repeating here):

". . . XP doesn't claim 'fabulous productivity gains'. We claim to tell you where you are. Have I published something to the contrary? Let me know, I'll correct it."[15]

—Ron Jeffries

"Once you accept that scope is variable then suddenly the project is no longer about getting 'done'. Rather its [sic] about developing at a certain velocity. And once you establish a velocity then the schedule becomes the customer's problem."[16]

—Robert C. Martin

15. Ron Jeffries posting to OTUG (http://www.rational.com), subject: "C3 Project Terminated," October 10, 2000.

16. Robert C. Martin posting to OTUG (http://www.rational.com), subject: "Scope Creep," October 11, 2000.

Well, constant velocity on a project isn't a great achievement if the velocity achieved is a snail's pace.

So, let's be clear about where we stand:

- **Unit tests:** Very important.

- **Acceptance tests:**[17] Also very useful.

- **Writing the test before coding the method:** Fine by us.

- **The tests are the design:** Nope.

- **The tests are the requirements:** Nope.

Fangs for the Memories

The stories and tests "snake" is driven by these issues:

- User stories have a totally amorphous definition.

- Coding everything for the sunny-day scenario will come back to bite you with both fangs.

- Good luck finding a customer who can code executable acceptance tests.

Regarding Robert C. Martin's quote at the start of the chapter, we could say, with tongue placed firmly in cheek, that XP prioritizes stories with the just slightly arbitrary mechanism of whether the customer can remember each story or not. So if the on-site customer wants his stories to be taken seriously by the team, he needs to have a pretty good memory.

User Stories Defanged

To "refactor" XP's approach to project requirements, we need to address these three issues:

- User stories do not define requirements in sufficient detail.

- With the greatest respect to all customers everywhere, human memory is neither reliable nor machine-like in consistency, and customers' memories are no exception.

---

17. You can find some examples of acceptance tests at
    `http://c2.com/cgi/wiki?AcceptanceTestExamples`.

- Acceptance tests are not the ideal medium for capturing and validating customer requirements. We can think of many customers we have dealt with who would simply refuse to work this way.

So we need a better way of capturing requirements than "2-bit" user stories, customer memories, and executable tests. Quite simply,

- Define the requirements in detail. Treat an incomplete requirement as a risk—something that could delay the project because it may hide many other requirements, which in turn could result in a rethink of the architecture.

- Write "4-bit" use cases (see the definition earlier in this chapter) to define the behavioral requirements. Capture all of the alternative flows. Leave no stone unturned.

- Write acceptance tests to verify that the requirements have been implemented, not that they have been thought of.

Automated acceptance tests are still useful for proving that the requirements have been correctly implemented, but they should not be confused with actual customer requirements. Acceptance tests bring the requirements too close to the solution, the implementation, to be useful as a specification. Requirements are there to define the problem rather than the solution.

Summary

In this chapter, we compared user stories with use cases and "traditional" requirements. We questioned whether the XP approach of writing a user story in a sentence or two and leaving the details for later conversations with the customer is a sufficiently robust approach to software development. We compared this approach with "vague" requirements as handled in non-XP projects.

As we hope we've demonstrated, there are reliable means of establishing a set of requirements early in the project that are correct or very close to being correct. This isn't folklore: There are documented ways of sniffing out incorrect requirements and getting agreement from all the various customer representatives.

There are, of course, cases where the requirements just aren't known early in the project, and in such cases, agile methods can prove to be a useful supplement to effective requirements elicitation. In most cases, however, the issue is simply that the requirements are there waiting to be got at—the team just needs to know how.

In the next chapter, we examine the notion (prevalent in the Extremo world) that "software is never done."

Part IV

The Perpetual
Coding Machine

CHAPTER 11

Software Is Never Done (The Schedule Does Not Exist Per Se)

Software Is Never Done
(Sing to the tune of "Happiness Is a Warm Gun" by The Beatles)

Soft-ware
Is never done
Ooh ooh yeah

So-oft-wa-aa-are
Is never done, mama

When I'm coding
With my pair
And I feel . . . her fingers on my keyboard
Then I know
The project should go on and on
Because

Soft-ware
Is never done
Ooh ooh yeah

 "Once you accept that scope is variable then suddenly the project is no longer about getting 'done'. Rather its [sic] about developing at a certain velocity. And once you establish a velocity then the schedule becomes the customer's problem."[1]

—Robert C. Martin

---

1. Robert C. Martin posting to OTUG (http://www.rational.com), subject: "Scope Creep," October 11, 2000.

"There is a difference between 'Schedule' and 'The Schedule'. In XP, 'Schedule' is very important, but 'The Schedule' doesn't exist per se."[2]

—Robert C. Martin

This chapter might just turn out to be the most controversial in this book, because it describes a curious paradox that is central to the way that XP works: fixed deadlines versus no schedule.

The XP literature is quite clear that XP does contain schedules and that it's possible to set fixed milestones for project completion. However, this doesn't sit well with the Extremo philosophy that "the schedule doesn't exist per se." XP approaches each iteration with a view toward swapping stories in and out (at the start of the iteration), reprioritizing stories as the project progresses. As we explore in this chapter, this approach can result in an unfocused project without a clear direction or sense of completion.

In this chapter, we begin by exploring this aspect of XP together with the curious Extremo concept that software is never done. We then contrast this with the XP approach to project contracts (in which *time*—the deadline—may be fixed, but *scope* is the biggest variable).

The Schedule Doesn't Exist Per Se

The following is Robert C. Martin's (not yet famous) "the schedule doesn't exist per se" posting to OTUG.

"There is a difference between 'Schedule' and 'The Schedule'. In XP, 'Schedule' is very important, but 'The Schedule' doesn't exist per se.

"The notion of having 'The Schedule' is related to the notion that a software project reaches a point where it is 'Done'. The notion of 'Doneness' pervades our thinking and our communications. We say to each other things like 'When this project is done . . .' or 'When will this project be done . . .', etc, etc.

"The reality, of course, is that a software project is never done until it has been terminated. So long as the market is active, the project will continually evolve. Certainly it will reach points where it is releasable; but at each release there will be a whole list of things that need to be done to it."[3]

---

2. Robert C. Martin posting to OTUG (http://www.rational.com), subject: "Estimates and Promises," October 13, 2000.

3. Ibid.

We think it's important for people—especially clients—to realize before they sign up to using XP with an optional-scope contract that they're freeing themselves from the notion of "doneness" that pervades our thinking and communications. Because some gold owners might find "doneness" to be a valuable notion. Like maybe somebody who was building a Y2K payroll replacement system?

Rejecting the Notion of Doneness

It's worth emphasizing this point, because it seems that anyone who wants to run a software project free of accountability can just reiterate the phrase "The schedule is the customer's problem." So that's okay then. Suddenly, the project isn't about getting "done" but is about developing at a certain velocity. Although consistency and repeatability are important factors in any software development process, they aren't really the *goal* of the project. The goal (as other XP authors have correctly noted) is working software.

Refactoring the Agile Manifesto

To rewrite one of the Manifesto for Agile Software Development's values[4] (with tongue in cheek):

- We value **meeting deadlines** over constant velocity.

   That is, although there is value in the item on the right, we value the item on the left more. And as somebody once pointed out (thanks, Rob): constant velocity == zero acceleration.

This line of thinking—rejecting the notion of doneness—pervades the theory behind XP. For example, much of the discussion surrounding C3's "inexplicable" cancellation centered around the concept that termination can be success: A project runs through however many iterations and releases, and (if it's successful) it simply keeps going, spinning round, and churning out small releases until the customer eventually pulls the plug.

In XP's favor, if/when the project is suddenly cancelled, it should be in a state where at least what has been written is releasable (depending on how effective the team has been at combating emergent entropy through simple design and refactoring). However, XP teams, simply by following the XP practices, are putting a huge amount of effort into being constantly prepared for the risk that the project might be canned at any moment. The XP life cycle (and all the effort that the team must put into it) is very much centered on the notion

---

4. See the Manifesto for Agile Software Development at http://www.agilemanifesto.org.

that the software is never done, it just runs until it suddenly, without warning, gets inexplicably cancelled.

In the real world things are slightly different. The real world runs on deadlines. For example, in the real world the new product has to be on the shelves in time for the Christmas shopping season, or the new air traffic control system needs to be online by the year 2005, or the payroll has to run if the mainframes drop dead on January 1, 2000.

Imagine if you had spent several million dollars funding a payroll project to protect your company from dead mainframes on January 1, 2000, and then the project manager said to you, "The concept of 'schedule' depends on the notion of doneness, which pervades our thinking." You might expect the team to be frog-marched from the building (or quite inexplicably terminated).

Voice of eXPerience: Recovery via "Not XP"

The November/December 2001 issue of *IEEE Software* magazine contained a case study of a troubled software project (run by ThoughtWorks, Inc.) that was "rescued" by XP. In fact, the team saw this as an opportunity to "test-drive Extreme Programming in a project recovery setting."[5]

Two things are striking about this case study. The first is that the team quickly realized that XP just wasn't suited to rescuing a project with a fixed deadline:

"As the severity of the matter quickly became apparent, we were forced to concede that the impending deadline did not allow us the luxury of XP. Instead, we cut up the application and parceled [sic] *it out by areas of expertise: servlets, documentation generation, business engines, database, and so on."[6]*

Despite this, the article was introduced and titled in such a way that it appeared, at first glance, as if XP had saved the project. By the end of the project, the team had *not adopted* these XP practices: small releases, metaphor, and 40-hour week. The team had only *partially adopted* these XP practices: planning game, pair programming (30% of the time), on-site customer, and coding standards.

The second striking thing is that (reading between the lines) the team appeared to regard the customer as unreasonable for not wanting to budge over the fixed deadline. Damn that pesky customer for wanting software delivered by a specific date! For example, the team blamed its failure to adopt small releases on the fact that it "could never get client buy-in."[7]

The fixed deadline was also given as the primary reason for not adopting XP before the software was released:

---

5. Peter Schuh, "Recovery, Redemption, and Extreme Programming," *IEEE Software* magazine, November/December 2001, p. 2.

6. Ibid.

7. Ibid., p. 5.

"The client's refusal to budge on the delivery date was the single greatest contributing factor to this outcome. Groundhog Day [the case study author's name for the project deadline] meant that the team could not step back and reassess the situation."[8]

However, it wasn't until after the initial deadline had passed and the software had been released (and hence entered maintenance mode, with real live customers to support and train) that the team felt able to begin gradually, painfully adopting the XP practices. By this stage, XP was doing what it is best suited to: maintaining existing systems.

 We discuss XP's suitability for maintaining legacy systems in the section "When Refactoring Is Useful" in Chapter 9.

This does raise the issue that XP is simply overdesigned, too high-maintenance in its practices, for developing new systems from scratch. There are more efficient ways of doing this.

While Management Gently Weeps
(Sing to the tune of "While My Guitar Gently Weeps" by The Beatles)

The clock on the wall
Shows the schedule slipping
While management gently weeps

We've got unit tests
But the design is missing
While management gently weeps

You know that schedule is
The customer's problem
Requirements are too

You just can't let
The schedule control you
Code tells you when it's due

Look at the code
Smell the bugs we are shipping
Still management gently weeps

My pair programmer
Decided to go fishing
Still management gently weeps

---

8. Ibid., p. 4.

Embrace Rampant Scope Creep Regularly

"How stable is the release plan? Not at all. The only thing we know for certain about a plan is that development won't go according to it. So release planning happens all the time. Every time the customer changes his mind about the requirements and his priority, this changes the plan."[9]

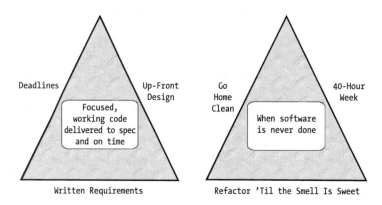

Deadlines   Up-Front Design

Focused, working code delivered to spec and on time

Go Home Clean   40-Hour Week

When software is never done

Written Requirements   Refactor 'Til the Smell Is Sweet

Figure 11-1. Two very different approaches

It's not surprising that the XP methods promote scope creep. The whole "go home clean," "40-hour week," and "refactor 'til the smell is sweet" triad of Extremo philosophy is completely bogus in the real world.

As we will discover in Chapter 13, the Extremos see scope creep as a positively good thing that should be embraced in any project.

And without that triad, the only hope of fighting rampant scope creep and endless refactoring is detailed written requirements, schedules with deadlines for deliverables, and up-front design (see Figure 11-1). Fangs is running rampant, because the software engineering practices (written requirements, deadlines, and up-front design) that mitigate risk in the areas of estimation and scheduling have been vaporized in Extremo-land and replaced by aphorisms such as "schedule is the customer's problem" and "the schedule doesn't exist per se."

The problem isn't with refactoring as a technique. The problem is refactoring in the absence of deadlines, especially because refactoring in XP isn't a scheduled task—it runs concurrently. It's just a thing that happens all the time and is

---

9. Kent Beck and Martin Fowler, *Planning Extreme Programming* (New York, NY: Addison-Wesley, 2000), p. 41.

expected to take up time in each iteration. If refactoring was scheduled as a story (or, more likely, as one or more tasks), and programmers signed up for it each iteration, then it could be more manageable.

What happens instead is that the amount of refactoring being done affects the project velocity, so a team that diligently refactors every day would be perceived to have a lower velocity because (for a few iterations at least) the team completes fewer stories. Conversely, a team that does very little refactoring might complete more stories for a while, but soon the increasing "spaghettiness" of the team's code would make it very difficult to implement new stories.

Because of its emergent design approach (coupled with its dislike of deadlines), XP is a constant fight against emergent entropy, in which its chief weapon is refactoring.

However, refactoring isn't scheduled by the customer. It's up to the programmers to decide how much to refactor. The customer will be told by the team how many stories the team can implement in this iteration. So the decision of how much code quality to "add" to the product (stir in 3 ounces . . .) isn't a managed decision—it's a decision that's left to the programmers to make.

Managing Change Through Up-Front Design

XP advises teams not to schedule specific refactoring tasks, but instead to treat refactoring as an integral part of the development process. The benefit of constant refactoring is that design flaws are caught early. Big refactorings are difficult; it's better to catch flaws early and so keep the refactorings small.

As we've maintained elsewhere, however, spending more time on up-front design (and following a logical design process) helps to drastically reduce the amount of refactoring needed later. Catching design flaws before coding keeps the refactorings almost microscopically small.

Because our refactored process doesn't rely so heavily on refactoring, we can afford to schedule it as an engineering task (e.g., a half-day task here or there). This also enables requirements change to be managed, because specific refactoring tasks can be traced back to a particular change in requirements. This makes the process more predictable and controllable, and (non-extreme, though it is) gives control of the team back to the project manager.

Also see the section "Use Up-Front Design to Enhance Agility" in Chapter 13.

One analogy is of a news anchor reading from a teleprompter. In his velvety-smooth voice, the anchor reads out the news at his own pace, and the teleprompter speeds up or slows down accordingly. The pace of the news report isn't set by the teleprompter (which supplies the stories) but by the anchor. Similarly, the customer supplies the user stories, but the programmers set both the pace (schedule) and the quality.

We cover refactoring further in Chapter 9.

Customers of XP might be surprised to learn, therefore, that quality *management* is very much in the hands of the programmers. That is, unless they specifically tailor XP to make quality schedulable and therefore estimable.

Quality tends to be the first thing that suffers with tight deadlines, so, without time on the XP team's side, the practices start to slip and the circle of snakes breaks loose. In Chapter 14, we discuss a case study of an XP project that was conducted by ThoughtWorks, Inc. In this project, the deadlines were tight, so what the programmers sacrificed (whether intentionally or not) was code quality. They didn't have time to clean up the stinky code that did the simplest thing that could possibly work, so they ended up with spaghetti code, and at the end of the project the code was in a worse state than when the team first adopted XP.

Refactoring Iteration

A discussion on the C2 Wiki concerns the concept of a refactoring iteration:

"XP requires you to EmbraceChange. Sometimes you have to rip the crap out of your design to meet some changing requirements. When you need to make a fundamental or global design change and some external force beyond anyone's control is driving you to get it done now. You need a RefactoringIteration where refactoring is the theme of the entire iteration."[10]

In many ways, we feel that the sentence "Sometimes you have to rip the crap out of your design to meet some changing requirements" proves our point regarding the benefits of up-front design and detailed requirements elicitation, versus the dangers of emergent design and brief user story exploration. So some XPers (including Don Wells on the VCAPS project) have found that sometimes the design degrades to such a state where they need to stop for a whole iteration and simply refactor—that's one or more pairs, refactoring, not producing any new functionality, for 1 to 3 weeks.

Not surprisingly, even Kent Beck sees this as a very bad idea (see the referenced discussion page). However, his proposed "solution" concludes with the characteristically mystical (for Beck) comment:

"Whenever we could, we made progress towards our ultimate goal. But we didn't let our fear overcome our desire to serve our customers."

---

10. See `http://c2.com/cgi/wiki?RefactoringIteration`.

Voice of eXPerience: eXtreme Road Building

Emergent design isn't just difficult in the software world, as this excerpt from a news item in the *Arizona Daily Star* shows:

"Six years ago, county officials pegged the cost to widen the stretch of Skyline at $10.8 million. On Tuesday, the county Board of Supervisors approved an amended contract for the project that adds another $10.6 million.

"The total tab is now $21.4 million.

"The cost overrun makes the 2.2-mile road project the most expensive per-mile project in the history of road construction in unincorporated Pima County. Reasons for the cost increase include:

"The county's trial of the 'design-build' method of road construction in which contractors design and build the project at once to save time.

"County officials didn't know the Skyline widening cost had doubled until recently because the contractor couldn't calculate the entire cost until doing a sizable amount of design."[11]

But If We Don't Acknowledge the Existence of Deadlines, Nobody Will Force Us to Meet Them, Right?

"One of the most important principles in planning for Extreme Programming is that the dates are hard dates, but scope will vary."[12]

The variables that govern every software project—time, effort, scope, and quality—are handled in XP by fixing time but varying scope (and as we discussed earlier, quality in XP varies in an ad hoc way determined by the programmers). XP uses fixed iterations and releases to the customer often. This can mean that it's very difficult to say specifically, "X piece of functionality will be delivered to you by Y date," because the scheduling process is so fluid. Instead, the team can at least say, "*Some* functionality will be delivered to you by Y date, but we're making no promises about exactly what it will be."

If we reverse the equation, we can see that this is roughly equivalent to saying, "We will deliver you specifically A, B, and C requirements, but we're making no promises about exactly *when* they will all be delivered."

---

11. Tony Davis, "Widening cost double for Skyline," *Arizona Daily Star*, February 5, 2003.
12. Kent Beck and Martin Fowler, *Planning Extreme Programming*, op. cit., p. 84.

To adopt an approach that starts out with the presumption that deadlines are meaningless is like an ostrich thinking no one can see him because his head is stuck in the sand. Interestingly, XP acknowledges the existence of deadlines (e.g., on page 1 of *Planning Extreme Programming*), but XP's particular approach to software agility makes it very difficult for the team to actually stick to a pre-ordained schedule. In other words, in XP the schedule is secondary to embracing change (or, if Robert C. Martin is to be believed, "the schedule doesn't exist per se").

Agile planning—that is, reprioritizing the requirements at the start of each iteration—is proving useful for certain types of project. As we explore in Chapter 4, for example, XP's arrival was very well timed with the emergence of the dot-com mentality ("We have a business plan, kind of, now let's build us some software!"). In projects where market forces are sufficiently volatile to lead to frequent changes in requirements, or where the survival of the company depends on being first to market, then XP's approach could make more sense than a traditional BDUF approach. However, as we discussed earlier in this chapter, most business projects just don't work that way. Most business projects are driven by fixed deadlines.

This is really the crux of the problem. When the simple concept of deadlines is added to an XP project, look what happens: The team can't refactor indefinitely anymore. So, surprise, surprise, quality suffers. So they'd better not have all their code do the simplest thing that could possibly work for the current iteration. So they'd better do some detailed, diligent, up-front design. So they'd better write down the requirements (in detail—not just as promises for future conversations).

Voice of eXPerience: Estimation and Short Time Frames

by David Van Der Klauw

David worked on an XP project at a company referred to here as "CompanyXYZ."

XP concentrates on the extremely short time frame to the exclusion of other time frames. XP says that programmers tend to waste time planning for a future that never occurs. In my opinion, this is a serious fault and a case of throwing out the baby with the bathwater.

Short Time Frame

Spending within a business hinges around payback periods. Whether the spending is dollars or time, the decision to spend or not should always be done on its payback period. A common payback period to use within business is 2 to 3 years.

The short time frame of XP makes the serious error of eliminating many fruitful tasks that would pay themselves back in a few short months or years. I don't deny that most software development work should pay back in days or weeks. However, the flaw I'm highlighting is that XP excludes valuable tasks with a medium or long payback period.

One symptom of the short time frame is that CompanyXYZ is neglecting all learning exercises in favor of completing immediate customer tasks. Many CompanyXYZ programmers feel that their skills are being used up and not replenished. Like a foolish farmer who eats his breeding stock or his seed corn, CompanyXYZ isn't allowing its programmers to take time to learn anything that doesn't have an immediate payoff to a customer.

In business, there are many techniques that will give a short-term boost to productivity but with long-term damage. These techniques are often pushed by consultants or managers who can come in, quickly show a short-term gain, cash out, and then leave the problems behind for someone else. I believe that XP is one of these quick-fix fads.

The short-term emphasis leads to low quality of coding. There are many altruistic reasons for writing quality code, but one benefit of the conventional code ownership is that it forces you to write good quality code so that you won't be stuck with a mess in a few months' or years' time. With conventional code ownership, if you failed to plan ahead, you would be dragged back in to fix the design. With XP, however, any problems down the track are not your problem. In practice, this results in less care and lower quality results.

 For a discussion of what can go wrong with collective ownership, see the section "What If Programmers Take Ownership of Code?" in Chapter 3.

Estimation and Spikes

Estimating the time a job will take is one of the most difficult aspects of software engineering. XP attempts to solve this problem by demanding accurate estimates for routine work and requiring investigative "spikes" for tasks that cannot be accurately estimated. I believe this is a serious flaw in XP.

Estimating software is so hard to do because, unless you are a complete idiot, every job involves something you have never done before. After all, if you have done it before, a copy and paste from your archive will take only seconds.

XP pretends that work can be conveniently divided into routine work that can easily be accurately estimated (yet too hard for a single person to do by herself) and groundbreaking work that will always require doing an investigative spike, then throwing away code, then estimating, then writing tests, and finally performing the task. If only life were so simple.

Perhaps your car's accelerator could be replaced with two speed buttons: one speed for highway cruising and one speed for local roads. In reality, there is a full spectrum of routine/experimental work that is experienced throughout just about every task, just as your car experiences a range of speed on every journey.

For example, as I code a FOR loop it might be 100% routine. I use a familiar API function but in a new way: 50% experimental and 50% routine. Then I try to cast the return to an unfamiliar type and it is 100% experimental.

The distinction between spikes and production code is not a useful distinction. The two are heavily entwined and cannot be separated.

I am not saying that there is no value in making an estimate and reevaluating when the time is up. Estimating is worthwhile, but it will never be accurate. Trying to make it so with the worthless distinction of a spike is futile.

I am not saying that there is no place for dedicated spikes, nor am I saying that work is never 100% routine. What I am saying is that a great deal of work cannot sensibly be divided into the categories of experimental and routine, because it is a mixture of both. Forcing this distinction is a flaw in XP.

Estimation in Practice

XP involves breaking down every task into very small sections and estimating the time needed very accurately. Should an accurate estimate not be possible, an investigative "spike" is first done, then an accurate estimate is made, and then the task is started.

In practice this does not work. It was interesting to see the various ways our developers defeated this system:

- Some simply did the work, and after completion they did a task breakdown and entered the time actually taken (as their estimate).

- Some wrote the first thing that came to mind, estimated it to take 4 hours, and then started the task. If it took longer, then they simply added further tasks of 4 hours until the job was done.

- Some gave a generous 4-hour spike for each task. In this time they performed the task and then allocated half an hour to finalize their work.

Optional-Scope Contracts

There are, of course, many different types of project contract. What each type of contract has in common is that it attempts to define the project in terms of the four variables that we introduced earlier: time, effort, scope, and quality. (Cost is often seen as one of these variables, though it is essentially a combination of time and effort.)

Some project bids are won on the basis that "we'll do it more cheaply and in less time than our competitors." This usually means that both the cost and deadline are set before we know exactly what needs to be delivered. The result is that postbid negotiations take the form of an almost desperate wrangling of the project scope, where the customer wants as much as possible out of the deal, and the supplier (that's us) tries to cut down the scope as much as possible—at least to a sensible amount. What if the customer wants to fix scope as well as time? Then you've got a problem. And in fact the fourth variable, quality, tends to be the one that gets sacrificed.

XP attempts to counter this by using *optional-scope contracts*. The theory is that the customer will be prepared to sign up for a project that runs for a fixed amount of time for a fixed price, without any commitment as to what is actually delivered. This premise is central to XP. Without an optional-scope contract, where scope is the biggest variable, XP cannot function.

Note that treating *scope* as the biggest variable is in contrast to Extremo Robert C. Martin's viewpoint, where *time* is the biggest variable because the schedule doesn't exist per se. So it's interesting that one of the fundamental aspects of XP is open to interpretation (and, in fact, is given conflicting interpretations by its own authors). But it's worth reemphasizing a point we made earlier: *Fixed deadlines with variable scope are equivalent to fixed scope with variable deadlines.* Phrase it how you will, it's still the same thing: no commitment to being done with a job while meeting a deadline.

 For a discussion of these opposing sides of the same coin, see the section "But If We Don't Acknowledge the Existence of Deadlines, Nobody Will Force Us to Meet Them, Right?" earlier in this chapter.

Whichever rocky road you choose to follow, there are potential pitfalls in contract negotiation. The customer may regard your sales team as "slippery" because the team members refuse to commit to any sort of concrete plan while apologetically explaining that "it's just the way our software process works!"

Of course, the supplier can commit to a fixed-scope contract anyway, but then that isn't really XP, and the team would then be better off using a process that's tailored to fixed-scope projects. From *Extreme Programming Explained*:

> *"XP can accommodate the common forms of contract, albeit with slight modifications. Fixed price/fixed scope contracts, in particular, become fixed price/fixed date/roughly fixed scope contracts when run with the Planning Game."*[13]

This is contrasted with a discussion on the C2 Wiki,[14] in which it's postulated that XP's planning game isn't compatible with fixed-price contracts. The problem is that in the real world (there's that pesky real-world thing again!), management prefers to allocate the budget for a project up front, or it may even decide whether or not to give the go-ahead for the project based on its estimated cost.

---

13. Kent Beck, *Extreme Programming Explained: Embrace Change* (New York, NY: Addison-Wesley, 2000), p. 159.

14. See http://c2.com/cgi/wiki?PlanningGame.

This doesn't sit well with XP's "plan a bit, estimate a bit/plan a bit more, estimate a bit more" system. XP's approach does result in more accurate estimates over time, but at the start of the project, the estimates tend to be way off-target, and it's impossible to know (even at a broad level) how much the project is going to cost.

This is, of course, a problem with agile methods in general, not just XP, because a process that doesn't go to reasonable lengths to pin down the scope of the project just can't be accurately costed up front.

In fact, off-target cost estimates are a notorious problem in "traditional" software projects as well. It's a thorny issue because software is inherently difficult to predict and estimate. However, Ron Jeffries' suggested solution (in the PlanningGame C2 Wiki page referenced earlier) of a "paradigm change" at the management level wouldn't go down well at most companies (certainly not at the companies where we've worked—or with those companies' customers, for that matter). Once again, the pesky real world gets in the way.

Optional-Scope Contract
(Sing to the tune of "Octopus's Garden" by The Beatles)

I'd like to be
Coding in C
With the optional-scope contract
That we made

No work gets done
We'll just have fun
We can just eat snack food and get paid
(Just eat snack food and get paid)

Oh we would be so happy, you and me
No management can tell us what to do

I'd like to be
Coding in C
With an optional-scope contract
With you

Voice of eXPerience: Stumbling About
by David Van Der Klauw

I was calmly discussing XP with our tracker, MG, and coach, BM. I said I didn't feel that I had learned anything properly while doing pair programming. BM contrasted that he had learned things:

BM: Take SQL Server and stored procedures, for example. Before I came to this team, I knew nothing about them.

Me: Well, could you write me a simple stored procedure that–

BM: No I can't, it's just that I feel that with my partner I would be able to.

Me: Well, what happens if your partner knows as little as you? You'd have two people stumbling about and nobody really knowing what he is doing.

MG: Dave that's the whole point—really knowing. If two people stumbling about is what it takes to write software that meets customer requirements, then that is what we should be doing.

Me: Well, 13 years of software development experience tells me that is *not* the way to do it.

A Night at the Payroll Project: Optional-Scope Contract Scene

Many people credit Kent Beck with inventing the optional-scope contract, which is a cornerstone of the XP philosophy. Along with the famous statement "software is never done," it provides justification for an infinite amount of Constant Refactoring After Programming. But in reality, the optional-scope contract was invented by Groucho Marx in *A Night at the Opera*.[15]

Here we imagine how it might have been at a seminal moment in history as the world of software engineering became infused with Marxist philosophy.

The setting: Groucho plays Otis P. Extremo, an extreme programmer currently working under contract to provide a replacement payroll system to a major automobile manufacturer. Chico plays Barry GoldOwner, the project sponsor. It's early 1999 and, having realized that the team isn't on the imagined schedule, Extremo is seeking to change the scope of his contract with GoldOwner.

---

15. If you've never seen *A Night at the Opera*, you can enjoy the original classic scene in RealAudio at `http://www.nightattheopera.net/nato16.ram`.

Extremo and GoldOwner are standing next to each other, and each is holding a long scroll of fax paper that has the contract printed on it.

Extremo: Now, this thing here about a weekly payroll . . . YAGNI to that, okay?

GoldOwner: Who'sa YAGNI?

Extremo: YAGNI, you know, you aren't gonna need it. YAGNI. Where have you been? Can't they live in Detroit with just the monthly payroll?

GoldOwner: Well, I only getta paid once a month, so I guess that's okay.

Extremo: Fine, fine.

[They each rip a page off the contract.]

Extremo: Now, it says here we've got to code income tax, and federal tax, and state tax, and city tax, and sewer tax. That's too many taxes. Can't we run this payroll program with fewer taxes than that?

GoldOwner: Well, we could move from taxes to Oklahoma, would that help?

Extremo: No, no, I don't think that would be OK. We only want to code the simplest thing that can possibly work, you know.

GoldOwner: *[Suspicious]* The simplest thing that can possibly work, huh?

Extremo: Well, you wouldn't want us to code the simplest thing that didn't work, would you?

GoldOwner: *[Satisfied]* Well, I guess you're-a right . . . *[Ripping the contract]* yeah, thatsa no good.

Extremo: Fine, now we're getting someplace!

GoldOwner: Where?

Extremo: What?

GoldOwner: Where are we getting?

Extremo: Why, Ypsilanti, of course.

GoldOwner: Why didn't you say so?

Extremo: All right, enough of that—now look, this bit here about being done before January 2000, that's just the imagined schedule.

GoldOwner: The imagined schedule?

Extremo: Yeah, you know, because the concept of schedule depends upon the notion of doneness.

GoldOwner: Doneness? You mean like a steak . . . medium rare?

Extremo: You *do* know that software's never done, don't you?

GoldOwner: Oh yah, ha ha ha! *[Slaps knee]* That'sa right, how could I forget. Software's never done. Ha ha. How silly of me. I guess we gotta rip that out too.

Extremo: *[Ripping page]* But we've still got a contract, right? No matter how small, it's still a contract, right? So when are you going to have those acceptance tests ready?

GoldOwner: I thought you were gonna do the testing.

Extremo: You don't seriously expect *me* to do the testing, do you?

GoldOwner: No, I guess not.

Extremo: I should say not! The very idea. Having me do the testing! See, it says right here, acceptance tests are the customer's responsibility. Say, do you smell something?

GoldOwner: You mean your cigar?

Extremo: No, no, not my cigar, something else. . . . It has a delicate fragrance . . . like . . . lavender.

GoldOwner: *[Sniffs]* No, I just smell your cigar.

Extremo: What about Smalltalk code?

GoldOwner: Does Smalltalk code smell like a big stinky cigar? What'sa Smalltalk code?

Extremo: You know, Smalltalk code, don't you have any Smalltalk code?

GoldOwner: C'mon . . . what am I gonna do with Smalltalk code?

Extremo: Well, you smell it of course—how do you think you know if it needs to be refactored? *[Exasperated]* What are they teaching in school these days? Look, can't you smell?

GoldOwner: I haven't smelled anything yet . . . did you code anything?

Extremo: I didn't code anything worth smelling.

GoldOwner: Well, that's why I didn't smell anything.

Extremo: Well, that's why I didn't code anything.

GoldOwner: That's all right, I fool you—there were no requirements, anyway.

Extremo: Well, I fooled you, too—I don't even know how to code.

[They pause and look at each other.]

Extremo: Say, that reminds me, it's time to rotate our pair programmers!

GoldOwner: Why, don't you want 'em facing the desks?

Extremo: No, you see, we don't want people to get into the habit of pairing together for any length of time, because that way one of them might actually learn what the other one is doing, so we rotate them. It's kind of like changing the tires on your car. Every 30 classes or 10 refactorings we rotate the programmers.

GoldOwner: I get it, you don't want the programmers to get bald. But I still think they oughtta face the keyboards. So, how does that work?

Extremo: You know, the first programmer from the first pair becomes the second programmer of the second pair.

GoldOwner: What about the second programmer?

Extremo: Of the first pair or of the second pair?

GoldOwner: Of the first pair.

Extremo: *[Scratches head]* Let's see, the, uh, second programmer of the first pair becomes the second programmer of the second pair.

GoldOwner: Whaddya you crazy? You just said the first programmer of the first pair becomes the second programmer of the second pair. You can't have both the first programmer of the first pair and the second programmer of the first pair become the second programmer of the second pair—there aren't enough chairs at the desk!

Extremo: You know, I never thought of it exactly that way.

GoldOwner: *[Smiles]* Sure.

Extremo: I guess you're right, I guess the second programmer of the first pair becomes the first programmer of the second pair. Yes, yes, I'm sure that's right.

GoldOwner: Now you're talkin'. What about the third pair?

Extremo: There are three pairs?

GoldOwner: Sure, because three of a kind always beats two pairs.

Extremo: Finally, we agree on something. Listen, with three pairs it doesn't work. The third pair will have to integrate.

GoldOwner: All day?

Extremo: Sure, why not? It's constant integration, you know. Everything is always integrated.

GoldOwner: Even on Thursday?

Extremo: No, of course not. On Thursday we all play pinball. It's right here in the contract, see?

Fangs Is Running Rampant

SoftwareIsNeverDone. Believe it, and be prepared to renounce "the concept of doneness" if you decide to try XP. It's a Zen thing: The journey is the reward. Who needs projects to get finished, anyhow?

As soon as deadlines are added to an XP project, time becomes a fixed variable. This can cause time-consuming XP practices (particularly refactoring) to slip, and inevitably code quality suffers.

Because the level of code quality is controlled by the programmers, quality management is never quite under the bourgeois management's control.

The Planning Game Defanged

If "software is never done," then most customers would have a serious problem.

Adopting a process that embraces fixed deadlines instead of embracing change is a major step toward reenabling the concept of doneness.

Although changes in requirements can be beneficial (and can even be of major commercial benefit to the customer) and shouldn't be prevented, the *likelihood* of change can be significantly reduced by improving the up-front requirements elicitation process. Learning to extract the correct requirements from the customer and users, and to validate the requirements in the context of the problems they're trying to solve, reduces the amount of churn due to wrong or misunderstood requirements.

Summary

In this chapter, we discussed a surprising aspect of XP, that of the concept of "doneness" (or lack of it). We contrasted this with XP's optional-scope contract, which at first glance appears to contradict the Extremo attitude to doneness— but turns out to be the opposite side of the same coin.

We also discovered that the emergent design approach runs a high risk of leading to emergent entropy, where the design quickly breaks down into spaghetti code unless it is constantly fought with the chief weapon of refactoring. We discuss emergent design in more detail in the next chapter.

CHAPTER 12

Emergent Architecture and Design

I Can't Get No Architecture
(Sing to the tune of "(I Can't Get No) Satisfaction" by the Rolling Stones)

I can't get no
Architecture
I can't get no
Architecture
'Cause I tried
And I tried
And I tried
And I tried
I can't get no
I can't get no

Well I'm refactoring my code
Yeah I'm movin' this and I'm changin' that
Every time I get the urge
But I'm still sittin' here waiting for
The architecture to emerge

I can't get no
No no no
Hey hey hey
That's what I say

I don't need no
Infrastructure
I don't need no
Infrastructure
'Cause I tried
And I tried
And I tried
And I tried
I don't need no
I don't need no

When I'm posting to the newsgroup
And a man comes on and tells me
That I should not say YAGNI
But he can't be a man cause he does not write
As much C code as me

I don't need no
No no no
Hey hey hey
That's what I say

"Get a few people together and spend a few minutes
sketching out the design. Ten minutes is ideal—*half an*
hour should be the most time you spend to do this.
After that, the best thing to do is to let the code participate in the design session—*move to the machine and*
start typing in code."[1]

—Ron Jeffries

"The larger the scale, the more you must rely on
emergence."[2]

—Kent Beck

Emergent architecture (also called *emergent design* by XPers) is central to the XP
way. The question is, in a complex, real-world project, does emergent design
provide a sufficient substitute for planning ahead?

In this chapter we discuss emergent design from a few different angles. We
start by revisiting YAGNI, the XP design mantra that in many ways sums up
emergent design. Then we critique the description of emergent design given in
the book *Extreme Programming Installed.* Finally, we compare emergent design
with its deadly rival, up-front design with early prototyping (our colleague Mark
Collins-Cope recently gave up-front design its own acronym, JEDI—*Just Enough
Design In-front*).

But before we get serious about emergent design, because we have the
power of satire on our side, here's a little story that was inspired by the previous

1. Ron Jeffries, Ann Anderson, and Chet Hendrickson, *Extreme Programming Installed*
(New York, NY: Addison-Wesley, 2000), p. 70. (Emphasis ours.)

2. Kent Beck posting to the C2 Wiki page Can An Architecture Emerge, http://c2.com/cgi/
wiki?CanAnArchitectureEmerge.

quote about "letting the code participate in the design session" (all right, we admit it, we've just spent too many hours reading the Wiki Web while writing this book, and it's beginning to affect us just a bit).

The XP Society's Annual Picnic

(All the characters in this story are fictional.)

The members of the XP Society were extremely excited at the prospect of their first-ever annual picnic, to be held the very same day that it had been announced.

"What should the picnic involve?" Society Chairman Ronnie Lips asked.

"None of us know," the picnic crew's unofficially elected spokesman, Tom Bradshaw, replied morosely.

"Well, never mind," Chairman Ronnie empowered. "We don't have to plan that far ahead. The main thing is to get the picnic underway, then we can decide what we need at a more appropriate time."

"Great!" Tom exclaimed, chirping up immediately. "Now, let's have a quick think tank to get some initial ideas, then we'll get going."

"That's the spirit!" encouraged Ronnie. "Now, what's the first, most important thing that any picnic should have?"

Tom frowned, suddenly a little unsure of himself. Then his worried expression cleared and he quipped, "Food! We want food, so let's bring food."

"Excellent!" confirmed Chairman Ronnie. "That's more than enough detail to get us started. Now, I'm going to gather everyone around for their early-morning stand-up show and tell them today is a special day: the last day of Planet Irk. No more irksome problems for us—it's all plain sailing from here. And that's why this will be the best picnic in the whole world . . . ever!"

"But where should the picnic be?" asked Tom.

"Don't worry," Ronnie chuckled. "Remember, you have the Power of XP on your side. Just tell everyone to meet at the picnic site. When it is time to know where it is, they will know."

"Master, you are truly wise," Tom replied.

"Yes, yes. Now get your thinking cap on, there's a picnic project to kick off!"

Chairman Ronnie departed to round up the rest of the team, leaving an air of hushed intoxication in his wake. Tom immediately telephoned his friend Jim and breathlessly told him the exciting news.

Jim was not so enthusiastic, though, because (he explained) today was his 1-year wedding anniversary and he already had plans.

"Jim," Tom admonished in a mock-stern voice, "remember this is XP—and you're not allowed to say no!"[3]

So poor old Jim reluctantly left a note for his wife, grabbed some randomly chosen food from the kitchen (some sausage rolls and a cake with "Happy Anniversary, Bunnikins" written on the top in special colored marzipan), and sped over to Tom's place.

---

3. See http://www.objectmentor.com/resources/articles/xpepisode.htm.

"Now," enthused Tom once Jim had arrived, "we need to think this next stage through. Do you think we ought to have something to carry all the food in?"

Jim seemed slightly gloomy at first but was soon swept up by Tom's infectious enthusiasm for the project. "Perhaps a picnic hamper," he offered.

"Can you eat a hamper?" Tom immediately challenged. "No, I didn't think so. Our customer's one requirement was that we bring food—edible things. Our first and primary test for this is whether everything we bring is edible. And our tests are, after all, our picnic specification. Now, I rather think a picnic hamper would fail that test, don't you?"

So they gathered up as much food in their arms as they could without dropping any and stumbled out to Tom's station wagon as best they could.

"Fear my agile palm solution!" Tom chuckled proudly, as an unboiled egg slipped out of the pile of food balanced precariously in his arms and hit the asphalt with a messy splat. "Who needs frameworks? We're doing the simplest thing that could possibly work!"

"We sure don't! We sure are!" Jim responded, trying to get into the spirit of the occasion.

Once they had made about 20 short trips back and forth to the station wagon, they piled into the vehicle and got underway. "That was a lot of work," Jim commented, wiping perspiration from his brow.

"Yes," Tom responded with his unrelenting enthusiasm, "but we were sure as heck moving fast, weren't we?"

"We were the best!" agreed Jim.

"Now, once we've been driving for about 20 minutes, we'll decide where we need to go," said Tom.

About 20 minutes later, as Tom drove in silence and Jim furiously studied a battered old roadmap, Jim said, "Well, there's Jimbo's Picnic Area about 20 minutes' drive from here. In fact, it's right by your house. If only we'd studied the map before we set off!"

"Oh, you and your grand designs," snapped Tom. "You and your stupid, old-fashioned ivory tower logic. Well that's not how we do things here. See, there's no time lost really. I can turn the car around—for free! Now we're simply heading back in the opposite direction."

"Well," Jim replied, bristling, "if we'd thought this through from the start, we could have gone to the Grand Conifer Nature Reserve and eaten our picnic with the tame bears! But no, it's too late for that. Jimbo's Picnic Area it is."

They arrived at Jimbo's Picnic Area about 40 minutes later (having taken a few wrong turns). To their delight, Chairman Ronnie was already there, waiting for them with a broad, beaming grin on his shiny face. Behind Ronnie, the entire XP Society stood grinning. Tom and Jim cheered up at once and quickly forgot their earlier quarrel.

"Where's Bill?" Jim asked as they bounded out of the station wagon.

"Bill's pair-programming from home today," Ronnie explained. "Although . . . we haven't quite worked out how tele-pair-programming is going to work yet. Anyway, let's get this picnic set up!"

Singing and cheering happily, they brought out the food: Jim's anniversary cake and sausage rolls, plus some canned fruit, a microwavable suet pudding, a frozen chicken, three dozen half-baked baguettes ("Mmm, you should taste these ultra-fresh dough treats once they're fully baked!"), a bottle of undiluted orange-squash cordial, and several bottles of fizzy wine.

They started with Jim's sausage rolls but were appalled to discover that the rolls were uncooked.

"Yes," Jim explained enthusiastically, "they're much fresher this way. You just heat them in the oven for 40 minutes. Oh, hang on . . . we need an oven."

Standing in a circle, the group descended into a slightly depressed hush.

"I tell you what," Tom offered. "My house is just around the corner. Why don't I take the sausage rolls home now, cook them for 40 minutes, and bring them back when they're done?"

"Splendid idea!" Chairman Ronnie exclaimed. "Except . . . I'm sure Derek over there has a fan-assisted oven. He could get them cooked in half the time."

"That's right!" Derek quipped, stepping forward. He grabbed the sausage rolls and drove away in a cloud of dust.

"But doesn't Derek live an hour's drive away?" Tom queried, sounding hesitant.

"Excellent point," Chairman Ronnie confirmed. "Still, not to worry. We can eat the cake while we're waiting."

They quickly discovered that they didn't have a knife with which to cut the cake, so another XPer was sent away to find a cake knife. When he returned an hour later, they discovered that they had no paper plates on which to put the slices of cake. Another XPer was sent away to find some paper plates.

That XPer arrived back at about the same time as Derek, who proudly showed everyone his stack of sausage rolls (which by this time had cooled down and turned slightly rubbery).

They stood around in a disconsolate circle and munched the cold, rubbery sausage rolls.

Minutes later, Derek was sent away again to "quickly" defrost and cook the frozen chicken.

"Anyway," Chairman Ronnie announced, sensing that his troupe was in need of some morale boosting, "it's time for the cake! Jim kindly informs me that he has probably sacrificed his marriage and future happiness to bring us this cake, so I am sure it will taste quite nice."

"Do we have any plastic forks?" someone asked from the back. "I don't like to get my hands grubby with cake goo."

An increasingly disillusioned Jim was sent away to find a shop that sells plastic forks.

As the afternoon wore on, various Society members were, in turn, sent away to find paper napkins, a can opener, small plastic bowls, a corkscrew, folding chairs for everyone to sit on, a small foldaway table to keep the food away from the ants, cups, mosquito netting (as it was long since dark by this stage and the mosquitoes were having a heartier feast than the increasingly morose Society members), and—the last straw—a shotgun to fend off a nearby bear.

As the picnic drew to a natural close and wrapped up, the disgruntled members began to pack up their things and go their separate ways. It was midnight by this stage, and no one was really speaking to anybody else. Almost everyone had mosquito bites, and one member had been badly mauled by the bear.

As they departed, a frustrated-looking Derek returned and announced that despite his best efforts, the chicken was still frozen solid.

"Never mind," offered Chairman Ronnie. "If any task looks as if it's going to take too long, we just don't have to do it. That's one of our most important rules. And anyway," he added, in a last-bid attempt to rally the silently departing Society members, "I have decided that tonight's grand finale shall involve fireworks! The grandest fireworks you have ever seen! And . . . and a 40-piece orchestra."

The rest of the Society members just ignored him and silently departed, their heads hung low.

The following week, the Society Web site described the annual picnic as "a bit chaotic, but a roaring success nonetheless," and urged everyone to bring a friend along the following year—same date, same place.

"That is," the Web site blurb added, "assuming that we choose the same venue and date. We will let you know on the day."

XP Design Mantra: YAGNI

YAGNI
(Sing to the tune of "Let It Be" by The Beatles)

If you think of building architecture
But you're feeling lazy
You can just skip it
YAGNI

If you think you might need infrastructure
You don't have to worry
Go ahead and skip it
YAGNI

YAGNI
YAGNI
YAGNI
YAGNI

Don't worry 'bout tomorrow
YAGNI
You aren't gonna need it
YAGNI

"XP is making a bet. It is betting that it is better to do a simple thing today and pay a little more tomorrow to change it if it needs it, than to do a more complicated thing today that may never be used anyway."[4]

—Kent Beck

---

4.   Kent Beck, *Extreme Programming Explained: Embrace Change* (New York, NY: Addison-Wesley, 2000), p. 31.

The XP mantra "you aren't gonna need it" (YAGNI) is about not adding a feature until the iteration it is needed. YAGNI also sums up the XP practice of emergent design. It is in some ways the antithesis of up-front design: not thinking ahead versus thinking ahead (see Figure 12-1). YAGNI represents a myopic approach to software development.

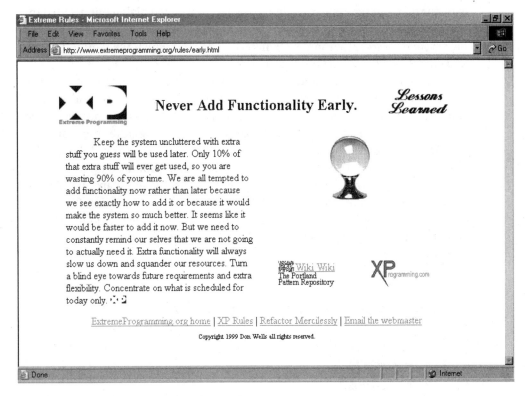

Figure 12-1. Never add functionality early

YAGNI is really a product of the parallel Extremo culture (even though it also crops up here and there in the XP books). As such, it gives a stronger, almost militant message than "new XP"—YAGNI is a product of the Old Testament, the angry years, when XP was new and a vengeful, no-nonsense god was needed to communicate a clear and unambiguous message to the unwashed. Anyway, where was I?

We discuss YAGNI in the context of Extremo culture in Chapter 4.

As the previous quote from Kent Beck suggests, XP is making a bet. We would say, better still, don't bet! If you have planned, architected, and designed properly, you're much less likely to have to throw away any work.

In fact, Beck's quote plays down the amount of rewriting that typically takes place in an XP project. To justify this approach, Beck (in *Extreme Programming Explained*) uses the example of a general-purpose dialog for displaying text. He explains that a programmer needed to display a message dialog but decided to make the dialog multipurpose "in case anyone else would like to use it." Two days were then spent writing the "smart dialog," after which the requirements had changed and it wasn't needed anyway.

This is a fine example, and of course it would have been much better to simply write a single dialog to display that one message (probably one line of code). Nobody else had asked for a multipurpose dialog, after all. This example is used as the basis for Beck's simplicity value (i.e., code only the features that you need).

Of course, you don't need to be doing XP to do that. The main difference is that without XP, you would have a documented design produced up front; hence, you would know simply by checking the design whether anyone else was going to need the same dialog. It's then possible to make a pretty intelligent decision about whether the time spent coding a smart dialog is justified. With XP, you just can't do that because tomorrow's design document doesn't exist yet. You're still coding it.

Top 10 Emergent Architectures We Hope We Never See

10. Payroll

9. PC operating system

8. Telephone switch

7. Electronic funds transfer

6. LASIK beam control software

5. Autopilot

4. NORAD early warning system

3. Space station environmental control

2. Missile guidance

1. Air traffic control

Building an Infrastructure with Emergent Design

> *"What about that database you need to build first? What about that framework? What about that syntax-directed command compiler? Get over it!"*[5]

Chapter 26 of *Extreme Programming Installed* (we'll call it "XPI26" for now, because we refer to it quite a lot) gives a fairly succinct description of the theory behind emergent design. XPI26 also mentions and reinforces the Extremo yell of *"YAGNI!"*

Similarly, XPI26 pulls no punches in the message that it communicates (we're talking here about transitioning the developer mind-set from the more traditional up-front design, or "look before you leap" approach, to emergent design):

> *"As you go along, put more and more simplicity in at the beginning, relying on your ability to refactor to add the generality—or the general tools—that you'll need."*[6]

The concept of "putting simplicity in" struck us as a conceptually backward thing to do—rather like opening a window to "let the cold in" rather than "let the heat out." Perhaps it's a Zen thing. Regardless, the emergent design approach is backed up by XP author Martin Fowler, who (talking about the joys of refactoring) said the following in an interview:

> *"I let most of the design flow from the evolutionary process. So I feel that there's been a shift in balance. Before, I might have preferred—and these percentages are purely illustrative—80% of my design in planned mode and 20% of it as the project went on. Now I'd perhaps reverse those percentages."*[7]

This is a startling ratio, illustrative or otherwise. The implication is that very little time is spent on up-front design—less than a quarter of the overall design, in fact. Ron Jeffries (quoted at the beginning of this chapter) takes this to even further extremes by stating that *10 minutes* of up-front design should be sufficient.

---

5. Ron Jeffries et al., *Extreme Programming Installed*, op. cit., p. 189.

6. Ibid., p. 192.

7. Bill Venners, "Flexibility and Complexity: A Conversation with Martin Fowler, Part IV," http://www.artima.com/intv/flexplex.html, November 5, 2002.

This approach might just work on very small projects, where 10 minutes of thinking is likely to generate a workable design. However, on complex projects, on the bleeding edge, it might take a lot longer to get in touch with reality, no matter how much we'd like it to be otherwise.

Here's another quote that made us scratch our heads:

"Emergent architecture relies on looking at a solution with a poor architecture and making a better architecture."[8]

We wonder, why deliberately start with a poor architecture? What's the benefit of starting with a poor architecture? Wouldn't we want to start with the best architecture that we can?

Why XP Deliberately Starts with a Poor Architecture

The philosophy behind XP's emergent design approach is somewhere along these lines: We start with a poor architecture because we don't know yet what the best architecture is; we learn only by doing; and maybe the first-pass architecture will suffice after all, and if so, we haven't wasted time in speculation. Furthermore, in the Test ➤ Code ➤ Refactor cycle, you do, according to Extremo theory, end up with the best architecture that you can, and it has taken, if all goes well, less time than Prototype ➤ Analyze ➤ Design ➤ Code.

This philosophy is based on the (erroneous) assumption that you can't get the architecture and design right by designing up front. In this book, we're making the case that by following a logical design process and by prototyping during designing, it's possible to get the design a lot more "right" than Extremo wisdom would suggest.

See later in this chapter for more about the benefits of combining prototyping with up-front design. Also see the section "Is Up-Front Design Sufficient to Avoid Large Refactorings Later?" in Chapter 9 for more about the benefits of applying a logical up-front design process.

Using XP's approach, you don't set out to design a good architecture first and then code it. You just leap into the code with minimal up-front design (as described by Ron Jeffries in XPI26) and wait for the architecture to emerge. Spending time

---

8. Kent Beck posting to the C2 Wiki page Can An Architecture Emerge, http://c2.com/cgi/wiki?CanAnArchitectureEmerge.

thinking about the design first is denigrated by the Extremos as Big Design Up Front (BDUF), another XP design mantra.

We discuss BDUF further in Chapter 8.

On first scan, XP's design approach does make sense. Designing for something that you might not need *is* often a bad idea, and leaving that part of the design until later can definitely save time, even if it turns out you do need to add that something in after all. However, XP once again takes things to extremes, and this is where the idea of emergent design (in the XP sense, at least) goes awry. We cover the reasons why in the remainder of this chapter.

Frameworks: What If Your Code Has Design Value Instead of Business Value?

In XP, the disparagement of up-front design extends to framework design and implementation (i.e., spending extra time putting code infrastructure in place). You might end up with a framework (of sorts) at the end of an XP project, but you certainly don't start out by writing or designing a framework.

This approach is described in XPI26. The driving force is that all the code you write should provide immediate business value to the customer. All code must start off with a user story, which the customer will have chosen to be developed next. Frameworks tend to be "behind-the-scenes" code—the underpinnings—so they aren't directly attributable to business value.

If you need to create a nonvisual component, which doesn't itself provide immediate business value (perhaps it provides support for some other component), then of course it needs a user story of its own. The user story should describe the new component so that the customer thinks, "Gosh, I really do want one of those after all!"

The same goes for generic code that applies to more than one user story but doesn't itself qualify as a user story. Thus, it would be nearly impossible to justify starting a parallel project (however small in scale—for instance, a week's work) to produce some common code that can be shared by different modules or even shared between projects.

The stumbling block is that anything that doesn't provide immediate business value to the customer (i.e., that doesn't get written as a user story) can't be justified. Therefore it's considered to be low priority and gets pushed to the back of the queue or dropped altogether. If you think about it, this means that sometimes *the customer must think like a designer* in order to justify whether a user story is worth including in the next iteration.

There are two issues to explore here:

- **The customer must sometimes make design decisions (despite the fact that the XP literature preaches otherwise).** Often, even minimal infrastructure code can make a program simpler and reduce development time. This sort of code provides design value rather than business value. However, for such code to be written, it would need to be written up as a user story and signed off first by the customer. This may seem contrary to XP *theory*, but we will attempt to explain why *in practice* this would turn out to be a customer decision.

- **An up-front design would make planning (therefore prioritization of features) more predictable.** If the infrastructure code is quite small scale, it could be refactored into existence without the need for a user story, but as the infrastructure gets bigger, project velocity will drop. From the customer's point of view, the software is just taking a lot longer to write than had been anticipated, but with no real feedback on why. Instead, more code is being produced that doesn't relate directly back to any particular user story. An up-front design would have allowed the team to better predict what needs to be written and how long it would take—cutting a straight line from A to B.

It's worth walking through a brief design example to illustrate both points.

Example: A Services Framework (Nothing to Do with Web Services!)

Suppose your project consists of many interrelated GUI dialogs that link to common services behind the scenes. Services might be for anything: printing, linking to a remote EAI hub, connecting to a banking system to transfer funds, and so on. These services communicate with and delegate to each other to provide responses to GUI events.

The simplest possible design would be for each service to know exactly which other service it needs to delegate to in order to get the job done. This is great, and it should give us a clear and simple design—at first. However, as the system grows in complexity, we quickly discover that it's difficult to add or extend services, because each caller (the class that invokes a service) must be made aware of the new or changed services as well.

Not Much Functionality at First: Nice and Simple

Let's say that our mythical application is a content management system in which the static parts of the Web site are designed offline and then uploaded to the public Web server.

To facilitate this, we would need a service that connects to the Web server in order to upload the static files (HTML files, images, etc.). This Web Server Upload Service is in turn called by a service that is responsible for publishing all recently modified files for a Web site. This Web Publisher Service is in turn triggered directly from the GUI. Figure 12-2 shows the basic class structure.

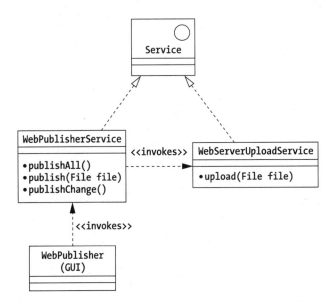

Figure 12-2. The basic class structure, early in the project

Adding More Services: A Bit More Complex Now

Now let's say that the customer has identified a need for a new upload mechanism to upload via a secure connection. This Secure Web Server Upload Service extends our existing WebServerUploadService class. This is fine—a simple if statement in the Web Publisher Service will determine which upload service to call, depending on a global user setting. Now let's say we want to add another upload type (an FTP upload, for instance) so our if...then statement becomes a little more complex. Figure 12-3 shows the new class structure.

The WebPublisherService class is now a potential minefield of complexity— and all because we wanted to keep things simple. Now every time we want to add a new upload service, we need to modify WebPublisherService to make it aware of the new service to call.

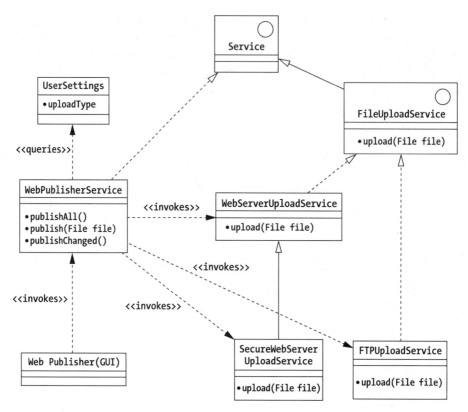

Figure 12-3. The class structure a bit later in the project—not quite so neat and tidy now

The obvious solution is to make the choice of service implementation transparent to the WebPublisherService class—in other words, that all WebPublisherService knows about is the FileUploadService interface. Now, however, things get a little more complicated. WebPublisherService itself needs to know which service to delegate to, without knowing what those services are. And we especially want to avoid the very non-object-oriented situation of a stream of if...then...else statements to determine which service to call.

As the overall system gains complexity, it's likely that the exact same problem is cropping up in many different parts of the system. We need a proper way of extending the system with new services, without breaking existing code—ideally so that the caller can't tell that it's using a different service.

Adding a Little Complexity to Make the Solution Simpler

One solution would be to introduce a new back-end module—a generic mechanism for looking up services, say. Of course, we can't justify this extra module without a user story, so XPers should just skip to the end of the chapter now. . . .

In fact, it would be pretty much impossible to write a "genuine" user story that asks for a design feature. (Of course, we *could* write such a user story that purely adds design value, but then—hey, guess what, the customer is now thinking like a designer!)

Anyway, back to the example. Using our generic lookup mechanism, the caller would simply pass in the details of the type of service (e.g., the interface of the required service) that it wants and be handed back a concrete implementation of that service. So to round off this example, the caller could pass in a service interface called FileUploadService and receive back one of the implementation classes (e.g., WebServerUploadService), depending on the user configuration. The caller is none the wiser about which implementation it receives—all it needs is the FileUploadService interface. The resultant class diagram would look something like the one in Figure 12-4.

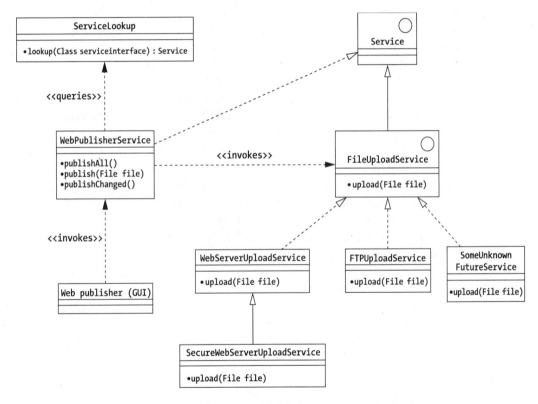

Figure 12-4. The class structure with some added infrastructure. Ah, that's better!

The addition of a little extra infrastructure would almost certainly provide savings in terms of time spent on development, because it results in a much cleaner overall design. But it would need time spent up front creating it, without any appreciable new functionality appearing. In fact, it might take an entire

1-week iteration to code the basic ServiceLookup class and its associated support code.[9]

And Then the Rest of the Design Falls into Place–Isn't It Great When That Happens?

With this infrastructure in place, we begin to see other benefits emerge—and before any code has been written, too!

For example, each service would need to handle its life cycle (i.e., starting and stopping, and multiple instances—for connecting to different servers, for example). Using XP's emergent design technique, life cycle management would be added to individual services, initially the service for which the need is first identified, then the next one, and so on. This would continue until after a while somebody notices that each service is doing something similar (life cycle management) and the design could be simplified a lot by having some sort of centralized service manager that handles life cycles for all the services in a consistent way (e.g., calling startup() and shutdown() on each service object at the correct time, and handling failure modes). It's time to grab our pair-programming buddy, refill the snack bowl, and start refactoring!

The trouble is, having evolved independently of each other, each service would be handling its life cycle in a slightly different way, probably having been written by different people (but we're forgetting this is the Borg collective, and everyone here thinks alike).

This inevitable (and subtle) divergence of the code can make refactoring much stickier. This sort of problem—unstitching similar, but not *altogether* similar, code—can make refactoring a progressive, time-consuming chore. Each individual service must be re-analyzed (there's no logical design to refer back to, after all), and each service's start/stop behavior must be picked apart and all its semantics deciphered so that we don't accidentally remove any essential behavior by "commonalizing" the code.

Meanwhile, if we had simply taken the up-front design approach and been able to put our Service Lookup infrastructure in place, all this would have been solved already. By assigning behaviors to the classes in Figure 12-4 (possibly via a sequence diagram), we would have identified almost immediately that each service will have startup() and shutdown() methods (plus a need to exist as more than one instance).

There is obviously some common behavior here, so it makes sense for some of this code to go into a new superclass called AbstractService and for the life cycle management to be controlled centrally by the ServiceLookup class, which basically becomes a Service Factory (to use the Factory design pattern).

---

9. Well, okay, for this example we could get away with a simple HashMap, but this is a simplified example, right?

By identifying this right at the start, the design has been kept simple before any code has been written—before the code has even had a chance to diverge or for duplication to appear. So . . . no need for all that time-consuming refactoring!

But How Do We Justify This to the Customer?

In an XP project, this extra infrastructure might never be added because *it isn't directly attributed to a user story*. The Service Lookup infrastructure doesn't provide direct business value to the customer, so we can't justify allocating resources to code it.

Therefore, we'll just have to rely on the code gradually, painstakingly being refactored into something similar in perhaps a year's time (with all the associated pain of a bad design in the meantime), when it is blatantly obvious, from looking at the design model, that spending time coding this up front would save a *lot* of time, even in the short term.

In a non-XP project, no such restriction exists: The customer defines the requirements, and the programmers design the solution. This is supposedly the same in XP (in fact, division of responsibility is central to XP rhetoric). However, as we've demonstrated, sometimes the customer sits a little too close to the programmers and may be required to make design decisions in order to keep the XP flag flying.

And as we discussed in Chapter 5, the customer is already over-loaded with responsibilities without having to become a software designer as well.

It might be possible to add a user story that says, "Write something that gets me the finished system several months sooner," and then the programmers can implement their Lookup mechanism. But then we enter the realm of controlling the planning game with "meta" user stories, which XP certainly doesn't cover.

We're not suggesting that these problems are insurmountable in an XP project. In the kind of scenario we just described, any development team with a collective ounce of common sense would realize that they need to spend at least a portion of their time producing code that isn't directly attributable to customer value (at least not without some pretty contrived user stories).

In such cases, the most likely course of action is that the team will estimate the amount of time it will take to produce the additional infrastructure and schedule it as one or more "rogue" user stories (i.e., ones that don't have immediate business value but instead add *design* value). However, in this case it's important to understand that the team is no longer performing XP. The team has strayed from the path, however deliberately. It is effectively tailoring the process: producing a customized version of XP that's adapted to the needs of its own project.

However, tailoring XP is actually much riskier than it at first seems. The circle of snakes is already complex and insidious without adding our own customizations, and it's all too easy to let the snakes unravel.

Using our "circle of snakes" metaphor, we describe the risks involved in tailoring XP in Chapter 3.

From A to B in a Straight Line

A key point to the services example is that the design was evolved and refactored before a single line of code was written.

The equivalent (taking an emergent design approach) would have involved writing unit tests, writing some code, realizing the code was wrong, changing it, fixing it because the tests caught errors introduced by the change, adding more tests, changing the code again, and so forth. Test-first design[10] is useful when used in conjunction with up-front design (because they address different aspects of the design), but on its own, emergent design is too high-discipline and not as efficient as it should be.

We discuss test-first design in Chapter 8.

Up-front design is agile in the sense that nothing we write down is fixed. Diagrams are, simply, easier to change and update than source code.

Up-front design (done properly, of course) isn't speculation; it's thinking and planning ahead. As such, up-front design provides us with a roadmap. Having produced the design, we don't need to implement everything in it right away. Instead, we can prioritize engineering tasks, where each task traces back to one or more customer requirements. (Note that this isn't dissimilar to XP's approach, with user stories broken down into tasks and stories penciled in for each iteration.)

---

10. A key component of emergent design.

The services example shows us that a services lookup framework isn't particularly complex. For example, we may not need database persistence (yet). With emergent design, we would assume at every stage that we need only the simplest possible design for now, even if we need to rewrite it later.

Conversely, with an up-front design, it's possible to make a much more intelligent decision about whether to code something simple for the time being, part of which might need to be rewritten when we implement the rest of the design. It all rests on if the customer really needs this simpler functionality sooner, or if he would prefer to wait and get more functionality delivered in a shorter time frame (with less rewriting).

Time to market might appear to be everything, but this isn't always the case. Often it pays to spend more time getting the product right first.

 Keeping the Design Agile

Looking at the UML model in Figure 12-4, it becomes obvious that passing File objects back and forth isn't a particularly abstracted solution. The java.io.File class is essentially a handle to a file system resource, so this ties the design into a files-only solution. What if we want to upload something that isn't a file? There could, for example, be a concept of a "virtual file-system" (e.g., hierarchical configuration details).

One possibility would be to replace the File parameter with an InputStream. This would cover pretty much all eventualities without adding any real complexity.

This is where up-front design (especially when combined with prototyping) has great advantages over emergent design. We get to see patterns emerge and consolidate the design into something both simpler and more generic before any production code has been written.

Is this the same as "guessing ahead" to future requirements? Of course the answer to this will vary. The amount of guesswork depends partly on the volatility of the requirements and also on how far ahead you're trying to design. The skill is in not guessing, but in learning to identify real requirements based on real problems that the customer needs to have solved—then to build a high-level design around those requirements—and then to prioritize implementation of the design into short iterations, which are in turn designed up front in more detail.

Up-front design helps us to quickly massage the design into something that is modular and therefore malleable. And because this needn't take very long, it helps the project to be more agile. If the requirements change or new features are added, the documented design helps us to quickly identify dependencies before any code is written.

Up-Front Design Is Not "Big Delay Up Front"

It's important to make this point. Producing a comprehensive design up front, done properly, doesn't have to take a long time.

The extreme that we all want to avoid is the one where no code is written for a year or more because the architects are still perfecting the design documents. The ideal middle ground is where the design takes one or two iterations (in "XP time")—maybe about a month, including prototyping. Of course, this is still a lot longer than XP's recommendation of 10 minutes of design up front.

Starting with the high-level architecture also helps, because individuals (or individual teams) can then get started on different areas of the detailed design in parallel. Coding can also begin on individual subsystems before the big design is finished, as long as the team has a very clear idea of what it is doing.

Meanwhile, testers can get started writing test scripts from the requirements, and programmers can write prototypes that are immediately fed back into the design. This all helps to make the design more stable, and it ultimately saves a lot of time and effort (we discuss this in more detail in the next section).

Is it really that important to give the customer working code a couple of weeks into the project? If the customer is prepared to wait just a few weeks extra, she will get a much more robust design and functionality—delivered incrementally—that gets delivered faster and is less buggy.

Going into more detail about the design earlier can also help the team to produce a more accurate set of estimates earlier—that is, the team can better predict, at an earlier stage, when the project will be completed.[11] The team can do this because the design process involves breaking down the requirements (e.g., use cases) into schedulable, estimable engineering tasks.

eXtreme Building (XB)

by Mark Collins-Cope

There's a new construction (of the building type) method out called XB—*eXtreme Building*. Basically, a lot of brikkies (bricklayers) grew frustrated that architects, civil engineers, electrical planners, etc. earned a lot more money than they did, and they decided that they were a redundant waste of space. So XB was born.

With XB, buildings can be put up in much less time. XB teams consist of a small number of talented brikkies who go on site, discuss what they're going to build informally (over a cup of tea in the tea hut), and then get to it.

Initial results are amazing. One team managed to construct a small 10×10×10 room in less than a day. They're now starting to think about what the rest of the house is going to look like, but initial indications are good, and the building team is very happy with its initial display of progress.

---

11. Note that this is still very much subject to the usual uncertainties that afflict many software projects, but with a decent design process, these uncertainties are more easily controlled. In fact, ignoring the benefits of detailed up-front design because design is "difficult to get right early on" is (to use a cliche) throwing the baby out with the bathwater.

One recent innovation is refactoring the building. It turned out that the $10\times10\times10$ room had the door in the wrong place (initial thoughts on the position of the second room were changed). But this wasn't a problem. They refactored the room in no time. Basically, every brick in the new door position was meticulously moved to the old door, and voila! Everything was all right.

Unfortunately, this took longer than it took to build the initial room, but heck, at least the construction manager had something concrete to show his clients on day one!

Plans are now afoot to build the first XB skyscraper (or is it a bridge?). Anyway, more news as it arrives. . . .

Emergent Architecture vs. Early Prototyping

Emergent design (also referred to as *emergent architecture*) is an evolutionary prototyping technique used in XP to "evolve" a design through refactoring from code, with little or no significant up-front design.

Conversely, *early prototyping* is a technique that involves creating lots of small, transitory programs and "program fragments" as an integral part of the up-front design process.

These two approaches are almost diametrically opposed in the philosophy that drives them, and yet in some ways they're grounded in the same set of goals.

Early prototyping traditionally fits into supposedly less "agile" methodologies that take a design-up-front approach. However, it also provides many of the benefits of the agile approach (e.g., early feedback), while retaining the more rigorous benefits gained from designing a system before coding it. The key benefit of early prototyping is that it provides a mechanism that helps to get the architecture and design right very early in the project.

Contrast this with the XP approach of emergent architecture. The theory here is that it should be possible to launch straight into the project without spending time up front (before production coding begins) thinking the architecture through. Done the XP way, the architecture itself would (in theory, at least) arise spontaneously as the codebase evolves.

In a discussion on Usenet regarding emergent architecture, XP author Robert C. Martin wrote the following:

> *"The fact that the architecture arises spontaneously does not mean that the architecture doesn't take work to derive. It does! Lots of work. It's just that the developers have more and more information with each new iteration. Each new batch of information solves more of the architecture puzzle. I agree, architecture requires up-front planning. However, I don't define 'up-front' as meaning 'pre-code'. I think you have to write some code up front to find the real architecture."[12]*

---

12. Robert C. Martin posting to the newsgroup comp.software.extreme-programming, subject: "XP and Rational Unified Process," August 19, 2002.

I almost choked on my cup of tea when I read the brilliantly circular "I don't define 'up-front' as meaning 'pre-code'." We agree with the kids, smoking cigarettes isn't at all bad for you, but then we don't define smoking as meaning "inhaling cigarette smoke."

This reply to Martin's message was posted by David Van Camp:

"Sorry, I simply don't buy it. I've been though this 'evolution' too many times. I call it 'redesign'. It is painful and labor intensive. To call it 'refactoring' is not to give it justice."[13]

These two messages highlight the differences between the two approaches. In XP, "emergent architecture" is achieved via evolutionary prototyping. With this approach, the prototype itself becomes the production code.

Conversely, with "traditional" early prototyping, the prototype is largely abandoned. It's kept for reference, but the production version is begun afresh. No time is wasted trying to refactor the prototype code into something more acceptable: Its place is simply to explore, to find out what's possible, and to get some idea of what's going to be involved in the real thing. That isn't to say that some code won't be cut and pasted from the prototype. However, the main thing that's kept is the knowledge and insight into the solution that the prototype gives us.

Combined with up-front design, we feel that this is a much more realistic approach to *getting the architecture right* than its evolutionary cousin.

Early prototyping is discussed in more detail in the online article titled "Emergent Design vs. Early Prototyping."[14]

Emergent Fangs

Emergent design relies on many XP practices/values being followed to the letter—in particular, pair programming, unit tests, collective ownership, coding standards, and simplicity. If anyone on the team starts to slip, code quality could immediately start to suffer (e.g., making changes to the design without full unit test coverage could result in undiscovered bugs slipping through).

Emergent design ignores the benefits of up-front design, instead using the erroneous assumption that you can't get the design right early as a reason not to do up-front design at all (or at least to reduce it to a 10-minute design workshop).

---

13. David Van Camp posting to the newsgroup comp.software.extreme-programming, subject: "XP and Rational Unified Process," August 20, 2002.

14. Matt Stephens, "Emergent Design vs. Early Prototyping," http://www.softwarereality.com/ design/early_prototyping.jsp, May 26, 2003.

Emergent Design Defanged

XP is very much opposed to adding extra layers of code "just in case" we need it later. We're 100% in agreement on this. We do, however, make the distinction between that and adding in code because we've designed for it and because we know that it's going to be an essential part of the system.

A documented up-front design provides a roadmap, with customer requirements broken down into engineering tasks. These tasks are estimable and schedulable, and so can be prioritized across iterations. Taking this approach lets the team make an intelligent decision regarding what to implement now based on how much of it would need to be rewritten later.

One of the most-feared problems with BDUF—that the customer doesn't get to see visible signs of progress for a long time—can be reduced in a couple of ways:

- Breaking the design into iterations, producing a high-level design (architecture) that can then be divided into subsystems, each of which is then designed in more detail. The subsystems may be designed and implemented concurrently, or sequentially in separate iterations.

- Showing the customer the early prototype. Remember the "prototype" may be many disparate pieces of code, each intended to explore a different area of the design.

A truly powerful approach would be to combine effective up-front design modeling techniques with XP's unit testing and refactoring techniques. The trick is to get the balance right: to spend sufficient time on architecture and design up front (precode) so that the design doesn't "churn" and spin out countless refactoring eddies (which create an illusion of progress when the project is really stuck in neutral).

More about this combined approach in Chapter 15.

Summary

There's a lot to be said for emergent design when it's used in moderation and under the correct circumstances. We've noticed a common reaction in people when we describe the concept to them: "Woo-hoo, on the face of it this makes so much sense! When you think about it, your understanding of the design really does change once you start programming! The design *does* evolve!" Then, when they really do think about it, they realize that there's something missing. Even if they use the full XP design arsenal—emergent design, refactoring, test-first design, YAGNI, and so on—they miss out on an essential and timesaving aspect of software development.

XP appears to be stuck in the initial "on the face of it" reaction. Dismissing the benefits of up-front design and early prototyping is just plain unwise, because it *is* possible to get a design pretty close to correct if you use the right approach. That isn't to say that the design will be perfect, but it will be stable enough, for example, for multiple teams to begin coding to the same design.

It has been argued that emergent design is a good approach for a project where the requirements are not clearly defined (i.e., they keep changing). We examine this aspect of XP in the next chapter.

CHAPTER 13

Embracing Change (Embrace People, Manage Change)

Changes
(With apologies to David Bowie)

I still don't know what I'd need design for
And my code was running wild
A million dead-end arraylists
Every time I thought I'd got it made
It seemed the code smell was not so sweet
So I turned my pair to face me
But I've never caught a whiff
Of how the others must smell the Smalltalk
I'm much too fast to unit test

Ch-ch-ch-ch-changes
(Tryin' to embrace change)
Ch-ch-changes
Don't want no specifications, man
Ch-ch-ch-ch-changes
(Tryin' to embrace change)
Ch-ch-changes
Just gonna have to toss that code and start again
Got no deadlines
So I can waste time

I watch the iterations change their size
But never leave the stream
Of those acceptance tests and
So the code floats past my eyes
But still the days all seem the same
And this snack food that we munch on
As we try to embrace change
And receive congratulations
On the marvelous agility we're going through

Ch-ch-ch-ch-changes
(Tryin' to embrace change)
Ch-ch-changes
Don't tell them to pair up and where to sit
Ch-ch-ch-ch-changes
(Tryin' to embrace change)
Ch-ch-changes
The planning game
You've left us up to our necks in it
Got no deadlines
So I can waste time

Strange code smells, fascinating me
Changes are shaking the code I'm going through

Ch-ch-ch-ch-changes
(Tryin' to embrace change)
Ch-ch-changes
Oh, look out you junior coders
Ch-ch-ch-ch-changes
(Tryin' to embrace change)
Ch-ch-changes
You just need to get a little bolder
Got no deadlines
So I can waste time
We do XP
So we can waste time

"Requirements creep is perfectly reasonable and rational, even valuable."[1]

—Kent Beck/Martin Fowler

"A project *without* rapidly changing requirements is a project that nobody cares about and nobody really wants."[2]

—Robert C. Martin

---

1. Kent Beck and Martin Fowler, *Planning Extreme Programming* (New York, NY: Addison-Wesley, 2000), p. 71.

2. Robert C. Martin posting to the newsgroup `comp.software.extreme-programming`, subject: "Why eXtreme Prejudice against XP?" August 8, 2001.

"Please tell me a story where the moral is, 'And that's why I am ever so happy that I tracked requirements changes'." [3]

—Ron Jeffries

The primary message in XP is to "embrace change." It's the maxim that appears on the front cover of the first XP book, *Extreme Programming Explained*. Despite occasional protestations to the contrary, the Extremos encourage us to embrace change and to follow a software process that makes changes to requirements almost a certainty.

In this chapter we examine this aspect of XP.

Constantly Fighting Emergent Entropy

The more code that has been written, the more difficult, time-consuming, and error-prone any change is likely to be. XP attempts to reduce this problem with constant refactoring, pair programming, unit tests, and so on, but as we will soon see (and as we will also see in the case study in the next chapter), emergent entropy (in which the code breaks down over time) is a likely outcome of the emergent design approach. So, as the codebase becomes more complex, the cost of making a change to the code increases.

The Cost of Change Curve (aka the Cost to Fix Defects Curve)

"XP puts the program into maintenance on the first day, and keeps it there forever. That's how we know XP produces maintainable code." [4]

It's been generally accepted for a long time that the further into a project, the more expensive it becomes to fix defects. If a design needs to be changed to accommodate new requirements, then similarly the cost is higher. In this section, we discuss the ways in which XP attempts to turn this "cost of change curve" on its head.

---

3. Ron Jeffries posting to the C2 Wiki page Requirements Tracking, `http://c2.com/cgi/wiki?RequirementsTracking`.

4. Ron Jeffries posting to the newsgroup `comp.software.extreme-programming`, subject: "Is XP Early Maintenance?" October 19, 2001.

In *Software Engineering Economics*, Barry Boehm writes the following:

"If a software requirements error is detected and corrected during the plans and requirements phase, its correction is a relatively simple matter of updating the requirements specification. If the same error is not corrected until the maintenance phase, the correction involves a much larger inventory of specifications, code, user and maintenance manuals, and training material.

"Further, late corrections involve a much more formal change approval and control process, and a much more extensive activity to revalidate the correction. These factors combine to make the error typically 100 times more expensive to correct in the maintenance phase on large projects than in the requirements phase.

"The total economic impact of leaving errors to be found after the software has become operational is actually much larger, because of the increased operational costs incurred by the error."[5]

In his 1999 *IEEE Computer* article "Embracing Change with Extreme Programming," Kent Beck raises this question: "What if we got good at reducing the costs of ongoing changes?" This became generally accepted as gospel to the tune of "XP reduces the cost of ongoing changes." (Note that many of XP's claims are actually made in "WhatIf" form.)

Boehm presents a logarithmic curve based on actual project data showing how cost increases from the requirements phase to the maintenance phase. Beck presents a what-if speculation that the curve could be flattened. And how does Beck propose to flatten the curve? *By eliminating all of the low-cost places where requirements errors can be corrected, releasing software to the client almost immediately, and operating the entire project in "maintenance mode"—the exact mode that Boehm's data shows to be the most expensive.*

Have the Extremos ever provided any real data beyond what-if speculation? Well, generally, they've pointed at C3. And guess what, this doesn't really make a very strong argument in their favor. *What if* it's still really expensive to skip requirements definition and up-front design and operate continually in maintenance mode?

 Well, we'd like to propose a few what-if speculations of our own (read the ^. notation as "leads to"):

```
WHATIF (CustomerBifurcation^.
    GoalDonorAndGoldOwnerDisagreement)?
    then ASSERT TerminationCanBeSuccess
```

---

5. Barry W. Boehm, *Software Engineering Economics* (Upper Saddle River, NJ: Prentice Hall, 1982), pp. 39–40.

```
WHATIF((SquadronOfOnsiteCustomers^.
    CustomerDoesNotSpeakWithSingleVoice)&(OralDocumentation))^.
    MassiveConfusionAboutRequirements?
    then ASSERT ItsTheCustomersProblem
WHATIF(LackOfUpfrontDesign^.
    ConstantRefactoringAfterProgramming)?
    then ASSERT RewritingCodeIsLotsOfFun
WHATIF(ConstantRefactoringAfterProgramming^.
    RefactoringInACircle^.
    SoftwareIsNeverDone)?
    then ASSERT GoodThingTheresPlentyOfSnacks
```

Release Early, Release Often

"We want to get a release to the customer as soon as possible. We want this release to be as valuable to the customer as possible. That way the customer will like us and keep feeding us cookies."[6]

—Kent Beck/Martin Fowler

"The customer will like us and keep feeding us cookies" for a while, anyhow. See the section "Generate a Quick Illusion of Success" in Chapter 2.

XP encourages teams to release code into the wild as soon as possible. By getting the product into the hands of the users very quickly (and then every few weeks from then until the project is cancelled), the team can start to get user feedback early in the project life cycle.

Thus, the users will have the latest version of the software installed "live" the day after it was written, and they'll get to say, "I don't like the way this works, can you change that?" or "This doesn't work the way it needs to." This is rather like crashing cars to work out how to make them safer, except the real users are being used as crash-test dummies.

It might be more sensible to take an interaction design approach (as described by Alan Cooper in *The Inmates Are Running the Asylum* and *About Face 2.0*). This approach is a very effective way of working out in advance what the users really need. By taking a goal-driven approach to human-computer interaction (HCI) design (rather than a feature-driven approach), the design is much more likely to

---

6. Kent Beck and Martin Fowler, *Planning Extreme Programming*, op. cit., p. 64.

fall into place early on (a good indication that this has happened is when both the technical design and the user experience design just *feel right*).

Getting feedback from the users at this early stage is also vital, but the distinction is that the users are being fed prototypes and drawings, rather than real software that must be tested out on real data in a live environment.

Another point made by Cooper is that paradoxically, the users aren't always the best people to decide what features to include in the product. Of course, their input is essential because they'll be the people using the software—the software is intended to solve their problems. However, the end users are typically not interaction designers. Users tend to suggest features or changes based on what they believe is reasonable.

The experienced interaction designer is likely to come up with a much better, more integrated set of features to fulfill the users' *goals* than the users themselves. Thus, while the users' feedback is important, they're best suited to contributing the goals of the software, rather than dictating the user interface design. And these goals (typically based on the problems that the users are facing with their current system) are just as easily identified prior to code being written than after.

Note that XP and some interaction design critics counter this by saying that discovering goals is hard, and users sometimes don't know what they want until they're using the software "for real." This is precisely why an experienced interaction designer is so important, because she understands how to identify the goals early on and she can help the users understand what they're getting. There's nothing arcane or magical about this approach; it's well documented.[7]

Luckily, interaction design and agile development aren't mutually exclusive. We combine them in our refactored process in Chapter 15.

Small Releases Can Delay the Minimum Feature Set

One of the purported advantages of small releases is that the software can begin earning its keep by providing business value to the customer straightaway. Although desirable, this isn't always as useful or practical as it sounds. Sometimes, time to market is less important than taking the time to get the product right first. And sometimes the customer needs a certain minimum level of functionality to be achieved before the software is really useful.

---

7. For example, read Alan Cooper's books (referenced in Chapter 15). Also see Jennifer Preece, Yvonne Rogers, and Helen Sharp, *Interaction Design* (New York, NY: John Wiley & Sons, 2002); Hugh Beyer and Karen Holtzblatt, *Contextual Design: Defining Customer-Centered Systems* (San Francisco, CA: Morgan Kaufmann, 1997); John M. Carroll, *Making Use: Scenario-Based Design of Human-Computer Interactions* (Cambridge, MA: The MIT Press, 2000).

If this turns out to be *most* of the product's functionality, then the team would do better to design and write the software as quickly as possible—cutting a straight line from A to B.

For some reasons why this is a faster approach, see the section "Building an Infrastructure with Emergent Design" in Chapter 12.

Although the "small releases" approach (coupled with emergent design) may seem to reduce risk, sometimes it can increase a project's likelihood of early cancellation because it actually delays the first useful release—when the product has achieved its minimum level of useful functionality.

Sometimes small releases can be useful, though. The point is to appraise the nature of the project at the start and tailor the process accordingly—and not to simply "go for it" with frequent small releases whether the customer needs them or not.

The benefits of small releases (primarily, early feedback) can still be achieved in a wider range of projects by taking an up-front design approach (as we discuss in Chapter 12). This does, of course, depend on whether the customer is prepared to wait a little longer (say, a month or two) for the first release—in our experience, we have found that this is almost always the case. In the few cases where the customer needs something working as soon as possible, a smaller interim release will often do. This keeps the customer happy and provides a breathing space to design the "main" product properly.

An example of this "interim release" approach is given in the case study in Chapter 15. See also the section "The Stopgap" in Chapter 15.

Another, major problem with releasing the system early is that it puts the software into maintenance mode very early on. This effectively slows development down; in certain circumstances it can slow development to a crawl. From now on, the party's over—you have real live customers to support. This means no more quick changes to the database or sweeping application programming interface (API) changes. Any such modifications now come at a price—several prices, in fact: reinstallation of all or part of the product, database update scripts, update scripts testing, user retraining, user manual or help screen rewriting, and regression testing, to name a few.

See Chapter 9 for more detail on the problems of refactoring a system with an installed user base.

Remember that live systems must also be supported on a day-to-day operational basis, and this can often involve your programmers, who would otherwise be better spending their time writing the other 90% of the product.

If the benefits outweigh the problems, it's worth doing; otherwise, you should ask yourself whether the project really needs to be in the customer's hands *just* yet.

Release Planning

Everything in XP revolves around user stories. The programmers break stories up into tasks and sign up for those tasks; acceptance tests are driven by the stories, with more detail added; and conversations with the customer are triggered by requests for more detail for individual stories. If the system contains bugs that need to be fixed, then they are written up as stories.[8] And planning in XP, in particular, revolves around user stories.

More specifically, *release planning* in XP is based on which user stories to implement and release to the customer in which iteration. The stories are estimated by the programmers in terms of "perfect weeks"[9]—that is, the amount that a programmer feels he could get done in a week with no interruptions, no distractions, and a mind focused purely on the story at hand. By tracking these estimates over time and comparing these with the actual time that each story takes to implement (which will inevitably be more time due to all the interruptions and distractions), the project velocity can be measured.

In XP, this is known as the *planning game*. Essentially, XP's planning game is a way to do "agile planning" so that change can be embraced. The team (including the customer) plans several iterations and at least two releases ahead. At the start of each iteration, the stories may be reprioritized.

Although this approach has merit for certain types of projects, in most business organizations the customer would almost certainly prefer to take a "fixed scope, fixed budget" approach, in which the customer works out in advance what is needed and the supplier (the XP team) tenders for the contract.

---

8.   Kent Beck and Martin Fowler, *Planning Extreme Programming*, op. cit.

9.   The term "perfect weeks" or "ideal days" is used less often these days. Most XP teams now use "story points" or "gummi bears" or some other arbitrary measure to distinguish between estimating and scheduling.

XP is optimized toward optional-scope contracts, but in many cases the real world just doesn't work this way. So in cases where a fixed-scope contract is required, XP's high-discipline collection of interdependent practices isn't the most efficient approach by any means.

 We discuss the merits and pitfalls of the various contract types in Chapter 11. And in pretty much the entire book (though particularly in Chapters 3, 11, and 12) we discuss why XP is high discipline and not the most efficient approach.

Iteration Planning

In the following quote, Ron Jeffries takes Kent Beck's Zen-like lead and adds further simplicity into XP by dropping task cards (as distinct from index cards for user stories) from the process:

> *"I don't use task cards any more, ever. The team might want to use some cards to write down notes about things they think need to be done. For anything that can be done in an evening, I'm not seeing why I'd need task cards.*
>
> *"Frankly I wish I had never written about them."*[10]

Despite this change of heart (tucked away as it is on the Extreme Programming message forum on Yahoo Groups), many XP teams continue to faithfully use task cards to help with iteration planning.

Iteration planning operates at a finer level of granularity than release planning. It involves breaking stories down into the aforementioned tasks, allocating tasks to programmers (rather, getting the programmers to sign up for the tasks they're interested in), and estimating the tasks (rather, getting the programmers to estimate the tasks they've signed up for).

The estimates are in "perfect days"—that is, the number of days it would take to complete each task if everything goes right and there are no distractions, no snack food mishaps, and so on.

The total estimated perfect days for all the tasks in an iteration might not add up to the same number of perfect days for the stories. This is because the stories were estimated before they had been broken down into tasks, and almost certainly before the tasks had been allocated to programmers.

---

10. Ron Jeffries posting on the Yahoo group Extreme Programming, http://groups.yahoo.com/group/extremeprogramming/message/70299, subject: "[XP] If you have time, could you comment on this...," March 1, 2003.

Note that (as the quote from Ron Jeffries suggests) many teams don't estimate tasks anymore. Instead, they base their estimates on the higher-level stories—they see task cards as unnecessary bookkeeping and have found story cards to be sufficient.

When Change Is Free

Loretta returns from a shopping trip to the new year sales at the local galleria, excited by the number of bargains she found. She finds JoJo at the snacking table and proceeds to tell him enthusiastically about her day.

"These shoes were like half-price, and this lip gloss was reduced, and this top was like buy ten get one half-price, so . . . just think about all the hundreds of dollars I've just saved! So I was halfway back here when I thought about it, and . . . seeing as I've saved all that money, I can go back tomorrow and find even more amazing bargains just like these!"

At that point, the on-site customer walks up to the table, hugely excited. "Guys!" he shouts, "I had no idea change was so free! With all the time that we've saved by not writing down any requirements or design, I can afford to keep changing my mind over and over again! XP is just like a trip to the new year sales!"

JoJo, finishing his snack, adds, "Those potato chips were reduced fat—so I can afford to eat another bag! Gosh, I love you guys . . .”

The Perpetual Coding Machine (Embracing Change)

"Even though you don't really have to release for six months or a year, releasing every couple of months can really pay off. You don't want to pass up the chance to learn what users really want. You don't want to pass up the increasing confidence that will come from showing people that you have done something useful. And you don't want to pass up the sheer thrill of releasing useful software into the universe."[11]*

Um, riiiiight.

In a project that is releasing early and often to end users, there is an increased risk that the software will never be done. This is because each iteration from the first release onward involves maintaining legacy code (which must in turn be changed because the users aren't happy with the first few versions). The Extremos' viewpoint, not surprisingly given their case history, is that a project that continually undergoes revisions until it is finally cancelled is a sign of success.

---

11. Ron Jeffries, Ann Anderson, and Chet Hendrickson, *Extreme Programming Installed* (New York, NY: Addison-Wesley, 2000), p. 50.

Ron Jeffries' sheer thrill of releasing useful software into the universe is tempered by the fact that the user is likely to want the software changed. Our own "sheer thrill" comes from delivering a piece of software to the user's satisfaction and from knowing that it's completed—that it's time to move on and deliver something else. This is the satisfaction of getting the job finished.

Why *do* XP projects risk going round and round, covering the same old ground? The evidence suggests that this is what happened on C3 (as we explored in Chapter 2). The problem that XP suffers from is that it spins at two levels: at the requirements (user story) level and at the design level.

Spinning a Story

> *"Requirements creep is perfectly reasonable and rational, even valuable. The requirements can creep wherever they like as long as we know where they are going and the customer is informed of the consequences. Indeed, we encourage the requirements to crawl around and find whatever it is the customer needs."*[12]

Surely (we would suggest), the requirements spin because not nearly enough effort is put into getting them right in the first place. Apart from the initial brief exploration phase, very little time is spent helping the customer understand what it is she is really asking for.[13] Instead, the XP mechanism to achieve this understanding is to release the project early and get user feedback on a working system.[14] The requirements for subsequent iterations may then change (or new requirements discovered) based on this feedback.

This sounds okay, except that in order to make this really work, XPers must accept scope creep as a natural part of the project. To an extent, scope creep is a natural part of any project, but XPers go several steps further and embrace scope creep as a good thing: a way to extract the body of correct requirements from the customer. We feel that these requirements should be identified much earlier.

---

12. Kent Beck and Martin Fowler, *Planning Extreme Programming*, op. cit., p. 71.

13. The customer also spends a lot of time writing tests, which in XP is considered to be discovering and writing requirements. More about that in Chapter 10.

14. It was suggested to us that acceptance tests are also a mechanism for this purpose. However, acceptance tests aren't a mechanism for *understanding* the requirements; they're a mechanism for verifying that the requirements have been implemented by the programmers.

Does Agile Mean Fast?

XPers see scope creep as being an important part of software agility.[15] The ability to accept new requirements late in a project is what makes a project "agile." However, this isn't the same as following a process that *causes* requirements to be discovered late in a project (and embraces the cause with "courage").

Instead, why not follow a process that accepts scope creep as an occasionally necessary evil and makes it possible to add requirements late in the project, but that doesn't go out of its way to make scope creep more likely?

A large part of XP is about planning and making estimates gradually more accurate by tracking the velocity of each iteration. However, XP's wholesale acceptance of scope creep kind of throws a wrench in the works and (for the reasons we've described) makes it more likely that requirements will lurk undiscovered until late in the project.

Spinning the Design

The design also gets spun perpetually because in XP coding is never finished. A task might be signed off and pass all its unit tests, and the overall story (or stories) to which the task contributes might pass all its acceptance tests, but the lid is never quite fully closed on the code. A different pair of programmers working on a different task might find that their task needs the "finished" code to be changed, or they might simply decide that the design could be refactored, without any particular goal in mind except to make the code cleaner.

We discuss the problem of Constant Refactoring After Programming in Chapter 9 and emergent design in Chapter 12.

This makes planning difficult. The team *might* eventually reach a constant velocity by factoring in the refactoring process[16] (seeing it as a constant, concurrent process that persists throughout the project), but the velocity is likely to be much slower than if the team had spent time getting the design right up front (as we discuss in Chapter 12).

The Extremos see the concept of "getting the design right up front" as something that just isn't realistic—something that would be great if this were a perfect

---

15. Note that many people might associate the word "agile" with the words "quick" or "fast." But the meaning is considerably different. Organizing your software process to embrace changing requirements means it takes a long time to get done!

16. Factoring in refactoring? Isn't it refactoring in factoring? This reminds us of Groucho Marx in *Horsefeathers*: "Anything further, father? That can't be right. Isn't it anything farther further?"

world but really just can't be done reliably. We've spent a lot of time in this book trying to convince you otherwise: that it *is* possible to get a design right prior to coding; that this can be done predictably, by following specific methods (a logical process); and that doing this minimizes the amount of postcode refactoring needed.[17]

Constant Refactoring Not Realistic in Small Companies

One of our "Voice of eXPerience" interviewees, Robin Sharp, suggested that XP might be better suited to large companies in which entire projects can hide behind department budgets and be left to linger for years at a time, blithely dismissing the notion of "doneness." In small companies (e.g., tech start-ups) where resources are tight (and probably paid for by venture capitalists), every piece of work needs to be budgeted for and fully justified.

In the latter case (as happened on the XP project Robin was involved in), the managers would be very happy to embrace the "no up-front design" and "no detailed up-front requirements capture" aspects of Extremo culture, but they would not be so keen on the "refactoring code that we thought was already finished" aspect.

Of course, this problem is not insurmountable. A lot depends on the mentality of the managers and on the extent to which they micromanage the programmers' lives. However, XP's emergent design approach does not fit comfortably with small company management dynamics.

Voice of eXPerience: The Simplest Build System

by David Van Der Klauw

Our build system had evolved over the years from BAT files to VBScript. Although it had become a bit complicated, it did have concise logging, checked for most errors, and immediately stopped and reported errors.

When XP was introduced, a new team needed a cut-down integration build. I suggested basing it on my build system but simplifying certain sections. This would have taken maybe 2 days of work.

The team members rejected this idea because my build system was too complicated and, in XP fashion, they were determined to do the simplest thing that could possibly work—BAT files, they thought.

Their BAT file build was simple, sure enough: no error checking, no logging, and pages and pages of useless output with a critical error buried in the middle. It was impossible to debug and never worked properly.

Various pairs spent 8 weeks on this abomination, adding more and more BAT files, more and more layers of simplest possible solutions, before it was finally scrapped.

---

17. Doug has actually gone to the trouble of writing two books that explain how to do this reliably. This topic is beyond the scope of this book, though.

Pair-Watching the Progress Bar

To maintain all development PCs at the same state, our team would create an image of a PC and load it onto a clean PC. Before XP, Nandor did a good job of all the imaging for the team.

Under XP, it was decided that everyone had to do imaging and it had to be done in pairs. Under XP, the team had only one PC per pair, so during the lengthy imaging process, there was nothing else to do, and you had two people sitting there watching a progress bar move for half an hour.

Every half hour the coach insisted that a new member swap in to the pair. So the new member could watch the progress bar move from, say, 30% to 70% in that half hour.

Anyway, some weeks after this nonsense had occurred, it became necessary to update the image. I asked the team, "Who can tell me how to do the imaging?"

It turned out that no one could. Each person had been swapped around so much that no one had seen the whole process, nor understood it, nor remembered it. I had to go outside the team to find the expertise. Fortunately, Nandor was still with the company at this stage.

Project's Not Going Too Far
(Sing to the tune of "Back in the USSR" by The Beatles)

Overtime is evil when you do XP
Gotta leave at five PM each night
Schedule's not our problem because change is free
Man, Kent really got it right

Project's not goin' too far
Find out how lucky you are, boy
'Cause your project's not goin' too far

This code has been refactored by a chimpanzee
Maybe it needs a rewrite
What that ape was thinkin' about I just can't see
Maybe he's just not too bright

Project's not goin' too far
I dunno how lucky you are, boy
'Cause your project's not goin' too far

We put code in and we rip it out
We leave a mess behind
Refactoring's what it's all about
Ain't no time for design-nine-nine-nine-nine-nine-nine-nine-nine

Going round in circles each and every day
Is not a cause for alarm
When we throw the stack of index cards away
We're not doing any harm

Project's not goin' too far
I dunno how lucky you are, boy
'Cause your project's not goin' too far

What Is This *Change* of Which You Speak?

Change in XP (and, in fact, in every other software process ever) operates at two levels:

- Changes to requirements

- Changes to architecture/design

Changes to requirements usually involve some form of impact analysis, where the customer is given enough information to decide whether the change is worth pursuing. For example, adding this module will take an extra 2 weeks; or deciding that the system must cope with up to 10,000 transactions per hour, not 100 as originally decided, will involve a significant architectural change that could add an extra 6 months to the project. Given such information, the customer may decide to go ahead, or to postpone the change until a later release, or not to make the change at all.

Changes to architecture/design are often a direct result of a change in requirements. Also, a design change can be a result of increased understanding of the solution (whereas a requirements change is a result of increased understanding of the problem).

In XP, changes are handled by dividing the project into short iterations of 1 to 3 weeks. A shift to a completely new architecture would involve many, many short "baby steps," gradually changing the design until the new architecture is reached. Of course, baby steps may not always be possible. At some stage (for example) a giant leap might need to be made if the change is as fundamental as a migration from .NET to a J2EE architecture.

See Chapters 9 and 12 for more about refactoring and emergent design.

Use Up-Front Design to Enhance Agility

Detailed up-front design can actually be used as a tool to increase agility. This might sound self-contradictory at first, but let's explore whether software agility really can be enhanced with the right kind of up-front design.

Manage Change

This might be seen as a controversial statement, but we believe that the best way to be agile is simply to do the following:

1. Develop software really quickly. Then there's less chance that it will need to change midproject.

2. Don't code each module until you have your design (see Chapter 8 for a discussion on knowing when the design has enough detail). It's much easier to change a diagram than to change source code.

The easiest way to develop software quickly is to code to a known design. Then you know exactly how to get from A to B in the straightest possible line. Everyone is working from the same version of the same design, so there is no confusion.

Developing software rapidly is effectively shielding the project from the forces of change. This is the bipolar opposite of the Extremo definition of agility we cited earlier.

Of course, this doesn't make the project *impervious* to change. When change happens, you still need to be able to respond to it without the entire project shuddering and falling over.

A couple more items could be added to the list:

3. Keep your design simple. Changes will be a lot easier to handle.

4. Break the architecture down into smaller modules, delivered separately in small increments (ideally about a month each).

Simple design and small releases are also central to XP, but if we combine them with the first two items, the result should be a process that is lightning fast, robust, and responsive to change. We have our Holy Grail.

Refactoring the Design Before Code—Surely That Would Be Too Extreme?

Yes, it's true. Refactoring is hard work, and when you don't keep your code in a well-factored state, it's just too easy to let that next iteration deadline creep in and keep you from doing the refactoring you need. And, you know, you can't ever have too much refactoring. Yes indeed, refactoring's a good thing, and so we can't have too much of it.

So we're going to introduce a *new* concept that we believe to be even more eXtreme and agile than Constant Refactoring After Programming. Because we're all agreed that the earlier we start refactoring, the better, what if we started our refactoring *before* coding?

Wow, you say, that really *is* eXtreme! I mean, how can we refactor code before code exists? Certainly we couldn't start refactoring before we have some stinky code to refactor, could we? Seriously, don't we have to code the simplest thing that can possibly work, and *then* refactor it?

But here's a thought: Every time we refactor, we have to write new tests and rerun all the old tests. Because we always have to keep the code in a state of 100% unit-test correctness. But *what if* we could refactor the *design*, without all the overhead of first writing bad, stinky code; and then making sure the bad, stinky code passes all the unit tests; and then cleaning up the bad, stinky code so it smells better and making sure that the sweeter-smelling code passes all of its tests, all the while worrying about that next iteration deadline for delivering new functionality that's always within a week or two of making us late on our stories?

What if there was time budgeted into the development process where we could think about getting the design right, without that next iteration deadline looming on the horizon? *What if* we had *frictionless refactoring*, where we didn't have all the overhead of testing and integration getting in the way of our refactoring? We could turn the dial all the way up to ten on refactoring! Wouldn't that be eXtreme?

Striking the Balance of Design Abstraction

Good design documents are much quicker to update and refactor than code. This means that not only can you refactor the design very quickly before the code is written, but also—should you need to update the design once you have begun coding—you can do so equally quickly. The robustness diagram, as defined in Chapter 4 of *Use Case Driven Object Modeling*, is ideal for this task.

The skill is in knowing how abstract the design should be. We sometimes see sequence diagrams where the designer appears to have tried to write a detailed program (with the minutest code logic) into the diagram. Diagrams are intended to convey sufficient information so that the program can be coded from them,[18] but they aren't intended to be the program themselves. In other words, they're written at a level of abstraction away from the code.

Getting the level of abstraction right means that the design can be updated quickly and minute changes to code don't render the design obsolete in a nanosecond. The design needs to be decoupled from the code but not made so far removed that it's meaningless. There is obviously a balance to be achieved.

---

18. And sequence diagrams in particular are intended to model a scenario—a single pass through a collection of objects for a specific set of data—rather than a complex web of conditional logic.

Embracing Fangs

If it sounds too good to be true, it probably is. Changing the requirements during coding is expensive, and changing the requirements once the product has shipped is even more expensive. Always has been, always will be. Smell the hype.

Change Defanged

In any project, it's worth questioning how soon it really needs to go into maintenance mode (i.e., how soon the first live customer release should happen). If the reason for an early first release is simply to gain better user feedback, there are other ways of achieving this.

Rather than evolving the requirements based on a process of early feedback from the user, it's better to use more effective techniques to get the requirements in the first place. Use an interaction design approach, analyze the users' goals, and gain the users' insight into their ideal solution using prototypes and storyboarding techniques. The requirements will never be 100% correct at first, but we can nevertheless take great steps toward reducing requirements churn.

Similarly for design, effective up-front design techniques can help to reduce the need for Constant Refactoring After Programming.

That isn't to say that the requirements should be *locked down* once programming begins. Many projects have failed because the requirements changed (e.g., due to a change in market forces) but the project team didn't react. As with XP, the customer should be allowed to change the requirements at any stage, but he should also be made aware of the cost of such changes, and the effort should still be made to get the requirements right as early as possible.

Summary

As we discovered in this chapter, as long as change is managed and not actively embraced like a long-lost lover, and as long as your development process doesn't increase the likelihood of requirements changing late in the project, then change can be used to good effect. The competitive advantage that can come from last-minute changes should not be ignored. However, it is also important to understand that change is not free. Simply rewriting something (however efficiently) can only add to the time that was taken to write the first version.

Therefore, accepting change and managing it appropriately is rather different from the XP approach of embracing change and encouraging scope creep.

As the project grows larger (either in team size or functionality), it becomes even more important to manage change, as we explore in the next chapter.

Part V

The Big Picture

CHAPTER 14

Scalability

Big Projects Got No Reason to Live
(Sing to the tune of "Short People" by Randy Newman)

Big projects got no reason
Big projects got no reason
Big projects got no reason to live
If you got too many coders
To fit in a room
You know that your project
Is destined to doom
So we don't want no big projects round here

Big projects got no reason
Big projects got no reason
Big projects got no reason to live
When you smell the code
You know you got to inhale
We like small projects
'Cause XP don't scale
So we don't want no big projects round here

"It is difficult to build extensive tacit knowledge without good osmotic communication, and that is hard to do with more people than conveniently fit in a room."[1]

"Code is definitely worse than we started."[2]

"Metaphors are unrealistic with large projects. They are just too complex. Period."[3]

---

1. Alistair Cockburn, *Agile Software Development* (New York, NY: Addison-Wesley, 2001), p. 169.

2. Amr Elssamadisy, "XP On A Large Project—A Developer's View," http://www.xpuniverse.com/2001/pdfs/EP202.pdf, paper presented at the 2001 XP Universe conference.

3. Ibid. We analyze the paper containing this quote and the last in the "Painting Over the Cracks" section in this chapter.

In this chapter, we analyze the difficulties faced by XP teams when dealing with scalability. For the purposes of our discussion, there are two types of scalability:

- The ability of the product being delivered to scale architecturally

- The ability of the development process to handle larger projects. Larger projects could be

  - Larger in team size

  - Larger in terms of the amount of functionality being delivered

Most of this chapter is concerned with the second type: process scalability. (Although we will also discuss some ramifications that emergent design may have on architectural scalability.)

But before we look at either of these scalability types, let's examine some important available research.

Painting Over the Cracks: XP on a 50-Person Project

What really happens when XP scales up to large projects? In this section we analyze a case study of a 50-person XP project (with the team referred to as ATLAS). The case study can be found online here: http://www.xpuniverse.com/2001/pdfs/EP202.pdf.

The ATLAS project was conducted by ThoughtWorks, Inc., an XP "shop" and home of Extremo author Martin Fowler. In this project, we see the circle of snakes really come to life.

See Chapter 3 for our "circle of snakes" metaphor.

Note that when Matt wrote the original "The Case Against Extreme Programming" article http://www.softwarereality.com/ExtremeProgramming.jsp and introduced the circle of snakes a few years ago, he had not seen this research. But, as you'll see, XP breaks down in just about all the ways you would expect it to as projects grow in size. In fact, some of the breakdowns would occur even on smaller projects.

The first thing to note about this particular study is that, after a year and a half of XP, the "code is definitely worse than [when they] started." Yet this is one of XP's biggest selling points: that repeated refactoring supposedly results in greater code quality. So, what went wrong?

Looking at the case study, it's quite obvious to us that the circle of snakes broke loose. One practice slipped, meaning that the next in line stopped working, and so on. The team, meanwhile, saw this as a sign that it needed to work harder at applying the XP practices. (In the words of Boxer the cart horse from George Orwell's *Animal Farm*, "The only possible answer is that I was not working hard enough. I *will* work harder!" Or, to put it another way, "The only possible answer is that I was not refactoring hard enough. I *will* refactor harder!")

XP is simply an impractical approach to follow on medium- to large-scale projects. Even a medium-sized, 50-person project like the one described in the case study quickly shows XP's shortcomings. To apply XP's practices effectively involves tailoring it, resulting in something that the team might prefer to call XP, but really isn't.

Dodging the Practices

Table 14-1 summarizes some of the ways in which we would expect the XP practices to fail as the project grows (either in scope or in team size). Just for fun, we've also summarized the corresponding problems that were reported on the ATLAS project (full descriptions can be found in the referenced case study).

Table 14-1. Problems Reported on the ATLAS Project

XP PRACTICE, TENET, OR MAXIM	HOW WE EXPECT XP TO FAIL AS THE PROJECT GROWS	WHAT ACTUALLY HAPPENED ON ATLAS
On-site customer	Difficult for the customer to speak with a single, unambiguous voice. A detailed requirements document would help.	One customer wasn't sufficient; instead, a team of analysts was needed.[4]
Iteration planning meeting	Communication less effective; risk of some key decisions being missed.	The meetings had to be split into smaller, more manageable meetings attended by different people (with "summary" meetings held later).

---

4. As we explored in Chapter 5, this has proved to be the case generally in XP.

Table 14-1. (continued)

XP PRACTICE, TENET, OR MAXIM	HOW WE EXPECT XP TO FAIL AS THE PROJECT GROWS	WHAT ACTUALLY HAPPENED ON ATLAS
Small releases	Larger pieces of work could be difficult to fit into a single iteration. This makes project velocity more difficult to measure (possibly less accurate over time).	The team worked hard to adhere to a fixed 2-week iteration, although larger pieces of work needed to span iterations.
Programmers test their own code	XP suffers from not stipulating a separate software tester. Having a separate QA team that is proactively involved in all areas of development helps to reduce the bug count and improve (and enforce) the development process. QA is especially important on large projects; leaving programmers to test their own code isn't sufficient.	Although the team members kept to this tenet, they also discovered that a separate QA team was essential.
Pair programming	Lower levels of communication, because there are more people to "pair-rotate" with (see the next entry on pair rotation).	The team pair-programmed religiously when new functionality was being added, but abandoned the practice when bug-fixing or writing "repetitive" code.
Pair rotation[5]	Lower levels of communication; programmers end up specializing in particular niches of the project, which in turn increases the risk of insufficient communal knowledge of a particular area if a programmer leaves the project. A documented design can significantly reduce this risk.	The team started out rotating pairs but stopped, citing the following reason: *"When you have deadlines— we find ourselves signing up for things we already know."* They added, *"Signing up for cards in several parts of the system in one iteration is definitely out of fashion these days."*

---

5. See the section "Extreme Programming in Theory" in Chapter 1 for a brief description of pair rotation. Also see Chapter 6.

Table 14-1. (continued)

XP PRACTICE, TENET, OR MAXIM	HOW WE EXPECT XP TO FAIL AS THE PROJECT GROWS	WHAT ACTUALLY HAPPENED ON ATLAS
Refactoring	The team may find itself relying more and more on refactoring to keep the code in shape (in other words, emergent design becomes harder and harder work).	A year into the project, *"Refactoring* [was] *being done much more often as code starts to spaghetti in some parts of the app."*
Sustainable pace (40-hour week)	As refactoring becomes more difficult (hence, time consuming), sustainable pace may as a result become more difficult to adhere to and overtime becomes the norm. The programmers become more tired. Tired programmers means more bugs and less effective unit tests, which in turn means refactoring with a safety net full of gaping holes, which in turn means more bugs. . . .	The team interpreted this practice as "minimum 40 hours." They claimed that working overtime did not adversely affect them (and yet, again, they later concluded that the code degenerated during the project).
Coding standards	Collective ownership becomes more problematic, because code written by different people would be inconsistent and hence more difficult to decipher.	Coding standards were very informal (i.e., not strictly adhered to). The team reports that this was not detrimental to its progress; yet the team later concluded that the code was in a much worse state than when the team started.
Collective ownership	Communication of the overall design decreases; knowledge of individual areas becomes highly specialized. Refactoring also becomes significantly more problematic, because it involves changing other parts of the system, which are "owned" by other teams but are affected by the code being refactored.	From the case study: *"Code owner-ship* [sic] *remains diluted. Developers start specializing in parts of the system again."*

Table 14-1. (continued)

XP PRACTICE, TENET, OR MAXIM	HOW WE EXPECT XP TO FAIL AS THE PROJECT GROWS	WHAT ACTUALLY HAPPENED ON ATLAS
The code is the design	As the project grows, code becomes less and less effective as a method of communicating the design.	The team discovered that the code is not sufficient design documentation, and the team members needed to regularly communicate the design through presentations.[6]
Stand-up meetings	Lower levels of communication, because the increased team size would make stand-up meetings for everyone involved less practical.	The team abandoned these in favor of "informal communication" and monthly team meetings. "Informal communication" is just another way of saying "We couldn't be bothered to document our design." On a large project, this is lunacy.
Metaphor	More misunderstandings (some of them probably quite insidious) could spring up.	The team found that a single unifying metaphor to describe the architecture just wasn't suitable for such a large project.

As you can see, most of the ways in which the team "tailored" XP resulted in lower levels of communication—exactly the opposite of what any team would *want* to happen in a large-scale project. Unfortunately, the way in which the team's practices slipped one by one is also exactly what you would expect to see as an XP project scales up (and hence its practices become steadily more difficult to adhere to).

For example (as we describe in Table 14-1), the XP metaphor practice (which many XPers see as a vital ingredient in XP's supposed ability to cut down on design documentation and up-front design) just doesn't work well on large projects—it's too simplistic. From the case study:

> *"Metaphors are unrealistic with large projects. They are just too complex. Period."[7]*

---

6. Presentations are useful to bring the design to life and communicate it effectively to developers. Writing the design down (and keeping it up-to-date) can also save a lot of wasted work and misunderstanding.

7. Amr Elssamadisy, op. cit., p. 5.

A documented (and maintained) domain model would have helped a lot. A domain model is a much more scalable and robust replacement for XP's metaphor.

Constant pair programming also turned out to be difficult to adhere to:

"Some are really just more talented than others and are slowed down by it—and it becomes obvious that it becomes a burden for these people."[8]

As mentioned in Table 14-1, the team abandoned pair programming when bug fixing or writing repetitive code. In some ways, bug fixing can be thought of as a surgical form of refactoring (albeit with a different goal: fixing bugs instead of tidying up code). So, to prevent the other high-discipline XP practices from slipping, the team should have adhered to pair programming even more religiously, not less.

Iteration planning meetings became more of a burden with more people involved. Meetings involving 50 people were found to be overwhelming (and were later abandoned altogether), but in the meantime, smaller groups of developers "prepped" each meeting in advance (resulting in more work, when the developers could have better spent their time designing and programming).

Collective ownership also showed signs of taking a back seat to the natural urge to simply make some progress:

"With specialization, there is a trend with a small set of developers knowing more about different parts of the code—so we tend to have them be more active in the continuing designs, but still communal ownership of the code."[9]

So there was an effort to retain "communal ownership." Unfortunately, having the specialized programmers be more active in the design work is missing the point of collective ownership: that in XP-land, every time somebody refactors a piece of code somewhere in the system, they're doing design work. If programmers are specializing in certain areas, blindly saying "we still have collective ownership" could lead to refactoring without a vital safety net.[10]

It gets worse. As we saw earlier, refactoring on ATLAS wasn't backed up by rotation of programmers to different tasks. The danger (particularly on large projects) is, again, that of decreased communication. Refactoring is hampered

---

8. Ibid., p. 4.

9. Ibid., p. 3.

10. At least, it's vital in XP because the practices are taken to extremes.

because it's more difficult to change other people's code, and diving in to change unfamiliar code will almost certainly result in a higher defect rate. Small wonder, then, that the team was relying so absolutely heavily on unit tests to save the day (as we explore in the next section). Nevertheless, the code quality still suffered.

If refactoring is hampered by other problems, then of course emergent design—one of the cornerstones of XP—also becomes problematic.

Emergent Design on ATLAS-Sized Projects

The ATLAS team correctly identified that simple design is essential for a large-scale project, and that refactoring is an important practice to keep the design in trim. This is true of any project to an extent, but much more so in XP, which places more of an emphasis on emergent design (as opposed to up-front design). Unfortunately, the article also highlights the inadequacy of emergent design when it comes to large projects:

> *"Code is definitely worse than we started. But is this because the project is larger? Or is it because many people* [that] *touch the code are first timers? A little of both—but at the same time we don't get islands of code that do not have anything to do with the rest of the application. There needs to be a constant cleaning up of code."[11]*

This suggests that Constant Refactoring After Programming just isn't sufficient to make up for the paucity of up-front design.

Let's revisit that preceding quote for just a second, especially the first sentence of it: "Code is definitely worse than we started." If XP has any purpose, isn't it to improve code quality? Isn't that *exactly* what XP is supposed to be all about? So, doesn't the sentence "Code is definitely worse than we started" pretty much tell the whole story?

Ironically, the team also showed signs of perhaps becoming too dependent on certain high-discipline XP practices. In particular, the article reveals the team's overreliance on unit tests and continuous integration when up-front design is skipped:

> *"Unit tests and integrated builds—are ABSOLUTLY MANDITORY* [sic]— *we would be stopped in our tracks and not able to deliver one piece of code if we could not rely on tests. As the application gets larger and larger it becomes almost impossible to add new code or refactor existing code without going through tests."[12]*

---

11. Amr Elssamadisy, op. cit., p. 4.
12. Ibid.

This highlights the true cost of the emergent design approach, particularly on large projects. The team also appears to have forgotten the benefits that a documented design would have provided when adding new code.

Summing Up

In conclusion, kudos to the team for writing such an honest and open appraisal of its experience with XP—although the conclusion surprised us (our emphasis):

> "XP, or our evolved version of it, *has done wonders for us as a team.*"[13]

This is a chilling example of Extremo logic and a shining example of another XP "success story" on a par with C3. Quite simply, the conclusion isn't borne out by the rest of the case study, which paints a much less rosy picture (although the article's author appears to be blinded to the signs that XP was causing more problems than it was solving). As a project increases in team size, the XP practices become more difficult to adhere to. The main deliverable—working code—inevitably suffers as a result. The ATLAS project is evidence that this really is the case.

In the next section, we shift topics slightly to look at the way in which XP handles architectural scalability (as opposed to project scalability).

Projects That Are Very Small
(Sing to the tune of "The Wall" by Pink Floyd)

We don't need documentation
We don't need no UML
We use our nose for quality assurance
We're sniffing out the code that smells

Hey
People
OMG can go to hell

All in all we just like
Projects that are real small

---

13. Ibid., p. 6.

We don't need written requirements
We don't need project control
We code in pairs in one big-assed room
We never ever code alone

Hey
People
We never code alone

All in all we just like
Projects that are real small

We don't need no architecture
It emerges from the code
We unit test, code, and refactor
Don't plan ahead, no, not at all

Hey
People
We don't plan ahead at all

All in all we just like
Projects that are real small

We don't need no project deadlines
We refactor every day
Schedule is the customer's problem
They can't replace us anyway

Hey
People
They can't replace us anyway

All in all we just like
Projects that are real small

All in all we just like
Projects that are real small

Architectural Scalability

The scalability of a system includes its ability to handle large numbers of active users. For example, a Web site that fails to respond if more than ten Web browsers request a page at roughly the same time isn't particularly scalable. Conversely, a Web site that can handle hundreds or even thousands of simultaneous users and can handle periods of peak usage without crashing or causing time-outs is scalable.

The level of scalability of a system needs to be decided early on in a project. Scalability is a nonfunctional requirement, and nonfunctional requirements are notorious for affecting the architecture in often quite severe ways. YAGNI, DTSTTCPW, and no BDUF[14] are very bad mantras for projects that need to scale.

So, at a very early stage, the project manager and programming team need to determine (whoops, this is XP—the *customer* needs to determine) how scalable the system needs to be. How many total users can it support? How many users can connect at the same time? Are there peak usage times?

Of course, these decisions can be reversed later, but at a cost. Despite the plethora of hype indicating otherwise, XP doesn't flatten the cost of change curve, particularly when it comes to nonfunctional requirements (the danger, of course, is that customers, believing the hype, might sign up for an XP project thinking that they *can* defer these decisions until much later. *Caveat emptor*—let the client beware).

Scalability Drives the Architecture

Changing a nonfunctional requirement can result in a complete rethink of the system architecture. The effect is on a different scale from functional requirements, which also affect the architecture but to a lesser degree. Unfortunately, XP makes very little distinction between the two: Everything's fair game, open to change (no, make that *embracing* change. Changing requirements during coding is *invited* in XP). It doesn't seem to matter that for nonfunctional requirements, the rules are very different.

The XP approach to design is as follows: Design what you need for the current 2-week iteration (test first) and code it. Design what you need for the next 2-week iteration, and code it, and so on. Incremental development includes incremental design.

Thus, if the current iteration will just be used by, say, five concurrent users, then the architecture should be targeted at five concurrent users—even if the team knows that the system is intended to be used for five *thousand* users in a later iteration.

The architecture for a 5-user system would be completely different from the architecture for a 5,000-user system. The choice of platform, programming language, hardware, tools, and frameworks might be different. Nonfunctional requirements—and scalability, in particular—have a huge effect on the system architecture.

---

14. The XP mantras "you aren't gonna need it," "Do The Simplest Thing That Could Possibly Work," and "[Don't do a] Big Design Up Front" are all described variously throughout this book.

Nonfunctional requirements are an extreme example of the shortsighted-ness of YAGNI—just designing for the current iteration. Let's take an example from *Extreme Programming Installed*, just to prove we're not making this up.

Example from Extreme Programming Installed: Patient Records Database

Back in Chapter 12, we gave a critique of Chapter 26 from *Extreme Programming Installed* (hereafter known as "XPI26").

The example of emergent design provided in XPI26 is an application that, through user stories, the developers have identified needs to store patient details for up to 10 million patients. It stands to reason that we would need to use a database for such a system. However, XPI26 suggests instead that you should initially (for the first few iterations, at least) target the system at a smaller number of patients (say, 1,000 or 10,000), and just use files for data persistence.

The purported benefit is that this should be easier, because writing to files is simpler than writing to a database, and that this gives the patient record structure time to stabilize. Fields can be added and removed more easily: "Just write little programs to do it." Then, when you're ready to add patient number 10,001 to the system, it should be really easy to migrate your file-based, proprietary storage system to a real database, because you also followed the "once and only once" rule (you did remember to follow that rule, didn't you?).

The implication in XPI26 is that if your code is well factored (so that there is no duplication of code—that is, each piece of functionality is written "once and only once"), then migrating the design from a 10-user system to a 10-million-user system would be as easy as changing the code in two places (one for reading the data, the other for writing). Of course, this is entirely fallacious, because it over-simplifies the issues involved in extending an architecture to make it scalable. Failover, transaction support, server clustering, and so on also play a part. In many such cases, the entire architecture can change dramatically, not just the little hole that the data gets squirted through.

Even if (for the sake of argument) changing the data access layer were the only issue, we would feel much more comfortable making changes in a database schema and letting a real database like Oracle or MySQL handle the adding or removing of columns, relationships, and constraints for us, while maintaining integrity of the existing data. Database engines are designed specifically for that sort of thing, after all. Why spend time writing your own file-based persistence mechanism (however simple) when you know that soon you will need to replace it with code that accesses a real database? More to the point, why do this when it in fact works out *simpler* to use the "more complex" database?

In this case, as in many others, the apparent simplicity of taking a "roll-your-own" approach turns out to be illusory. The effectiveness of a design isn't just about how simple it is to implement at the time, it's also about how easy it is to transition between different versions—something that, ironically, can be better achieved by spending more time documenting the design, thinking it through, and letting the emergent design take place in the class model—before spending time writing the production code.

It's true that databases are more complex than files; however, the database system has already been written for us. It's there, it exists. Pretending it doesn't exist doesn't make our job any easier. In fact, the proprietary file storage solution that Jeffries recommends can only result in a lot more coding, because there are issues such as concurrency, file locking, transactions, data integrity, data marshalling, constraints, and so forth that we would have to write ourselves for a multiuser system. This wouldn't be apparent at first; files would at first seem like the simplest way forward, assuming that the way forward is only for the next couple of weeks. However, gradually all of this extra code would need to be written as these problems pop up (most likely reported by users who are being forced to use our half-baked "database" system) until we suddenly find that we've written our own in-house version of SQL Server. If we chose instead to write to the "more complex" database first, all of this would have been taken care of for us.

Usually, the simpler option *is* the preferable one. It's possible to learn a lot from this area of XP's teachings—particularly simplicity, "once and only once," and simply how to refactor existing code. However, it's also important to take these teachings with a pinch of salt and not to get too carried away with them. If XP was simply saying, "Here's a nice, safe way to improve existing code," then we wouldn't have a problem with it. Instead, the overall process prescribed by XP leads to a design process that can fool the customer (and the programmers) into thinking the project is nearly complete when success is really a long way off.

The patient records example in XPI26 demonstrates that XP takes a "throwaway" approach; that is, XP encourages us to write code that we know is going to be thrown away later, as if it's free. In this example, Jeffries deliberately ignores the scaling issue. If the code were written to a database first, then it wouldn't have to be thrown away.

In the same way that C3 generated a quick illusion of success, emergent design generates a quick illusion of progress. The basic product is complete—all that's left is to write in the complex logic that takes care of alternative scenarios (such as when the user decides to click some buttons in a different order than the one that the programmers anticipated, or when two users try to access the same record simultaneously). We would say we're about 90% complete. . . .[15]

---

15. The first 90% is always easy. Fear might be the mind-killer, but it's that second 90% that is always the killer on software projects. To (mis)quote Marvin the Paranoid Android from Douglas Adams' *The Restaurant at the End of the Universe*: "The first 90% was the worst. The second 90%, that was the worst too. After that we went into a bit of a decline. . . ."

This can lead to premature boasts of success. "In 4 years' time I have won the Nobel Peace Prize. Can I have that book deal now?"

Throwing Away Code

As we've explored elsewhere in this book, throwing away code is a central theme of XP. Yet to evolve designs by repeatedly throwing away code ignores the fact that late projects get late a day at a time, then a week at a time, then a month at a time. Pretty soon they're 4 years late if they haven't been inexplicably cancelled by then.

We'd like to introduce a radical concept, though. *What if* we could throw away bad code *before* it ever got written? What if we didn't have to write unit tests for throwaway code? What if we could actually visualize a design before coding?

For more about this radical new concept, see the section "The Cost of Change Curve (aka the Cost to Fix Defects Curve)" in Chapter 13.

We Can Toss It Out
(Sing to the tune of "We Can Work It Out" by The Beatles)

If we code it your way
There's a chance the code will fall apart before too long
So let's code it my way
Then we can refactor it until the day is done
Then we can toss it out
We can toss it out

Days are very short, they end at fiiiive
So you'll have to toss that, my friend
I have always thought BDUF's a criiiime
Instead we'll refactor till the end

If we code it your way
There's a chance the code will fall apart before too long
So let's code it my way
Then we can refactor it until the day is done
Then we can toss it out
We can toss it out

The Piggy Scale of Process Robustness

Or, Striking the Balance: Finding the Sweet Spot Between "Speed and Agility" and "Process and Safety"

The Three Little Pigs were very excited, because today they were going to leave the safety of their uncle's home and find a place to live. In an early-morning stand-up meeting, they linked their little trotters together and collectively decided that they would each head off in a different but roughly similar direction and find a nice place to build his house. They briefly discussed the architecture—four walls, windows, that sort of thing—but were too excited to discuss the details any further. They just wanted to get building and move in as soon as possible.

The first little pig found a lovely spot in a delightful rural location on the top of a hill, with charming views and excellent potential for the budding DIYer. So he set to work, resolving to evolve the design of the house as he went along. With this in mind, he decided to build his new home out of the most agile material he could find, which just happened to be straw. After all, it never rained in these parts, and he knew that he would be able to build something really quickly out of straw—not to mention that he would be able to "embrace change" and "refactor the design" very easily.

Unfortunately, the reality turned out to be quite different from the theory, and the straw kept falling down every time a breeze blew up. The fact that he was on top of an exposed hill, with 20-mile-per-hour winds whipping around his chubby legs, did not help his progress or his mood. Soon he was thoroughly frustrated, and his little trotters had turned blue from the windchill.

Almost 4 years later, he was still busy embracing change and clutching at straws flying around in the breeze, but after only one-third of his straw house was built, he gave up, wrote a book about his success, and used the proceeds to buy himself a Winnebago.

On the morning that the second little pig began building, he found a nice picturesque glade in the middle of a forest, with excellent local amenities (it was near a babbling brook). He had decided enthusiastically to build his house out of wood, and—because he wanted to be able to change his mind about the design (or even the location) as he went along—he would skip the foundation and generate a "quick win" by quickly building the walls first.

He was concerned at first that there might be a big bad wolf lurking in the forest and that wood might not be the strongest material because the wolves in this area were notorious for blowing houses down. But the lumberjack from whom he bought the wood had assured him that he was being driven by *fear,* and that he should instead have the *courage* to build his house out of wood and to skip the foundation.

"Well," he replied, half-jokingly, "an agile material like wood is okay for small projects like mine, but I wouldn't want to build a skyscraper using it!"

The third little pig, meanwhile, decided to build his house out of bricks. He had also thought about what he wanted a lot more and did not rush into the construction of his house. Instead he decided that, although he wanted somewhere to live, he also wanted something with a decent investment potential.

After looking around for a while, he settled upon an interesting location in an up-and-coming area, with lots of room for future expansion. In fact, he decided to build a large block of apartments that he could sell off as the area gained in respectability. He knew that his house would take longer to build than the others, but then his plans were on a much larger scale. By taking the time to plan ahead, he was confident that his property would shoot up in value very quickly—although he *was* somewhat concerned that it would be another 12 years before he was finished.

Each pig's approach had its merits and its drawbacks, with the possible exception of the straw house, which—let's face it—only had drawbacks.

For the majority of projects, the ideal software process would be the equivalent of a wooden house, with a good foundation (because a wooden house without a foundation is just a shack), but nothing too elaborate. However, if you're writing a safety-critical system, for example, you might want some concrete and steel in your architecture.

When XP Starts to Fail

"Another question is one of scaling. It is certainly not possible to start up a 100 person project and use XP. Don't do it. Won't work. No discussion. However, it is certainly capable of organizing the work of 10 programmers. And 10 programmers going fast, doing what is valuable to the customer and not doing what isn't valuable to the customer, can get a lot done."[16]

The various "Voice of eXPerience" reports suggest to us that the cracks in XP show up even on small projects. However (as the ATLAS case study shows), the cracks can turn into gaping chasms as the project scales up.

Particular areas of concern are as follows:

- Hand-written story cards (if several programmers need to look at the same card, do they time-share?)

- Reliance on "oral documentation" to fill in the details

- Collective ownership

- The XP coach

- The on-site customer

- Communal coding room

- Emergent architecture

Let's look at each of these in turn, starting with the first two.

---

16. Kent Beck posting to OTUG (http://www.rational.com), subject: "XP and the real world," March 1, 1999.

Hand-Written Story Cards and Oral Documentation

A prime example of scalability problems in XP is the practical reality of hand-written story cards (as opposed to the theoretical advantages). Very little text gets written on the cards themselves. Story cards rely heavily on verbal communication (or so-called oral documentation) to fill in the large amounts of missing information. It's primarily this reliance on oral documentation that means an XP project doesn't work well on large projects. Success of the project relies heavily on the team communicating well and on the whole team being in a single room.

For more about the problems of oral documentation, see Chapter 7.

Collective Ownership

Collective ownership in a small-scale project has its impracticalities. However, the problems are more obvious in larger projects with separate teams. If the overall architecture is emerging and evolving, does that mean that team A is allowed to go in and change the code of team B? This question remains unanswered in XP.

The impracticalities of collective ownership in a small-scale project are discussed in the section "What If Programmers Take Ownership of Code?" in Chapter 3.

In XP, the programmer pair that refactors a piece of code is responsible for running the tests for the whole system and for fixing any part of the system that gets "broken" by their changes. In a large project, this would mean diving into another part of the project that is being handled by a separate team and changing that team's code. This would almost certainly cause problems, because communication between the teams is much lower than if they were a single, colocated team. So if the programmers can't "dive in" and change any part of the code, then their ability to evolve the architecture becomes severely stifled.

XP Coach

Another area that prevents XP from scaling well is the XP coach. Because so much of XP relies on the team's adherence to the 12 practices, it takes a dedicated, observant, and unfailingly diligent coach to keep the project on track.

The impact this has on scalability is described in *Questioning Extreme Programming*:

> *"The need for a coach may be a critical limitation of XP, if only because of the difficulty of locating qualified coaches. It may also put a restraint on how large an XP team can grow, because one coach can handle only so many people. After all, if there were 20 people in the team, at best the coach would have less than two hours with each person every week."*[17]

(Actually, the coach would have 4 hours, assuming he can see the people in pairs, but the problem is still a significant one.)

Of course, a large team with a serious "have-a-go" attitude could still bite the XP bullet and launch into an XP project, hoping that among them they have sufficient eXPerience so that the coach can concentrate her time on the XP "newbies" on the team. However, the coach's role isn't simply about teaching XP, it's also about keeping a close eye out for people who are beginning to stray from the path—catching deviations early enough to prevent them from impacting the project. Because the XP practices are high discipline, even experienced XPers will inevitably slip from time to time.

 For more about how the XP coach's performance can impact an XP project, see Chapter 6. Also see the section "What If the XP Coach Falls Asleep?" in Chapter 3.

XP Coach vs. Team Leader

In non-XP projects, the closest thing to the coach is probably the team leader. Just like the coach, the team leader wears many hats. His expert skill-set must include programming, architecture (to get the "big picture" and communicate this to the rest of the team), process engineering, and interpersonal skills.

One major difference, however, is that in XP the coach isn't specifically "in charge." His role could be thought of as "passive aggressive." In other words, he must keep the team on track and enforce the rules, but he must do it in such a way that he is suggesting the improvements rather than telling people what to do.

The coach is there as an advisor rather than a leader. He is the Spock (science officer) in a team of rampaging Kirks. ("Captain(s), I *strongly advise* you to raise shields.")

---

17. Pete McBreen, *Questioning Extreme Programming* (New York, NY: Addison-Wesley, 2002), p. 87.

This makes his job doubly difficult. Unlike the team leader role, the coach has no teeth (figuratively speaking). This, coupled with collective ownership, is another aspect of XP that increases the power of the "proletariat" programmer.

We discuss Marxist aspects of XP in Chapter 4.

A coach who "overrules" the programmers in an attempt to keep the project moving risks gaining a reputation as a control freak—domineering, inflexible, bossy—the complete opposite of what XP is trying to achieve. In a hostile team environment, the coach is in danger of always grappling for power, never quite being in control.

Conversely, because the team leader is afforded control by her job description (and assuming she is backed up by her managers), she doesn't need to *aspire* to be in control. Instead, she can approach team issues and conflicts from the opposite direction: She delegates decisions and offers compromises to the programmers as she sees fit. The difference, in terms of keeping the project efficiently on track, is profound.

On-site Customer

We covered the overworked on-site customer in Chapter 5, so for now we will simply ask, "In a project that has too many developers to fit in one room, where does the on-site customer go?"

Communal Coding Room

Many of XP's practices rely on the osmotic communication gained from cramming all of the programmers and analysts into a single room. As soon as there are too many programmers to squeeze in, then the benefits are replaced with risks (risks of lost information, misunderstandings, and so on).

Emergent Architecture

It is worth repeating this quote from Chapter 12:

"The larger the scale, the more you must rely on emergence."[18]

—Kent Beck

18. Kent Beck posting to the C2 Wiki page Can An Architecture Emerge, http://c2.com/cgi/wiki?CanAnArchitectureEmerge.

This is one of the more extreme of the Extremo quotes. It is also directly at odds with our own experience of design on large projects (Doug, in particular, has worked on some pretty large-scale projects[19]).

Emergent architecture can work, but realistically only for small-scale projects. The architecture could be divided into smaller subarchitectures that are then allowed to evolve incrementally (where each subarchitecture is handled by a different team). However, there isn't likely to be any real cohesion between the different parts of the project. It's quite likely that the teams will end up with an "alphabet-spaghetti" architecture in which nothing quite fits together.

XP counters this to an extent with its metaphor practice, the theory being that a common architectural metaphor will keep the different areas of design consistent. However, as we discussed in the case study of the 50-person ATLAS project, XPers have found the metaphor practice to be insufficient on large projects.

What is really needed for such a project is a single documented architecture that can be shared by all the teams involved. The architecture document *could* be produced incrementally, but this introduces its own problems as each team tries to pull it in a different direction.

We discuss emergent architecture further in Chapter 12.

SP: The Opposite of XP

Okay, so you say scalability isn't an issue for you because your projects are generally small. So, XP's still the best approach for small projects, right? Well, maybe not. Here, Doug describes a process that's almost the exact opposite of XP, showing that our refactored process in the next chapter is definitely just one out of myriad alternatives to XP. There are many different universes out there.

During my 15 years or so of actively writing code, I generally observed that about 5% of the programmers accounted for 95% of the meaningful work that got done. In my later years of programming, I modified this conclusion somewhat and became convinced that 5% of the programmers accounted for 110% of the meaningful work because the crew that hung around the coffee machine and the social butterflies who wandered around from office to office chatting generally didn't produce anything useful and distracted the folks who did the real work. I always

---

19. One of Doug's favorite mental images is to imagine emergent architecture on something like a really big jet-fighter project. Developed over a decade or so by multiple companies, with multiple teams participating within each company, all geographically distributed, building real-time embedded software that has to respond in the millisecond/microsecond time frame or people die—really quickly.

tried to be in the "good" 5% and had pretty reasonable success at doing so. I also found that people in that "good" 5% quickly learned to recognize one another. So, when I started working on a new project, I always learned to look for them right away (generally they were the ones with a line of people stretching behind their desk waiting to ask them how something worked). Over the years, I became friends with a lot of these folks.

Eventually I decided to start my own business, which originally involved me writing code in my living room. Gradually, I added a few other programmers out of my group of overachieving friends, and they all started writing code from home as well. As a couple of years progressed, I stopped writing code and spent more of my time managing what the other programmers were doing. I generally carved out particular "chunks" of programming tasks and assigned one to a programmer. For example, one person worked on a diagram editor, another worked on a multi-user dictionary, and another worked on an import/export/model merge utility program. Everybody worked from home, and everybody negotiated their interfaces with the other folks via e-mail and through me. We built about a quarter of a million lines of code this way over a period of maybe 4 years with a team of six people. Each programmer would come into the office and meet with me once every couple of weeks for an hour or two. We did everything else by e-mail. Everybody tested their own code, and we had very few integration problems.

I've often informally referred to this approach as *SP,* or *Small Projects.* And I think it's a perfectly good approach for small projects, although it wouldn't work for everything, nor would it work for everybody. Its strength is that it lets talented programmers work undisturbed in an environment they're comfortable in. It completely avoids the situation where the social butterflies on the project get to hitch a free ride on the backs of the talented folks and get equal credit for any success that might happen, which is guaranteed to be the case with constantly rotating pair programmers. It relies on having a chief architect who is capable of recognizing and hiring smart programmers, and capable of understanding enough of the programming details of each subsystem to ensure the overall integrity of the project. It's almost the diametric opposite of XP. And it works really well—at least it did for us.

The point really being that it's no big trick to come up with a process that works for tiny projects. Almost any process will do for a tiny project. The trick is coming up with a process that does scale. And that ain't XP.

Fangs Gets Too Big for His Boots (What Kind of Snake Wears Boots, Anyway?)

The scalability "snake" is twice as deadly as its brethren because

- The less up-front design you do, the more you must rely on refactoring.

- The larger the project, the more you must rely on refactoring.

As the project codebase increases, a little refactoring can work wonders on the design. In fact, this is an essential aspect of keeping the design simple and extensible. However, emergent design (which mainly involves refactoring) is labor intensive, very high discipline, and above all requires a high level of communication between all members of the team. It requires all the other XP practices to be in place to prevent all the other snakes from breaking loose.

So it stands to reason that the larger the project, the more you need to do up-front design (the project can still be broken into smaller iterations—just not run through a blender). However, the Extremo thinking is the reverse: The larger the project, the more you should rely on emergence.

XP's scalability problems occur because as the team size grows, the cost of communication increases. Osmotic communication, which XP relies upon heavily as a replacement for detailed documentation, becomes more difficult with more people in the room (or in different rooms). Osmotic communication is still important and its benefits shouldn't be ignored, but relying on it to keep the project from falling apart is a risky practice. It also becomes riskier as the team size gets bigger.

Scalability Defanged

The solution, we feel, is pretty obvious, really: Follow a development process that embraces requirements and design documentation. It's possible to do this and still keep the project agile.

Keeping design documentation up-to-date can be a burden (depending on how off-the-mark the original design was). This can be mitigated by doing the following:

- Maintaining only a core set of documentation (e.g., class and sequence diagrams), discarding diagrams that are no longer needed once the class model is fairly mature (e.g., robustness diagrams).

- Following effective design techniques (including prototyping) to get the original design right.

- Breaking the project into subsystems, individually designed. Produce an overall architecture up front so that everything will fit together and all teams involved are on a level playing field. Then break the project into subsystems spread over monthly iterations. Design in detail for the next two or three iterations. Besides the usual advantages of an iterative approach, this gives us the benefits that we would have got from XP's evolutionary design approach (only without the associated risks).

Summary

In this chapter we examined the concept of scalability (in terms of both the product and the project) and how well XP copes with it.

As we discovered, there are certain key stumbling blocks in XP that prevent the process from scaling up as the project increases in size. In particular, the on-site customer and the coach roles provide a natural ceiling to the size of an XP project. The case study of a 50-person project at ThoughtWorks, Inc., provides a classic example of the cracks in XP becoming more obvious as the project grows. Further processes and documents must be put in place to counter its shortcomings, but these in turn reduce XP's touted effectiveness.

A much better approach would be to start with a process that is effective with small projects but is designed to scale up easily as the project grows in size. As luck would have it, we describe just such a process in the next chapter.

CHAPTER 15

Refactoring XP

Hey Dude
(Sing to the tune of "Hey Jude" by The Beatles)

Hey dude
Your code smells bad
Go refactor and make it better
Remember
That tests are requirements
Then you can begin
To make it smell better

And if you say you need design
Hey dude
Don't whine
Make sure you don't put in
Any comments

Just code what you need today
Then go
And play
Remember the schedule
Is the customer's problem

La la la la la, la la la laaaaaaa

Hey dude

Your code smells bad

Go refactor and make it better

Remember

That tests are requirements

Then you can begin

To make it smell better

Back in Chapter 1, we asked what problems XP is attempting to address.[1] Through pretty much the entire book, we have discussed whether XP really does solve these problems.

As we've discussed, XP does raise some key issues regarding common development problems, and in some cases it provides some good answers. In particular, its emphasis is on feedback, feedback, feedback.

So the problems that XP has identified are sound, and some of its proposed solutions (used in moderation) are good. But, as we've discussed in detail, it gets us only partway to a viable solution.

The burning question now, of course, is this: Is it possible to take the good parts of XP, tweak them slightly so that they aren't such immense effort hogs, and supplement them with some better practices—and as a result solve the set of problems that XP originally set out to solve?

In effect, we would be refactoring XP—keeping it semantically the same (so that it solves the same set of problems), but tweaking its practices piece by piece, nudging it toward an altogether more robust design that fits a greater number of real-world project scenarios. The end result would, of course, not actually be XP, but we feel that it would be much less prone to failure. It should also be easier to introduce this refactored version into organizations that might otherwise resist an "agile" process (especially one that deemphasizes documentation and up-front design, relies on a permanent on-site customer, and so on). Let's give it a try.

This chapter is divided into three sections:

- **How to Be Agile Without Being Fragile:** A discussion of what an agile process should provide to avoid being fragile

- **Extreme Programming Defanged: Taking the "Extreme" out of XP:** A description of our proposed "refactored" process

- **Case Study: The Server Tools Project (Using a Defanged, Much Less Extreme but Still Very Agile Process):** A case study of a project that is very similar to our "refactored" process

Note that there isn't much very satire to be found in this chapter. This is the "but seriously, folks . . ." part of the night where we balance our guitars on our knees and adopt our sincere expressions. So with that in mind, let's begin.

---

1. A similar list of problems is also given in Chapter 1 of *Extreme Programming Explained*.

How to Be Agile Without Being Fragile

For a process to achieve the agile values and principles[2] without being fragile, we believe that it must provide operations and procedures that

- Provide the usual benefits of software agility (early and continuous delivery, reduced cost of communication, bringing businesspeople and technical people together, and so on)

- Decrease risk

- Encourage contingency

- Prevent fragility

The first item makes the process agile; the other three prevent it from being fragile. Analyzing those last three items should, then, help us to come up with a process that's agile without being fragile. So let's look at each of these in turn and see how XP compares.

A Good Agile Process Should Decrease Risk

For a process to be truly agile, it must provide operations and procedures that decrease risk. A *risk* is a thing, event, or trend that, unless properly addressed, could impact the project in a negative way.[3]

XP reduces risk by encouraging the use of unit tests, pair programming, acceptance tests, constant refactoring, very short iterations, frequent code integration, and so on. However, each of these practices comes at a cost in terms of the time taken to implement and maintain it.

However, XP increases risk because . . . well, because of all the reasons we've described in this book.

A Good Agile Process Should Encourage Contingency

For a process to be truly agile, it must provide operations and procedures that encourage contingency. This enables the project team to keep responding to

---

2. See http://www.agilemanifesto.org.
3. There's a good discussion of risk management in Chapter 5 of Steve McConnell's *Rapid Development* (Microsoft Press, 1996).

change (such as changes in requirements or changes in management, market forces, and so on that could adversely affect the project) without increased risk.

With any project, XP or otherwise, a question to ask yourself is, "What if something goes wrong?" For example:

- What if your chief programmer leaves?

- What if the on-site customer, who is essentially your walking, talking requirements spec, is forced to leave the project due to ill health? (Sure, you can get a replacement, but will he or she be as effective?)

- What if you discover late in the project that you need another subsystem to be written? (If your team is already up to its many eyeballs doing constant refactoring and constant integration with the current system, you may need to bring in a team from outside the project.)

- What if your targeted application server is suddenly taken off the market by its vendor? (It happens.)

- What if the janitor accidentally vacuums up your pile of story cards?

XP addresses the problem of the chief programmer leaving the project by encouraging all team members to know about all parts of the design and code in enough detail to be able to pick up where somebody left off at any time. This is a pretty robust approach, but it comes at a massive cost.

We discuss some of the reasons why the XP approach is costly in Chapter 3.

Contingency isn't just about having backup plans, it's also about lessening the likelihood that you'll need those backup plans. In addition, it's good to know that the alternatives have been thought about, should it come to that (but also see the comment about embellishment in the next section).

You can't plan for the unknown (at least not accurately). But you can prepare contingency, so that when things do go wrong, they don't take your entire project with them.

A Good Agile Process Should Prevent Fragility

For a process to be truly agile, it must provide operations and procedures that prevent fragility.

A development process is fragile (or becomes fragile) if

- **It has no contingency plans.** As we discussed previously in this chapter, if something goes wrong then it could take the whole project with it if your process doesn't provide a safety net or a backup plan.

- **It provides too *much* contingency, resulting in embellishment.** The problem is that people often mistake contingency for embellishment. *Embellishment* is unnecessary extra complexity; *contingency* is simply having a backup plan ready for when things go wrong and having practices in place that prevent things from going wrong. A large part of contingency is, therefore, risk management and prevention. We like Alistair Cockburn's statement, "Embellishment is the pitfall of the methodologist."[4] That is, it's easy to add extra practices and procedures because they might make the project more rigorous.

- **Its developers quickly get bogged down in analysis paralysis.** *Analysis paralysis* means being unable to move forward due to thinking too much about alternative designs or detailed edge cases. Processes that are overembellished are more prone to analysis paralysis. XP protects against analysis paralysis by using test-driven development (TDD), pairing, and YAGNI. Ironically, as a direct result, XP is more prone to the *programming* equivalent of analysis paralysis: Constant Refactoring After Programming.

We discuss XP's propensity toward Constant Refactoring After Programming in Chapter 9.

- **Its practices are high discipline.** XP takes a lot of sustained effort to keep to its practices. This would not be so bad, but the level of bite-back in such cases is too high. In fact, by stopping doing certain practices even for a short while, the whole project becomes unstable.

We discuss the high discipline aspect of XP in the section "A Self-Referential Safety Net (Circle of Snakes)" in Chapter 3.

---

4. Alistair Cockburn, *Agile Software Development* (New York, NY: Addison-Wesley, 2001), p. 142.

- **Its practices are not easily tailored.** Knowing which of XP's practices can be tailored and how to tailor them safely is the focus of the second part of this chapter (and the "Defanged" sections throughout the book). Tailoring XP is like defusing a bomb—we need to determine exactly which practices can be safely cut.

- **It can't grow as the project grows.** All processes are scalable, but some processes are more scalable than others. Most projects start out small and grow in size as more developers are added to the team, the customer asks for more features, and additional modules "spin out" to form subprojects. A good agile process should be able to take this in its stride. As the team grows or gets split into separate teams, extra procedures or documents may need to be added to the process. This shouldn't, however, require a complete reworking of the process, which in many ways XP does.

We discuss the reasons why XP doesn't comfortably "scale up" in Chapter 14.

- **A module has too many dependencies.** A project quickly becomes fragile if its modules have too many dependencies. In such cases, it becomes almost impossible to change some code without affecting a separate code module in some way, so the project grinds to a halt, at least until that module is complete. XP followed to the letter helps prevent this kind of fragility, as long as the team keeps on refactoring. XP encourages clean, loosely coupled designs with no duplication of code or code responsibilities. Unfortunately, for the same reason, XP also magnifies the problem. Many of its prescribed refactorings include changes to public interfaces; therefore, a refactoring in one piece of code will almost certainly break some code in a different part of the system. XP relies heavily on plentiful unit tests, continuous integration, and crossed fingers to mitigate this particular problem.

Contingency vs. Embellishment: Why XP Gets It Wrong

Somewhere, there has to be a compromise when weighing how much contingency to factor into your project. The XP ethos is correct, at least insofar as each project deliverable must be justifiable in some way. If you're spending time producing a document, you should be able to explain how it will benefit the project. Each document should return a profit in terms of the effort invested in it. Otherwise, why spend the time producing it?

But (there's always a "but") XP takes this too far by cutting out practices that are essential to any software project.

We discuss the practices essential to any software project (e.g., suffi-cient up-front design, precode interaction design, and in-depth requirements elicitation) in the "Extreme Programming Defanged" section in this chapter. We discuss the likely results of not using them in Chapter 3 and pretty much the rest of the book.

In fact, XP approaches contingency in the wrong areas. Specifically, all of XP's practices are geared toward making sure the software is fully functional and releasable at any stage in the entire project, just in case the project should be can-celled without warning. Although this is admirable, the result is a process that takes a lot of ongoing effort from the entire team just to keep the software releasable at all times.

Our refactored process relaxes contingency around the sheer effort involved in keeping the software constantly releasable. We focus instead on making the software releasable for certain key mile-stones. This frees up the team's time to concentrate on other, higher risk areas.

Extreme Programming Defanged: Taking the "Extreme" out of XP

Now that we've analyzed XP's many flaws and described some of the areas in which an agile process risks being fragile, let's try to put the pieces together into an agile process that's hopefully less prone to these risks.

We provide a brief summary of our refactored process near the end of Chapter 1. Also refer to the "Defanged" sections at the end of most chapters in this book—these combined with the process described in this section comprise our defanged, refactored process.

Many of the practices that XP promotes can be, and very frequently are, applied successfully to non-XP projects. For example, automated testing is grow-ing in popularity, because it really does help to stabilize code and catch bugs. If you have access to an on-site customer (at least for part of the project), that can have a beneficial effect too. "Agile" projects are not the only ones that benefit from such practices.

However, lifting these practices out of XP and putting them straight into another project, verbatim, isn't always such a good idea. This is partly because XP puts words like "always," "frequent," and "continuous" in front of many of its practices and recommendations.

If you remove the "push the dial up to 10"[5] modifiers, many of the practices can be safely applied. But which ones?

We've divided this section into these two areas:

- Refactored XP Practices/Xtudes[6]/Values/Tenets

- Additional Practices

Refactored XP Practices/Xtudes/Values/Tenets

In this section, we take the existing XP practices, etc. and tweak them (or, in certain cases, completely rewrite them) to provide something that should be suited to a wider range of projects.

The Values

There's absolutely nothing wrong with having a set of values to guide your work, or indeed your life. The four XP values—communication, simplicity, feedback, and courage—are worth keeping in mind.

Putting them into practical use is more difficult than simply accepting them as useful high-level guides. Putting the communication value into practice, for example, means actually making an effort to talk to people more (shudder!)—not just for a few days (like a New Year's resolution), but throughout the project.

We discuss simplicity in Chapter 12 and in the section "Example from Extreme Programming Installed*: Patient Records Database" in Chapter 14.*

Putting the simplicity value into practice means constantly thinking about how things can be simplified, although the trick is often knowing when to stop.

---

5. This is referring to a quote from Kent Beck in *Extreme Programming Explained*, in which he states that we should "take all these good things and turn the knobs up to 10"—in other words, do all of them all the time.

6. See http://c2.com/cgi/wiki?XpXtude.

A prehistoric hunter-gatherer looking for a way to simplify the amount of gear he has to take on a long day's hunt might whittle down his hefty spear until he has a sleek, ultralightweight toothpick that he can carry for miles, but that wouldn't even pick the gunk from between a woolly mammoth's teeth, let alone pierce its tough hide. So simplicity is something of an acquired art that involves not just keeping something simple, but also knowing when to stop and not make it *too* simple. You'll generally find, however, that it's more challenging to create a simple, elegant solution to a complex problem than it is to create a complex, unwieldy, overdesigned solution. The payoff for making the effort, though, is huge.

The listening value is also important. Eliciting feedback from the customer and from your peers and not being offended when you're criticized are valuable skills. Often you can engender more respect by admitting that you're wrong and giving your colleagues some credit for their own experience and judgment than by blindly insisting that you're right (and possibly leading the project down a blind alley as a result).

We suggest that maybe the courage value should be regarded with bemusement:

> *"Courage is the trademark of Extreme Programming. It is our goal. And, it is the yardstick we should use to judge a project."*[7]

Perhaps a more appropriate word would have been "confidence."[8] Soldiers and firefighters have *courage*. Despite this, though, it's useful to have both confidence in your work (and the work of others) and the confidence to make changes should you need to.

The Planning Game

XP's planning game offers some useful advice on structuring an agile project, namely planning ahead at a broad level of detail; dividing the project into very short, fixed iterations; and only deciding what you need for the next iteration. Tracking the project velocity is also a useful aid in estimating the time to perform individual tasks and for steadily improving the accuracy of your estimates (based on feedback for the current project).

---

7. Chet Hendrickson, "When is it not XP?" http://www.xprogramming.com/xpmag/NotXP.htm, December 5, 2000.

8. For an interesting discussion, see http://c2.com/cgi/wiki?XpCourageValue. We can see from this page that the Extremos were originally debating between courage and aggressiveness (not to mention confidence, fearlessness, boldness, and ruthlessness) as a possible name for the value. *"Our chief weapons are . . ."*

Projects that don't use user stories (e.g., they instead use formal require-ments or use cases) can similarly break these down into tasks of roughly equivalent size (in terms of the person-days it will take to implement them). Feature-driven development (FDD) takes a similar approach, breaking work into tasks that each take up to 2 weeks to implement.

Measuring project velocity is useful, but it's important not to mistake speed for distance.

Working Within Your Organization

Teams trying to introduce XP into their organization may face resistance because XP requires big changes to the way that the organization works. For example, XP doesn't work particularly well in projects that must deliver a fixed amount of func-tionality by a certain date. Unfortunately, this is the way that most companies do business. So our refactored process needs to take this into account and be more applicable to fixed-scope contracts.

One way to achieve this is to use a process that helps us to get both the requirements and the design right early, and to produce an architecture and decompose this into subprojects (also known as "subsystems" in RUP), each of which can then be designed in more detail. This approach helps to produce an accurate estimate of the project's completion date earlier in the project.

Also see the "Taking a Goal-Driven Approach" sidebar in this chapter.

Short Iterations

XP recommends iterations even as short as a week (although 2 to 3 weeks is also allowable). We've found 1 month to be the ideal iteration size (with working, functional software delivered at the end of each month). This keeps the team focused on delivery and allows the project velocity to be measured over time. Fixed iterations shorter than a month tend to be too distracting.

Having said that, progress *should* be tracked on a weekly basis. At the start of each week, each programmer is assigned (or signs up for) a set of tasks that's estimated to take 1 week in total. However, there doesn't need to be a releasable, working version of the software at the end of each week[9]— that's just too disruptive.

---

9. XP takes the approach that the software should be ready to release at any time, just in case the project is suddenly cancelled. We prefer to take a more realistic approach and plan ahead to specific release milestones.

Short Iterations
(Sing to the tune of "Revolution" by The Beatles)

You say you want short iterations
Well, you know
You really shouldn't skip design

You say since you got pair programmers
Well, you know
That everything will come out fine

But when you skip writing your requirements down
You know you're just setting yourself up to look like a clown

Don't ya know it's just XP
All right
All right

You say you like to do refactoring
Well you know
You could do it right the first time

You say you don't need documentation
Well you know
Because the code is the design

You're gonna have code that doesn't smell too great
But you got no schedules so you can't be late

Ya know it's just XP
Shoo be doo bop
All right
Shoo be doo bop
Mm hmm
All right
Shoo be doo bop

Small Releases

At the end of each month, the in-progress product is released internally to the company for user feedback, quality assurance, and tracking purposes. Actual "live" customer releases should be planned well in advance so that more effort can be put in to make the software releasable at the appropriate time.

Small releases can help your project because you get early feedback regarding such things as

- Usability of the system

- Usefulness of what's there so far

- Requests for new functionality (which otherwise might not have been discovered until later and could require a big design change)

Small releases also help to mitigate the problem that occurs when the programmer thinks the software is done and says it's done, but on delivery the customer discovers that it's really not done. Small releases catch this sort of problem early.

It's nice work if you can get it, but do bear in mind that for many project leaders, such an arrangement might be impossible. Your customer might have her own stringent acceptance testing procedure, which would make such a short cycle of releases impossible. The nature of the project itself could also make such short iterations and small releases impractical.

As we mentioned in the "Short Iterations" section, the project velocity should be tracked on a weekly basis, in addition to tracking the requirements that are completed for each monthly release. Interestingly, this allows *perceived* progress (tasks completed per week) to be compared with the project's *actual* progress (requirements implemented and released per month). Thus, if the project is "spinning"—completing many tasks (which include bug fixes) but not really getting anywhere (i.e., not completing many requirements)—then this would show up starkly on the project's monthly progress chart.

 We discuss some other aspects of planning and small releases (including the problem of a project going into maintenance mode too early) in Chapter 11.

Metaphor

Metaphor is not a replacement for architecture or for a decent centralized project glossary (or even better, a domain model that shows at a broad level the relationships between all the real-world objects in the problem space). However, it's definitely worth spending a little time thinking about one or more suitable metaphors to apply to your architecture. Often, this reduces ambiguity; it's surprisingly common for people to interpret the same name or phrase in different ways. Using a common metaphor consistently throughout the project helps to reduce the chances of such mix-ups.

Simple Design

There's nothing more time consuming than coping with an overly complex way of doing things. Code that's overdesigned, has one layer of indirection too many, or involves changes to a multitude of classes and XML files just to add a small field to the database (without really giving you anything back for your pains) is best thrown out or refactored into something simpler (depending how far gone the problem code is).

Better still, don't code this way in the first place. As we describe in Chapter 12 (and in the case study later in this chapter), some time spent architecting and designing the system up front helps you to identify patterns, simplifications, and easier ways of doing things. It's possible to do all this without writing any production code (which you would have had to spend time refactoring until you got to the design that you should have begun with).

Refactoring

Refactoring—used in the right context—is a valuable practice, especially as a supplement to detailed up-front design.

We cover refactoring in detail in Chapter 9, so for now we'll just conclude that it's worth keeping the refactoring practice from XP, but constant refactoring (or refactoring to produce an emergent design, "doing a little design every day") should be taken with a hefty dose of salt.

Testing

Should we test? Why, yes!

Automate as much as you possibly can. With testing, this means having unit tests that catch bugs and help to stabilize changes. This is especially useful during regression testing—if you invest the time to write a comprehensive set of unit tests, you'll thank yourself for it later when you need to quickly make some changes and the customer is waiting for them.

We discuss unit testing in more detail in Chapter 8.

If you're using refactoring for its intended purpose (improving the design of existing code) rather than as a means to produce a design from scratch, then you should find that you don't need to rely on unit tests quite as much. Moderation in all things—it's worth bearing in mind.

Requirements Documentation

XPers create very short user stories (two- or three-line requirements) that are placeholders, or promises, for future conversations with the customer.

We recommend something a little more rigorous: writing the requirements down in detail, up front, and getting them signed off by all the project stakeholders. The commonly associated drawback with this process is that the programmers might spend a few months doing nothing, waiting to be handed a specification (although this strikes us as much less of a price to pay than, say, having the project cancelled because of misunderstandings between individual project stakeholders later).

One way to get around this problem is to start with a short high-level spec and break this into parallel subprojects. The requirements for the subprojects can then be fleshed out in more detail. The programmers should also be spending this time prototyping and designing.

Of Course XP Works—We're Doing It!

Regarding the paucity of design documentation in XP (and the problems that this creates), a frequent comment made by pro-XPers who have read Matt's "The Case Against Extreme Programming" article is along the lines of

"You've obviously never worked on a real XP project! If you did, like I do, then you would realize that XPers do create lots of design documentation!"

One critic added, "90% of XP teams have a project wiki!"

This is fine, except that XP actually doesn't recommend that you create lots of design documentation. It recommends that you create "just enough"—the problem here being that "just enough" is entirely subjective, and the Extremo definition of "just enough" is quite different from ours. So teams that claim that they're doing XP but are also creating and storing lots of design documentation— and who are also creating all this documentation "up front"—aren't really doing XP. At least not in the pure, XP-as-defined-in-the-20-books-on-XP sense.

These are also the people who claim that XP does work because they're doing it, and their projects are succeeding (although, of course we just have to take their word for this. What we never seem to hear about is what happens in the maintenance phase, or what happens if something goes wrong, or why the project is taking so long).

What these people are doing is an adapted version of XP, tailored to the (rather common) local condition[10] that their project needs more documentation than XP prescribes. In fact, their project is closer to an Agile Modeling (built on

---

10. XP recommends tailoring its practices to local conditions, although (as we describe in Chapter 3) it contains little guidance for doing so, and in many ways tailoring XP can be a risky business.

XP) project than "pure" XP. That is, they're doing sufficient design up front to establish an architecture and set a clear direction for the remainder of the project. And they're identifying what documentation is purely transitory (following some analysis technique for getting the design closer to the code) and what documentation should be kept (and therefore kept up-to-date).

Colocated Team

Fitting all the programmers (and analysts) into one room helps to reduce communication costs. However, the downside is that the general noise level increases, and people may find it hard to concentrate.

This particular practice is really a judgment call, and it depends to a massive degree on the culture and preferences of your team. With the refactored practices that we discuss in this chapter (particularly the greater emphasis on documentation), the resultant process doesn't *rely* on having a colocated team—it's just a "nice-to-have."

Pair Programming

Again, we stress moderation in most things. Pair programming is a useful concept: Apply two minds to one thorny problem, and the chances are that a nice, simple solution will emerge. What we've found over the years is that pair programming happens naturally in just about every project. At some point, one programmer will call another one over, and they'll sit and peruse the same thorny problem together.

Pair Programming Refactored: A Flexible Approach to Pairing

When pair programming happens, let it happen. When it doesn't happen often enough, remind your developers that they are in fact a team, and they should use each other's strengths to their advantage.

However, don't force people to pair program. There's a serious law of diminishing returns. Remember, each person has a fully functional brain at his or her disposal.

The benefit that this flexible approach gives us is that we don't have to use collective ownership. This gives us individual accountability and individual pride in the code that we write (especially in how well it integrates with the rest of the system).

We discuss collective ownership in the section "What If Programmers Take Ownership of Code?" in Chapter 3.

Pair Programming Refactored: Programming and Reviewing Are Different Activities

XP promotes pair programming as a replacement for code reviews, the theory being that two people programming together (one typing, the other talking) is like reviewing *all* the time. Unfortunately, this misses the point of code reviews, which is that somebody who wasn't involved in the coding reviews the code. The benefit of code reviews is that a fresh pair of eyes can often spot problems that would have been missed by jaded programmers who are immersed in the task. Wood, trees, and all that.[11]

In addition, we've found that *precode* design reviews also help immensely to improve the state of the code even before it's written.

So, pair programming is worth salvaging from XP, but not constant pair programming—and it certainly shouldn't be mandatory!

We discuss the arguments for and against pair programming in Chapter 6.

Programmers Do Design

A valuable lesson to emerge from XP is that programming and designing are very closely related; therefore, it makes sense for the programmers to handle the designing (whether up front or evolutionary).

XP goes further to say that programming *is* designing (or, the code *is* the design). However, we still view designing as being at a higher level of abstraction than programming at the code level (this is why up-front design and test-first design are complementary disciplines). Designing is looking at the bigger picture (100 feet above ground level). There is also architecture, which is the 10,000-foot view.

The worst kind of antimethod is having software architects who produce a high-level architecture and then swan away to confuse the people on some other project. Because the architects don't get involved in the implementation of their architecture, there's nothing there to compel them to produce a workable design. Any old rubbish will do (they think).

So, programmers do architecture and design, but they do most of it precode.

---

11. In XP, collective ownership also helps, in that sooner or later someone else on the team will notice some bad code and refactor it. This is a little too ad hoc, though—it leaves a lot to chance. A more rigorous approach is to schedule regular reviews (not necessarily with a big group of people, because this can be demoralizing for the person whose code is being analyzed). This coupled with up-front design reviews helps keep your code in shape.

Programmers Write Their Own Tests

As in XP, programmers should write their own unit tests. This gets them thinking about code quality, which is definitely a good thing. There should still be a separate tester or testing team, though (in XP, the tester role is adopted by both the programmer [writing unit tests] and the customer [writing acceptance tests]).

Test-First Design Complements Up-Front Design

Up-front design and test-first design are entirely complementary practices, because they tend to address the design at different levels of detail and scope. Consider this paragraph from *Agile Modeling* (our emphasis):

> *"There is room for conceptual overlap* [between Agile Modeling and test-first design] *because test-first development clearly delves into the realm of detailed design since it provides developers with an opportunity to think through their code before they write it (as well as important feedback regarding their code). If you've chosen to do a little modeling before writing your code, perhaps to think through an issue larger than a single test case, then that's okay.* In fact, it may even make your test-first development efforts easier, particularly if you have adopted AM's *Consider Testability* practice."[12]

It's worth emphasizing that Agile Modeling (AM) isn't XP, because it emphasizes models and diagrams (which XP deemphasizes) and up-front modeling (which XP discourages). However, AM provides useful guidance on how to apply these disciplines within an agile context.

To get the bigger architectural picture, begin by creating an overall design, thinking it through, prototyping, drawing on whiteboards, arguing over the best approach, and getting senior engineers involved to incorporate their valuable feedback. This should culminate in an architecture document that will prove invaluable as development proceeds. The project is broken down into smaller areas, each of which has its own detailed design document. Each of these areas may be designed and implemented in parallel.

Taking this approach almost invariably produces a stronger design. Combine this with writing the tests before writing the code and you should end up with well-designed and planned-out code that is eminently testable.[13]

---

12. Scott W. Ambler, *Agile Modeling: Effective Practices for eXtreme Programming and the Unified Process* (New York, NY: John Wiley & Sons, 2002), p. 188.

13. For an example of test-first design in practice, see http://www.objectmentor.com/resources/articles/tfd.pdf.

Spikes

The XP *spike* is a quick, ad hoc prototype, the theory being that if you aren't sure how to code something, you try coding it one way for a day, then try it a different way, and keep the one that least makes your stomach turn.

As we described in Chapter 12, the process that we advocate includes a lot more prototyping than XP, because prototyping code is faster than writing and refactoring production code. Thus, you might find that you just don't need to write spikes once you get to production coding (though spikes can still be useful on occasion). If you find that you've reached a coding impasse, and you're unsure how to massage some code into the design, then it's time to question the design. Hold a quick review meeting with the team to work out what might have gone wrong and how to integrate the new code into the design.

Note that spikes are also used in XP as a way of exploring how long a particular task is going to take (i.e., they're part of the planning game). In this sense they're similar to the early prototyping technique we describe in Chapter 12, because for this particular purpose they involve "preproduction code" prototyping.

Continuous Integration

Before keeping this one, we would change it to "frequent integration" (which in practical terms is what it really means in the XP sense).

 See our description of continuous integration in the section "Case Study: The Server Tools Project (Using a Defanged, Much Less Extreme but Still Very Agile Process)" later in this chapter.

Continuous Integration Combined with Test-First Design

When using a dedicated build and test PC, teams that combine continuous integration with a test-first approach may find that the following problem occurs.

Because the tests are written first and deliberately fail, the code can't be integrated until all the tests pass, as the build PC (assuming it's regularly building the code and running the unit tests once an hour or more) will catch the failed tests very quickly. This might seem like a minor annoyance, but in practice it can start to hinder the team's progress. In XP, this problem is mitigated by breaking the development into smaller steps: Write a few small tests, write the associated code to pass the tests, integrate it, and then rinse and repeat.

However, we found in our Server Tools project (see the case study later in this chapter) that this approach quickly became inefficient, and we had to "think creatively" a bit too frequently to find ways to write chunks of code of a meaningful size and still integrate often. This became an annoyance because we wanted to spend sufficient time on a piece of code without worrying about making it work just so that it could be integrated within the next 20 minutes.

Instead, we settled on integrating working code *at least once a day if feasible* and taking slightly longer than a day if needed. This method turned out to be a lot more efficient for us.

Sustainable Pace (40-Hour Week)

Working a 40-hour week is good work if you can get it. Of course, that does mean not working the other 40 hours that your boss has penciled you in for. Even for people such as ourselves who "live, breathe, sleep" computers, you should find that your quality of life improves a whole lot if, more often than not, you give yourself the evening off. You'll find that weekends are wonderful little nuggets of long-lost freedom when you rediscover them. Use the time well: Take your family to the zoo. If you live alone, build a model ship out of matchsticks (we live exciting lives, as you can tell).

You'll probably find that there will be spikes in your working hours—sometimes, you just have to show some commitment to the company by staying late every now and again to get something finished on time. When deadlines loom, as customers become more concerned, you'll find yourself having to work late again. It's inevitable, but some of us prefer to have it this way than to work at a job that doesn't really matter to us.

The trick is to be able to achieve a consistent, sustainable pace: to work at maximum productivity without burning yourself out (or your team, for that matter). Monthly "sprints" (as in Scrum—see the reference at the end of this chapter) help to focus the team and maintain a healthy sense of urgency, as distinct from panic.

On-site Customer

The information you gather for your project's requirements will come from a variety of sources. If you can get a real customer representative to sit in with your team for a large proportion of the project, it's worth doing. However, the system isn't necessarily being written especially for the customer—specifically, it's being written for the people that will be using the system on a day-to-day basis. As such, the customer shouldn't be your sole source of information; you also need to talk at length with the users, the clerks, the supervisors, and everyone else who can be thought of as a project stakeholder.

What you do need from the customer is the final sign-off—not from the people who are telling you what needs to be in the system, but from the person who will be putting your payment check in the mail. In C3 parlance, this would be the gold owner. As C3 has shown us, it's vital to distinguish between the project sponsor and the information providers and to get sign-off from the right one. Always know your true master.

In certain situations, it still makes sense to have a customer representative on-site for some of the time. If that person has some real domain knowledge and has been authorized to make on-the-spot decisions about the scope of the project, then it's worth doing. It's a situation that needs to be handled with care, though. Not all programmers are suited to a "customer-facing" role. To use an extreme stereotype, imagine an unkempt hacker who hasn't washed his or her hair for several days and has yet to be sold on the idea of deodorant or toothpaste taking your key client out to lunch at the local Burger King.

In most cases, the reality will hopefully be a toned-down version of that scary example. However, asking a key client to sit in with your programmers for any length of time (even if they do wash behind their ears regularly) could be taxing the relationship somewhat. It won't always be this way: Often, the relationship can work very well, and the customer will come out of the deal feeling very good about his level of involvement. The trick is to make a judgment call at the time. Try not to rely on any software process that *requires* a permanent on-site customer for it to work properly. Life just isn't that straightforward.

Conversely, XP does make the provision for a customer role (we apologize on XP's behalf for introducing such a confusing and misleading role name). The customer role is played by a business analyst who isn't the real customer, but who talks to the customer regularly and is able to act as a customer proxy. Such a person is unlikely to be authorized to make actual decisions regarding project scope (this is particularly true with traditional bespoke projects that have one external customer). In this case, the analyst-customer can still be a hive of information ("Should the system do this or that?" "This! No, that!"), but in the case where actual decisions need to be made, there would inevitably be a delay while the analyst-customer contacts the mothership for instructions.

Collaborative Coding Standards

Coding standards are definitely worth salvaging from XP. A good standards document will explain up front why coding standards are so important (and what the programmer stands to gain from the deal). With such an arrangement, unequivocal buy-in from the people involved is essential. This isn't something that can be forced; someone who is bullied into doing something against her will is likely to get pretty demotivated. Instead, a team that has provided input into and fully understands the importance of a set of standards will actively conform to them and hopefully provide feedback to help hone and improve the standards even more.

A good standards document will also not just stop at such items as positioning of curly braces, but instead will provide advice about good programming style, best practices, identification of design patterns, and so on.

A good standards document won't encourage the programmer to overcomment his code.

Coding standards are especially important in XP projects, due to the XP practice of collective ownership. If everyone is responsible for all code, then it's doubly important that the code be written in a precise and consistent fashion. The act of doing this isn't such a big thing, but you should be wary of a process that *relies* on this practice being followed to the letter (especially because diversification—deviation from standards—is an almost universal human trait).

The Activities

All four of XP's activities (coding, testing, listening, and designing) are worth keeping. You need to code, you need to test what you've written, you need to listen, and, of course, you need to design.

Agile Goals, Fragile Practices

Notice that, as we get further from XP's concrete practices and closer to its goals, further into the abstract, we agree more with what XP is trying to achieve.[14] The agile goals of XP are sound—it's just that the implementation leaves something to be desired. Hence this chapter!

Listening, oddly enough, isn't just about listening—it's also about talking back, asking the right questions, then listening raptly to the answers, assuming nothing (as we describe in the "Listening Without Preconceptions" sidebar in Chapter 10), and then asking more questions. This is *requirements elicitation*. The programmers might not have time to do this properly, as they're more interested in getting back to the task in hand, which for them is likely to involve programming. This is why many projects employ a business analyst whose job is solely to elicit requirements from the customer.[15]

These people, if they're good at what they do, will also know how to treat the customer well: take them out to lunch, compliment them on their choice of car, that sort of thing. This is not a dig against programmers (we're programmers ourselves)—it's simply a statement that different types of people are better suited to different roles. Most business analysts couldn't shake a stick if it involved writing a program, but the chances are that they'll be very good at requirements management and elicitation.

---

14. Although we part ways again when XP goes *really* abstract and ascends into Zen-esque philosophy to justify its practices, as we discuss in the final chapter.

15. Luckily the Extremos have also seen the light and refactored the XP customer role to mean a team of analysts (as we discuss in Chapter 5).

Additional Practices

In this section, we add some practices that have also proven to be extremely useful outside of the documented XP world, but that we've found (as shown in the case study in the next section) to be a very effective fit with our refactored practices.

Note that some of these tenets are occasionally mentioned in XP and are generally not considered to be incompatible with XP (e.g., a separate QA department).

The Stopgap

Also known as "Giving the Customer Something Quickly Without Putting the Project into Maintenance Mode Straightaway." For projects where the customer really needs something up and running very quickly (like within the first month or two), a "stopgap" release is well worth considering.

This initial version of the product would contain maybe 10% or less of the eventual feature set, and it may not be particularly well designed. In many ways it's similar to XP's initial release, getting useable functionality into the hands of the customer/users early. As such, it should be produced with the same attention to code quality (extensive unit tests and so on). Something that XP doesn't emphasize (although it doesn't say not to do it) is that the stopgap product should also be run past QA, perhaps even more diligently than the main product (as if that were possible).

What we absolutely need to avoid, though, is putting the project into maintenance mode early. This is one of XP's major shortcomings.

Technical Team Leader

The team leader has greater authority to enforce certain decisions than the XP coach. This sounds dictatorial, but the alternative is the "quasi-Marxist" regime that we see in XP (which awards more power to the "proletariat" programmers).

You should find that if your practices are less severe than XP's (and therefore are more easily adhered to over long periods of time), there's less of a need for a full-time coach. Therefore, this role can be safely adopted by the team leader.

Introducing a team leader role can also mean that more time is spent actually programming than discussing the process and how to interpret the Extremos' teachings. Discussing how best to proceed is important, but if a roomful of people disagrees emphatically, then at some point it's useful to have someone in a position of authority who can say, "Enough! We're doing it this way. Now let's just get on with it."

We compare the team leader role with XP's coach role in the section "When XP Starts to Fail" in Chapter 14.

Quality Assurance

Although QA is deemphasized in XP (because the programmers write their own tests), we feel that a separate QA team is a vital component of software development. QA is a totally different mind-set from programming: QA destroys, programming creates.

A programmer wants his code to work, whereas a QA tester wants it to die—he actively wants to find bugs, errors, and ugliness. One person just can't wear both hats at once; it creates a major conflict of interest. A QA team member's job is QA: There are no other distractions, no need to fix bugs, and no ego to defend.

QA and programming are different jobs; hence, they should be done by different people.

There's a danger with QA that the programmers can quickly develop a "somebody else's problem" (SEP) mentality—that they don't need to test their code because QA will do it for them. As you'd probably expect, code quality can drop dramatically as a result. In our refactored process, this danger is balanced by the emphasis on unit tests (as with XP) and individual ownership (unlike XP). If the programmers have to achieve 100% test passes, code quality firmly remains their problem, not somebody else's.

Interaction Designer

HCI design is a fundamental aspect of software development, so it's strange that XP omits a specific interaction designer role.

This problem is mitigated to an extent because XP does promote close involvement with (and early feedback from) the end users, and if the on-site customer can be an actual user, then so much the better. This doesn't take the role far enough, however. An end user will know what she wants when she sees it, but she is unlikely to have the training needed for effective interaction design. So the job of user interface design is left to the programmers, who are really not the right people for the job.

The case for a full-time interaction designer (as a separate role from the programmer, whose goals are in almost direct opposition to interaction design and usability) is made very well in the book *The Inmates Are Running the Asylum* by Alan Cooper.

Taking a Goal-Driven Approach

When a design is unclear, estimates are sometimes given in ranges, so that the team doesn't unwittingly commit to a deadline it can't hit (e.g., "This module will take 3 to 6 days of programming").

Similarly, at an early stage, *functionality* can be specified in ranges. This can be achieved by taking a goal-centered approach to specifying the requirements. The high-level *goals* paint broad brush strokes (e.g., "I want a system that combines results from different search engines"). These goals can be steadily broken down into more detailed *tasks* (e.g., "I want to be able to combine search results from Google and AltaVista" and "I want to be able to sort the results in order of relevance").

Goals that haven't yet been fully fleshed out with specific details can be easily identified, because they wouldn't have very many tasks identified yet. As soon as sufficient tasks have been identified, then each goal can be estimated more accurately.

This isn't dissimilar to a use case-driven approach, which derives use cases (behavioral requirements—the *tasks*) from higher-level requirements (the *goals*). Interaction design also complements this approach rather well.

See Chapter 10 for more about user stories, use cases, and requirements.

Create Documentation As Part of the Design Process

As we discuss elsewhere, XP attempts to replace the effort that goes into producing design documentation with a combination of collective ownership and oral documentation. This combination of practices has its own special set of problems in an XP project that needs to scale up beyond, say, a roomful of programmers.

For a description of the sorts of problems we mean, see Matt's article "Collective Ownership, Oral Documentation, and Scalability: The Perfect Storm" at http://www.softwarereality.com/lifecycle/xp/storm.jsp.

As you might have gathered from reading some of the previous chapters in this book, we are in favor of design documentation produced as an integral part of the design process. However, it is worth stressing that design documentation *is not a replacement for oral communication*. It is still absolutely vital that everyone in the team talk to each other (and not just about football!). Conversely, so-called oral documentation is not a substitute for written design documentation. Writing something down in an unambiguous way removes ambiguity, funnily enough.

For any project, we don't see written design documents as an optional extra. An added advantage is that not everybody needs to know every aspect of the project's codebase in detail. It still pays for most people to have a broad overview of the architecture and to know as much of the project in detail as possible. For a person to know the *entire* project isn't always practical, though, particularly with large-scale projects.

So, a less extreme (and, we feel, a more robust and efficient) approach is simply to do the following:

- Document your design as you design it and keep it up-to-date (this doesn't take as long as some people would have you believe, especially if the documentation is effectively a by-product of the design process).

- Employ somebody who knows how to design software (many of the problems that XP sets out to solve can in fact be solved "magically" by employing people who have a clue[16]).

- Make sure everyone has a good knowledge of the high-level architecture.

- Make sure everyone understands the problem domain (in other words, what set of problems is this project setting out to solve).

- Make sure that each module or subsystem is understood in detail by more than one person.

Individual Ownership

This practice replaces collective ownership, but it certainly isn't mandatory. If collective ownership works well for your team, there's no reason not to continue. However, our refactored process gives you the choice, whereas in XP (as we've demonstrated elsewhere), there's a Hobson's choice of collective ownership or nothing.

If you do choose individual ownership, the following practices can help to make the process more robust:

---

16. This may sound blatantly obvious, but that's possibly because it is such basic, profound advice. We're still amazed at the number of projects we see or hear about that contain one or more bad programmers.

- Encourage people to find out about other parts of the system (but not to spend all day doing it).

- Promote the assertion that everyone on the team is responsible for overall product quality. This means that if someone finds a defect (whether at the code level or the end user level) in a part of the system she isn't directly involved with, it's her responsibility to log the defect and keep nagging the programmer responsible until the problem is fixed. Each programmer is a deputy of the QA sheriff. Note that this is very different from a programmer going in and fixing someone else's code on his behalf.

See the section "What if Programmers Take Ownership of Code?" in Chapter 3 for a comparison of collective and individual ownership.

Case Study: The Server Tools Project (Using a Defanged, Much Less Extreme but Still Very Agile Process)

In this section, Matt describes his latest project, which has many similar characteristics to an XP project, albeit with some key differences (detailed up-front design being one of them). As it turns out, it's very close to the "refactored" process that we're aiming for.

Brief Overview

The details of the project itself aren't important for this discussion, except for one or two items that help to explain why the process has been tailored the way it has. So a brief overview is probably useful.

The company is a technology start-up based in central London, with a server product that controls business processes via a Web-based front-end. The front-end is constructed dynamically from various back-end Web servers. So the server product is like a cross between an Enterprise Application Integration (EAI) server and a Web screen-scraper (although that does understate its role somewhat—the server contains a *lot* of very neat technology, written by some very talented people).

Initially, the server was being configured in-house by the engineers, via a combination of XML files and command-line tools. The next stage (and with a pressing need to get something released as soon as possible) was to produce some GUI tools for configuring the server and defining its business processes. The project I'm heading up is tasked with the job of creating these GUI tools.

The first tool was released very quickly (first a prototype, followed quickly by the real thing). It was basically just a GUI front-end on the most-used command-line tool being used by the engineers, with added functionality taking advantage of the graphical environment. This tool was essentially a stopgap that allowed the engineers to get their job done more quickly while they waited for the real high-level GUI tools to arrive.

The temptation was, of course, to rush out these high-level tools and then tweak them gradually based on the users' feedback. Luckily, we didn't need to rush to do a quick release because we had provided the stopgap tool straightaway. This gave us a breathing space to concentrate on getting the main GUI tools right, rather than launch the project straight into one long maintenance phase.

Given the intense focus of the project on user interfaces, much of our analysis work has involved use cases, user experience walk-throughs, UI "workshops" with some of the prospective users, and so on. We also have on-site HCI experts who play an important role in shaping the product's interaction design.

The team size is currently five programmers plus a tester, a dedicated interaction designer, and various analysts, product managers, and consultants who together form the on-site customer role—so about 12 to 15 people in total. This is quite a small size, but it is roughly the number that might be considered the "top end" for an XP project. Even at this size of project, we found it necessary to tailor many of the XP practices (as described in the next section).

As the project ramps up, the plan is to bring in more programmers and produce different tools in parallel. The insular nature of each tool means that each one can be treated as a miniproject (although they're all kept integral and consistent via a documented architectural framework and user experience spec).

Would XP Have Sufficed?

Many of the practices we follow as a team are pretty much the same as XP: unit testing; test-first design; pair programming; short, fixed iterations; small releases; and on-site customer team. The planning process is also quite similar: a detailed plan and task list for the next iteration and a broader plan for the long term.

There are, however, vital (and quite deliberate) differences:

- **The role of XP coach is filled by the team leader.** The main difference being that the team leader has greater authority (the team leader also performs some project management duties).

 Also see the section "Technical Team Leader" earlier in this chapter and the "XP Coach vs. Team Leader" sidebar in Chapter 14.

- **Interaction design is a "first-class citizen."** That is, we involve usability experts who don't themselves program (because the goals of interaction design and program design frequently conflict). There's also a full-time interaction designer on the team.

Also see the section "Interaction Designer" earlier in this chapter.

- **Pair programming is encouraged for solving difficult problems, but it isn't mandatory.** Each programmer gets to have a say in the way he works. (Also, some of the programmers like to work from home on occasion, so this must be taken into account.)

- **We do frequent integration (as opposed to continuous integration) once per day.** Toward the end of each day there is a build—all code is checked in, rebuilt, and unit-tested—and any integration issues are resolved then and there. This allows us to catch code divergence problems early enough to prevent them becoming a problem, without the added burden of continuous integration.

  Having said that, continuous integration *can* work well if it's sufficiently automated. We recently set up a low-spec PC to be a dedicated build machine. Once an hour, it rebuilds the system and runs the unit tests. If a test fails, the person responsible is e-mailed automatically. QA loves this setup because the QA team's functional tests get run on the same PC, including automated GUI "click" tests.[17]

  As the project really gets under way and increases overall velocity (as more people are now being added to the team), we're finding this level of automation to be a real bonus. That said, the team still keeps its routine of making sure all code is checked in and working at the end of the day. It provides an "amnesty period" to get everything integrated before people clock off for the day (or to make a note that someone is midtask and needs to integrate as soon as possible the following day).

---

17. QA also has its own separate test environment, but running the tests regularly in Engineering means that not only are the functional tests testing our software early, but also the software is testing the functional tests early as well. This virtually eliminates the "big bang" delivery problem, which affects test scripts equally as much as it affects production software.

- **Our iterations each last for exactly 1 month (a la Scrum[18]) rather than 1 or 2 weeks.** There is always a release (internal, at least) at the end of each monthly iteration. We are finding that this cycle is really helping to get everyone focused. The creation of these minideadlines creates a reasonable sense of urgency and encourages everyone to create that last push toward the end of the month to get the release ready.

Also see the section "Short Iterations and Small Releases" earlier in this chapter.

- **Test-first design complements our design process but doesn't drive it.** We have found that this approach works very well for us. The test-first approach (that is, writing the unit tests before you write the code, and driving the design from this) operates very much at a micro level ("designing in the small")—designing for one test case at a time.

Also see the section "Test-First Design Complements Up-Front Design" earlier in this chapter.

- **At the core of the project there's a designed framework.** Into this framework, we plug the tools that we're creating (e.g., to share data). The framework was designed up front but is being developed in parallel with the tools themselves. For more about this approach, see the next section, "Framework."

- **We use a combination of requirements and use cases instead of user stories.** A lot of the requirements actually "read" like user stories, but we have high-level requirements clearly delineated from behavioral requirements. This helps management to more effectively prioritize what it wants delivered each month.

---

18. See http://www.controlchaos.com.

For a comparison of use cases, user stories, and "traditional" requirements, see Chapter 10.

- **The requirements are stored electronically.** But they can be conveniently accessed by any of us via the project intranet.

- **Project velocity is measured in terms of the "formal" requirements completed per iteration, rather than user stories per iteration.** This is a subtle difference, but it means that when comparing the time taken to complete different requirements, we're more likely to be comparing like with like.

We round off this case study with descriptions of a couple of aspects of the project that differ significantly from XP and that warrant discussing in more detail.

Framework

Although XP isn't specifically against frameworks, it's philosophically against designing and building a framework up front. We were in the "lucky" position of not having to deliver something immediately, because we had given the engineers a stopgap tool in the meantime. This in turn meant that we could afford to spend some time getting the underlying framework right—paving the way. . . .

For more about applying the stopgap method, see the section titled (fittingly enough) "The Stopgap" earlier in this chapter.

To design our framework, we began with a quick-and-dirty prototype (including some prototype GUI-based tools) to get a feel for what we needed. Then we defined an architecture suitable for plug-in tools, shared data and services, and so on; documented it; and got as many people as possible to read through it, see the prototype, and give their feedback.

While this was going on, some necessary data analysis work was taking place to help define the server configuration data that the tools would be creating. Through a combination of luck and planning, these two activities finished at the same time. We then began to develop the framework in parallel with the first set of tools.

Ironically, we've found that taking the time to think through, prototype, and create a robust framework has made the project much more agile overall. One reason for this is that the framework is just plain *right* for what we need. It's also well designed (having been through a lot of iterative feedback from senior and junior engineers alike), hence it's easy to modify should we need to.

Another reason is that the source code for the tools themselves is generated automatically[19] from a very small set of definition files[20] and accompanying Java code templates. The generator itself was developed in-house and is really very simple for what it does: It just steps through the definition files and iteratively "munges" them with the Java templates, creating reams upon reams of lovely, well-formed Java Swing code (plus XML descriptors, manifests, and so on). The size ratio of generated code to definition files is roughly 100:1.

This code generation is probably the single most "agile" aspect of the project. It means that if the server product changes spec in any way, we just update the definition files and crank out a new version of the tools—within seconds!

Another way in which the code generator makes us more agile is that it wouldn't be a very tall order to switch frameworks if we needed to. Currently, our framework is based on the NetBeans platform, but (if market forces dictated) we could switch to, say, Eclipse, just by swapping in a different set of templates (e.g., to generate SWT code instead of Swing). The framework design also helps reduce the cost of change because it keeps the (code-generated) tools themselves nicely decoupled from the framework implementation.

More Than One Master

The people who drive the direction of our project are many and varied. Come to think of it, have you ever encountered a project where this wasn't the case?

The users, of course, have a big say in what goes into the product. Currently, the tools are being used by the team of engineers who produce the accompanying server product. Because they're in the same room, this gives us quick and valuable feedback whenever we release a new version. So essentially, the engineers are currently our "on-site customer."

However, our "customer" is also various other people—for example, the product management team located elsewhere in the building; the marketing team, who in many ways drive the direction of the product; and the team of consultants who will use the tools externally on customer sites.

So the majority of our customers are not colocated (at least, not in the same room). We do, however, meet regularly with them, send them screen shots, solicit their feedback, and so on. It's a good habit to get into.

There would be potential for chaos here if we followed the XP route of an on-site customer team drip-feeding us with requirement details. Instead, we

---

19. Matt Stephens, "Automated Code Generation," http://www.softwarereality.com/programming/code_generation.jsp, May 6, 2002.

20. We're using Java properties files for this purpose because they're much simpler to work with than XML (not to mention easier to read and edit). If the project increases in complexity and demands more flexibility, we will change as needed.

need to recognize that we have many masters, each one trying to pull the product in a slightly different direction (and with good reason). The only way we could possibly reach a middle line that everyone agrees on would be to elicit requirements from everyone involved, write them down in detail, and get all the on-site customers to sign them off. So that's what we do.[21]

It could be viewed that this is the least agile (certainly the least XP-like) of our practices, but quite frankly we don't care. All the customers involved are happy that they get to have a say in the direction of the project. (They would have their say anyway, but this way our process takes the fact into account.)

Summary

In this chapter we took everything we've learned throughout the book and refactored XP into something that we feel to be altogether more robust. The process that we ended up with, though it still has striking similarities, just isn't XP anymore. However, "son of XP" should be applicable to a much wider variety of projects than the original.

Of course, we aren't attempting to invent a new methodology in a single chapter. It's important to take our advice not as a definition of a methodology, but as a set of guidelines for what to look out for and tailor when applying an off-the-shelf methodology (or when creating your own). Some more advice for tailoring methodologies can be found in Alistair Cockburn's book *Agile Software Development*.

XP isn't the only fruit, even if it is the loudest. There are plenty of other agile methodologies to choose from: Scrum,[22] the Crystal series,[23] DSDM,[24] FDD,[25] and so on. Even RUP[26] can be made agile in the right hands. We would also point you toward Agile Modeling,[27] which addresses many of the weaknesses in XP in similar ways.

FDD, for example, offers a good mixture of up-front design and progressive design, and it has a much bigger emphasis on documentation than XP (in fact, as with ICONIX,[28] the documentation is produced almost as a by-product of the design process).

---

21. XPers tend to view this practice with quaint amusement, and yet this was a primary factor in the early termination of the C3 project (as we discuss in the sidebar "Did Oral Documentation Kill C3?" in Chapter 7).

22. See http://www.controlchaos.com.

23. See http://crystalmethodologies.org.

24. See http://www.dsdm.org.

25. See http://www.togethersoft.com/services/tutorials/jmcu/chapter6.pdf.

26. See http://www.rational.com/products/process.jsp.

27. See http://www.agilemodeling.com.

28. See http://www.iconixsw.com/ICONIXProcess.html.

Well, that's about it really. XP just isn't deserving of the hype, and you may find resistance introducing XP in its entirety into your organization. But there are parts of it that can be salvaged and wrapped up into a more rigorous process, while still achieving its agile goals.

We leave you with a conclusion of sorts in the next chapter, in which we examine some of the core philosophy that we're convinced led to XP being the way it is.

CHAPTER 16

Conclusion: Neutralizing the Reality Distortion Field

Imagine
(Sing to the tune of "Imagine" by John Lennon)

Imagine there's no requirements
It's easy if you try
Just a bunch of coders
Reachin' for the sky
Imagine all the people, coding for today

Imagine there's no schedules
It isn't hard to do
No silly project deadlines
No one supervising you
Imagine all the people, coding hand in hand

You may say I'm an Extremer
But I'm not the only one
I hope someday you'll join us
And make coding lots more fun

Imagine oral documentation
I wonder if you can
No need for UML diagrams
Just words passed, man to man
Imagine just refactoring, playing in the sand

You may say I'm an Extremer
But I'm not the only one
I hope someday you'll join us
And make coding lots more fun

Well, we've come a long way together (assuming you're not still standing in the bookstore deciding whether to buy this book[1]). In this, the final chapter, we look at the philosophy that is at the very heart of XP, and then we discuss, in our own philosophical way, what to do next.

Ethereal Wizardry in Action

The Extremo world contains a strange dichotomy. On the one hand, there's the good sense and pragmatism of unit testing, pair programming (because "two brains are better than one"[2]), short iterations, and so on. On the other hand, there's a certain mystique to XP that possibly attracts the wrong type of follower. The XP values, although not particularly mystical, are the first step away from the grounded (though often misguided) advice contained in the practices. The XP values are incorporeal, more akin to a "feeling" than a physical thing or situation. However, in terms of etherealness, the XP values are nothing compared with the surrounding mystique that we sometimes see in XP. In this sense, XP appears to have been designed from the ground up by approaching it from the sky downward—that is, the ethereal philosophy drives the values, and the practices are in turn created out of the thinking behind the values.

Fittingly, much of this "high-level mystique" is introduced by Kent Beck, XP's creator (we give some examples later in this chapter). The mystique is fundamental to XP, because it drives the core philosophy behind the methodology. Unfortunately, this core philosophy is occasionally at odds with the more pragmatic practices. It's possible that this is what creates the contradictions and paradoxes in the XP teachings, leading to many of the circular arguments that we've pointed out—for example, the Extremos' dislike of the word "methodology" because it feels as if it dictates practices to the XPers. In fact, XP tells us not to treat any of its teachings as gospel (or "prescriptive"). However, as we discussed in Chapter 3, XP's web of interdependent practices makes it eminently difficult (even dangerous) to tailor.[3] Perhaps this difficulty explains some of the mystique behind XP.

Let's briefly explore some of this so-called mystique.

---

1. If you *are* standing in the bookstore trying to decide whether to buy this book, the answer is obvious: Go to the cash register right now and buy it—you'll be glad you did (and so will we!).

2. See http://www.computer.org/SEweb/Dynabook/PairProg.htm.

3. It's worth mentioning that in *Planning Extreme Programming*, the chapter on tailoring XP (Chapter 27, "Your Own Process") is barely more than a few short paragraphs. On reading the "chapterette," we turned the page expecting an in-depth discussion of how to tailor the planning aspects of XP, but we were surprised to be met with an empty page!

Too Much Pebble Talk

In *Extreme Programming Installed*, Chet Hendrickson recites a "war story" regarding an event in the C3 project.

The problem was that the system was "about ready to launch," but the team still had one problem: the programmers were interfacing with the legacy system's reporting tool, which contained "several hundred poorly understood data items."[4] None of these items could have automated acceptance tests written for them, because they were poorly understood. Therefore, they weren't showing up on the team's plan anywhere or on the team's test completion charts. The resultant problem was that the system was at the infamous 90% complete stage, but it still had a huge amount of unreported, seemingly unreportable functionality that had yet to be implemented.

The team's solution was ethereal wizardry in action:

> *"I had an epiphany. I went back to where Kent was and said that we were just 'balancing hopes and fears.' We had focused on our hope that we could launch the system as planned and our fear that we wouldn't. Kent told me that I had just 'snatched the pebble from the master's hand.' We knew what had to be done. . . ."[5]*

If this is an example of oral documentation in an XP project, then we're worried. "The marmosets arrive by dawn. Too quickly? Sadly not yet. A stone tablet to cure all? No, trust the wind. . . ."

A solution in a more pragmatic software project would have been, "We have several hundred poorly understood data items. Let's write some of this down, then get someone to confirm that what we've written is correct. Let's do that before we waste any more time writing code that we know we're going to have to change." Writing things down first in order to capture and confirm our understanding of the problem might seem like a lot of work at first, but ultimately it can save a huge amount of time.

Understanding So Profound They Cannot Be Understood

And then there's this, which we found on the C2 Wiki Web (we can't claim the credit for this gem, which appears to be adapted from the *Tao Te Ching*). We suspect that this adaptation is tongue-in-cheek—in fact, it almost qualifies as a "Song of the Extremos":

---

4. Ron Jeffries, Ann Anderson, and Chet Hendrickson, *Extreme Programming Installed* (New York, NY: Addison-Wesley, 2000), p. 196.

5. Ibid., p. 196.

The ExtremeProgrammingMasters possess understanding
So profound they can not be understood.
Because they cannot be understood
I can only describe their appearance:

Cautious as one crossing thin ice,
Undecided as one surrounded by danger,
Modest as one who is a guest,
Unbounded as melting ice,
Genuine as unshaped wood,
Broad as a valley,
Seamless as muddy water.

Who stills the water that the mud may settle,
Who seeks to stop that he may travel on,
Who desires less than may transpire,
Decays, but will not renew.[6]

We were surprised to learn from the preceding verse that in fact Gandalf was the original XP master! (We always thought it was Yoda.)

Bad Advice by Any Other Name Is Still Bad Advice

Here's an extract of some advice from Kent Beck that we found on the C2 Wiki Web (check the referenced page for the full version):

"When you sit zazen (the Zen mediation technique (I don't know how much you know about stuff like this, so I'll make little explanatory notes until you tell me to stop)), I am told that bizarre things can happen to you. You can get sudden bursts of psychic powers-precognition, far-seeing, telepathy, etc. Lots of people would think that was cool. They would hold onto these powers (if they could). Zen teaches exactly the opposite. . . .

". . . Because envisioning feels good. It brings many of the good feelings that really programming brings, but it can't crash. So people pursue visions instead of code (lots of design before you code), and visions of visions instead of code (lots of object oriented analysis), and the worst of all are those who pursue visions of visions of visions instead of code (the methodologists).

---

6. See `http://c2.com/cgi-bin/wiki?ExtremeProgrammingMaster`.

"So—congratulations on having gained the ability to envision objects before you program. Take a moment to enjoy the feeling when it comes. Then knock it the hell off. Find the one piece of the vision that seems most compelling and do the least possible amount of that. Then bless and release the vision and get back to listening—to your code, your user, your partner, and yourself."[7]

Okay, don't get us wrong. We're not against Zen Buddhism. We think there are a lot of good ideas in Zen Buddhism. Way back when Doug was in college he used to read Zen literature while riding the New York City subways, clearing his mind and listening for the sound of one hand clapping. Now he listens for the sound of one man coding.

But there's just something wrong with couching a bunch of bad advice in catchy Zen-guru terminology. It's just wrong. Extreme Programming has about as much to do with Zen as Tammy Faye Baker has to do with religion. Is it Zen-like to write articles that proclaim you're "the best team in the world"[8]? Is that what the Zen masters teach? Is it Zen-like to defend a mandated noisy programming environment that isn't conducive to quiet thought by saying "concentration is the enemy"[9]? Is it Zen-like to pass off failed projects that refactor around in circles for 4 years as all being the responsibility of "fear, the mind killer"[10]? And whether it's Zen-like or not, is it fair to clients to advertise an "agile" process when the clients don't realize that the price of "agility" is that they must "free themselves from the concepts of doneness, and thereby schedules do not exist per se"[11]?

We believe that Kent Beck knows something about Zen. But we don't think that what he knows translates across to the legions of Extremo followers who dote on his every word. "The archer who shoots true to the target without aiming" is a nice poetic analogy, but as an excuse to avoid up-front design, it reeks. If we're managing a software project, give us a good design spec that can be reviewed by our senior engineers every time. And *please,* save us all from bad advice couched in catchy slogans.

---

7. Kent Beck posting to the C2 Wiki page To Ayoung Extremist, http://c2.com/cgi-bin/wiki?ToAyoungExtremist.

8. Chet Hendrickson, "DaimlerChrysler: The Best Team in the World," http://www.computer.org/SEweb/Dynabook/DaimlerChryslerSdb.htm (reprinted from *Computer,* Vol. 32, No. 10, October 1999).

9. Ron Jeffries, posting to the C2 Wiki page "Pair Programming Ergonomics," http://c2.com/cgi-bin/wiki?PairProgrammingErgonomics.

10. Chet Hendrickson, "When is it not XP?", http://www.xprogramming.com/xpmag/NotXP.htm, December 5, 2002.

11. Robert C. Martin posting to OTUG (http://www.rational.com), subject: "Estimates and Promises," October 13, 2000.

Voice of eXPerience: Packaged Dogma

by David Van Der Klauw

Let's hear from David one last time.

Thou Shalt Learn Speed Reading

As part of a task, my pair had to study some documentation found on the Internet. This had to be done in a pair, of course. As we read the document, I already understood some parts, but I had to wait while my partner slowly read and understood these sections. Similarly, at other points I was unfamiliar with the material and had trouble when my partner skipped ahead faster than I could take it in.

Later I complained to my manager, EI, that it was ridiculous to pair-read a document. EI said, "Do you mean to tell me that it is not your fault for not learning to speed-read so that you can keep up with your partner?"

I thought I had heard it all, but this XP zealot expected me to learn to speed-read so that two people could read a Web page together.

My Karma Ran Over Your Dogma

XP can be described as 12 principles that must be followed closely. Some obvious questions arise:

- Is it a good idea to replace common sense and judgment with close adherence to 12 principles?

- If so, are the 12 XP principles the best possible 12 principles to follow?

To put the questions another way:

- Should you follow a dogma?

- Is XP the best dogma?

To answer the first question, "Should you follow a dogma?": No. I believe that it's a great idea to try to follow several time-tested, basic principles as a guide, tempered by experience, judgment, and practicalities. Rigidly adhering to a dogma isn't the way to success in a complex and changing field such as software engineering.

To answer the second question, "Is XP the best dogma?": I don't believe that XP is the best dogma available. Imagine you have a friend who is going off to run his own software company. He asks you to give him 12 principles to follow in order to be a success. Would you give him the 12 XP principles? I think not. I would suggest something like this:

1. Know your market.

2. Hire the best people available.

3. Motivate your people.

4. Keep the customer happy.

5. Manage risk.

6. Plan ahead, short term and long term.

7. Maintain balance. Don't overemphasize any one aspect of software development.

8. Use incremental development.

9. Use recent hardware and technology, but avoid the latest.

10. Keep studying and learning.

11. Learn from your mistakes.

12. Make rules but trust the judgment of your people to break the rules when needed.

I spent just 10 minutes thinking of these rules. Even so, I'm sure that they're a better guide to success than the XP principles.

Imagine there was a competition where developers submitted their best 12 principles for software development. All entries were given a score by an expert panel of judges. How well would XP score?

My feeling is that XP wouldn't score highly at all when compared to other available principles.

The point I'm trying to make is that XP shouldn't be selected just because one or more of its principles have some merit. That isn't good enough. XP should only be selected if you decide to follow a 12-principle dogma, and if those 12 XP principles are the best 12 available.

My impression of XP is that it's a way of allowing software to be written by people who aren't really good enough to be writing software. By following these simple rules, novices can avoid disaster and get the job finished.

For novices, a 12-principle dogma like XP might be just what is needed to get them over the line. However, for experienced professional developers, I believe that a dogma and a one-size-fits-all philosophy is a major mistake.

Extremes Are Stupid

I believe that a major flaw in XP is that it takes things to an extreme. I believe in doing things in moderation and trying to optimize the value by trading off one factor against another. In life, I find that rarely is the optimum achieved at some extreme point.

From the preface of *Extreme Programming Explained*:

"XP takes commonsense principles and practices to extreme levels.

"... If code reviews are good, we'll review code all the time (pair programming)
... If testing is good, everybody will test all the time
... If design is good, we'll make it part of everybody's daily business
... If simplicity is good
... If architecture is important, everybody will work defining and refining the architecture all of the time

"I had the mental image of knobs on a control board. Each knob was a practice that from experience I knew worked well. I would turn all the knobs up to 10."[12]

Hello! Does anybody have a sound system at home? Can you tell me how good it sounds when you turn all the knobs to their maximum?

. . . If it's good to eat at lunchtime, then let's eat all of the time.
. . . If pay rises are good, then let's have a pay rise every month.
. . . If cleaning toilets is important, then we'll make it part of everybody's daily business.

Extreme Simplicity

There's a lot of sense in doing things simply. Einstein said, "We should make all things as simple as possible, but no simpler." However, let's use the example of taking simplicity to an extreme in order to show how taking something to an extreme narrows its range of applicability.

Here goes: Many software developers make things more complex than necessary. If I advise that developers should write slightly simpler code, then I'd probably be right in 99% of cases. Further, if I advise that developers should write moderately simpler code, then I'd probably still be right in 90% of cases. However, if I advise that developers should always write code that is extremely simple, then my advice would only be correct in very few cases.

The more extreme I become, the more I narrow the fit of my advice. It's a matter of statistics and bell curves and all that.

If the Shoe Doesn't Fit . . .

The result of combining several practices to extreme levels is that XP will only fit very rare situations.

The "white book" says, "XP is a lightweight methodology for small-to-medium sized teams developing software in the face of vague or rapidly changing requirements."[13] That's a very narrow focus. This is precisely the point I'm making. Extreme practices make for an extremely limited range of suitability. And I'm not convinced that much of the work done by the CompanyXYZ product development team fits within this narrow range. Last time I looked, CompanyXYZ was a large team programming for well-known, largely unchanging requirements. Why are we doing XP?

---

12. Kent Beck, *Extreme Programming Explained: Embrace Change* (New York, NY: Addison-Wesley, 2000), p. xv.

13. Ibid., back cover.

Neutralizing the Reality Distortion Field

Dooo doooooo doo doo doo doo doo . . .

Spock: Captain, our situation is quite precarious. All of our sensors are out, and our shields are down. We are quite vulnerable to attack, sir. I suggest we head for the nearest star base.

Kirk: That's . . . all right, Mr. Spock. Just sit in the lotus position and meditate. When the Klingon ships appear, we will know. Our photon torpedoes will fly straight to their . . . targets without aiming.

Spock: Highly illogical, Captain. My calculations indicate that our odds of survival would be 3872.6 times better if the targeting computer was working. I respectfully suggest that you allow me to initiate repairs, Captain.

Kirk: Permission denied, Mr. Spock. We *must believe* in the power of extreme guidance.

Spock: I've got some star charts here, Captain. There's a reality distortion field up ahead, and we wouldn't want to run into it.

Kirk: Documentation, Mr. Spock? I'm . . . disappointed in . . . you. You know all documentation is dated and obsolete. Meditation, that's the key. Meditation, not documentation.

At the End of the Day

The problem with life is that there's an answer to everything. Not an answer *for* everything, though. For any argument that someone wants to make, it's possible to find a credible source and quote it to "prove" his point. Studies are performed that prove just about anything that needs to be proved. Further studies prove that the previous studies got it wrong, and so on. Studies are even performed that question the effectiveness of studies.

It doesn't take a sophisticated understanding of the Heisenberg uncertainty principle to appreciate that whoever commissions the study influences the result.

Eventually, personal experience and your own set of values turn out to be a much more valuable orienteering kit to help navigate your way through the moors of conflicting advice, where cheery voices shout at you from out of the gloom, "There's a study that proves my point, you know!"

It's a complex world out there, and you would be forgiven for sometimes thinking that methodology authors are trying to shove their opinions down your throat. ("Swallow that bitter pill!") Of course, this book is no different. If you've reached this point (assuming you didn't just skip to the last chapter to find out who the murderer was), you might feel that we're just as guilty (probably more so) of being opinionated and trying to shout those opinions onto others.

Whether you agree or disagree with our arguments in this book probably has more to do with your own experience and reflection on life (i.e., whether our arguments resonated with your own opinions and experiences of projects past). It's likely that you set out to read this book with your mind already made up regarding XP. That's okay—it's part of being human. People very rarely change their minds about something as fundamental to the human psyche as how to develop software.

Not *everything* about XP is bad. In fact, XP has achieved many good things for the software industry. It has introduced the concept of refactoring to a wider audience, and it has helped to boost this concept even outside the XP world. It has also enforced key disciplines such as design simplicity, modularity, code conventions, and so forth that are not exclusive to XP, but about which it always helps to evangelize.

In fact, when we get right down to it, there is nothing particularly new in the individual parts of XP. The practices all existed before in various corners of the industry, and some of what XP preaches is even preached as good practice in the "nonagile" parts of the industry. What makes XP unique, though, is the combination of practices that its creators have put together into one process and the established practices that the XPers have chosen to leave out or modify almost beyond recognition. This is summed up rather nicely by David Van Der Klauw (who we have quoted in the "Voice of eXPerience" sections throughout this book):

> *"Imagine how angry Christians would be if I took the Ten Commandments from the bible, added two of my own, packaged it as a new religion, and then used the merits of the original ten to justify my additions. Something similar, I believe, is what has happened with XP."*[14]

XP has sparked some interesting debates about how software should be created, something that is really quite important for the software industry.

It has achieved these things with more than its fair share of controversy, for a number of reasons. Two of these reasons are as follows:

- Instead of simply using key disciplines to strengthen it, XP makes them a core part of its methodology, such that it *relies* on them in order for it to work. This sounds great, but it's then an anorexic process without effective contingency plans.

- Amid the good advice, XP also contains some bad advice. That is, it contains advice that doesn't make sense outside the XP world.

---

14. David Van Der Klauw, e-mail to author, May 2003.

Eventually, only you can decide what to do next. It's your project. We're not "empowering" you with this; it's just the way it is. However you decide to proceed (with XP, without XP, with only parts of XP), having listened to both sides of the argument and weighed the advice objectively, it's important to base the decision as much on your own gut feeling as on the opinions of others. Don't be taken in by all those impressive-sounding studies, though. Their experiences are their own. Yours might be similar, or they might be 100% different.

Perhaps that's why we've found ourselves to be so opposed to XP (even though XP's agile goals are about right). We've found our experiences to be wildly different from those of the XP authors. For example, they say (largely speaking) that project inception activities, requirements elicitation, fixed-scope contracts, detailed up-front design, and a decent change-management system (including traceability) are tiresome, optional, and too time consuming for most projects. On the other hand, we've found that these exact same things *save projects*. In most cases, these activities are essential to the initial and ongoing success of your project.

It's possible to denigrate these activities by saying that they're based on fear. We prefer to say that they're based on simple common sense. With the increasing number of XP projects that are being started, some of these projects will, of course, succeed. The risk is high, though. All these projects will be flying by the seat of their pants. XP claims to have a "safety net" in the form of unit tests. Even patched with XP's other practices, that's hardly sufficient to prevent most real project-failure modes (see the analysis of C3 in Chapter 2). Trying to reduce software development to a simplistic, naive formula based on one (dubious) success and then designing a methodology around it is bound to create problems and contradictions.

> *"Listening, Testing, Coding, Designing. That's all there is to software. Anyone who tells you different is selling something."*[15]
>
> —Kent Beck

In Closing

So, just what is XP useful for? XP is mostly suited to maintenance projects. In fact, it could have been tailor-made for projects that have legacy code being used in production environments but that have a fresh set of requirements waiting to be somehow shoehorned in. XP's refactoring approach and emphasis on "after-the-event" code quality is a good approach to such a scenario.

There are plenty of reports (e.g., in *IEEE Software* magazine) of projects under way that have adopted XP partially (but never in full, strangely), after at least one customer release has been made.

---

15. Kent Beck posting to the C2 Wiki page Extreme Programming, http://c2.com/cgi/wiki?ExtremeProgramming.

For all other projects, however, XP isn't the most efficient way to do it. And it's certainly not the most scalable software process on the block.

XP is still evolving, and we hope that this book will help to drive XP to a better place. It may be that another software process will take XP's place, or XP itself may evolve to correct its many flaws. If XP could lose the Zen-esque mumbo-jumbo that surrounds it, and not require great organizational change to be effective, and not be quite so extreme, *and* appeal less to the hack-and-whack crowd by placing a (much) greater emphasis on effective up-front design techniques, precode HCI design, and requirements elicitation methods, then we would feel like our job here is done and we can now safely retire to a small island in the South Pacific and spend the rest of our days throwing pebbles at small crabs. But we suspect that day is a long, long way off yet.

XP isn't about hack and whackery, but it seems to appeal more than other software processes to the hack-and-whack crowd. With that in mind, we'd like to leave you with these parting thoughts.

You Can't Always Hack All You Want
(Sing to the tune of "You Can't Always Get What You Want" by the Rolling Stones)

I found a pink slip in my mailbox
The letters were printed in gray
It was a note from the gold owner
And here's what he had to say

You can't always hack all you want
You can't always hack all you want
You can't always hack all you want

'Cause if you look sometimes
You might find
That change isn't free

You can't always hack all you want
You can't always hack all you want
You can't always hack all you want

You say that there is no real schedule
It does not exist per se
You say there are no fixed-price contracts
And at five PM you must go play

You can't always hack all you want
You can't always hack all you want
You can't always hack all you want

But folks might try sometimes
And you might find
They call it XP

Index

A

"A Day in the Code" (song), 204
"A Night at the Payroll Project: Optional-Scope Contract Scene" (satire), 263–266
About Face 2.0, 297
acceptance tests
  customers writing, 191–192
  defined, 228
  described, 8
  on-site customers and, 130–131
  vs. requirements, 242
  requirements as, 242–245
  timing of releases and, 303
  user stories vs., 228
acronyms, and Extremo culture, 103–104
activities
  extreme programming in practice and, 27
  extreme programming theory and, 16–18
  taming XP and, 357
"The Adventures of Uncle Joe and Jack the Siberian Code Hound" (satire), 145–146
agile methods
  agile, defined, 304
  managing change and, 308
  refactoring XP and, 339–343
    contingency vs. embellishment, 342–343
    decreasing risk, 339
    encouraging contingency, 339–340
    necessary operations and procedures, 339
    preventing fragility, 340–342
  up-front design and, 286, 287, 307
  XP as a people process and, 94–96
Agile Modeling (AM), vs. XP, 353
Agile Modeling: Effective Practices for eXtreme Programming and the Unified Process (John Wiley & Sons, 2002)
  pair programming and, 353
  principles in, 216
  up-front design and, 218
  XP documentation and, 166, 167
Agile Software Development (Addison-Wesley, 2001). *See also* Cockburn, Alistair

  customer responsibility and, 118
  feedback and, 6
  on software processes, 79
  tailoring methodologies and, 368
agility
  agile, defined, 304
  enhancing with up-front design, 307
  keeping design agile, 287
Alexander, Ian, 101
Ambler, Scott, 287. See also Agile Modeling: Effective Practices for eXtreme Programming and the Unified Process (John Wiley & Sons, 2002)
  "Why Data Models Shouldn't Drive Object Models [And Vice Verse]" (article), 223
  XP documentation and, 166
Application Development Advisor magazine, 109
architecture. *See also* emergent design
  architectural scalability, 322–328
    emergent design example, 324–326
    scalability drives architecture, 323–324
    "The Piggy Scale of Process Robustness" (satire), 326–328
    throwing away code, 326
  architecture-shifting requirements, 242
  poor architecture and XP, 278–279
Arizona Daily Star, 257
"Aspects of Testing" (VoXP), 192
asynchronous messaging, testing for, 188–189
ATLAS project, 314–322
  emergent design on, 320–321
  problems with, 315–320
  summary of, 321–322

B

"Bang! Bang! I Think We'll Refactor" (song), 74
BDUF, 187–188
Beck, Kent. See also *Extreme Programming Explained: Embrace Change* (Addison-Wesley, 2000)
  on activities, 16